Educating for Life

❖

A Spiritual Vision
for Every Teacher and Parent

Educating for Life

A Spiritual Vision
for Every Teacher and Parent

Thomas H. Groome

A Crossroad Book
The Crossroad Publishing Company
New York

The Crossroad Publishing Company
481 Eighth Avenue, Suite 1550
New York, NY 10001

First published in hardcover in 1998 by Thomas More.
First published paperback in 2001 by The Crossroad Publishing Company.

Printed in the United States of America

Library of Congress Cataloguing-in-Publication Data

Groome, Thomas H.
    Educating for life: a spiritual vision for every teacher and parent
/Thomas H. Groome.
        p. cm.
    Originally published: Allen, Tex. : T. More, c1998.
    Includes bibliographical references and index.
    ISBN 0-8245-1970-1 (alk. paper)
    1. Christian education. 2. Education – Philosophy. 3. Catholic Church –
    Education. I. Title.
    BV1471.2.G6874 2001
    268'.82–dc21

2001002921

1 2 3 4 5 6 7 8 9 10 04 03 02 01

For Colleen

Grá mo chroí

Table of Contents

PREFACE

I was weary when I arrived in Karachi but excited to be in Pakistan, eager to encounter a culture so different from my own. Without knowing the language, I had some apprehension about customs clearance and baggage retrieval. My host, an American nun working here almost forty years, had written to be sure to tell them at passport control that I was coming to St. Joseph's Convent School. Then "you'll have no trouble." I doubted, but did as she advised.

I was welcomed with a smile and waved through without question—leaving a long line looking enviously after me. That all my luggage was missing began to dampen my spirits a bit, but now Sister herself took charge, telling the baggage handlers that I was coming to St. Joseph's—as if announcing a celebrity. She said to me, without the slightest trace of doubt, "They'll find it," and they did. I learned later that I could have "dropped" the name of any of the well-known Catholic schools in Karachi with the same effect, they are held in such high esteem.

My sister chaperone had taken drivers ed as a young woman in Boston—no better preparation for driving in Karachi. The adventure of crossing this clogged and sprawling metropolis beside her remains indelibly etched as a vivid memory. She fought her way through the horde of all-male drivers, shouting exchanges in Urdu as we circled fender benders; stared down menacing trucks; and vied for the road with crammed buses. When two other sisters welcomed me to St. Joseph's, I replied with more than politeness, "I'm so happy to be here."

The first Catholic school in Pakistan was founded in 1856 at Sialkot by the Sisters of Jesus and Mary, a French order, and the system burgeoned thereafter. It now numbers about 550 schools of various kinds, many of which are huge institutions, providing schooling from kindergarten to college. St. Joseph's, Karachi, is more than one hundred years old and has over three thousand students. Clearly a jewel in the crown, yet it is only one example of what is widely considered the best educational system in Pakistan.

Many Catholic schools were nationalized in 1972 and are now funded by the Pakistani government. A few are still private and charge full tuition, and some, like the Urdu-medium schools, charge a minimal fee and are subsidized by the church.

All are predominantly Muslim in faculty and enrollment. Most have less than 5 percent Christian students. In deference to their communities, these schools display none of the symbols of Catholic Christianity. They scrupulously avoid proselytizing Muslim children to Christian faith and, in fact, require them to take a religion curriculum in Islam. Muslim parents vie to enroll their children in Catholic schools knowing that they will receive an excellent education and formal instruction in their own faith tradition. I became intrigued by the fact that, although showing none of the outer trappings of Christianity and providing religious education in Islam, these schools are readily recognized within Pakistani culture as very "different."

Upon inquiring about what makes them different, it became evident that many commitments combine to create the distinctive ethos of Pakistan's Catholic schools. They promote the value of the person, emphasizing the equal dignity of boys and girls—exceptional in this society; they encourage a positive outlook on life and challenge the fatalism that pervades the surrounding culture; they build up a sense of school community and promote friendship across class and ethnic divides. They also encourage students to develop a personal spirituality, to commit to justice and peace, to respect those who are different. They have strong academic curricula that encourage critical thinking (the government schools favor rote learning).

In sum, these schools provide a *humanizing* curriculum, educating *for life for all*. The values they reflect cannot be taught overtly from the perspective of Christian faith—as a catechesis—but they permeate the ethos and style of the schools. As one sister explained, "Though we cannot instruct in Christian faith, we see to it that gospel values pervade the life of the school and the general curriculum."

I was intrigued by how this system of education can function by a humanizing philosophy that clearly has its grounding in Christian faith and yet remains open to all and without any trace of evangelizing to Christianity. How does it maintain its distinctly Catholic character with a predominantly Muslim faculty and student body, making a singular and yet highly appreciated contribution to this rigorously Muslim society?

On a number of occasions, my sister hosts and I talked late into the night about their philosophy of education and sociocultural situation. When I inquired if they felt their mission was compromised by the exigency to avoid evangelization, the principal, seeming a bit surprised by my question, responded immediately, "Oh no, to educate well is always to do God's work—that is enough!"

And I, embarrassed by my own question, remembered the long tradition to which these women belong—the Catholic Christian commitment to provide quality education for its own sake, as a work of salvation in and of itself.

Yet, I continued to wonder how this Christian system of education maintains its vitality, especially with a dwindling number of vowed religious to staff the schools. From visits to many of them, it became clear that the sponsoring sisters have their own faith-inspired philosophy of Catholic education. But beyond this, they have also devised an approach to education that although inspired by the depth structures of Catholic Christianity can be embraced by their large Muslim faculties without threatening their Islamic faith.

It seems that what is operative in these schools is both *a philosophy of Catholic education* and *a "Catholic" philosophy for educators*—of any persuasion. Or, I began to surmise, they have tapped into some depth structures of Catholic Christianity and found there a spiritual vision for education that could have universal appeal, that could be embraced by people from other religious traditions, albeit for their own reasons. It was certainly clear that these schools have found ways to induct their Muslim faculties into their educational vision and to elicit the support of Muslim parents as well.

The Twofold and United Purposes of This Book

My experience in Pakistan crystallized in a compelling way the possibility of articulating what amounts to both a philosophy of Catholic education and a "Catholic" philosophy for educators— teachers and parents—regardless of their religious background or affiliation or, indeed, the social context of their educating.

I call the latter philosophy "Catholic" because although it is suggested by core convictions of Catholic Christianity, it can have general appeal and be persuasive apart from confessional Christian faith. It reflects catholicity as in the etymology of the term *kata holos*—"welcoming everyone." When such catholicity is the intent the particularity of Christianity can contribute most richly to the universal enterprise of education.

Upon further travel and research, I became aware that the Catholic schools of Pakistan are not unique. They have analogues in other cultures that are predominantly Buddhist or Hindu or Shinto or whatever. Nor is Catholic Christian education the only faith-inspired pedagogy that has appeal and finds proponents beyond its own confessional adherents. I have a Catholic friend who teaches at a Quaker college. She is deeply committed to the Quaker-inspired philosophy of her school and finds it an enrichment rather than a threat to her Catholic identity. During her junior faculty years, she had an excellent mentor who enabled her to grow and develop as a "Quaker" educator. She was surprised to discover that he was a devout Lutheran.

Educating for Life reflects twofold, and yet united, purposes and, correspondingly, two potential audiences—that also overlap and have common bond. First, I intend to propose a philosophy of Catholic education, one relevant to any and every instance of education carried on by Catholic Christian communities. This audience includes every Catholic parent in home schooling and family formation—the "domestic school"; every educator—teachers, administrators, and parents—involved with Catholic schools at any level (primary and secondary, colleges and universities); teachers, administrators, and parents in parish catechetical and religious education programs and in every expression of Catholic faith education (e.g. seminary and ministry education, catechumenal and lay leadership programs). It seems reasonable to expect that Catholic education and catechesis be carried on in ways consistent with the tradition itself.

Second, and reaching from the depth structures of Catholic Christianity toward the universal discourse about education, even to engage contexts where explicit faith commitment and religious language are excluded, I hope to make a "Catholic" contribution to the philosophy of education, offering a vision that can engage educators of any or no religious persuasion.

Rippling outward, this audience includes Catholics working in public schools who wish to allow their spirituality to inspire their educating, and educators of other religious traditions working in Catholic schools who subscribe to a "Catholic" philosophy of education. Indeed, some of the latter might choose to place themselves in my previous category of audiences. One of the finest educators I know is a Lutheran friend who teaches in a Catholic school and has embraced its philosophy of Catholic education. Upon reading a previous draft of this preface, she insisted that she is a Catholic educator—Capital C and without quotation marks.

Then, mainline Protestant Christians may identify with much of what is here and might consciously allow its spiritual vision to influence their educating—in family or congregational programs, in public or religiously sponsored schools; recognizing that whatever they do not identify with may help to clarify their alternative perspectives. (In 1996 there were one and a half million students in Christian sponsored schools—other than Catholic—throughout the United States.)

Lastly, I hope what is here might contribute to a humanizing education, proposing a vision of educating *for life for all* by educators in any school, program, or family. I am sustained in this hope by my own experience of studying the great Jewish educator Martin Buber (1878–1965). Since I first encountered his writings as a young graduate student, Buber has set my soul on fire.

This great philosopher and educator, writing out of the depths of Judaism and even more particularly from its Hasidic and mystical traditions, touched in lasting and life-giving ways the heart of a young Catholic educator. I was inspired, too, that Buber could write out of his own particularity and yet have appeal far beyond his community and tradition. I remember wondering if it might be possible to make a similar statement out of the depths of Catholic Christianity. My effort is here.

Both purposes—a philosophy of Catholic education and a Catholic-inspired contribution to the philosophy of education in general—are united by their common intent, namely a *spiritual vision of education that is humanizing,* a curriculum that educates *for life for all.* And both audiences are bonded in that *Educating for Life* will constantly reach beyond theology and philosophy to nurture the spirituality of teachers and parents, regardless of their background.

Herein lies the bedrock intent of *Educating for Life*—to propose a spiritual vision for every teacher and parent. Convinced that when spirituality is grounded in a particular tradition it is also most likely to have universal appeal, I draw upon the depth structures of Catholic Christianity for inspiration. In consequence, the spiritual vision proposed may most readily inspire Catholic educators—teachers and parents who are Catholic Christians by faith confession and educate in schools (public or parochial), parishes, or families.

I am convinced, however, that the vision of *Educating For Life* can have an even broader appeal. It reflects spiritual values that find echo across a broad spectrum of religious traditions and could inspire the work of any educator, regardless of religious identity. And though few may call theirs a catholic pedogogy—even with a small c—they will experience what is proposed here as a humanizing one, a way of educating *for life and for all.*

So although a little pretentious in scope perhaps, my intended readership is everyone involved in education of any kind or context, as teacher, administrator, or parent. And in some way at some time, most people function as educator.

Spirituality will be the central theme of chapter 7, but the whole book is about a spiritual vision. *Educating for Life* reflects the conviction that the ultimate foundations of education are spiritual, given the nature of what educators effect at "the deep heart's core" of learners (Yeats) and if they are to educate *for life for all.* For now, by the spirituality of educators I mean the operative commitments from a faith perspective that undergird and permeate their educating—the deep-down things that persons really believe and that shape how they educate.

The core curriculum of this text, then, is to invite you the reader to look at your own spiritual foundations for educating, to reflect on them contemplatively and critically, to renew old or make new commitments around issues crucial to education and from your own faith convictions. The encounter with Catholic Christian spiritual foundations will be the catalyst for such review much as Buber and the spiritual resources of Judaism occasioned in me as a young graduate student.

My hope, then, is to stimulate the philosophical but more significantly the spiritual reflections of teachers and parents as educators. Since the resources of the text are drawn primarily (although not exclusively) from Catholic Christian faith, such reflections may come most readily to designated Catholic educators, and in this I would achieve the first of my two coprimary purposes. My hope, however, is to reach out from my particular faith community to propose a spiritual vision that can inspire "every teacher and parent." I wish to make explicit and articulate what my friends in Karachi have been doing more implicitly and by intuition.

Given my social context, the conversation partners I most often have in mind beyond my own Catholic community are the educators—teachers and parents—of American public schools. I am not naive about the historical resistance here to spiritually-based conversation about education. We Americans, although a deeply religious people, have created a constitutional separation between Church and State. The opening lines of the First Amendment to the U.S. Constitution read, "Congress shall make no law respecting an establishment of religion."

Since it was passed in 1791, there has raged a debate whether the separation should be a "wall" or a "line;" in the initial controversy Thomas Jefferson (1743–1826) favored the former; James Madison (1751–1836) was the great exponent of a "line of separation."[1] Although interpretation of the First Amendment has generally tended to see-saw back and forth, in matters regarding education it seems that a "wall of separation" ever prevails. It is as if Americans say as a nation, "In God we trust," and then add, "except in education."

Although other Western democracies have flourished without it, undoubtedly this "wall of separation" has had some positive consequences. An unfortunate one, however, has been to insinuate to American educators that their educating must transcend the influence of their own spirituality, thus excluding what should be consciously present to them as a prime source of humanizing education. I am convinced that the lack of a spiritual vision is an Achilles heel of "the American experiment" in education.

The fear encouraging "the wall," of course, is that some one religion might control public education. If warranted at one time, today's threat would seem to be the opposite—a system purged of all spiritual influence. And surely to constitutionally exclude an established religion should not prevent teachers from drawing upon their own spirituality as a resource to their educating—should not deny them their spiritual vision. Without spiritual foundations, educators are left with only philosophical ones, and although the latter are necessary and valuable, they are neither "innocent" by way of objectivity nor "sufficient to the task." Ironically, American education has drawn most heavily, almost exclusively, from one school of philosophy—pragmatism—and yet has been phobic about its spiritual neutrality.

Surely some of what ails American education needs spiritual address. I propose that public school educators be encouraged to reflect upon, probe, and consciously allow their spirituality to serve as a humanizing foundation for their educating. To this end, I raise up out of Catholic Christianity—a faith tradition with an enduring commitment to education—some spiritual resources that may serve as a conversation partner "for every teacher and parent." For readers from other traditions, encountering what is different, whether it spurs agreement or disagreement, can help to clarify their own spiritual vision.

It should go without saying, too, that rich spiritual resources for educating could be drawn from many other traditions. For example, if American education would allow the influence of Native American spirituality, it would likely teach a much keener ecological consciousness and more concerted care for the environment. If the "Protestant principle" truly permeated education, learners would have less difficulty with critical thinking. And the examples could go on. For too long the foundations of American and Western education in general have been drawn exclusively from philosophy. But no one school of thought nor all of them combined can provide educators with the foundations they need. The educational work of teachers and parents is ultimately and essentially spiritual. They need a spiritual vision.

Apart from my persuasion that every attempt to engage conversation with "neighbors" must be "made from one's own backyard," the following two strong convictions encourage me to propose a philosophy–cum–spirituality of education out of the depths of Catholicism:

• Catholic Christianity has some "substantial" characteristics that are deeply life-giving and have universal appeal.

• These characteristics can support a humanizing philosophy of education, one that transcends confessional Catholicism and can inspire educators of any tradition—nurturing their spirituality.

"Substantial" Characteristics that Are Humanizing and Universal

For many people outside of it and within, Catholicism appears at best as a mixed bag. Throughout this book, I frequently point to ways that Catholic Christian communities and people like myself fail to live up to their best traditions of faith. In these comments I have particular eye to my own Roman Catholic communion. It seems that all religious institutions fall short of living their "creed," but this is small comfort and should not bless complacency in any person of faith. I pose my critiques out of deep care for the Church and the conviction that recognition and repentance of sins—personal and communal—is integral to Christian faith. Rather than thinking of the Reformation as one time period in its history, the Church, to quote St. Augustine writing about 1600 years ago, must be *semper reformanda*—"always reforming" itself. And rather than thinking of only one half of Christianity as "protesters," the original Protestant principle—to protest anything in Church or society that is not of God's reign—is the baptismal mandate of every Christian.

All this being said, the fact remains that Catholicism seems to have an unrivaled ability to invite negative stereotypes of itself. Included among the current favorites—all of them having some warrant in Roman Catholicism—are the following: an authoritarian monolith with absolute norms that presumes to possess the fullness of divine truth; a patriarchal system that favors men and discriminates against women; a structure scarred by racism, classism, and many other "isms" besides; a religion obsessed with issues of sexuality—of any kind; an old-world monarchical leadership exercising supreme legislative, executive, and judicial powers; a papacy that encourages a cult of the person, stifles dissent, and forbids open discussion of controversial issues; a secretive bureaucracy with too much power, property, and possessions—and all the corruptions attendant thereto; and the list could go on.

Loyal Catholic Christians like myself recognize such negative stereotypes as either exaggerations or humbling evidence of how much the Catholic church is ever in need of reform—to practice what it preaches. Defenders also rightly insist that for every pompous cleric, one can find many priests, sisters, and pastoral ministers who follow the servant model of Jesus Christ. For every authoritarian hierarch, there is an Oscar Romero (1917–80), archbishop of San Salvador, who gave his life in his people's struggle for justice or a Cardinal Joseph Bernardin (1928–96) of Chicago, whose open heart and holiness of life made him "Brother Joseph" to all.

Against attempts at knowledge control there is the "fresh air" and openness of the Second Vatican Council (1962–65), as well as the great vibrancy and diversity that prevails throughout contemporary Catholic theology. Even on women's rights, to focus alone on present exclusion from priesthood can overlook the significant contribution by Catholic Christianity to women's equality throughout history and the world.

And those of us still deeply nurtured by the tradition and who work in hope for its institutional renewal would certainly claim that there is more richness, nuance, and multivalence at the depths of Catholicism than the negative stereotypes convey. Otherwise, it would not have survived so long or given life to so many. In fact, some of its most controversial aspects, and usually the ones that get attention in the media, are "accidental" rather than "substantial" to this tradition of Christian faith.

Here I use an old philosophical distinction that I learned from Aristotle (384–322 B.C.E.). the great Greek thinker whose writings covered every branch of human knowledge known to his time. "Accidentals" are aspects of something that are not essential to what it really is, that could be otherwise. "Substantials" are aspects that are fundamental and abiding. They belong to the very nature of something. That I needed breakfast this morning is a substantial aspect of my humanity. That I had a muffin was an accident—it happened to be there.

My focus in this book is the substantial aspects of Catholic Christianity that could lend themselves to a humanizing philosophy for teachers and parents—and nurture their spirituality. These substantials are like great rivers of faith and commitment that flow consistently through Catholic Christian tradition in every time and place. I will use other phrases too like "core convictions" or "depth structures," but they, too, refer to substantial features that give Catholicism its distinctiveness within Christianity and among religious traditions in general.

The most essential substance of all Christianity—Catholic and Protestant—is faith in God and in Jesus Christ. Like adherents of all the great theistic religions, Christians believe they are to live as a people of God. Then, specifically, they are to live their faith in God as disciples of Jesus, the Christ, following "the way" that he modeled, living their faith in the midst of the world and through solidarity with a Christian community—the Church. Jesus is the "foundation stone," to use the New Testament term, of Christian faith. Besides discipleship to Jesus, many other beliefs, morals, and practices are shared by all mainline Christian denominations—symbolized in their regular recitation at Sabbath worship of the same sixteen-hundred year-old Nicene Creed.

Although all Christians share a common faith, there are configurations of belief and worship, practice and discipline within the Christian Church—distinctive traditions. In the early Christian communities, we already notice different perspectives, beginning with the fact that there are four gospels rather than one—each with its own emphasis in telling and interpreting the Jesus story.

As Christian faith became inculturated into different contexts and cultures, further diversity emerged as richness in the midst of unity. In time, however, instead of being enriched by diversity, the unity became rent by divisions, the deepest emerging between Protestant and Catholic Christianity at the time of the Reformation in the sixteenth century.

With the ecumenical spirit of our time, there are hopeful signs that the wounds of division are being healed. As the Christian Church slowly returns to "unity in diversity," every communion in the Body of Christ has greater access to the richness of each other's theological and spiritual traditions. Meanwhile, although hardened division is disappearing and awareness growing of common spiritual heritage, a distinctiveness remains to both Catholic and Protestant Christianity—substantial characteristics that give each its rich identity. As I will often note, many of these characteristics overlap—with lots of individual Catholics and Protestants "switching" on particular issues—and yet each has a distinct configuration that lends its uniqueness.

Catholic Christianity's substantial characteristics coalesce as the particular spin it puts on the great human questions about meaning and purpose and how to live. They weave together into a philosophy of life, with its grounding in faith also encouraging a spirituality. Catholicism has a long tradition of partnership between theology and philosophy, between revelation and reason.

Among other things, this reciprocity encourages composing its faith as a philosophy and stating faith convictions in philosophical as well as theological terms. Many Catholic scholars, most notably the greatest of them all, Thomas Aquinas (1225–74), have been as much philosophers as theologians, with little to distinguish in their writings where one begins and the other leaves off. True, some central doctrines—like the Blessed Trinity—are suggested first by divine revelation, but many of Catholic Christianity's core convictions about life—its meaning and purpose, how to live responsibly and find happiness—can be discerned "naturally" and presented as a philosophy without requiring confessional faith in Christian revelation or in Jesus Christ. For example, to the "natural law" tradition of ethics so favored by Catholicism, people can know that murder is wrong, in and of itself, and not simply because the Bible condemns it.

That Catholic Christianity finds warrant for many of its core convictions about life in a kind of "natural" theology can lend it appeal to people of other traditions—simply on human grounds—enriching their own spirituality. And surely this is what all great religious traditions can share most readily with each other—what seems true on their common footing of experience and reason. As a Christian, I do not profess Mohammed to be God's greatest prophet, but I have long been persuaded and inspired by the Muslim example of compassion for the poor. Similarly, someone outside of Christianity could draw inspiration from its substantial commitment to justice without sharing its confession of Jesus Christ.

A Humanizing Approach to Education

My second conviction is that just as the substantial characteristics of Catholic Christianity can be woven together into a life-giving philosophy, so, too, they can suggest a humanizing approach to education.

Take, for example, Catholicism's core understanding of the human condition—its anthropology. Essentially, it holds to a positive and hopeful sense of ourselves. The conviction is that people, although all too capable of evil, are more disposed toward doing good. What a difference this conviction might make to how one educates, in contrast to the attitude that persons are essentially bad and not to be trusted.

So many of the great movies on teaching (like *To Sir with Love, Stand and Deliver, Dead Poets Society, Mr. Holland's Opus*) are about the difference a teacher can make who appeals to what is best in students, to their highest aspirations, refusing to bow to negative attitudes or social circumstances.

Or take the Catholic depth structure of sacramentality. When philosophically stated, it encourages people to see "the more" in the everyday, to find joy in the ordinary, to appreciate the aesthetic, to relish life's giftedness. Imagine how this conviction could shape the style of a teacher or parent, regardless of religious tradition or where she or he educates.

This book will review eight core convictions of Catholic Christianity that seem particularly relevant to a humanizing philosophy for educators, to a spirituality that supports educating *for life for all*. Hopefully, every teacher and parent can take its spiritual vision to heart if only to enhance or bring to consciousness what is already there.

Clarification of Terms and Language Use

I will explain many technical and uncommon terms as they occur, but what I mean by some key and often used ones should be rendered here at the outset.

I use *Catholic*—without quotation marks and typically adding Christian—to refer to persons or communities, parish programs, families, or schools that can be designated as Catholic because of their confessional faith. Therefore, a Catholic parish program is one sponsored from within a local Catholic Christian community. A Catholic school is one sponsored or managed by a Catholic diocese, parish, organization, or by one of Catholicism's vowed religious orders. On the other hand, any school, program, or family could be inspired by a "Catholic" philosophy or spirituality of education—as are the Muslim faculties of Catholic schools in Pakistan, and elsewhere.

And what of *Catholic Christian?* I write consciously out of my own Christian tradition of Roman Catholicism, committed to representing faithfully its depth structures, their concomitant spirituality, and the implications for education of any kind. Then, beyond the Roman rite and the various rites in the Catholic Communion of Churches (e.g., Maronites), Catholic Christianity also includes the several Eastern Orthodox rites (e.g., Greek Orthodox) and, spiritually at least, the various expressions of the Anglican communions (e.g., Episcopalian).

Then, by tradition as well as from a growing ecumenical sentiment the core convictions of Catholic Christianity are shared also to varying degrees by mainstream Protestant Christians. In fact, many old lines of demarcation have become blurred. There seems to be a great increase of what could be called Catholic Protestants—people who appreciate and draw upon the legacy of Catholicism and yet by polity and/or conviction remain identified as Protestant Christians.

Likewise, there are growing numbers of what could be called Protestant Catholics—people biblically centered in their faith, committed to reforming the Church, more autonomous in their decision making, and yet, by polity and/or conviction remain identified as Catholic Christians.

Even when identified by denominational membership, many Christians on various issues "switch" positions, especially at a spiritual level. I think of a Methodist minister friend who has a decidedly Catholic anthropology. This is not unusual since John Wesley (1703–91), the founder of Methodism, was an ordained Anglican priest and retained a quite Catholic understanding of the person. I think of a Congregational minister colleague who has been learning the art of spiritual mentoring at a Catholic retreat center and of a liberal Catholic theologian friend who "protests" the shortcomings of the Church as concertedly as any Luther ever did.

There are also many Christians who embrace some or all of the substantial characteristics of Catholicism but may not locate themselves institutionally within the Catholic church for disciplinary reasons. I think of a woman raised Roman Catholic who became Lutheran out of a desire for ordained ministry. Sometimes Protestant Christians can be more faithful in practice to the sentiments of Catholic Christianity than self-identified Catholics, and vice versa.

For example, many Protestants in the Calvinist tradition no longer subscribe to the theological notion of predestination—that God predestines some people to be lost and others to be saved—whereas I know Catholics who would seem to subscribe to it, if only by overemphasizing the importance of church membership to salvation!

On the other hand, in the aftermath of the Second Vatican Council, Catholics often seem more committed to "ever reforming" the Church than mainline Protestants.

With ecumenism encouraging the demise of hardened divisions, it is not easy to find precise language to name "who's who." When describing a belief or practice shared generally by Christians, I will refer to it simply as Christian. On the other hand, there are constitutive aspects of Catholic Christianity that could not be attributed—even spiritually—to all Christians. For example, a strong sense of sacramentality.

In general then, to highlight the fundamental bondedness between Catholic and Protestant Christians—in reciting the Apostles' and Nicene Creeds, all confess faith in the Church as *catholic*—and to signal that Catholic tradition is a deep river from which all Christians can refresh themselves as desired, I tend to favor the term *Catholic Christian* throughout. It could be said that I am proposing a broadly Christian philosophy–cum–spirituality of education, giving it a Catholic "spin" when a foundational issue (e.g., anthropology) engenders a variety of positions within Christendom.

On occasion, I use *"Catholic"*—with quotation marks—to reflect a philosophy and spirituality that, albeit suggested by substantial characteristics of Catholicism, could be embraced by anyone so persuaded or inspired by its implications for education, apart from one's own confessional faith. I will sometimes refer to a "Catholic" philosophy—or spirituality—for educators to capture with one phrase the twofold purposes of this book, namely, a philosophy of Catholic education and a Catholic-informed contribution to education in general. *"Catholic"* with quotes is to signal a breadth of meaning beyond, and yet including, the intracommunal interest of Catholic education. The opening story of chapter 9 may provide a helpful clue to the overall sense of Catholic that underlies *Educating for Life*.

I use Vision in the title and throughout because what I propose is much more a hope than a claim, more a promise than a report, more a vision than a story of what has ever been achieved in the educating by any Catholic Christian community, or indeed by any educating community at all. As a vision, it is an ideal, and although never realized completely by any school, parish program, or family, I hope at least some aspect of *Educating for Life* may inspire every teacher and parent.

As may already be evident, it is not easy to find terms that encompass all the agents and sites of education which this book intends to address. Thus, I stay with fairly traditional words but intend their broadest meaning—sometimes overlapping. Generally, I use *school* to designate any kind of formal and institutionally based educational environment. This includes the obvious candidates like primary and secondary schools, colleges and universities, but also any other school that has an institutional life. I use *program* as a generic term for intentional but community-based curricula and usually in faith education, such as a parish religious education or catechetical program.

I use *Church*—capitalized—when referring to the whole Christian people. On the other hand, I favor *church*—lower case—when referring to a particular Christian community, as in Catholic church or Protestant church. I follow this usage so that the term Church may remind all Christians of the unity to which we are called as the one Body of Christ in the world. Many of the texts I quote, however, do not follow this pattern, so Church/church may be a bit confusing at times—but so it may always be!

I use *parish* to designate a distinguishable and local Christian faith community. Although "parish" is a more Catholic word, for brevity's sake I do not usually add the more Protestant term "congregation," hoping that people from other traditions can read parish to mean a local faith community. I use *family*—not in the "nuclear" sense—to indicate any intimate and sustaining network of personal life. A central proposal throughout the book is that family is to participate intentionally in the nurture, growth, and learning—the education—of its members.

Family education always includes the formation that parents provide to children through the ethos of their home, and then can range from tutoring with homework and being a partner in the work of a school or parish program to full-fledged homeschooling.

From the above, it is already clear that education includes more than schooling and educator more than teacher. Although I sometimes use *teacher* and *educator* interchangeably, *educator* is the broader term, including parents as well as designated teachers and people who administer any school or parish program. On the other hand, I use *teacher* to include people who teach in parish catechetical programs— paid or volunteer—as well as in schools. *Teacher* also includes parent and most notably in a homeschooling situation. And by *parent,* I mean any primary agent of family nurture and maintenance.

When I use the term *students,* I typically refer to participants in a formal school. For all participants in education of any kind, I prefer the term *learners* in that it seems broader than students in its connotation, the latter being so closely associated with schooling. I never intend either *student* or *learner* to be hierarchically lower in relation to teacher, educator, or parent. As I elaborate, those latter terms all refer to "leading learners," and the universal human vocation is for all to remain perennial students and lifelong learners. It is just that in particular circumstances, some may be designated as learners and others as educators—though they ever remain learners, too.

I will often use the word *curriculum.* As I intend the term, there are four aspects to an educational curriculum: the explicit content that is taught; the pedagogy or teaching/learning process that educators employ; the environment in which the education takes place—with its own implicit curriculum; and lastly, the purpose that permeates the whole effort—the "intended learning outcome," to use a traditional phrase.

Note too that the translation of the Scriptures most often cited is the *New American Bible.* However, on a number of occasions—when a translation seems more apt to my purpose—I use some others, most notably the *Jerusalem Bible* and the *New Revised Standard Version.*

I am committed to an inclusive language pattern—one that excludes no one, especially on the basis of gender. Inclusive language is an issue for becoming catholic—for "including all."[2] Since some works I quote were written before awareness of exclusive language, I take the liberty to adjust some quotations inclusively, placing the interposed word or words in brackets. Typically, I follow the lead of the U.S. National Council of Teachers of English, which now permits the use of *they, their,* or *them* to refer to an indefinite singular pronoun—a return to the practice of Medieval English. As Shakespeare wrote, "May God send everyone their heart's desire."

In modern English we were taught "send everyone his heart's desire" and then, of late, began to add "or her"—a rather awkward construct. Although not yet common usage, it now seems permissible to return to the Shakespearean pattern—and to let "everyone have their heart's desire" again—or at least for "each one to decide for themselves."

Why Teachers and Parents

At the outset I should explain why I explicitly include parents in a philosophy of education—addressing them "in the same breath" as teachers. The very need to explain their inclusion reflects how far Western education has strayed from its ancient awareness that parents are the primary educators of their children. That schools and parishes should replace the educational and catechetical work of parents is a recent notion and one much in need of review.

First and foremost, parents educate by osmosis—through the process of socialization in the shared life of the home. The family's entire ethos and lifestyle, its relationships and conversations, its attitudes, outlooks, and values, its faith—just about everything that goes on there—educates its members in the most foundational sense of influencing and sustaining their identities. We emerge into the consistent sense we have of ourselves as persons, we absorb our particular self-understanding, perspective on life, and ethic of living—we glean our identity—from the primary socialization of "the home." As the word *education* is expanded to mean more than schooling and imparting knowledge, one recognizes that the socialization of the original family is the most consequential "education" people ever receive.

That families educate through socialization is inevitable. That they educate in humanizing ways is far from inevitable. The socialization of the home can be and needs to be fashioned intentionally if it is to educate *for life for all*. I recently observed a mother playing in a public park with her three-year-old son. Everything he saw was of curiosity and led to a question—not only about things, but about people ("But why's that lady wearin' a funny hat?") and about life ("But why do we hafta not do dat?")—dominated by that greatest of a 3-year-old's questions, "But why?"

I was impressed by the care and thoughtfulness the young woman took to answer her son's questions, engaging him in conversation and inviting his own reflections as well. It was quite evident that she was making a choice to take his curiosity seriously—in fact, encouraging and delighting in it. I reflected on how positive this moment of socialization must have been for the child, just as to dismiss his questions and discourage his curiosity would have been a negative pedagogy.

Parents, especially of younger children, have a hundred educating opportunities every day, not only in explicit conversations but in the curriculum implicit throughout the shared life of the home. And parents, as much as any teacher, must make curriculum choices about their educational approach—how and what to teach within the family and to what end. A parent's approach to socialization can be more consistent and life-giving if grounded in a humanizing philosophy–cum–spirituality that enables them to educate *for life for all*. They are as much in need of such a spiritual vision as any educator. This book is certainly not a "practical guide to parenting"— valuable as that might be—but it will suggest to parents some operative faith commitments to bring to socializing children.

What then of parents' participation in their children's formal schooling? Is the parents' function as educators limited to primary socialization with no responsibility for their offspring's schooling other than seeing to it that they get there and back safely, and, as required, that tuition is paid? Clearly not! Conscientious parents see that their children complete assignments and give help with homework. Likewise, they usually have some level of partnership with their children's schools through "home and school" associations, parent-teacher conferences, and so on. Valuable as such participation may be, there is growing consciousness that much more is both needed and possible from parents in the formal education of children, especially in the early years.

More is needed because too many schools in Western society—for whatever reason—seem less capable of providing quality education to their students. Parents are foolhardy to totally transfer the education of children to schools/ They need to reclaim a more active role themselves. I say "reclaim" because when the "public school" system of the West was founded—schooling provided by the State—it was never intended to replace the primary role of parents.

In 1524, the great Protestant reformer Martin Luther (1483–1546) wrote his "Letter to the Councilmen of the Cities of Germany," urging them to sponsor schools for all and to take education out of the hands of the Church—a document often considered the Magna Carta of public education in the West. Luther said that the State should intervene but—and he was adamant—only to supplement the work of parents, not to replace it. For this reason, he advised that boys attend school for no more than two hours each day and girls for only one, so that their schooling would not unduly interfere with their education at home and in the world around them.[3] In short time, however, schools did replace parents as primary educator. But parents can no longer afford to settle for such an arrangement—if they ever could.

Even more is possible on the part of parents with the advent of new technologies of communication. Just think of the vast supply of high-quality books that are readily available to every family—in local libraries if they cannot afford to buy them. What an educational influence parents have when they encourage their children to read good books.

Then add in the potential of television and the educational possibilities of cyberspace. A friend Marjorie told me that her eleven-year-old daughter Helen—who heretofore had "hated" English composition—has been writing and swapping short stories on the Internet and that she cannot wait to get home from school to see what awaits her on e-mail and to send a new story to a friend.

To take advantage of such new possibilities for home-based education, parents must be intentional about it—be mentors, encouragers, resources to their children of how to use modern media to educational advantage. Statistics indicate that American elementary school children watch about thirty hours of television each week. It undoubtedly requires much attention on the part of parents, but surely they can ensure that at least some of their children's viewing is educational.

The most notable instance of parents as educators is the "homeschooling movement"—now estimated to embrace one million families in the U.S. alone and expanding rapidly. Homeschooling is a very diverse movement, spanning the ideological spectrum from the Christian far right to the radical social left. Essentially, homeschool students attend no formal school at all; their parents take complete responsibility to resource and supervise their education within the home and community.

When I asked Carol why she and her husband Peter choose to homeschool their five children, she said that two considerations had originally prompted their decision: First, homeschooling seemed more likely to enable the children to become who they were born to be—to honor their own abilities and talents, interests and gifts. Second, it was more likely to encourage them to "learn how to learn" and ever to remain curious explorers of life. Carol uses some curricula materials published for homeschooling contexts, but much of the curriculum emerges from the children's particular interests at any given time. Being the parent at home during the day, Carol sees to it that they have the resources they need to pursue whatever they desire to learn or helps them to seek out the resources within the community.

Carol's rationale echoes the work of American author John Holt (1923–85), leading philosopher of the homeschooling movement. Holt had a rather strident critique of traditional schooling as "compulsory, coercive, and competitive" and "cut off from active life and done under pressure of bribe or threat, greed and fear." By contrast, he was convinced that homeschooling could encourage "self-directed, purposeful, meaningful life and work" based on learners' own interests and self-initiated activities.

Holt was convinced that children have a natural capacity for learning, often socialized out of them by schooling; that

> [they learn best] if they are allowed, encouraged, and
> helped . . . to think, talk, write, and read about the things
> that most excite and interest them. In short, if they are
> able to explore the world in their own way, and in as
> many areas as possible direct and control their own lives.[4]

The homeschooling movement is the most eminent instance of parents taking primary responsibility for the formal education of their children. In this, it is prophetic to all parents, challenging them to reclaim the explicitly educational aspect of their vocation.

I am not as critical as Holt was of systems of schooling and, by implication, parish religious education programs. Given the sociocultural circumstances, however, it is true that much more is now asked of parents as educators, inviting them to be more intentional about the socialization within the home and to reclaim a proactive role in their children's formal education. This is eminently true in the case of religious education—always and appropriately a special interest throughout this work. As parents reclaim their rightful role as educators, they too will need a humanizing philosophy, to tend to their own spiritual foundations. So, I address *Educating for Life* to the obvious candidates like teachers and educational administrators, *and* to parents as well—to all who educate.

Acknowledgments

For whatever the personal reasons may be, I first acknowledge that *Educating for Life* has not been an easy book to write—hopefully, it will be a little easier to read. One challenge has been to make a statement that is both a philosophy of Catholic education and a "Catholic" contribution to the philosophy of education in general.

Likewise, it has been challenging to write out of the depths of Catholic Christianity and yet do so in a way that reflects deep ecumenical sensitivity, that proposes a spiritual vision which is eminently *catholic*—welcoming all. Now only the reader can judge how well I have succeeded; hopefully with a modicum of success because educating *for life for all* requires as much.

Throughout the project, I have had the support and help of a great number of people. Although I alone am responsible for what is here, I should acknowledge my indebtedness to them. In that much of what I have written reflects my own biography, I begin by thanking the great host of family and "old" friends along my life's journey—my own "communion of saints and sinners." I think especially of the Groome family in Ireland and here in the United States and of the Griffith family who have welcomed me as one of their own. After that, the "old" friends are too many to name, but a host of their faces returned as I searched out the many personal stories I recount here.

I thank the many people who shared stories and suggestions with me. Although my list is surely partial, my indebtedness requires that I take the risk. So, I thank: Fred Poole, Austin Groome, Janice Webb, Florence Trahan, Jeanne Snyder, Jane Silk, Doreen Groome, Laura Dahlke, Carmen Torres, Marcelline Koch, Carol Delaney, Thomas Griffith, Peter Benson, Marybeth Griffith, Teddy Gorman, Roseanne Quinn, Paul O'Conner, Andreas Perdikis, Tom Beaudoin, Barbara Redmond, Russ Butkus, and John Manganzini. I thank Margaret Wuelfing, Briedge Vallely, Richard Kohut, Stephen Minnema, Marin Fortune, William Grogan, Francis Blighton, Keith Anderson, Columba Byrne, Catherine Cronin Carotta, Mario D'Souza, Mary Hess, and indeed all the participants in my summer school course at Boston College, 1997, who read and offered many comments on a penultimate draft of the manuscript.

I thank Paula Jurigian for some bibliographical research and Dermot Groome for his friendship, helpful comments on the manuscript, and "being there" at the end—when most needed—to help finalize the bibliography. I express deep gratitude to Annette Francis who has been not only an extraordinary editor but also an encouraging friend throughout the writing process. Whatever grammatical errors or inelegant prose may be here are in spite of her valiant efforts. I cannot imagine a more competent and caring editor!

Finally and without adequate words, I thank my beloved spouse, Dr. Colleen Griffith. She lent me her own theological and educational expertise as I talked through with her many of the ideas that are here. Throughout the most struggled times, her vital and infectious spirit has enlivened mine—she is ever "the rainbow 'round my heart." Colleen's enduring love continues to sustain as first sacrament of God's love in my life. I am abundantly blessed and deeply grateful for her companionship in *educating for life* together. To her, Cailin *grá mo chroí*—woman love of my heart—I dedicate this book.

Thomas H. Groome

Notes

1. For a discussion of both positions, see McBrien, *Caesar's Coin,* 63–67.
2. See my short book, *Language for a "Catholic" Church.*
3. See Martin Luther, "To the Councilmen of All Cities in Germany that they Establish and Maintain Christian Schools" in Cully, *Basic Writings in Christian Education,* 137–149.
4. See John Holt, *Instead of Education,* 1–7.

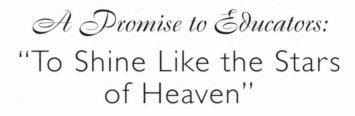

CHAPTER ONE

A Promise to Educators:
"To Shine Like the Stars of Heaven"

'No Brighter Star'

"Hello, Maggie. God bless the work!" This was John's greeting to my mother as he sauntered by my childhood home with a nonchalant air—like a man of leisure out for a noontime stroll. She invariably responded, regardless of the weather, "It's a grand day that's in it, John. Always a good day when we have our health." And he would agree enthusiastically, with more benedictions.

John Finnan, with his tattered clothes and raw-boned appearance, reminded my childhood imagination of a scarecrow—the kind we put up in the fields at sowing time to frighten the birds away. A bachelor all his life, he lived alone in a small dilapidated cottage—barely a roof over his head.

Because he owned his own small plot of land, local folklore ascribed the suspicion of "plenty of money" to him—and perhaps for his context, he had—but truth was that he barely eked out a living for himself and certainly had never learned to cook. For as long as anyone could remember, he relied on my mother and Bride Fox, another good neighbor in the village, for daily food.

In their routine exchange, John always managed to look as if he just happened to be passing by—at lunch time—and indeed intended to go further. My mother would say, "Beg yer pardon, John," as if she might be delaying him from important business, and then continue, "I cooked too much meat and potatoes again today, and I hate to see them wasted. You'd do me a great favor to come in and finish them up for me."

John's standard response was, "Well, Maggie, I've had plenty t' eat already, but, like yerself, I hate to see good food go to waste."

Then inside he'd come to our kitchen and finish off a fine lunch, with my mother thanking him for the favor, and he regaling her with the momentous news from the village—like whose cow had calved, who was tilling ground or sowing potatoes—his gratuity. To her stock question, "Any news, John?" I never once heard him say "No." And when I'd sit still long enough, he'd have some great story for me, too, about "th' ould times."

Even as a child, I was awed by their finesse in playing out the roles so credibly—when they both knew what the other knew. With my child's sense of "reality," I often wanted to protest, "But Mammy, I heard you say you were puttin' on extra spuds and meat 'cos John would be comin' by," but somehow knew to hold my tongue—and, anyhow, I loved to watch the little drama unfold.

One summer's day, after John had left, I finally asked my mom why she didn't just come out and say, "Hello John, lookin' for yer lunch again? I have it ready for yeh."

I have never forgotten her response. "Well, it might hurt John's feelings to say that. And I could begin to think that he's in my debt. The poor are their own gift to us, and we owe them!" She said no more.

Recalling the story now, so many years later, I recognize that I continue to mine and try to live the wisdom that she taught—an untold treasury. Not least of which, that day, was how to be partners with those we help, affirming their dignity and not inflating our own ego—a lesson that both individuals and societies need to learn, and educators to model and teach. She taught mostly by her life, occasionally with a little instruction.

I have never had a better teacher, a "star of heaven" forever!

Privilege and Responsibility

It is a sacred privilege and an awesome responsibility to be an educator. And it may be the closest we have to a universal human vocation. They are few who do not fulfill the function of educating at some time in one way or another. Of course, to appreciate its breadth of participants, one must expand the notion of education far beyond "schooling." For most it includes the latter, albeit with sympathy for Huckleberry Finn's sentiment that he tried not to let his schooling interfere with his education. But we are educated by far more than formal schooling.

Pause for a moment to remember the myriad people from whom you have learned in your life, and you will recognize that you have had a host of educators. As human beings, we are forever teaching and learning from each other!

American intellectual historian Bernard Bailyn offered such an expansive horizon with his now classic definition of education as "the entire process by which a culture transmits itself across generations."[1] I am traditional enough—or is it vested interest?—to keep designated teachers at the center of this expansive enterprise, with parents alongside them and being teachers in their own right. Then, rippling out into society, just about everyone participates, however obliquely, as educator—to transmit the culture across generations. And certainly no one in a society can afford not to care about the quality of its educating.

Another expansive way to think of education is as an "ontological" affair. This auspicious sounding word is from the Greek *ontos* for "being" and has the dual sense of both noun and verb, as in human *being* and how I do *be*—to take a grammatical liberty. A moment's reflection brings the realization that education, at its best, molds the very "being" of people—both who they become and how they live in the world. It is ontological.

So, regardless of what teachers teach, they teach people, and the better they teach the more they influence the whole person—head, heart, and hands. To be educator is to stand on holy ground—people's lives. No wonder the Bible promises that those who do it well, "shall shine like the stars of heaven forever" (Daniel 12:3).

The work of educators is much in need of affirmation. Even professional teachers can forget the significance and value of what they do. And it can be difficult to remember. Many of the "results" of teaching are a long way down the road—usually far out of view. At times, too, students are capable of a deadening indifference, enough to threaten any teacher's sense of self-worth. And the doubts within can be fanned by a commodity culture that values people's work by how much they "make"—always meaning money. Since career teachers "make little" compared to other professions, teaching must not be that valuable.

There can even be elements in society that prefer teachers and parents not to take their educational work too seriously—apropos critical thinking and social reform. All societies are tempted to prefer a domesticating brand of education that prepares "good citizens" who "fit" into the status quo and help to maintain it. Even the Church can be blind enough to prefer congregants who simply pray, pay, and obey. In fact, there is little welcome anywhere for "boat rockers" who challenge "the authorities"—as good education would encourage.

Teachers and parents, of course, should be concerned to enhance learners' lives in the world. Everyone needs their education to help them find food and shelter, work and security, relationships and community, self-esteem and aesthetic fulfillment—the basics of life. No instance of education can ignore such a reality principle. It is surely a poor education that prepares learners to be no more than social misfits. On the other hand, it is a travesty for teachers and parents to be co-opted into programming social automatons.

Consider the worthiest purpose of education as that learners might become fully alive human beings who help to create a society that serves the common good. As the reader will have already noted, I often summarize this personal and social purpose of education with the pithy phrase *for life for all*—or sometimes as a humanizing education.

For now I suggest—and elaborate throughout—that such a vision calls for ways of educating that engage people as active agents in their own learning, instead of passive recipients; that help them to develop all their gifts and abilities, especially their capacity for freedom and responsibility; that give learners access to the legacy of humanities, arts and sciences bequeathed by generations before them; that are designed to inform, form, and transform participants and society toward wisdom of life and social well-being.

I also understand such a sense of purpose and process for educating to be most likely inspired by if not synonymous with a spiritual vision. For there is an ultimacy to such educating; it enables persons to become fully alive human beings, to fulfill their utmost human vocation with a horizon that stretches into eternity and toward the Transcendent. Such humanizing education seems more likely if educators have an abiding faith—faith in the worthwhileness of their vocation, faith in the potential of learners, and faith in Gracious Mystery that is ground and horizon of all. And if, then, they can verify such faith as a religiously held conviction—for example, that all people are made in God's image and likeness—how more likely that it become an operative commitment in their educating.

The purposes and mode of educating I am proposing here are certainly in contrast to the pragmatism that presently reigns in Western education. But why should educators settle for less than a spiritual and noble vision—given the holy ground from which they look into the horizon?

This book raises up such a vision from the depth structures of Catholic Christianity, but it finds warrant in many other sources as well, including the whole humanist tradition of Western education. In fact, every teacher and parent can find within their own heart the vocation to be a humanizing educator, to teach with a spiritual vision. Such a "calling" (*vocatus*) is heard, indeed, from one's own depths, but also comes *from beyond the self,* as not of one's own making. This is why its best philosophers and exponents have understood educator as a spiritual vocation, implying that its surest foundation is the educator's own spirituality. I cite a few notable spokespersons.

The greatest Greek philosopher, Plato (ca. 428–348 B.C.E.), described teaching as "turning the soul" of learners,[2] and he meant touching and shaping their innermost "being"—their identity and agency. For Plato, we become and act most humanly as our souls are turned toward the true, the good, and the beautiful, and education is a crucial catalyst in this "turning." He was also convinced that the outcome of humanizing education is wisdom lived as virtue, which in turn renders the life of true happiness. For Plato, because educators are attendants to the deepest human desire—for ultimate happiness—they fulfill a religious service, a priestly function.

Aristotle was Plato's finest student and became a great philosopher in his own right. Significantly, and following the lead of his mentor Plato, Aristotle favored the word *morphosis* for education. Its literal meaning is "formation." More than dispensing knowledge, education forms character, or what people come to know should shape their "being"—who they are and how they live.

Agreeing with Plato, Aristotle said that the best life and the one that brings true happiness is the life of virtue, again making happiness in life through virtuous living the ultimate purpose of educating. Aristotle claimed that the loftiest outcome of human cognition is spiritual wisdom, which he called *sophia* and described as the most God-like way of knowing. He was convinced that humankind is capable of *sophia* "in virtue of something within us that is divine."[3]

So, for Aristotle, too, to educate is ultimately to nurture people's divine potential.

Confucius (551–479 B.C.E.), the great philosopher of China and writing some twenty-five hundred years ago, had a primarily political sense of purpose for education—to transform society into a moral and harmonious community. To this end, the process of educating must be such that it forms people in *jen,* a word that translates as both benevolence and humanness. Confucius was convinced that as people become more benevolent they become the human beings they should be, and, likewise, their society becomes humane and harmonious; note how his political purpose merges into an ontological one.

For a person to become benevolent, however, knowledge alone is not enough. One must be led to wisdom. In fact, Confucius often used benevolence and wisdom as symptomatic of each other: a person who "cannot be said to be wise . . . cannot be said to be benevolent."[4] So the work of the educator is to promote wisdom and benevolence and, thus, personal and social harmony—as strongly as an ethical humanist could state a spiritual purpose.

The most frequent title of address for Jesus in the Gospels is "teacher" (*didaskalos* in all four and also *rabbi* in John). He frequently referred to himself as a teacher, and more than fifty times the Gospels describe his work as teaching. Scripture scholars often summarize Jesus' lifework—in word and deed—as one great act of teaching.

From his first appearance in public (see Mark 1:14–15), Jesus made clear that he intended to teach people how to live for the reign of God—with love and compassion, peace and justice, holiness and freedom. His ultimate intent was that all might come to fullness of life—here and hereafter for eternity. "I came that you might have life and have it to the full" (John 10:10). No educator ever had a more spiritual purpose than Jesus.

In Jesus' culture, students typically sought out their teachers. Jesus, by contrast, took the initiative and went recruiting disciples—the Greek word *mathetes* also means "apprentice" or "learner." And he was totally inclusive in whom he sought out and welcomed as apprentices—women, tax collectors, those of other races, public sinners, the outcasts of society. His pedagogy, epitomized in the parables, deeply engaged the everyday lives of learners—farming and fishing, cooking and homemaking, robbers and taxes. He challenged old perspectives—both religious and social—and proposed new ones. And always he invited people to change their hearts, their lives, and their world by following his "way"—again ontological, political, and spiritual.

The Gospel of Mark notes of Jesus that "the people were astonished at his teaching, for he taught them as one having authority and not as the scribes" (1:22). This is amazing since Jesus had no official status as an educator in his society, whereas the scribes did. His authority was the integrity of his own life. He encouraged disciples to be the same kind of educators, promising, "Whoever obeys and teaches these commandments will be called greatest in the kingdom of heaven" (Matthew 5:19).

The final mandate of the Risen Christ to the assembled community was "go teach" how to live as people of God (Matthew 28:16–20). It would seem that all disciples are to be educators and to teach as Jesus did.

Many great educators of the contemporary era echo the ancient sentiment that education has ultimate purpose, and should be *for life for all*. The great Italian reformer Maria Montessori (1870–1952), whose significance for early childhood education is unparalleled, described teaching as "practicing the great art of companionship" in order to draw out "the life already within" the child. For Montessori, education should enable learners to grow in responsible freedom and boundless creativity.[5]

With similar grandeur of purpose and rhetorical flourish, the greatest American philosopher of education, John Dewey (1859–1952), wrote in his Pedagogic Creed, "I believe that the teacher always is the prophet of the true God, and the usherer in of the true kingdom of God."[6] Seldom are the echoes of Jesus so evident in Dewey!

And some twenty-five hundred years after Plato wrote about education "turning the soul," Alfred North Whitehead (1861–1947), the British genius mathematician and metaphysician with a lifelong passion for education, reechoed this enduring theme:

> We can be content with no less than the old summary of educational ideal which has been current at any time from the dawn of our civilization. The essence of education is that it be religious.[7]

The pantheon of witnesses to the ultimacy of education could go on. St. Irenaeus, bishop of Lyons (ca. 130–200) and ranked the greatest theologian of his era, wrote to Christian educators (ca. 190) urging them to be empowering catalysts in learners' lives because "the glory of God is the human person fully alive."[8] My sister friends in Pakistan were correct. To educate *for life for all* is ever to give glory to God.

The vocation of educator, however, is not for the fainthearted. St. James offered enough caution to give every pedagogue pause: "Not many should become teachers because you will be judged more strictly" (James 3:1). But lest we be daunted by the possibility and responsibility of this sacred calling, I repeat God's promise through the Book of Daniel. As an old translation ran, "Those who teach others unto justice shall shine like the stars of heaven forever" (Daniel 12:3).

For Reflection

- Take a few moments and write down your own sense of what it means to be an educator. "Being an educator means . . ." Then reflect on what or who has influenced your understanding.

- Defining *educator* very broadly (e.g., as in my opening story of my mother), think back on some of the great ones you have encountered. Dwell in the memory of them again. What phrase or metaphor might describe their vision of education?

- What can you learn from such great educators for your own vocation as teacher or parent?

"Catholic" Education: Some Preamble Points

This book's intent is to give parents and teachers—regardless of religious persuasion—access to the rich spiritual reservoir of Catholic Christianity as a resource to their own philosophical and spiritual foundations for education, hoping to enhance their educating *for life for all*. But the previous section surely attests that words like *teacher, educator,* and *education* can stand alone in their own ultimate significance. So, why insert a qualifier—like "Catholic"—before any of them? Why indeed interface education with an explicit spiritual tradition like Catholic Christianity? It will take the remainder of the book to respond, and at the end much will remain unsaid! There are preamble points to put in place before proceeding. I begin with some serious cautions about "Catholic" education.

Cautions to the Qualifier

Such a qualifier may be considered only if alert to avoid two pernicious prejudices it could encourage—sectarianism and parochialism. To stumble into such pitfalls would defeat the very purposes of a "Catholic" philosophy of education—and of this book. The caution cannot be taken lightly.

As always with any community naming its particularity, those within—and their neighbors—must be alert to avoid such dangers, forward and in reverse. The fear that schools sponsored by a faith community would encourage alienation and fragmentation and thus be inimical to the common good is precisely why American government has refused them public funding.

An intent throughout this text and accented in chapter 9 is to indicate how people can be grounded in a particular religious identity in ways that enhance their bondedness with all humankind—and serve the common good. And yet, although they can be avoided, no one proposing a spirituality of education out of a particular religious tradition can be naive about the dangers of sectarianism and parochialism. I should explain how I use both terms, beginning with sectarianism.

I accent immediately that there is a rich and valuable tradition of sects within Christendom. As the famous German sociologist Ernst Troeltsch (1865–1923) pointed out, both "church" and "sect" are valid social forms of Christianity, each with deep roots in the New Testament. I would venture that every Christian community needs both expressions of itself—"church" being an open kind of fellowship that welcomes all, saints and sinners alike and "sect" a more strict and committed group of adherents.[9] Certainly within the Christian Church as a whole, many sectarian traditions have given prophetic witness to the radicalness of Christian discipleship. As authority in the Church need not become "authoritarianism," so sectarian bonds need not lead to "sectarianism."

In historical point of fact, the best sectarian traditions have been most free of sectarianism—more free than many churches. I am thinking of Christian sects—in Troeltsch's sense—like the Mennonites and Brethren who are committed pacifists and give prophetic witness to the universality of God's love. And surely every defined community of faith needs a sectarian sentiment apropos its particular identity—having ways to know who belongs and who does not—even as it maintains a universal sentiment of welcoming and caring for all.[10]

In contrast to a valuable sectarian Christian tradition, and a danger for all religions and religious communities, is sectarianism. By this I mean *a bigoted and intolerant exaltation of one's own group that absolutizes the true and the good in its members, encouraging prejudice against anyone who has alternative identity—especially immediate neighbors.* Religious sectarianism, perhaps the most dangerous kind, can even murder the "other" while justifying it in the name of heaven.

One need look only to the pages of history or the morning newspaper to find evidence of religious sectarianism. A recent count revealed—and the statistics are likely constant—that of the violent conflicts presently raging in our world, 96 percent of them draw upon religious legitimation and some are directly caused by religion. Although much of this is undoubtedly the manipulation of religion by self-serving politicians, yet every religious group must be alert to avoid sectarianism, and this requires eradicating it from how it educates. Every religious community and tradition needs to claim its identity but is surely bound—in heaven's name—not to encourage sectarianism. This is an imperative for Christians if they are to honor their doctrine of the universality of God's love.

The key to avoiding sectarianism, it would seem, is to resist absolutizing one's own tradition and community and never to legitimize prejudice on any grounds. Surely one avoids exalting any group by recognizing its shortcomings. Besides the hope of renewal, I often note the failures of my own Catholic Christian community as an antidote to sectarianism. Nor is it sufficient to recognize shortcomings—as if breast beating is enough. Every Christian community must lament and repent of its communal sins and constantly recommit to reforming its ways. The Second Vatican Council (1962–65) declared that "the Church . . . is at the same time holy and always in need of being purified, and incessantly pursues the path of penance and renewal."[11]

A most forthright call to communal repentance for past sins and renewed conversion was issued by Pope John Paul II in his apostolic letter on preparing for the third millennium. He wrote:

> The Church should become more fully conscious of the sinfulness of her children, recalling all those times in history when they departed from the spirit of Christ and his Gospel and instead of offering to the world the witness of a life inspired by the values of faith, indulged in ways of thinking and acting which were truly *forms of counter-witness and scandal.* . . . The Church cannot cross the threshold of the new millennium without encouraging her children to purify themselves, through repentance, of past errors and instances of infidelity, inconsistency, and slowness to act.[12] (emphasis in original)

Regarding society, "Christians need to place themselves humbly before the Lord and examine themselves on the responsibility which they too have for the evils of our day."

Regarding the Church, Pope John Paul II emphasized the need to repent of sins of division among Christians—"for which both sides were to blame"—and to renew efforts for Christian unity. Second and contra sectarianism, the Church must repent "of the acquiescence given . . . to intolerance and even the use of violence in the service of truth."[13] Such repentance and *metanoia*—the Gospel word for conversion that entails a deep change of heart and way of acting— directly pertains to the Church's mission of education.

Much of the "downside" of Catholic Christianity has had negative and debilitating effects on its educational practice. Contrary to its own core tenets that I set out in subsequent chapters, Catholicism has shown itself capable of making people feel like hopeless sinners instead of affirming their essential goodness (chapter 2); of controlling their experience of God's presence instead of nurturing their sacramental consciousness (chapter 3); of encouraging sectarianism, racism, and patriarchy instead of communities of openness, equality, and mutuality (chapter 4); of repeating as closed a culture-bound tradition instead of drawing new life from it (chapter 5); of practicing authoritarianism and blind obedience instead of a chosen faith and an informed conscience, (chapter 6); of practicing shallow pieties instead of deep spiritualities (chapter 7); of working hand-in-glove with oppressive regimes and acquiescing in privileged social status instead of working for justice and social transformation (chapter 8); of encouraging parochialism instead of catholicity, narrow mindedness, exclusion, and prejudice instead of openness and hospitality (chapter 9). And the list could go on.

I proceed, then, determined to avoid sectarianism while affirming identity, ready to recognize, lament, and repent of the past and present sins of my faith community—in which I am an accomplice, and yet with humble hope for and recommitment to what might be—at its best—a "Catholic" philosophy and spirituality for educators.

Like sectarian, *parochial* can also be a positive term. It refers simply to a parish (Latin *parochia*) in the sense of a local area. So, a parochial school is one sponsored by a parish. *Parochialism,* on the other hand and like sectarianism to which it is closely related, *reflects a narrow-minded, self-sufficient, and insular mentality that closes up within itself, is intolerant to or oblivious of other perspectives, and conceited about its own.* It is sad but true that the very Christian community which puts explicit emphasis on claims to catholicity—universal in perspective—has often, in fact, fallen into parochialism. Parochialism and "Catholic" education should be an oxymoron—a contradiction in terms.

To be particularly avoided here is implying that "Catholic" education is the only way to do good education or that it should draw its foundations exclusively from Catholic Christian theology and church teachings. I hope indeed with this book to help promote good education, but as much can be achieved—and with many of the commitments espoused here—by a great variety of approaches and can be inspired by many different philosophies and religious traditions.

Every time and culture has had its great educators—a handful well-known and lauded, but the majority unheralded and unsung. Fine educators emerge in every context because God forever calls people to this noble vocation and gives them the requisite charisms to do it well. In addition to God's grace working in their lives, they draw inspiration and philosophical foundations from a variety of sources, or more accurately, God's grace works through the sources available to them.

Although I draw explicitly in this text from Catholic Christian theology and church teaching, the possible sources for a humanizing education are very diverse. The pragmatism of Dewey stands in stark contrast to Montessori's emphasis on contemplation and play, yet great teachers and parents have been inspired by both perspectives.

Similarly, although not always footnoted, the philosophy I propose here has been influenced by a wide array of authors and traditions—as should be the case for its catholicity. Besides the great Jewish author Martin Buber, the Quaker educator Douglas Steere has influenced my pedagogy, likewise, the political philosopher Jurgen Habermas, contemporary feminist thought, and an array of ancient and modern writers—that I footnote more adequately elsewhere.[14] As Catholic Christianity is a broad and deep river from which all may drink deeply, likewise, it can receive from many sources.

Educating for Life symbolizes my conviction that the pitfalls of sectarianism and parochialism can be avoided and that Catholicism's "underside" notwithstanding nor denied, ample historical record attests that its substantial characteristics can motivate great teachers and encourage good education. This is to say no more or less than that Catholic Christianity, at its best, can inspire a humanizing education and can enliven parents and teachers with the passion and faith commitment they need to educate *for life for all*. I believe it can do so precisely because it offers a spiritual grounding for education, and my primary focus in turning to Catholic Christianity is to glean its spirituality for the work of teachers and parents.

I referred in the Preface to the stout resistance that any mention of spirituality will surely meet within the context of American public education. Interpreting the First Amendment as requiring a "wall of separation"—at least in matters of education—has given rise to the debilitating views that publicly funded schooling should be "secular" in its inspiration and implementation, and concomitantly, education which claims a spiritual or religious basis must be excluded from government support as inimical to the welfare of society.

In consequence, debates about the reform of American education are invariably limited to technical problems (like how to raise test scores) or social ones (like how to cope with drugs and crime). Never does the public discourse allude to the need of teachers and parents for spiritual resources in their vocation as educators. Could there be a trace of reverse sectarianism and parochialism here—ironically against religious faith—that in fact may work contrary to the common good?[15]

Catholic Education: A Case in Point

Educating for Life will often read like a theology that leads to a philosophy and then reaches on to a spirituality for teachers and parents—faith-inspired operative commitments that might ground a humanizing education. While it draws a spiritual vision out of the depth structures of Catholic Christianity, it also has an empirical backdrop in the "case study" of Catholic education over its history.

This seems not only fitting but necessary lest the vision proposed appear "purely theoretical" and too far removed from reality. Catholic education and a "Catholic" contribution to education in general should both find warrant in the fruits borne by Catholic education over its history. Not that any practice lives up to its theory—all efforts fall short of their ideal. Yet, the old gospel criterion is that everything is best measured by its "fruits." (See Matthew 7:20.) The humanizing outcomes of Catholic education should be self-evident over time or all proposed here is a pipe dream.

Throughout its history, Catholic Christianity has reflected a deep commitment to education, from the beginning seeing it as an expression of God's "work of salvation." Christianity's Jewish roots surely inspired commitment to education and scholarship— something that Judaism has retained throughout history. Then Christian faith lent its own reasons for the Church becoming an educator. I think of the following three: a positive understanding of the human condition which gives rationale and hope to the work of educators; a this-worldly as well as other-worldly understanding of salvation which lends spiritual motivation for trying to improve the quality of people's lives now as well as preparing them for eternity; and perhaps most importantly, the conviction that revelation and reason are partners—that far from being antagonists, both faith and understanding are gifts of God and need each other.

This third conviction allowed Catholicism to educate in academic topics and yet do so from a faith perspective that lent integration to the entire curriculum. There were, of course, Christian leaders who opposed the marriage of faith and scholarship. Note the defiant stance of the great Carthage-born theologian Tertullian (ca. 160–225) that "Jerusalem has no need of Athens."[16] But a more balanced view won out in Catholic Christianity, well summarized in a classic statement of

Aquinas: "Just as grace does not destroy nature but perfects it, so sacred doctrine presupposes, uses, and perfects natural knowledge."[17]

From Monasteries to Universities

The marriage of faith and reason in a system of Christian education was first realized in the Church's monasteries. As these great powerhouses of prayer and holiness emerged (St. Anthony, d. 356, is generally regarded as the founder of monasticism), they soon took on the work of education as well, building upon and Christianizing the legacy of classical curriculum from Greek and Roman culture.

It was the monastic schools that met the challenge of the Dark Ages as Europe was invaded by "barbarian" tribes, preserving the culture and eventually incorporating the invaders through education. As Christendom emerged—the fusion of church and society, epitomized in the Emperor Charlemagne (742–814)—the sentiment was that every large church should also run a school alongside of it, taking for granted now the partnership of faith and education. By the Middle Ages, there was a vast network of monastic and cathedral schools, with the Church the primary educator of the Western world and the savior of its civilization.

Early in the second millennium, universities began to emerge in the West. Each one grew out of a leading monastic or cathedral school which supplied its students and faculty. Around 1150, the first two of these great institutions of higher learning were founded at Salerno and Bologna, dedicated to the study of medicine and law, respectively. The University of Paris followed shortly thereafter and then Oxford, Cambridge, Padua, Pisa, Salamanca, Lisbon, and many others.

The university movement was, more than anything else, the work of the Church. Each had a chancellor who was ecclesially appointed; the power to grant degrees was by papal charter; the professors were clerics, especially Dominicans, Franciscans, and Augustinians. Christianity lent the common faith and language that enabled faculty and students from diverse cultures to study together. Even theology, moving beyond its moorings in the monastery, went off to university. Of all things, it became the "queen of the sciences." Some Christian authors protested with good cause that the marriage of revelation and reason had gone too far!

The Reformation and Education

The Protestant Reformation made its own great contribution to Western education. It returned Christendom again to the Bible as its primary text, insisting that everyone read it for themselves, thus providing the impetus for universal literacy. Likewise, the Reformers' commitment to personal interpretation of Scripture sowed the seeds of autonomous and critical thinking that flowered in the Enlightenment era.

The Reformation was also the catalyst of government-sponsored education for all. Martin Luther recognized that for the reform movement to succeed, it had to wrest control of education from the church of Rome. Condemning the monastic and cathedral schools as "the tools of the devil," he wrote a groundbreaking educational manifesto in 1524, in which he argued that everyone is entitled to an education, urging civil rulers to establish schools funded and run by the government—both novel ideas.[18] Luther helped to launch the "national school system" throughout Europe and, later, the world.

Even after primary responsibility for Western education was transferred from Church to State, Catholicism continued to sponsor a huge network of schools at every level, staffed by its myriad religious orders of women and men—many founded precisely to educate. Catholic schools and universities continued to spread both in the old Western cultures and now throughout the mission lands, sometimes with state funding and often without. The intention always was to provide a "liberal" education—in the sense of humanizing—continuing to see this as a "work of salvation" in and of itself.

Typically, Catholic schools would also instruct in Christian faith. However, in many mission lands, a large percentage of students would not choose to become Christian, as in the example cited of Pakistan. Regardless, they received a good education, beginning with a strong curriculum in the basics—the four R's of reading, 'riting, 'rithmetic, and rhetoric.

When one considers the influence of Catholic Christianity on Western education and civilization and adds in its missionary work throughout the world, it does not seem an exaggeration to claim that no single agency in human history has educated more people than Catholicism—and done so in a life-giving way. Although undoubtedly falling short at times of its own ideals, nevertheless, Catholic education can claim a rich legacy.

Catholic Schools in the United States

A notable instance of this legacy is Catholic schools in the United States. As the young nation emerged, American Catholic bishops favored a truly "public" school system, one free of undue influence from any particular religion, and yet allowing for faith and moral formation. Unlike in other Western democracies, however, and for a variety of reasons, such an American public system of education did not materialize.

The first Catholic school in America was opened by Franciscan missionaries at St. Augustine, Florida, in 1606. Thereafter, the initial Catholic schools had a variety of relationships with local governments, from open hostility to significant financial support (e.g., in New York). By the mid-nineteenth century, however, public schools gained control over public funding for education, and all subsidies to Catholic schools ceased.

The Catholic bishops were wary that the curriculum of the emerging public system was permeated with religious values that threatened the Catholic Christian identity of children. For example, the famous *McGuffey Readers,* the standard texts of the nation from their publication in 1836, taught a strong Puritan ethic and outlook through their vocabulary, sentences, and stories. In addition, anti-Catholic sentiment was running high in mid-nineteenth-century America, epitomized in powerful "nativist" groups like the Know Nothing Society. The latter's publicly stated purpose was "to rid the country of foreign influence and Catholicism."

In response, the American bishops determined to make Catholic education available to every child, without support of public funds if need be. This would be a mammoth task. The Catholic population had jumped through immigration from one-half million in 1829 to eight million in 1884. Undaunted, at the Third Council of Baltimore (1884), the bishops mandated that "near each church, where it does not exist, a parochial school is to be erected . . . ." Thereafter, the number of U.S. Catholic schools skyrocketed.

Statistically, the U.S. Catholic school system reached its peak in 1964, with over 13,000 schools and 5.6 million students. A significant decline followed that heyday, yet in 1995 there were still 8,500 Catholic grade and high schools and over 200 Catholic colleges and universities in the United States, educating almost 3 million students.

A new sign of hope, too, is the increasing enrollment of non-Catholic students. In some cases, as high as 75 percent of the student bodies are from backgrounds other than Catholic Christian.

U.S. Catholic schools still comprise the largest independent and privately funded educational system in the world, and perhaps in human history. In all other Western democracies, church-sponsored schools are financed by public funds. In the United States, however, they continue to be denied state or federal funding, the peculiar counter argument being—and against all evidence—that such funding would not serve the common good.

Since its inception, the American Catholic school system has been built and maintained by the commitment of parents who make significant financial sacrifices to provide a Catholic education for their children. Throughout the system's history, too, the generosity of parents has been matched by the dedication and service of vowed religious women and men. Until the mid-1960s, sisters, brothers, and priests made up 95 percent of the faculty and staff of U.S. Catholic schools. Not only did their strong spiritual formation assure the schools' Christian identity, but they also received minimal stipends, thus making the entire system more financially feasible (but, sadly, now impoverishing many of them in retirement).

In a rapid reversal of circumstances, by the mid '90s the faculty and staff of U.S. Catholic schools were 95 percent laypersons, with the schools intensifying their efforts to pay something akin to a living wage. Although surely required by justice, this has put a huge financial strain on many schools, especially in inner-city contexts where they are most needed. Regretfully, too many have already closed. Yet, a great number continue to survive, and there is ample evidence that lay faculty and staff are strongly committed to the Christian identity of the schools and to offering "Catholic" education. There are even some hopeful signs that the attrition of the 1970s and 1980s is being reversed. Between 1990 and 1997, the number of students in U.S. Catholic schools increased by over 100,000—some of the upturn due to reopening ones previously closed.

Assessing U.S. Catholic Schools

Extensive research has been done on the quality of life and education in U.S. Catholic schools.[19] It now seems beyond challenge that

(1) American Catholic schools have a configuration of characteristics that make them distinctive from other public or private schools, and an attractive alternative.

(2) Their "learning outcomes" often excel those of comparable systems in the same social context.

(3) They function at about half the cost of local public schools—although some of their economy is due to limiting "nonessential" programs.

It appears from the research that the combined features which lend distinctiveness to U.S. Catholic schools are the following:

• They provide a holistic curricula that embraces the totality of the person—intellectual, moral, social, aesthetic, physical, and spiritual.

• They have a significant "social capital" of support provided by the sponsoring faith community.

• They offer a structured curricula with emphasis on core studies in the liberal arts and a strong commitment to academic rigor.

• Good collegiality exists among faculty and staff, with broad commitment to forging the schools into caring communities.

• Their decentralized governance makes them more responsive to local needs. "Virtually all important decisions are made at individual school sites."[20]

• In a concerted effort, they nurture social consciousness in students through justice activities, with outreach and service to the local community—especially to people in need.

• They have a compelling spiritual vision that is shared by faculty, staff, and parents.

By way of the learning outcomes of American Catholic schools, again the research points to notable success. At about half the cost, they have significantly higher academic achievement scores than public schools with students of comparable backgrounds. They have more effective discipline, with fewer problems or incidents of crime within the schools, and they have very high levels of teacher commitment and student engagement.

Catholic high schools have about one-quarter of the national dropout rate and a far higher graduation ratio among "students at risk" because of race or economic class (usually in inner cities). Over 80 percent of graduates go on to college—again, higher than the national average. Such research encourages Bryk, Lee, and Holland to argue in *Catholic Schools and the Common Good* that these schools in fact make a major contribution to the common good and that the public schools of the United States have much to learn from them.

Arguments can be made challenging the "success" of U.S. Catholic schools. For example, one reason that they operate at less cost is that typically they do not offer special programs for students with learning challenges. In consequence they can be less inclusive than their public school counterparts. But perhaps this highlights that the government should fund such programming for every student regardless of their school context.

Or, again, the vitality of Catholic schools may have less to do with Catholic Christianity per se than with the fact that they generally have a cohesive spiritual vision and the "social capital" of a supporting community. The implication is that the same could be provided by any life-giving faith community. This is surely true! For example, I fully suspect that the Lutheran school system (with almost half a million students in the U.S.), has comparable results. However, this affirms rather than belies the asset of a spiritual foundation for educating.

And note well that *Educating for Life* is not a polemic on behalf of Catholic schools. As the Preface broadened education beyond schooling, I emphasize here that by Catholic education I include schools but reach far beyond them to every instance of education by Catholic Christian communities—general or religious, in parish and family, program and pastoral center. Rather than a polemic, then, my intent is (1) to encourage that all instances of Catholic education—in schools and institutions, parish catechetical programs and families—be carried out in ways faithful to the foundations of Catholic Christian faith and (2) to share with any and every educator some of the wisdom about educating *for life for all* that can gleaned from Catholicism's depth structures and long history of educating.

As a worldwide network, Catholic education may well be the most effective agent remaining of humanistic education. As such, it is an antidote to some ominous sentiments. For example, leaders of the

"New Right" movement in education argue that schools and programs should be conducted on the principles of what they euphemistically call "free-market economy." They oppose the long-held democratic consensus that education is a public good which should be provided equally to all at the expense of the State. Instead, the New-Right proposes that education be treated as a commodity in the marketplace, allowing market forces to decide its participants, means of delivery, and quality.[21] Such sentiments are scarcely based on a life-giving spirituality or intent. With their rise, however, it behooves all committed to educating *for life for all* to pool their wisdom, supporting each other in a humanizing vision of education.

Characteristics of Catholicism Relevant to Education

My rather self-evident thesis is that *the foundations of a "Catholic" philosophy-cum-spirituality for educators are suggested by substantial characteristics of Catholic Christianity and that these characteristics can be reflected as educational commitments throughout an entire curriculum—its content and process, its environment and purpose.*

My thesis begs the question, "What are the characteristics of Catholicism that combine to constitute its distinctive character?" Before responding, it is important to emphasize what Catholic Christian faith has in common with other great religious traditions. It is because of so much held in common that we can be enriched by what is distinctive.

Common Ground With the Great Religious Traditions

Christianity in general shares with all traditions of faith an understanding of the person as essentially spiritual, with an affinity to reach out toward Reality that is more than ourselves and yet defines our very "being." Although variously understood and expressed, this human reach is for the Transcendent. Further, we share the conviction that people live more humanly and meaningfully, with more integrity and compassion, by being "anchored" (*re-ligare*) in some experiences, understandings, and symbols of Ultimacy, by living as spiritual beings with a conscious sense of our Spirit milieu.

Our spiritual affinity is universal in that all humankind encounters an original outreach from the Transcendent toward them. The diversity of religious traditions emerges as the original divine-human encounter is personally experienced, appropriated, and responded to with different systems of understanding, symbols of worship, and ethics of living. To use an oft-cited analogy for the diversity of religious traditions: although there are many paths, there is one mountain top. Therein lies our spiritual bondedness as humankind!

With the great religious traditions that believe in a personal God—with Islam, for example—mainline Christianity has a deep bond of faith in a Divine Being who loves all humankind with unconditional and everlasting love. With these traditions, it also shares the conviction that God reveals Godself to humanity and continues to be actively involved within history on behalf of human welfare. Note, too, that all the great theistic religions emphasize that God is compassionate and so expects compassion from God's people, especially for those most in need. Likewise, they share belief in an afterlife and the conviction that the conduct of this life affects one's eternal welfare.

With Judaism in particular, as the Second Vatican Council declared, there is "a great spiritual patrimony common to Christians and Jews."[22] We share faith in God as Creator who makes us in God's own image and likeness, who lovingly sustains humankind, and actively cares for all creation. Both traditions emphasize that God's will for all is *shalom*—justice and peace, love and compassion, freedom and fullness of life, and the integrity of God's creation.

Further, God takes humankind into covenant to live this vision as "people of God" with the shalom that God intends for all. Both traditions revere the Decalogue—the Ten Commandments—as summarizing the law of their covenant with God, not as a whimsical test to win reward later, but as a gift that directs now toward true freedom and happiness. Both believe that with God's help, people can be faithful to their covenant and live as a "people of God"—allowing their faith to permeate daily life.

Catholic Christians and Jews share an understanding of the person as essentially good, although capable of evil. Both view creation and life as great gifts of God and believe in God's presence and loving outreach through the ordinary things and experiences of the everyday. Both Judaism and Christianity emphasize membership in a faith community—on being a "people of God"—convinced that typically God finds us and we go to God together.

Both Jews and Catholic Christians share a similar theology of the relationship between "grace and nature," insisting that God's help and human efforts work in partnership. Although we need God's help, we must also make our own best efforts and are held responsible for how we live our lives. Both traditions know deeply that offering true worship to God requires living the covenant, and especially its mandate of justice for all.

With All Members of the Body of Christ

I once began an undergraduate theology course entitled "Catholicism" by asking the students—all raised as Catholic—how many thought of themselves as Christian. Sadly, only a few said yes. Perhaps they grew up with the word *Catholic* standing alone to describe their religious identity—indicating that my frequent use of *Catholic Christian* here is well-advised.

Catholics ought to always think of themselves first and foremost as Christians, claiming their deep bond within the Body of Christ with Protestant brothers and sisters. To be disciples of Jesus is the first vocation of all Christians. This common covenant of Protestants and Catholics is symbolized, as Vatican II stated, by "the sacramental bond of baptism."[23] By common baptism and the same discipleship, all Christians are partners in the one Christian Church. Their unity should far outweigh their differences.

With all mainstream Protestant denominations, Catholic Christians cherish the Bible as the inspired "Word of God" in human language. We share the same Magna Carta of belief, expressed in both the Nicene and Apostles' Creeds and their Trinitarian summary of Christian faith. Together, we confess our faith in God as loving Creator of all that is; in Jesus as fully divine and human, and the promised Messiah, the Christ; in his life, death, and resurrection as making possible the salvation of humankind; in the Holy Spirit "the giver of life," who "with the Father and the Son is worshipped and glorified." Our common commitment is to become Church that is one, holy, catholic, and an apostolic community of Jesus' disciples in the world, looking with hope to the same communion of saints. We share one baptism for the forgiveness of sins; we await the resurrection of the dead and the promise of eternal life. All Christian disciples must commit themselves to living "the way" of Jesus to fulfill their covenant with God.

Within Catholic Christianity

Observe, too, that within Catholic Christianity itself, there is great diversity of traditions, and yet enough common bond to lend a shared and distinctive Christian character. As noted in the preface, it has three major expressions—Anglicanism, Eastern Orthodoxy, and Roman Catholicism. Then, within these, there is an array of "rites"— each with its own distinctive style and emphasis about being human, religious, Christian, and Catholic.

Even within Roman Catholicism, there is great breadth of theological position and pastoral practice, ranging from conservative to liberal to radical, with many variations in between. And remark, too, Catholicism's cultural diversity that seems endless. Compare the stoic aura of German Catholicism to the festive style of Hispanic Catholicism, or compare the traditional Irish Catholic acceptance of Church authority with the democratic spirit of American Catholicism.

Catholicism's tendency to "inculturate" itself within each time and place also leaves it open to the various movements of history, to be affected by the emerging consciousness of humankind. For example, currently, the women's movement is having a profound impact on Catholic theology and pastoral life, and rightly so. On this issue in particular, the institutional expression of Catholicism—its church— often fails to reflect the emancipatory power of the tradition at its best.

The diversity of Catholic Christianity makes the point that its substantial characteristics are not abstract ideals above the fray of history. In fact, they must be vital, varied, and alive in their realization if the tradition is to remain a living one instead of becoming a museum piece. And yet, although affected by local culture, Catholicism retains substantial characteristics that combine to lend a distinctiveness for being human, religious, and Christian. As depth structures, these characteristics often exist beneath Catholic Christianity's institutional expression or accidental features. Much as the deep patterns of people's characters shape who they are, so the depth structures of Catholicism combine as its distinctiveness, albeit with varied expressions. What might they be?

For Reflection

- Take a few moments and jot down some associations that emerge for you when you hear the word *Catholic*.

- Uncover some of the story behind your associations. Where do they come from? Which ones are stereotypes? Which seem authentic?

- What might be some implications of the authentic characteristics of Catholic Christianity for teachers or parents?

A Configuration of Characteristics

Richard McBrien, a leading American theologian, writes that there are "various characteristics of Catholicism, each of which . . . it shares with one or another Christian Church or tradition." Although these characteristics are not uniquely Catholic, they have a distinctive combination within Catholicism. McBrien explains,

> Nowhere else except in the Catholic Church are all of Catholicism's characteristics present in the precise configuration in which they are found within Catholicism.[24]

Oftentimes it is a matter of emphasis. For example, all Christian denominations have some appreciation for the Church in the life of Christian faith, but Catholicism emphasizes its importance more than most. In other words, although Catholicism shares particular features to varying degrees with other Christian traditions, their configuration and level of emphasis within Catholic Christianity make up its distinctiveness.

"To see ourselves as others see us" is always helpful when considering one's identity. Honoring this wise aphorism, the work of Langdon Gilkey is particularly helpful on Catholic Christianity identity. A world-renowned senior theologian, Gilkey is an American Baptist. In the aftermath of the Second Vatican Council (1962–65), Gilkey—as a Protestant brother in the Body of Christ—rejoiced at the spirit of renewal sweeping Catholicism—*aggiornamento* (literally "bringing up to date") as the good Pope John XXIII (1881-1963) called it.

However, as a Protestant who has a genuine appreciation and affection for Catholicism, Gilkey also became concerned that it not lose any of its distinguishing characteristics—that no baby be thrown out with the bath water. So he wrote a fascinating book, *Catholicism Confronts Modernity*, in which, among other things, he set out his Protestant understanding of Catholicism's distinguishing characteristics and his proposal for how they could be renewed rather than lost in "the crisis of modernity." His schema struck a resonant chord, and many authors have subsequently used it. It has the added credibility of "a neighbor's view."

Gilkey outlines five characteristics of Catholicism that he summarizes as

> the people as *community*, the reality of *tradition*, the grace of *caritas*, the *sacramental* sense of the living presence of God, and the *rationality* of the traditional faith.[25] (emphases added)

In brief, he explains the *community aspect of Catholicism* as its emphasis on the role of the Church and on membership in a "people" of faith. Catholic Christianity is marked by a deep conviction that people work out their salvation together through "grace in the communal life." Within its community emphasis, Gilkey cites the "Catholic protest against what is evil and destructive in present human society" and Catholic leadership in the struggle for "justice and liberation in the world."[26]

Regarding *tradition*, Gilkey notes that Catholicism has a strong "sense of the reality, importance, and 'weight' of tradition and history" in forming its identity. Appropriately, he cautions Catholic Christians that if tradition is made absolute or given too much weight, it can become "stifling and corrupt." But if properly appreciated, tradition "can be a source of vast strength."[27]

The *caritas* characteristic is not easy to capture, but essentially Gilkey is highlighting Catholicism's positive, even benevolent, attitude toward the human condition. The Catholic attitude is to embrace one's humanness as gift, celebrate it as essentially good, relish its joys, and be merciful to it when sinful. Gilkey describes *caritas* as "the love of life, the appreciation of the body and the senses, of joy and celebration, the tolerance of the sinner."[28]

The *sacramental principle of Catholicism* is its insistence that "the presence of God and of grace" are "mediated through symbols to the entire course of ordinary human life . . . through a wide variety of symbols—material, sensuous, aesthetic, active, verbal and intellectual."[29] Catholicism surely has a depth conviction about the sacramentality of life, that God comes looking for us and we respond through the experiences of everyday.

Gilkey's fifth characteristic of Catholicism—*rationality* —may surprise some, even Catholics. Clearly, he is thinking of Catholicism in its richest tradition rather than as a stereotype of authoritarianism—a sad impoverishment and yet not without warrant—which forbids people to think for themselves in matters of faith. As noted already, when at its best, the tradition is to maintain a partnership between reason and revelation, between understanding and faith. Gilkey writes,

> There has been throughout Catholic history a drive toward rationality, the insistence that the divine mystery manifest in tradition and sacramental presence be insofar as possible penetrated, defended, and explicated by the most acute rational reflection.[30]

Gilkey goes on to wonder, however, if the speculative reason so favored by Catholicism in the Scholastic era can now embrace the critical rationality of the modern world. Later on (chapter 6), I propose that it can and must make this advance!

Chapters 2 through 9 of *Educating for Life* will reflect on eight substantial characteristics of Catholic Christianity that seem particularly relevant to a philosophy for educators and to weaving a spiritual vision of educating for life. Five are suggested by Gilkey's schema, with my elaboration and update. Then I add three others that Gilkey often mentioned but did not develop explicitly.

The first five substantial characteristics of Catholicism for attention will be the following:

- its positive anthropology—a benevolent or *caritas* understanding of the human condition;

- its conviction about the sacramentality of life—that there is always "the more" to be found in the ordinary and everyday;

- its emphasis on relationship and community—the conviction that humankind is "made for each other";

- its commitment to history and tradition—honoring the legacy of wisdom, arts, and sciences, including the Scriptures and traditions of Christian faith left by generations before us; and

- Catholicism's appreciation of a wisdom rationality—favoring a reflective way of knowing that encourages responsibility and wisdom for life.

I add three other substantial characteristics that permeate the life of Catholicism. Echoing the old distinction of the virtues into theological and cardinal, we can call these three "cardinal" characteristics in that they are "hinges" (Latin, *cardo*) that bind the five more theological characteristics together. All the other five must participate in realizing these three, and yet they can be distinguished as points of emphasis that run through Catholic Christian identity. They are emphasis on:

- spirituality—on seeking "holiness" of life;

- working for justice and the social values of God's reign;

- catholicity itself—hospitality for all and, as St. Augustine emphasized, being open to truth wherever it can be found.[31]

These three substantial characteristics will be our focus in chapters 7, 8, and 9. I conclude in chapter 10 with a review of the spiritual vision of *Educating for Life* and some reflections on how to "keep on" as educators *for life for all*.

Engaging The Text

The contemporary French philosopher Edmond Jabes suggests that when we encounter a book, there are always two texts involved—the one we are reading and the one we are writing ourselves. I agree—if we enter into a conversation with the text, listening to our own thoughts and insights, observing our feelings and sentiments as we read. I have tried to style this book to encourage the reader to write your own in reading mine, presenting much as "a proposal for consideration" and never pretending to be exhaustive. My hope is that you will sometimes agree with, sometimes disagree with, and often add to what I propose.

Each of the eight main chapters (2 through 9) follows a fairly consistent pattern, and it may help to outline it now. I begin with an opening story from my life as an educator (except, perhaps, chapter 3—more from my spouse, Colleen). Each is a parable-like expression of what the chapter is about. I hope the story can personally engage the reader with the theme of the chapter, encouraging you to remember and associate stories from your own life, and likewise for the many shorter stories and examples shared throughout.

Then, each chapter establishes a focus on a human issue or question (e.g., "Who are we?") addressed by a particular depth structure of Catholicism and foundational to education. After focusing the theme, I pose questions to elicit the readers own initial thoughts and feelings.

A similar set of questions is offered at midchapter and additional ones at the end to encourage your ongoing conversation with the text, moving to discernment and decision making. I urge you to pause for these moments of reflection. It will be even more fruitful if you can have a conversation about them with other teachers or parents.

The body of the chapter summarizes a substantial aspect of Catholic Christianity, giving some of its biblical and theological warrants and suggesting the human outlook—the philosophy—it would recommend to educators. For my theology of each depth structure, I draw predominantly upon official statements of Catholic church teaching.

One could make a far more conservative, or liberal, or radical statement by drawing upon a broader continuum of Catholic theology. However, there is something even more persuasive in finding grounds for humanizing education in the consensus statements of official Catholicism. My two most frequently cited sources are the *Documents of the Second Vatican Council* and the *Catechism of the Catholic Church.*

Vatican II was the most recent general council of the Catholic church held from October 1962 to December 1965. The documents of a general council are considered among the weightiest authorities in Catholic church teaching. The English translation of the new *Catechism of the Catholic Church* was issued in 1994 and offers in declarative form what Pope John Paul II described as "a statement of the Church's faith and of Catholic doctrine," to be used as "an authentic reference text."[32] (Hereafter, for brevity sake, I refer to this text as the *Catechism*.)

Although I draw heavily from these official sources, I do not pretend to offer an exhaustive review of Catholic beliefs and practices. My interest is more spiritual than doctrinal. Far from a complete statement of Catholic Christianity, my quest is to unearth what eight of its depth structures might suggest by way of a philosophy and spirituality for educators.

The second half of each chapter reflects on what the particular substantial aspect of Catholic Christianity might mean for teachers and parents. Here again, my proposal is only partial. I subdivide the second part of each chapter into three headings: "For the Educator's Soul," "For the Educator's Style," and "For the Educational Space." All of them, however, pertain to the educator's spirituality—to encourage faith-inspired commitments to educating for *life for all*.

I reflect on implications of each depth structure for the "educator's soul" so that such spiritual commitments might permeate the lives of teachers and parents and thus their whole vocation as educators. The "educator's style" will accent the pedagogy recommended by a particular characteristic (e.g., sacramentality suggests engaging learners' imaginations). I use the generic "style" to indicate more of a general approach than specific teaching methods. A point of "style" could be realized by a great variety of "methods"—depending upon age level, context, and theme.

Under "educational space" I reflect upon implications for the educational environment—for the ethos of the school, parish program, or family. My proposals on environment reflect concern for education's task of character formation. However, because character entails educating people in knowledge, conviction, and behavior—in knowing, desiring, and doing what is ethical and virtuous—concern for character formation runs throughout the book.

For Reflection
- What seems most important for you to take away from this opening chapter?

- Is there a decision or sense of renewed opportunity emerging for you?

Notes

1. See Bernard Bailyn, *Education in the Forming of American Society,* 14.
2. See Plato, *The Republic,* 518 B–D. For this point and reference I am indebted to the dissertation of Christopher Murphy, *An Interpretation Approach to Religious Education,* Boston College, 1997.
3. Aristotle, *Nicomachean Ethics,* 10: 7: 8.
4. Confucius, *The Analects,* 79.
5. See Maria Montessori, *The Montessori Method,* 115 and passim.
6. John Dewey, "My Pedagogic Creed," in *Dewey on Education,* 32.
7. Alfred North Whitehead, *The Aims of Education and Other Essays,* 14.
8. St. Irenaeus, *Against the Heretics,* 4: 40: 6. It is interesting for teachers to note that St. Irenaeus was writing against the Gnostics, people who, among other things, put too much emphasis on knowledge *(gnosis),*thus failing to honor the whole person.
9. See Ernst Troeltsch, *The Social Teaching of the Christian Churches.* Troeltsch also described a third possible "type" of Christianity: "mystical communion"—an informal grouping emphasizing spiritual experience and personal holiness.
10. On this point see the very insightful essay of Walter Brueggemann, "The Legitimacy of a Sectarian Ethic: 2 Kings 18–19" in Boys, ed., *Education for Citizenship and Discipleship,* 3–34. For this endnote, I am indebted to Briedge Vallely.
11. "Constitution on the Church" #8, Abbott, *Documents of Vatican II,* 24. Hereafter all references to the documents of Vatican II will be to this edition and will be referred as *Documents.*
12. Pope John Paul II, *On the Coming of the Third Millennium,* #32 and 33.
13. Ibid., #36, 34, 35.
14. I carefully footnote the many authors who have influenced my educational philosophy in two previous works, *Christian Religious Education* and *Sharing Faith.*
15. For a fine elaboration of this point, see Bryke, Lee, and Holland, *Catholic Schools and the Common Good.*
16. Tertullian, *The Prescription of Heretics,* 7.
17. Thomas Aquinas, *Summa Theologica,* Ia, I, 8 ad 2.
18. See Martin Luther, "To the Councilmen of All Cities in Germany that They Establish and Maintain Christian Schools," in Cully, *Basic Writings in Christian Education,* 137–149.
19. A most significant study is Anthony S. Bryk, Valerie E. Lee, and Peter B. Holland, *Catholic Schools and the Common Good.* This work has been appreciated by both advocates and critics of Catholic schools for its quality of research and balance of presentation.

    The sociologist and pastoral theologian Andrew Greeley has conducted many significant and scholarly studies on Catholic schools, beginning in 1966. (See *The Education of Catholic Americans* with Peter B. Rossi.) Greeley offered a helpful summary of his research over the years in "My Research on Catholic Schools" in *Chicago Studies,* 1989, vol. 28, 245–63.

    The research associated with the work of James S. Coleman has also been compelling because of its perceived independence of any Catholic sponsorship or interest (based primarily at the University of Chicago). See, for example *High School Achievement: Public and Private Schools* with Thomas Hoffer and Sally Kilgore. For a helpful overview of a great deal of research literature see John J. Convey, *Catholic Schools Make a Difference: Twenty-Five Years of Research.*

20. Bryk et al., *Catholic Schools and the Common Good,* 299.
21. For a critical analysis of this movement, see David Bridges and Terence H. McLaughlin, eds., *Education and The Market Place.*
22. "Declaration on Non-Christian Religions," #4, Abbott, *Documents,* 665.
23. "Decree on Ecumenism," #22, Abbott, *Documents,* 364.
24. Richard P. McBrien, *Catholicism,* New Edition, 1189.
25. Langdon Gilkey, *Catholicism Confronts Modernity,* 23.
26. Ibid., 17 and 19.
27. Ibid., 17.
28. Ibid., 18.
29. Ibid., 20.
30. Ibid., 22.
31. I will often cite St. Augustine for this conviction, so let me endnote it here. Openness to the truth as an aspect of Catholicity was a frequent theme throughout Augustine's writings. A classic statement is in his text *De Doctrina Christiana*—"All good and true Christians should understand that truth, wherever they may find it, belongs to their God." Saint Augustine, *Teaching Christianity,* 144.
32. *Catechism of the Catholic Church* (hereafter *The Catechism*), 5.

CHAPTER TWO

A Good People:
"God's Own Image and Likeness"

Who Told Joe?

They fancied themselves as "The Fabulous Five"; the rest of the school had other names for them. But they had the grudging respect of most, and in a tough, boys' boarding school—Dublin, early '60s—that was hard-earned.

Everyone called the senior prefect in charge of study hall "Hokey"; most thought of him as a likable nerd. The "Fab Five" weren't into study much; they mostly read trashy novels and kept other students from doing their work. Hokey warned them repeatedly about disrupting study hall, but they ignored him. All varsity athletes, they felt untouchable—above the law. Then it happened!

"You're nothin' but lousy bums," yelled Smithsy, as he threw their books out the door of study hall. "Now get t' hell outta here and don't come back!" Hokey had gone to Smithsy, the president, who personally supervised their eviction. How humiliating! "But where'll we go for study time?" one bewildered lad asked with a whine. "I don't care," said Smithsy as if he really meant it, "but I'd prefer never to see your faces 'round here again. Why don't you go home? You're wasting your parents' money and you're a bad influence on this school." Clearly, the president didn't understand their importance to the football team.

In a deserted part of the huge, old building, they found an unused classroom—dirty, with poor lighting and no heat. But everyone kept up a bravado: "What a lark!" "Great to get out of that stupid study hall!" "Now we can read all the novels we like!" They blew off the time the first few nights. The other students nicknamed the place the "Leper Colony." The third evening, in stormed "Joe"—though no one dared call him that to his face; students who had incurred his wrath also called him "Attila"—as in Attila the Hun. Everyone said Joe was a bit crazy, but they revered him; as head football coach, he had put this school on the map. A towering hulk of a man, he was tough—no one crossed Joe twice. He blew his stack. "What the hell are five of my football players doin' in this dump?" he bellowed. Joe got that famous red face and mad look in his eyes that every student hoped would never be directed at him. "You're a disgrace to the team, and to me personally."

They tried to offer an explanation, but there was none. At the end of the tirade, Joe yelled, "Smithsy's right, you are a bunch o' bums. He should have expelled you from the school!" From Joe, that really hurt; no one could remember the last time someone got expelled—the ultimate disgrace. He stormed out, then stuck his head back in again and said, "Of course, there still might be time to prove him wrong. . . ." and was gone. Dazed at first, they regrouped, held a summit, and decided to fight back. "Smithsy had no right to call us bums," Paddy, the ringleader, said defiantly. The boys cleaned up the place and put themselves on a strict study schedule. A rigorous discipline descended on the Leper Colony. They worked together and helped each other out with assignments.

That was when the one I know best began to read for the first time, really read, and to write too. Their grades improved and their demerits decreased. They began to participate in their classes and had clearly done the homework. Their image as a clique dissipated, and they cautiously grew comfortable with new-found acceptance among classmates—some even becoming leaders in the school. The night they were allowed to return to study hall people stood and cheered to welcome them. All five graduated well. They did OK in life too—not a permanent bum among them. And that one I know best has continued reading and writing ever since. Years later at a reunion, one of them asked Joe, "Who told you we were in the Leper Colony?"

Joe said, "Someone who thought you could still be turned around." Their vote was Smithsy. But maybe Hokey?

The Ultimate Human Question

Who are we—really? Beyond the immediate and obvious—such as name and family, age and address—what is the nature of us, of me as a person, and do we have anything in common as humankind? We refer colloquially to "human nature," but what is it? Or do we even have one—some depth characteristics that are shared, more or less, by all of us? If so, what are they? And does our nature allow that we be "turned around" or are we socially and/or genetically programmed for a particular path?

Every person must wonder about this human condition in some way and at some level. And maybe the fact that we can even raise the question of our "selves" at all is already a hint of our "nature." We seem to be the only earthly creatures with the self-reflective capacity to ask, "Who am I?" Surely any attempt at response requires some depth reflection. When we make ourselves the "subject" of our own thought, we use our consciousness to examine our consciousness, we think about our thinking—something like Norman Rockwell (1894–1978) painting himself painting himself. With even a little such probing, we could meet ourselves coming in circles!

This is probably why we do not often take the time—nor have the energy—to intentionally raise the question and dwell on it; it brings us to ultimacy, and no one can live at the edge for very long. So we pull back and occupy ourselves with the daily tasks of living as persons, preferring to take for granted that we know what all this means.

But the question cannot be suppressed for long, at least not entirely; inevitably, it comes back—as if our very "being" demands that we ask it. It can take many forms, such as, "What's it all about?" or "Why do we exist at all?" or "Who is the real me?" or "Can I trust anybody?" or "What's that other person really like?" or "Is eat, drink, and be merry our highest possibility?" or "Why should I try to be ethical?" or even, "Why should I get out of bed in the morning?"

Such questions can be prompted by a thousand different human experiences—by love or hate, courage or cowardice, compassion or cruelty; at moments of peace or war, joy or sorrow, birth or death; when we are touched by the beauty or threatened by the destructive power of nature; at moments of inspiration before human creativity or horror at human destruction; at encounters with art and beauty or with the banal and ugly. Whatever response we make with any consistency can be called our *anthropology,* literally, our "understanding" (*logos*) of the "human person" (*anthropos*)—what we think of "the condition" we are in.

Contemporary philosophers called "postmodernists" or "deconstructionists" claim that there is no common *nature* to us at all, that what we refer to as "human nature" is simply a social construct. Who a person is or becomes—what modern philosophers call "the subject"— is shaped entirely by their cultural and social context. We are merely the creatures of our environment, and there is nothing "essential" to us at all. Further, we are not even capable of knowing the truth about ourselves, for truth, too, is a construct of the historical context.

A battle cry of the postmodernists is that there are "no metanarratives," meaning that there is no overarching or coherent way of understanding ourselves. But, ironically, such a postmodernist deconstruction of human nature and of "the subject" is an anthropology of sorts, albeit by default. A less extreme but still contemporary perspective grants that we are indeed malleable and much influenced by our historical context and by genetic dispositions, that our nature is not a static thing given at birth (the classical view) but a lifelong project to be realized over time and much influenced by our own efforts. Yet, the consensus is that becoming human is grounded in capacities and potentials, depth characteristics and abiding vocations that are shared by all humankind to one degree or another; there are things that can be said of us all, of who we are and are called to become—gifts of a common nature.

I am confronted by the challenge of postmodernists and learn from them (more in chapter 6); for example, traditional anthropologies have canonized racism and sexism as if they are dictated by nature, whereas they are social constructs—or destructs! But, as making anthropology the focus of this chapter suggests, I come down on the side of what is now regarded as a more traditional view: though genetically predisposed in certain ways and though forever being shaped, buffeted, and changed by the conditions of life, there is a "center that holds" (William Butler Yeats) for all humankind—even if we seldom live up to our best possibilities.

Regardless of what philosophy one claims, the fact remains that every teacher and parent—indeed, every person—has a "functioning anthropology," whether we advert to it or not. In other words, we have a working sense of our own "selves" and an opinion of others. This general perspective on "the human condition" shapes our way of life, our way of relating to self, others, and the world—our entire modus operandi as human beings.

Our functioning anthropology is shaped by many influences: by family circumstances—its ethos, values, worldview, its financial status, gender roles, and even our birth order within it; by everything about our society and culture; by our genetics; by our physicality and the attitudes toward bodiliness in our sociocultural environment; by all the experiences that come our way and the activities we initiate; even, the social scientists tell us, by our geographical location and climate. Think about it: people who live in a climate of 110° in the shade are less likely to emphasize human agency and "getting things done," whereas a harsh New England winter without relief can encourage a rather dismal anthropology— certainly in February!

Because the configuration of each person's circumstances and experiences is unique, so is the "spin" to everyone's functioning anthropology. And yet, surely we share enough depth characteristics to construct a shared understanding of ourselves. This is the explicit purpose of the social science of anthropology which, with its companion sociology, interprets observable human behavior in its cultural and social settings, thus throwing much light on "the condition" of humankind. But, in one way or another, all the sciences attempt to understand ourselves and our lives in the world. Each has its own method of investigation; each has its own interpretive lens for looking at the "data"—giving rise to many proposals. Note the difference in how the biologist and the psychologist study human life, yet each perspective amplifies something important about us. And even the cumulative insights of all the sciences do not provide an exhaustive understanding of the human condition; mystery ever remains—as it must—given in whose image we are made; but now we are getting ahead of ourselves!

The cry "know thyself" goes back to the beginning of formal philosophy and has motivated philosophical reflection ever since. And, of course, all the great religions—even ones without an image of a personal God—reflect an image of the human; each one is, among other things, an anthropology.

Likewise, Christianity, from its perspective of faith in God and in Jesus Christ, proposes an understanding of ourselves. Within this, Catholicism puts its own particular "spin" on a Christian anthropology. Appreciative of human ways of knowing, Catholic Christianity can draw insights from all philosophies and sciences, but comes at the question and responds to it primarily as a theological and spiritual one. And is it not possible that a spiritual perspective may come closest to an adequate portrayal of the human condition?

Regardless of the personal or general sources from which teachers and parents garner their anthropology, this chapter—and indeed the entire book—reflects the conviction that there is no more foundational issue for educators. Their understanding of who people are and can become is fundamental to how they educate. A moment's reflection on your own experience will verify this. Educators who approach learners with a positive attitude, confident that they have great potential and challenge them to their own best efforts, typically receive as much—whereas educators with a negative attitude toward learners usually get what they are expecting too.

In chapter 1, I described education as an "ontic" affair in that, at its best, it reaches into and helps form the very "being" of people. Clearly, then, how educators understand human "being" will influence every aspect of their curriculum—what, how, and where they teach, and what they are teaching for.

I also proposed the worthiest "what-for" of education as that *learners might become fully alive human beings who contribute to a society of the common good*; I summarize this personal-cum-social purpose of education with the phrase *for life for all.* But what it means to become a *fully alive human being*—a "person"—shapes everything done toward such an end. (A society of common good is our theme in chapter 4.) Anthropology is the horizon that shapes every curriculum choice, the goal that evaluates all the means taken, the hope that permeates the entire enterprise. Educators' operative anthropology is likely the greatest influence on how they fulfill their teaching vocation.

Throughout this chapter and book, I deliberately prefer the term "person" for naming ourselves—over individual, self, the subject, and such terms—because *person* connotes both autonomy and relationality, individuality and partnership, of being an agent who initiates one's own actions and yet finds human identity only within and through relationships. It is significant that the Latin *persona* has its root in the Greek *prosopon,* which literally means "face to face."[1]

The human person is always both an individual self and yet turned toward "the other." I am ever a "person in community" (our focus here), making up with others a "community of persons" (our theme in chapter 4). Being autonomous and relational, individual and partner, free and responsible, however, is neither a static given nor an assured achievement. Rather, becoming "person" is a lifelong journey. Humanizing education offers provisions for the pilgrim way, and the educator's vision influences both the traveling and the destiny.

Although what it means to educate for a society of common good will be elaborated on in other chapters (especially 4 and 8), I should note here that making anthropology so foundational to education highlights the profoundly political nature of it and emphasizes the educator's role as social agent. This is not a new insight but an ancient one recently rediscovered.

Almost twenty-five hundred years ago, Plato and Aristotle—the great architects of Western philosophy—were both convinced that education is an aspect of politics in that it is sponsored by the state and intends to influence how people live in society. Confucius, of similar vintage but writing in China, understood education first and foremost as a political act. For him, whoever educates the person— and he gave priority to parenting—educates the society. If we ignore the chauvinism of his culture, we can appreciate Confucius's conviction that, "Simply by raising a good son . . . a man exerts an influence on government."[2]

The correlation of anthropology, education, and politics becomes self-evident when we recognize that all social injustices are undergirded by erroneous anthropologies. What else are racism, sexism, and ethnocentrism but ideologies that certain people are more human than others and, therefore, the "others" need not be accorded the dignity and rights due to full humans?

Yet these social ideologies are passed on from generation to generation—Bernard Bailyn's broad definition of education. Perhaps this is the most persuasive argument against the postmodernist posture that we do not have a common nature—and the most urgent reason favoring some sense of a universal anthropology that grants equal rights and the dignity of personhood to all. Without as much, educators especially are in grave danger of victimizing instead of humanizing, of failing in their personal and social responsibilities. Nothing is more urgent for clarification and choice by teachers and parents than their anthropology.

For Reflection

• Take time for some notes on "my own understanding of the human condition." Free-associate and notice what emerges. (Caution: Do not overlook "the obvious" about us—it could be most significant.)

• Reviewing your own sense of ourselves, uncover some of the background that has shaped your anthropology—influential people, significant experiences, cultural conditions. Note the insights that emerge!

• Think now of some consequences your functioning anthropology has for how you educate.

A Catholic Christian Anthropology: One Proposal

I do not pretend to make an exhaustive statement about the human condition in this chapter—indeed anywhere, given that the mystery about us always remains. However, more will unfold in later chapters on sacramentality, communality, rationality, and spirituality; these substantial characteristics of Catholicism also reflect its anthropology. Meanwhile, we can at least lay some foundations here that will suggest the contours of the "dwelling" that a Catholic Christian anthropology understands as the "home" of human "being." First, a few etchings to bring with you as an overall blueprint. Bernard Lonergan (1904–84), ranked by many as one of the greatest theologians of all time, (he ended his career as a senior professor at Boston College), summarized Catholic Christian understanding of the human condition as a "realistic optimism." It comes down essentially on the side of optimism—and by how much of a margin, Lonergan never suggests—while retaining a healthy measure of realism about ourselves as well. Lonergan represents the tradition accurately in making optimism the defining noun, because it clings tenaciously to a positive and hopeful view of life and yet is never pollyannish—sickness, sin, and death are reality checks that dissuade naiveté. Smithsy was realistic in expelling us from study hall, but his optimism remained that we might still be "turned around."

Another overall view! In chapter 1, we noted Gilkey's use of *caritas* to capture the esprit de corps of Catholicism's positive, even benevolent, attitude toward the human condition. The Catholic Christian disposition is to embrace one's humanness as gift, to celebrate it as essentially good, to relish its joys, to be tolerant of its imperfections and merciful when it sins. There is an even more sensual term within the tradition, however, that captures this humane attitude—the Latin term *humanitas*. It is difficult to translate, but perhaps the English author Hilaire Belloc captured the joie de vivre it connotes when he wrote:

> Wherever a Catholic sun doth shine,
> There's plenty of laughter and good red wine.
> At least, I've always found it so:
> Benedicamus Domino.

By way of a more complete statement, I suggest ten aspects of the human condition that may serve as an initial description of a *humanitas* anthropology. I use *aspect* because these are "ways of looking at" (the Latin *aspectus*) ourselves, "angles of vision" each adding a slight variation to the view. Many overlap or echo each other, and only their cumulative gives an overall sense of who we are. Most of them can trace their origin to a Catholic interpretation of the opening stories of the book of Genesis—of creation and the saga of Adam and Eve.

My frequent references to these early stories do not imply that they represent the entire anthropology of the Bible. As regarding all the ultimate questions of life and faith, the Bible reflects much diversity and complexity on the question of human nature; its various types of literature reflect differing perspectives. For example, the historical, wisdom, and prophetic literatures of the Hebrew Scriptures, and the Gospels, Pauline, pastoral, and apocalyptic literatures of the New Testament each has its distinct emphasis on what it means to be human.

Yet, throughout Jewish and Christian history, the consistent sentiment has been that the great faith questions about ourselves and the decisive foundations of a biblical anthropology are reflected in the opening stories of Genesis. Nor am I implying that these memorable myths explain the human condition—as cause and effect; few Christian scholars today would take them as literally true. But they are truth-laden in that they accurately reflect profound and perennial truths about ourselves.

1. Person as Essentially Good and Dignified—Though Capable of Sin, Remaining in the Divine Image

In the first story of creation from chapter 1 of the Book of Genesis, we read that God creates humankind as male and female, making both in the Divine image and likeness (see Genesis 1, especially verses 26–30). Up to this point, after each act of God's creation, the sacred author notes that God saw that "it was good." After the creation of man and woman, however, who are clearly the high point of God's creation—equally cherished in God's eyes and equal partners to each other—the text says that God looked upon this work as "very good" (Genesis 1:31). Only of humankind does the text add the superlative *very*.

Though many religious traditions embrace this story as reflecting their faith in God as Creator, Catholicism has clung more tenaciously than most to the interpretation of the abiding and essential goodness of the human condition; that the divine image and likeness are never lost to us. It does so under duress from another symbolic tale that soon follows—of "The Fall" into sin by Adam and Eve through disobedience and their banishment from "the garden" to live "east of Eden" (see Genesis 3:24).

In a sense, the Catholic view chooses to emphasize chapter 1 of Genesis rather than chapter 3—the more classic Protestant position; some of the story behind this tipping of the scales I relate presently.

From the Genesis 3 story of the Fall, Christian theologians extrapolated a "doctrine of original sin"—that by "origin" we are "prone to sin" was the old language—and Catholicism embraces this perspective too. However, as a matter of emphasis in contrast to classic Protestantism, theologically it manages to affirm divine likeness over human sinfulness, "original grace" over "original sin."

Though our divine reflection may be battered and bruised by the sinful condition of the world and by our own personal sins, it is never entirely lost to us. The classic Catholic Christian position is that humankind always remains in God's own image, having the vocation and capacity—by God's grace—to grow in divine likeness.

For Christian faith, the ultimate affirmation of the human estate— after the Fall—is God becoming human in Jesus. How could God take on our humanity if we are essentially evil? And after the Jesus event, the affirmation of humanity is sealed irrevocably by the death and resurrection of Jesus. Although Christians have many metaphors for expressing the consequences of Jesus' "work of salvation," each reflects the conviction that all humankind was subsumed in Christ's rising and has become a "new creation" (2 Corinthians 5:17).

The *imago Dei* tenet witnesses not only to the essential goodness of persons, but also to the equal dignity of all human beings—men and women; people of every color, class, and creed. As reflections of God, all have an essential dignity that gives them the "birthright" to be treated with reverence and with the dignity befitting a daughter or son of God. All human beings have innate rights to what is needed to become fully alive persons, and they have corresponding responsibilities to maintain the rights of others—to live *for life for all.* As the *Catechism* summarizes well, "Created in the image of the one God and equally endowed with rational souls, all [people] have the same nature and the same origin . . . all enjoy an equal dignity."[3]

Catholicism is not naive about the sinfulness of the human condition; it simply chooses not to emphasize it or, better still, to hope that it is not more decisive for humanity than an essential goodness. But in response to the ancient question "Why did God become a person?" all Christians accept the metaphor that Jesus came to free us from the slavery of sin. And apart from any biblical stories, a look into our own lives or world reminds us that something is awry, that we are badly in need of help—salvation of some kind. It seems that from our origin, we have the capacity and even a "proneness" to sin, a condition which the story of the Fall reflects accurately.

And our sinful proclivity is both inside of us—in our human dispositions—and in the world outside of us—in sinful social structures and cultural mores. However, Catholic Christianity has always stopped short of claiming that we are essentially sinful, that we

77

are more prone to evil than good. As the *Catechism* notes, when the early Reformers proposed "that original sin has radically perverted" people, leaving "a tendency to evil" that is "insurmountable,"[4] Catholicism rejected the notion of total depravity and taught instead that we are essentially good, that we are more capable of good than evil precisely because the *imago Dei* is never lost to us.[5] While human "nature bears the wound of original sin," we still "desire the good" and "remain an image of our Creator."[6] Though eminently capable and often the perpetrators of great evil, the more basic human sentiment and orientation is for good and for God.

2. Person as Body-Soul Union Alive in God's Spirit

The second story of creation in Genesis 2 gives symbolic detail— beyond the first account—of how God created humankind, with further clues to our "condition." God is depicted as crafting from clay "a person of the earth" (gender-inclusive)[7] and then blowing into its nostrils God's own breath of life (see Genesis 2:7).

Notice first how the story reflects our corporeality; we are physical beings of material substance—the earth. And it includes our bodiliness in the divine assessment of being "very good." Then, God's breathing of divine vitality—or of "divine energy" as Eastern Orthodoxy says—into the "earth person" reflects that our human life is a sharing in the very life of God. Our "being" is the advent of God's own "Being" into the created order; we are alive by divine life.

The traditional name for this "life" of God in humankind is the soul. As this second creation account reflects, it is the animating principle of humankind—our aliveness aspect. The soul defines our personhood precisely because it is our sharing in the life of God. It is the divine life that lends us the ability to know and become wise, to imagine and become creative, to choose and become free, to relate and become responsible, to do good and become moral, to love and become as human as we are meant to be.

Christian anthropology has a long tradition of affirming that our body and soul are not separate entities but constitute what Aquinas called "a single substantial unity." Even death represents no more than a temporary suspension of their union. As Jesus rose from the grave with a new body beyond death, so too, Christians, as they confess in the Creed, believe in "the resurrection of the body." In death a person's soul retains its individuality, and each unique person will be reunited as risen body and soul—one entire person in eternity.

As body-soul persons made in God's own image and likeness, we have an affinity for God as "like for like." As the contemporary Jewish philosopher Emmanuel Levinas wrote so insightfully, the person "is the irruption of God within Being" and likewise "the bursting out of Being towards God."[8] In Christian tradition, few have expressed this sentiment more eloquently than St. Augustine (354–430) with the stirring and oft-quoted lines with which he began *The Confessions:* "You have made us for yourself alone, and our hearts are restless 'till they rest in thee."[9]

The divine life in humankind gives us a "homing" instinct for God or, to use the lovely metaphor of Jacques Maritain, the human soul constitutes "our society with God." Therein lies the bedrock of divine/human partnership—the next aspect to be noted.

3. Person as Partner with God and Ever in Need of God's Grace

The primary biblical metaphor for the relationship between God and humankind is that of covenant—a partnership. This, too, is reflected in the first biblical stories, with God bringing the animals to the "earth person" for naming (see Genesis 2:19–20) and giving the first man and woman responsibility for stewardship of the earth (see Genesis 1:26 and 1:28). Then, God makes a covenant with Noah and his descendants—in other words, with all humankind—and places the rainbow in the sky as "the sign of the covenant I have established between myself and all mortal creatures that are on the earth" (Genesis 9:17). This first covenant, and every covenant thereafter, places responsibilities on both parties; though God is clearly the primary agent, God's commitment never lessens the responsibility of the human partners to live as a people of God. But, the theologians debate, given our "original sinfulness," are we capable of keeping our side of any covenant? Can we be faithful partners with God?

Throughout history, the best Catholic Christian response has been to say a resounding "yes" and then to immediately add "by God's grace." Grace is simply a coded term for God's help and care that is ever turned toward us without our deserving it; it is gift or favor (*gratia*).

In Christian faith, Jesus is the ultimate catalyst of God's grace in human history and now symbolizes God's unbreakable promise to sustain humankind in living as people of God. And yet, God's grace, rather than lessening our responsibility or freedom, heightens both; it empowers us to respond and to do so freely. To the paradox of how to affirm both God's grace and human responsibility, perhaps Karl Rahner offered the most lucid explanation. Rahner points out that God's grace is simply another name for God's love, and like all true love, it enhances the recipients, empowering and setting them free to respond. Like true parental love, rather than suspending our responsibility or programming our choices, God's grace/love is precisely what enables us to be responsible and free (more on this later).

4. Person as Partner in Community

That we are "made for each other" is also reflected in the Genesis accounts of creation. God saw that it was not good for the earth person to be alone, and so differentiated the one into two—now called man and woman (the first time the gender terms are used), and set them to be equal partners to each other (not the woman as "helpmate" to the man, as the old translations had it).[10] We are essentially relational, and intended for "right relationship."

The communality of the person is the main theme of chapter 4; it should be noted here, however, simply because any description of our nature would be egregiously incomplete without it. For though each person is a "whole" instead of a "part," we are ever related to others and responsible for them as well as for ourselves.[11] Our very personhood is inherently social. Yet this need not mean loss of agency and autonomy as person. Throughout Christian tradition, Catholicism has made particular effort to hold together the personal and social aspects of human existence.

In its dual affirmation of "person-in-community," a Catholic Christian anthropology is a counterpoint, on the one hand, to totalitarian regimes and philosophies and, on the other hand, to the individualism so championed by the Enlightenment. In totalitarian Communism, for instance, a person is simply a "part" of the society, a cog in a large wheel. Likewise, the Confucian attitude, so pervasive in Asian cultures, can emphasize the social entity to the loss of an autonomous sense of the "self."

Catholic Christianity also resists the individualism still championed by modern capitalism. As individual persons we are always partners in society, and the personal and common good are simply aspects of the same reality—our human condition. To cite Maritain again, "There is nothing more illusory than to pose the problem of the person and the common good in terms of opposition"; instead, Catholicism maintains, "The person is for the community and the community is for the person."[12]

As I will elaborate in chapter 4, philosophical insistence on the union of our personal and social aspects is also reflected and supported by a communal theology of the Church. Perhaps this is captured most graphically by the Pauline image of the "body of Christ." As Paul elaborates, each organ of the human body is important unto itself, even "the less presentable parts" (Romans 12:23). All of them must work together as one body; likewise, every member of the faith community is valued and important unto themselves and yet they find their Christian identity only by functioning together as "Christ's body" in the world—the Church (Romans 12:27).

Stated philosophically, each individual has dignity and value in and of themselves, but becomes fully a person only through relationships and community. We have our identity, but we have it in community; our autonomy, but in interdependence; our freedom, but with responsibility—our next aspect to highlight.

5. Person with Freedom, Rights, and Responsibilities

The Genesis accounts of creation reflect great freedom on God's part, choosing to create whatever pleases. The unfolding biblical narrative makes clear that God adamantly favors freedom for all humankind. The paradigmatic story of the Hebrew Scriptures—Exodus—is of a God of freedom who looks upon the Israelite people in slavery and intervenes in human history to set them free. Similarly, the central story of the Christian Scriptures—the death and resurrection of Jesus—is of God intervening in Jesus to set all humankind free—free *from* the power of sin and death, and free *for* living in right relationship with God, self, others, and creation. St. Paul, echoing the memory of Exodus and interpreting the meaning of Jesus, summarized with these stirring words: "Freedom is what we have, Christ has set us free. Remain then as free people and do not become slaves again" (Galatians 5:1)

Christian understanding of the freedom that God intends for all humankind has traditionally taken God's own freedom as a model for ours; human freedom is analogous to God's. This means that authentic freedom is always directed toward the true, the good, and the beautiful, and is essentially the freedom to become our most human selves—most like our God. It is not an individualistic freedom whereby we can choose as we please and according to our own preferences. Indeed, it includes freedom *from* internal compulsion or external constraint but reaches beyond to freedom *for* becoming most authentically who we are invited to be—fully alive human beings to the glory of God. Such freedom is not a fait accompli but a task to be realized within history, and it is to permeate every level and arena of human existence—the personal, interpersonal, and sociopolitical.

One way of explicitly naming the freedoms that are inalienable to all human beings is with the language of "rights." Drawing upon a long tradition, Pope John XXIII (1881–1963), of happy memory, described well the essential human rights as: to life and to a worthy manner of living; to respect as persons without discrimination on any basis; to pursue and express the truth; to be informed and educated; to worship God freely; to choose a state in life; to have gainful employment, decent labor conditions, and just compensation for work; to organize, meet, and associate with others; to participate in public affairs and to contribute to the common good.[13] But because our freedom is analogous to God's own freedom, such rights are never for ourselves alone but bring corresponding responsibilities to promote the same rights for all humankind. Rights and responsibilities are two sides of the same coin—of personhood! A defining aspect, then, of the human condition is that we have responsibilities. Our very personhood renders us responsible; no other aspect of God's creation is held so accountable for its actions. As persons, we are responsible to live with integrity to our own best selves, to care for the neighbor, and for the common good of all. Chapter 4 will elaborate specifically on the common good and chapter 8 will take up the theme of social justice, but all such responsibilities are grounded first in our personhood. As persons, we must act for the well-being of self and neighbor, responsibilities that cannot be delegated to someone else.

Much as no one can replace me in death, so no one can replace my responsibilities in life. Oh, I am ever in need of help to fulfill them, and I must always proceed in partnership with others and with God. But ultimately, *I am responsible to and for myself, to and for others.* This is what it means to be human; to renege is to be less than the person I am invited to become.

6. Person as Becoming, Knowing, and Creating

"Being" in the divine image, the person has unending capacities for *becoming* fully human; the ability to realize ourselves has a never-ending horizon. The ultimate expression of boundless human potential in Christian tradition is the Eastern Orthodox theology that, having originated in God's image, human life is a journey into divine likeness, into *theosis*, which literally means "becoming God-like." It is in this light that the Orthodox tradition understands the meaning of the Christ event, and the "difference" Jesus makes to the human condition. In the famous phrase of St. Athanasius, "God became human so that humans could become like God."[14]

And the emphasis must be on *becoming;* human nature is never "given" as a finished product, but comes as a lifelong journey that unfolds with the help of God's grace, partnership with others, and our own best efforts. This becoming bridges here and hereafter; what begins within time as growth toward fullness of life is completed in eternity. Along the way, our horizon should be nothing less than our limitless potential. As Jesus announced of himself and his function in human history, "I came that you might have life and have it to the full" (John 10:10). Could he have meant anything less than *theosis?* In the second creation myth of Genesis, we find the fascinating detail that Adam and Eve were forbidden to eat of "the tree of knowledge of good and evil"; the threatened punishment for disobedience was immediate death (Genesis 2:17). Well, now that we know the rest of the story, it was an idle threat! Succumbing to the temptation to have "knowledge like unto the gods," they ate the forbidden fruit and still lived—or did not die immediately. Can we not presume that their descendants, too, are capable of knowledge reaching into ultimacy?

However we interpret the story, it reflects that humankind has an extraordinary capacity and a stubborn will to know. Rahner referred to our potential for knowledge as an "existential," meaning that it is a permanent aspect of human existence—it comes with the turf. We are always capable of knowing, and—as far as we know—can do so in ways beyond every other instance of God's creation.

As knowers like God, we can use our reason, memory, and imagination to attend to and take in the data of the world and life, then push on to understand it, to make judgments and decisions about it—ever reaching for what it all "means." And not only can we make meaning out of life, but our capacity for self-reflection enables us to try to make sense of ourselves, to reflect on our own existence. This ability to rise above ourselves in the sense of being able to think about our own thinking is a transcendent reach, enabling us to keep on reaching for the Transcendent. Why, we can even come to "know" God—of course, never completely and only in our human way! But as Jesus taught, such ultimate knowing holds the promise of "eternal life" (see John 17:3).

In the first account of creation in Genesis, the Creator creates everything by the power of divine word—by *fiat* of "let it be." In the second account, God is more anthropomorphic, a craftsperson who takes some clay and begins to shape it (Genesis 2:7). It represents God fulfilling the functions of any person who creates something new—imagining what form it might take or discovering this in interaction with the materials, crafting the objet d'art with—may we presume—some playfulness, changes, adjustments, and finer touches, and setting it out in its own reality—as is.

Then observe that God immediately invites the "earth person" to "name" the animals—an exercise of human imagination. Clearly, God has found a like-partner in the work of creation. Taking, then, what is surely the decisive endowment of human creativity, God differentiates the "person of the earth" into male and female, fashioning them to participate in human procreation. God designed humanity to procreate itself; nothing could more fully symbolize that we are creators like our Creator.

7. Person with Divine Law Written in our "Nature"
The ethics of Catholic Christianity has a strong tradition of insisting upon a "law" written by God within human nature. Because we are not depraved, we have, by nature—which means by God's design—a reliable sense of right and wrong. This natural law reflects God's

intentions for humankind which we can know by reason alone. Though natural law ethicists now see "nature" as evolving rather than as static and hotly debate its extent and content, nonetheless, a strong conviction remains that there are universal and binding moral principles which can be known by human reason, unaided by any special revelation. In fact, Catholic Christian ethics is based as much on natural law as it is on the biblical word, with the latter confirming and, at times, amplifying the former (e.g., the natural need for rest amplified as keeping the Sabbath holy). For the classic Protestant ethic, murder is wrong because the Bible condemns it; for the classic Catholic ethic, because murder is wrong, the Bible condemns it.

8. Person as Agent-Subject Who Can Make History

There are many systems of politics, philosophy, and belief that diminish the significance of the human person and of history. They look upon this world as an end in itself or, alternatively, as a place simply of trial for the next; for whichever attitude, human efforts are, as a friend of mine often says, "no more than basket weaving." To such nihilist views, people have no contribution to make to improving their earthly lot and no worthwhile legacy to leave behind.

In contrast, the Catholic Christian view is that the person is always an "agent-subject"—someone who has autonomy to choose, decide, chart their own course, and make a difference in human history. Working with each other and empowered by God's grace, our human efforts, creativity, and ingenuity can be significant for the well-being of self, others, and creation. We can be "agents" rather than "dependents"—"subjects" rather than "objects" in our time and place.

Persons deserve autonomy and can be full players in the unfolding historical event, with each one capable of making a significant contribution. No life is useless or meaningless, for simply by being alive, we give glory to God. Although people are much influenced by their historical context, they need not be only the creatures of it but can become its creators and recreators as well.

9. Person Made from Love and for Loving

At the end of the New Testament, we find St. John's culminating three-word description of God that had been unfolding throughout biblical history—"God is love" (1 John 4:16). If we make a rainbow from the

Genesis stories of creation to this affirmation of St. John at the end, we realize that God's own life in us is, in fact, God's love for us. God literally made us out of love—God's own love. Every human is alive by the love of God; our very lifeblood is God's love coursing through our veins.

Following on, with our "being" sprung from Love, the highest calling of humankind, the truest realization of who we are meant to become is lovers. Since God's love is the model for humanity's, we are called to no easy romanticism but to the "tough" love that requires "right relationship" with God, self, others, and creation—that demands the works of justice and peace. This is the kind of love that Jesus, echoing his Hebrew faith, made the greatest commandment: a radical love for God with all one's mind, heart, strength, and soul, and of one's neighbor as oneself—with "neighbor" including even enemies.

10. Person with Eternal Destiny

All the religions of the world address, in one way or another, the ultimate issue of death. All of Christianity shares the deep conviction that our lives have an eternal destiny: to return to the Source from whence we came. As a Preface for the Mass of the Resurrection expresses it, "The sadness of death gives way to the bright promise of immortality," for in death, "life is changed, not ended."

Even as death "changes" life, there is continuity between how we have lived here and how we may dwell in eternity. For we will be judged and held responsible for our lives—anything less would not honor who we are. St. Matthew's Gospel has a riveting description of the Last Judgment which it attributes to Jesus. It seems that the decisive criterion by which our lives will be measured for eternity is how we have cared for the neighbor most in need.

Some of the Historical and Theological "Story"

Historically, Catholicism has often failed to live up to its own best theology of the human condition, practicing a negative anthropology instead. A friend Jenny, raised Catholic but now a member of the United Church of Christ, told me that she left Catholicism because, "I needed to get away from the dour and dismal attitude toward myself and all things human that the Catholic Church drilled into me since I was a little girl."

Jenny's experience is far from unique. It is significant, too, that she should find a more positive anthropology in the United Church of Christ whose Puritan roots might suggest otherwise. This reflects my point in chapter 1 that many Protestant denominations may adhere to a more "Catholic" anthropology than some expressions of Catholicism. As I will repeat often throughout, Catholic Christian perspectives are certainly not limited to—and are often poorly practiced by—identified Catholics.

Various historical influences help to explain—though not excuse—why the Catholic Church has often failed to live up to the optimistic sense of the person as favored by its own best tradition. For example, throughout Christian history, there have been many heretical movements claiming that the physical aspect of human existence is essentially sinful. In the early centuries, the Gnostics, Docetists, and Manichaeans (to which St. Augustine belonged for many years) were right-wing Christian groups that, among other things, saw the material world and especially the human body as evil.

More recently, a seventeenth-century Catholic reform movement called Jansenism taught a very negative understanding of human nature, coupled, ironically, with a puritan ethic; for instance, it discouraged frequent reception of the Eucharist by ordinary people, presuming their sinful state. Though it started in France and the Low Countries, by some quirks of history Jansenism had a pervasive influence on my own tradition of Irish Catholicism, helping to explain its common image as penitential and rigorist, with a less than healthy attitude toward the human body and sexuality. Coupled with such negativity, Catholicism has often overemphasized the decisive nature of "good works"—as if people must earn God's grace, work to deserve God's love, with the terror of hell-fire as the threatening backdrop for those (likely the majority) who fail in this "Catch 22."

The "fire and brimstone" sermon in James Joyce's *Portrait of the Artist* is a riveting example of the Jansenist and "good works" perspectives combined; imagine what it taught people about their human condition! And Irish Catholicism is certainly not unique in its traces of Jansenism and the "heresy of good works"—as if everything depends on our own efforts.

In fairness to mainline Catholic Christian tradition, it is important to note that the Church always, if sometimes belatedly, recognized movements like Jansenism as inconsistent with Christian faith and condemned them as heresy. Yet, some of their attitude "rubbed off," compromising, at least in pastoral practice, what should have been a *humanitas* anthropology. Catholic communities should not be sanguine about teaching, preaching, and practicing a positive anthropology—given past failures and old heresies still around. They must also guard against new heresies, most notably "free-market globalization" that reduces the person to a profit-seeking producer and consumer—an inhuman fate for us all.

I have already suggested some of the classic biblical and theological sources of what could be described philosophically as a *humanitas* anthropology. Beyond this, it may help to review briefly some of the fires of controversy in which it has been forged. As the Catechism notes, two extreme and contrary proposals about the human condition forced Catholic Christianity to its own most precise theological articulation, namely: the human self-sufficiency proposal of the Celtic monk Pelagius (early 5th c.) and the antithetical position of total human depravity taken by Calvin and the more radical Reformers (16th c.).[15] For Catholic sentiments, Pelagius was overly confident in human abilities—posing total independence of God's grace—whereas Calvin exaggerated human depravity—and so total dependence on God's grace. The Catholic Christian position attempts a middle ground between these two extremes.

Pelagius, at least as he was interpreted by his great opponent Augustine, claimed that by our own abilities, and without the help of God's grace, people can lead a good and moral life; that the sin of Adam was no more than bad example, reflecting no permanent debilitation of the human condition. This would mean that we can save ourselves by human effort alone; for Pelagius, all the eggs are in the human basket!

Augustine convinced the Church to condemn Pelagius for heresy; not, however, before some of his influence had rubbed off. In pastoral practice, Catholicism has often fallen into over emphasis on "good works;" yet theologically at least, it has insisted in one way or another, echoing the original condemnation of Pelagius, that "people cannot rise from the depths of sin by their own free will unless the grace of the merciful God lifts them up."[16] In other words, human agency for good is always by the power of God's grace.

On the other hand, for the great reformer John Calvin (1509–64), or at least as his Catholic opponents interpreted him, the human condition is *massa peccati*—a mass of sin (actually, Calvin borrowed the phrase from Augustine). Humankind is inherently depraved and so can contribute nothing to the work of its salvation, depending entirely on God's grace.

It should be noted that Calvin's intent, in reaction to undue Catholic emphasis at the time on good works to earn salvation, intended to make a pastoral more than a theological point, to emphasize that God's grace is free and unmerited. However, in a polemical situation, it was the theological position that drew attention.[17] When one combines radical human sinfulness with total dependence on God's grace, then the logical conclusion—reached by Calvin too—is that some people are saved and some are lost by "predestination." This means that God makes a prior election of both the people to receive salvation and those to suffer damnation.

At the Council of Trent (1545–63), held to respond to the Protestant Reformation, Catholicism denounced again Pelagius's exaggeration of "the powers of human nature" and then, as the opposite position, condemned the Calvinist claim that "free will was destroyed and lost" by Adam's sin.[18] For if this be so, then humankind has lost all responsibility and freedom in its response to God—leading indeed to "predestination" of who is lost or saved.

Trent roundly rejected this logic and reiterated that, though "fallen" and ever in need of God's help, humankind remains inherently good and thus capable of partnership with God—by grace—in saving ourselves and the world. Human efforts and cooperation are essential, even though ever prompted and sustained by the grace of God. If one were to put the Council of Trent's teaching on a bumper sticker, it might read: "Without God, we can't. Without us, God won't."

As a parenthetical note, Catholic Christians should learn to take with great seriousness the classic Protestant insistence on the reality of human sinfulness. It is held in good faith and with almost incontrovertible historical warrant, as a review of the morning newspaper still attests. It can seem that an abiding sinfulness reigns in the world, taking many personal and social expressions, causing dreadful suffering to people and destruction of the environment; all of us have complicity in some aspect of this "mass of sin."

Rather than overwhelming into paralysis, however, or abandoning human effort to depend totally on "grace alone," such realization should bring people to lament and repent their sinful condition. And true repentance is *metanoia*—a change of heart and life—which demands, in the words of the old Act of Contrition prayer, that we "firmly resolve to sin no more." By God's grace, such resolve and the effort it demands are not beyond the reach of our hope.

A number of contemporary theologians propose that the balance of cooperation between God's grace and human effort is reflected in the biblical notion of covenant—previously referred to. In all the covenants, including the new one made in Jesus, God bonds humankind with each other and with Godself and empowers people to live according to God's desires for creation. Both divine and human partners in a covenant commit themselves to playing their parts in fidelity to the agreement, signifying that humanity, with God's help, is capable of as much. Only a cynical and capricious God would demand more of humankind than we are capable.

Contemporary theology also looks to the life of Jesus for its "clue" to the human condition, beginning with the symbol of the Incarnation—God becoming human in Jesus. In Christian faith, Jesus was the fully human presence of God—"made flesh, to dwell among us" (John 1:14). The Incarnation forged a "new covenant" of divine/human partnership. As also already noted, that God entered fully into the human condition affirms unequivocally its innate goodness and thereafter assures its capacity for partnership with God.

Turning then to the person and preaching of the historical Jesus, a current theological sentiment is that Jesus not only embodies the revelation of God to humanity but reveals us to ourselves, epitomizing our true nature and possibility as persons and modeling how to live for fullness of life.

On the one hand, Jesus taught us to put our faith and trust only in God, to turn to God often in prayer, to depend on God's providence and grace; on the other, he constantly modeled how to live as a person of God and called people to discipleship as followers of his "way." Through his whole life, Jesus taught that humankind depends entirely on God and, paradoxically, human effort and cooperation with God's intentions are essential. Truly, Jesus reflected the covenant theology of his Hebrew roots.

It appears that the central theme and purpose of Jesus' entire life is captured well in his use of the symbol the *reign of God*. He lived and died that God's desire of peace and justice, love and compassion, holiness and fullness of life for all might be realized. And this shalom of God is not simply for later, but is to begin now, being done on earth as in heaven.

Jesus preached the law of love as the greatest commandment of God's reign, but although echoing the Hebrew Scriptures (see Deuteronomy 6:5, and Leviticus 19:18), he seems to have made the love command more radical by bonding love of God with love of neighbor and authentic love of self and by making explicit that "neighbor" means everyone—even enemies. Christians are to live in right and loving relationship in the community of all humankind.

At the beginning of his ministry, as recorded in Luke's Gospel, Jesus presented himself as fulfilling the Jubilee Year promise found in Isaiah 61—that God had anointed him to bring "good news to the poor," "liberty to captives," "recovery of sight to the blind," and "to let the oppressed go free"—to proclaim a time of God's special favor for all (see Luke 4:18–19).

In the Beatitudes, Jesus proposed the path to true happiness as dependence on God, opposing sin and evil, living with gentleness and patience, working for peace and justice, being merciful, putting God first in one's life, and being willing to suffer in witness to one's faith (see Matthew 5:3–10). He preached that our final judgment will be based on our compassion for the poorest and neediest—in whom God is present (see Matthew 25:31–46). What a worthy agenda for being human and living humanly!

When Christian tradition interpreted the meaning of Jesus' life, death, and resurrection, there was consensus that he achieved some major change for the human condition. There are many models for expressing what this might be. Some of the favorite titles attributed to Jesus—Savior, Redeemer, Liberator, and Divinizer—summarize four understandings of what he brought about: that he saves, redeems, frees, and empowers *theosis*—becoming God-like.

But all agree that Jesus made God's saving grace more readily available to all humankind. However, the classic Protestant position is that God's grace in Jesus covers over human sinfulness, making us, as the great Lutheran theologian Paul Tillich (1886–1965) expressed it, "acceptable to God in spite of our unacceptability." Surely a consolation upon recognizing one's sinfulness!

In contrast, however, the classic position of Catholicism is that God's grace in Jesus works an inner transformation in humankind—a "renovation" as Aquinas called it—that builds upon and improves the "original grace" already there "in nature." In Aquinas's classic summary, "Grace works through nature"—or, in more colloquial terms, God helps us to help ourselves.

A key point then is that God's help does not violate human freedom nor alleviate responsibility. Drawing upon some old theological categories, God's "operative grace" works as an original and saving outreach to humankind, whereas, with the help of God's "cooperative grace," people choose to respond to God's initiative. A fine precis of this grace/nature partnership is reflected in the Eastern Orthodox notion of synergy, summarized as "the affirmation that while human beings can do nothing without God, God does nothing regarding goodness, righteousness, and holiness without human cooperation."[19]

A Philosophical Summary

Without theological basis or argument and on purely philosophical grounds, it is very possible to embrace the *humanitas* anthropology just outlined, finding it a compelling and humanizing attitude toward one's own and other people's existence. So because it encourages a stance of *for life for all*, one can be wisely convinced that:

- Though capable of evil, the person is essentially good, should be treated with dignity and respect, and every human being deserves as much.

- The whole person—mind and body—is to be cherished, developed, and cared for in a life of balance and integration.

- We live most humanly in partnership with others, in community and interdependence rather than in isolation and rugged self-sufficiency, when we work for the common good as well as for our own and with a sense of participation in Something greater than the sum of the parts.

- The person has inalienable freedoms, rights, and responsibilities—essentially to become a fully alive human being committed to the same freedoms, rights, and responsibilities for all others.

• Each person is capable of lifelong growth, of being an active agent of knowledge rather than only a recipient, and of creating what would not otherwise exist.

• People have a "native" compass of morality, a conscience that alerts them to what is right and wrong, and lends a sense of mandate to choose what is moral over immoral.

• Each person is to live as a "whole" rather than a "part," as an interdependent agent rather than a dependent individual and is capable of making their own unique contribution to society and history.

• Our highest human calling is to love and be loved, with love that demands the works of justice and peace.

• Our lives have a lasting worth and are ultimately worthwhile, having a purpose that reaches beyond ourselves and our own time.

For Teachers and Parents

Regardless of the theological or philosophical arguments that can be made on behalf of a positive anthropology, the most persuasive argument for an educator is that it is more likely to generate positive outcomes in the lives of learners. The social sciences support this contention, advising that society generally receives back from people what it has projected onto them. Educators—significant social agents—are likely to "get what they expect" from learners; so, better by far to expect more than less! A negative attitude will engender as much.

What does a "realistic optimism" anthropology mean for teachers and parents and for how they educate? What does it ask of educators' own souls? What does it recommend for their teaching style? What does it suggest for the educational space they help to create? What are some implications for education—anywhere or anytime by anyone—if one opts for a humanitas anthropology?

To respond adequately will take the remainder of this book, and even then, leaving much to be said. At the outset, I offer only a few suggestions—leaving something for later chapters. You likely already know from your own experience as learner and teacher that both a positive and a negative anthropology make for corresponding educational outcomes. First pause to reflect a little on that experience.

For Reflection
- From your experience, think of one notable situation in which a positive anthropology was working. Then think of an instance where a negative one was dominant. What do you learn from each instance for your own educating?

- Imagine some likely consequences if you approach your teaching with a consistently positive anthropology.

- What are some roadblocks that you experience to implementing a humanitas anthropology? Think of deterrents inside and outside of yourself, both psychological and in your social context.

For the Educator's Soul

A *humanitas* anthropology suggests perduring commitments for the educator's heart, convictions that should permeate one's whole vocation as a teacher or a parent. I propose three attitudes for educators as persons in their general outlook on life, and three commitments that pertain more specifically to their educating. Let my suggestions only stimulate your own.

An Affirmation of Persons

Teachers and parents need a bedrock attitude that affirms the essential goodness and giftedness of people. This should not cancel out a healthy measure of "realism" but it should lead them to approach learners with an abiding attitude of affirmation, a deep-down sentiment of positive esteem. This includes respecting their dignity and valuing each one as a unique person whose life is a gift, cherishing and defending every person's basic human rights, affirming the whole person—body and soul—and the innate goodness of both. The world-renowned Spanish cellist and conductor Pablo Casals (1876–1973) once wrote:

> Each second we live is a new and unique moment of the universe, a moment that will never be again. . . . And what do we teach our children? We teach them that two and two make four, and that Paris is the capital of France. When will we teach them what they are? We should say to each of them: Do you know what you are? You are a marvel. You are unique. In all the years that have passed, there has never been another child like you. Your legs, your arms, your clever fingers, the way you move. You may become a Shakespeare, a Michelangelo, a Beethoven. You have the capacity for anything. Yes, you are a marvel. And when you grow up, can you then harm another who is, like you, a marvel?[20]

Casals was urging that the symphony of education be conducted by a *humanitas* anthropology.

On the other hand, learners are served poorly by a naive romanticism on the part of educators. The famous French philosopher Jean-Jacques Rousseau (1712–78) was so confident in the innate goodness of human nature that he proposed in his famous book on education entitled *Émile* that children be allowed to grow up in a "state of nature," with no intervention of teachers or parents by way of discipline or character formation, instruction or guidance. This is not the attitude I am recommending at all; it would be irresponsible on the part of educators. People's capacity for goodness must be nurtured and formed into character, their gifts and potencies fostered into realization; and everyone needs access to the knowledge, art, and wisdom of the ages in order to make and keep life human for self and others.

These significant interventions in learners' lives are the "designated" responsibility of educators. They serve learners best by maintaining a balanced realism—for example, gentle and respectful discipline if needed; and yet, their decisive attitude must be affirmation and esteem.

Amy, with the reputation of a great science teacher, was designated to a course on self-esteem with a class of "behavioral problem" students in a Connecticut middle school. Later she commented, "When I saw the 'I am lovable' curriculum that was assigned, I just knew instinctively that it wouldn't work, that their best hope was to find and develop their gifts."

She set out to uncover something that each person was good at and began to weave individualized curriculum accordingly. Her classroom could have puppet theater, science experiments, writing projects, math assignments, storytelling, and more—all going on at the same time. She found "field placements" where the students could share their talents and gifts with others. Gradually, the "behavioral problems" receded and the class became a model to the school.

In describing her educational philosophy, Amy said, "Instead of concentrating on their dysfunctions and trying to correct them, I focus on their gifts. And as they find an identity beyond their dysfunctions and develop their gifts as persons, their self-esteem also improves." Amy's undergirding anthropology is a "realistic optimism."

Remaining faithful to a *humanitas* anthropology can require a generosity of the educator—even a largess—toward the human condition. It enjoins not focusing on shortcomings as if they define persons, expecting the best rather than the worst, challenging and developing gifts more than trying to correct faults, favoring forgiveness over punishment. Yet it stops far short of a Rousseau-like romanticism; it is not naive about human capacity for bad choices and our need for character formation, and it never means excusing evil actions. In theological terms, this attitude recognizes the reality of sin and judgment but prefers to emphasize, as does the Bible, God's mercy and the hope that God's love holds out for humankind.

The art of Norman Rockwell is a lovely expression of such benevolence toward the human condition, often depicting its foibles but never with cruelty or despair. To see the painting of Casey deflated on election night creates sympathy for him but leniency, too, for the supporters who are abandoning him, probably for the winner; as a slice of life, *Before and After* reflects a *humanitas* anthropology. Educators are wisest and most likely to educate *for life for all* when they embrace the same.

An Anticipation of Persons

Educators should be able to see great possibilities in people. They need a perennial attitude that all persons can become fully alive human beings according to their own God-given potential. It is easy and so tempting for a teacher to look at a group of students and subdivide them, if only subconsciously, into "the bright and promising," "the mediocre who may get by," and "the rest—predestined for failure." But how shortsighted, biased, and unjust this is—and, of course, dangerous as a self-fulfilling prophecy.

Surely one of the most inspiring "educational" stories of our century is that of Helen Adams Keller (1880–1968) and her teacher Anne Mansfield Sullivan (1866–1936). Helen was only nineteen months old when stricken with an illness that left her deaf and blind, and mute shortly thereafter; but Annie Sullivan, herself a graduate of Perkins School for the Blind in Boston, refused to accept that Helen could not be educated. Through a remarkable and loving relationship, and beginning by pressing the manual alphabet into Helen's hand, Annie taught her the names of objects and, within two years, how to read and write in Braille. Then Annie taught Helen to speak by having her place her fingers on Annie's own larynx to "hear" the vibrations. Helen went on to graduate cum laude from Radcliffe College (1904) where Annie "spelled" the lectures into her hands.

Helen spent her life working and writing on behalf of handicapped people, becoming a widely read author. Helen and Annie were the subjects of an award-winning television play *The Miracle Worker* by William Gibson, rewritten by him for the Broadway stage and later made into a Hollywood film. If Annie Sullivan had not been able to anticipate and hope for what Helen Keller could become, the world would never have been blessed by such an extraordinary life. All educators are called to the kind of hope for people, the anticipation of their possibilities, that Annie Sullivan had for Helen.

Every person is a "work in progress" and remains so this side of eternity. Our personhood is never a fait accompli as if we ever exhaust our capacities for personal growth, learning, discovery, and creativity. Every day is a fresh gift that brings new promises and possibilities. For an educator, this conviction translates into an attitude that sees people as agents of knowledge rather than simply recipients (the theme of chapter 6) and as creators of new expressions and possibilities for themselves and others.

And these capacities are not simply for a season or an era in one's life—e.g., "school days"—but are lifelong. Life itself is "continuing education," and the educator needs to look upon everyone as a "lifelong learner" who is ever capable of growing into fullness of life—

reaching into eternity—and of making a lasting contribution to the human family, leaving the world a better place for being here. What "malpractice" it is if educators conspire with people to settle for less than who they can become.

Love for Persons

Affirmation of persons asks of the educator a profound faith, anticipation a perduring hope, but, as St. Paul intimated, faith and hope are at their best when suffused by love. Paul says that the fruits of all three "endure" forever, but "the greatest is love" (see 1 Corinthians 13). Surely to educate well invites love from the soul of teacher and parent.

A university class of sociology students were assigned to do a survey of 200 young boys in a Baltimore slum and to project their likely future: in every case the students reported, "He hasn't got a chance." Twenty-five years later, another class decided to do a follow-up study of the 180 men who still lived locally; they found, to their amazement, that 176 of them had achieved significant success as lawyers, doctors, businessmen, and in other careers.

When asked to account for their success, so many of them said, "There was this teacher. . ." and all talked about the same one. Since she was still alive, the researchers sought her out to ask what magic formula she had used to give hope to those young men slotted for failure. Her response was, "It was really very simple. I loved those boys."[21]

That love is asked of the educator's soul is accentuated by remembering that teaching is, essentially, "a way of being with" people. At its best and fullest, education is a relational encounter—an I/Thou relationship—intended to influence who each other becomes; it reaches into the very souls of people to affect their "being." Educators walk always on "sacred ground"—people's lives. What a hazard if they do not tread lovingly and with deep care for their well-being and becoming!

Though the teacher or parent may never realize it completely, their inspiring ideal is an *agapaic* love—love that chooses *to be generous and not for recompense*. What a far cry from a sentimental niceness or a glib feeling of liberality—these can amount to indifference. The love of teacher or parent must at times be a tough one, a love that challenges and makes demands, sets boundaries and lays down a just discipline as necessary. Love, by its very nature, demands integrity in concrete situations, truth to what is best for people. But the toughness should be suffused with the largess that goes the extra mile. Agapaic love is the ultimate expression of holiness of life (theme of chapter 8); yet, to think of education as requiring less is to diminish it.

Pertaining more specifically now to teaching and what a *humanitas* anthropology asks of the educator's soul, I suggest the following three commitments; you will imagine others!

Relate with Learners as "Agent-Subjects"

The great Jewish philosopher of education Martin Buber said that we can choose between two primary modes for relating to each other: either as things or as persons. The choice is between an "I/it" or an "I/Thou" relationship; no one has made a stronger argument than Buber on behalf of the latter. He insisted that relating person-to-person is the only way to realize one's vocation as a human being.[22]
In the context of teaching, educators can choose to view learners as "things" that depend on them for knowledge and formation—as "dependent objects"—or they can relate with learners as persons who have their own capacities, who can initiate and be full players in life, with all the dignity and respect that is their right—as "agent subjects." Surely, the educational encounter should reflect an "I/Thou" relationship!

In the delightful book, *Chicken Soup for the Soul,* a teacher tells the following story: "I had a great feeling of relief when I began to understand that a youngster needs more than just subject matter. I know mathematics well, and I teach it well. I used to think that was all I needed to do. Now I teach children, not math. . . . The youngster who really made me understand this was Eddie. I asked him one day why he thought he was doing so much better than last year. He gave meaning to my whole new orientation. 'It's because I like myself now when I'm with you,' he said."[23] Here is a teacher who knows that "the subjects" he teaches—in the personal sense—are students; math is the "object."

Relating with learners as "agent subjects" is to enable them to become as much. All of the pedagogical proposals made throughout the remainder of this book can be summarized as commitment *to educate people as "agent subjects" to live in "right relationship" with self and others, with society and creation, and with their God*—so we will return to this theme from many angles. Teachers and parents must be catalysts in learners' lives who enable them to become "fully alive to the glory of God" (St. Irenaeus writing circa 175 c.e.).[24] It is nigh impossible for learners to live into the wholeness of their humanity, to have a sense of ultimate meaning and purpose, to engage in their world as initiators and creators, to make a difference for human well-being, unless they have teachers and parents who so educate them.

Here I accent only one intent of an "I/Thou" relationship between educators and learners, and may we not consider it the crowning purpose of all, namely to educate people as *lovers*! St. Augustine, writing around 400 c.e. proposed as much when he responded to a deacon of Carthage named Deogratias who inquired of Augustine how best to educate: "With love set before you as an end to which you may refer all that you say, so give all your instructions that they to whom you speak by hearing may believe, and by believing may hope, and by hoping may love."[25] Augustine was equally convinced that the educator must teach students what and how to love, to love well and wisely, because "we become what we love."[26]

Nurturing learners as lovers surely includes: to love self and others as a "gift" not needing to be earned; to love nature and to care for creation as good and responsible stewards; to love truth and beauty—in their simplicity; to love authentic freedom as the entitlement of all people; to love peace and justice as the abiding desire of humankind; and, ultimately, to love God.

Foster All the Gifts of People
People are multifaceted mysteries; we have gifts in common and particular ones as well. Teachers and parents are to help develop all of learners' talents and possibilities, to commit themselves to *an integrated education of the whole person*. We have: physical gifts for manual labor, sports, and entertainment; moral gifts for discerning and choosing what is good; spiritual gifts for compassion, love, and reaching for the Transcendent; social gifts for relationship and service; intellectual gifts for pursuing truth and wisdom; and aesthetic gifts for creating and appreciating the beautiful.

Within any of these there are particular expressions; note the variety of aesthetic gifts—for music, art, poetry, dance, design, and more. Or within the intellectual, research scholars now propose that we have multiple forms of intelligence instead of the one alone as measured by IQ tests. Howard Gardner, Harvard professor of educational psychology, lists as many as seven intelligences: linguistic, musical, logical-mathematical, spatial, bodily-kinesthetic, interpersonal (ability for relationships), intrapersonal (ability to gain and use self-knowledge).[27] Beyond this, the work of psychologist Daniel Goleman is heightening consciousness of "emotional intelligence"[28] and may I add spiritual? The list could go on. A *humanitas* anthropology recommends education for the harmonious development of all human gifts, to inform and form people's various talents into realization. Of course, different instances of education specialize in a particular aspect of human "being," but should do so in ways that contribute to an integrated education of the whole person.

No gift is beyond the reach of education. People should be able to bring together into a coherent and integrated lifestyle all that they learn from the sciences of knowledge, expressions of art, and ways of wisdom—and a faith perspective is surely a fulcrum of such integration. Likewise, holistic education should enable people to recognize and function with integrity in the interconnected web of human existence.[29]

Commit to Human Freedom, Rights, and Responsibilities

These three belong together because to consider them apart can be distorting; authentic freedom, human rights, and historical responsibilities are symbiotic to each other. Commitment to freedom is asked of the soul of every teacher and parent to ensure that learners can live with freedom in free societies. As noted earlier, human freedom means becoming free like God; this is far from license or rugged individualism to do as one pleases, but freedom *from* inner compulsion and external oppression, and freedom *for* becoming fully alive persons who fulfill their responsibilities for the well-being of self and others, for the personal and common good.

As noted already, Pope John XXIII listed the basic human rights as: decent quality of life, freedom from discrimination, to pursue the truth, to be informed, to worship freely, to choose a vocation, worthwhile work, just compensation, to organize and assemble, and to participate in society for the common good. Every educator should be committed to promoting these rights for learners.

Later chapters on community and social justice will focus on the political responsibility of teachers and parents to promote their realization in society. Here I stress that teacher and parent must first be committed to realizing the rights of learners within the very event of education itself; the teaching dynamic, the environment, and the example of the educator should reflect and respect basic human rights. I once had a high-school teacher who talked much about the need for justice in society, but we experienced him as often unjust and abusive to students. His actions were so loud that it was difficult to hear his words.

Educators' "way of being with" learners should reflect commitment to their human rights as persons. The entire curriculum (content and process, environment and purpose) should enhance learners' quality of life and be free of all semblance of discrimination. It should reflect instead a deep respect for each participant, epitomizing the human search for truth and the right to be well-informed. Under no circumstance may an educator violate a learner's ultimate right to choose religious identity or vocation in life. All educators should help prepare their students for gainful employment, to participate effectively in their local communities, and to contribute to the common good.

And education for human rights should reflect commitment to human responsibilities. Every teacher and parent, regardless of where, what, who, or how they teach, are entrusted to educate the character of learners to fulfill responsibilities corresponding to their rights. This means forming them to be deeply committed to promoting a decent quality of life for everyone, opposing all forms of discrimination, enabling others to pursue the truth and be well-informed, worshipping freely, being able to choose a vocation in life, having worthwhile work, receiving just compensation, forming communities, and forging a society where everyone can participate fully—receiving from it and contributing to it according to need and ability.

As such general and particular commitments become established in the souls of teachers and parents, they are to permeate how and what they teach, and the educational environment they create. What prevails in the educator's soul should become functional in one's teaching style and space. And yet, we can say something more specific about style and space that may further clarify the implications of a positive anthropology for teaching and education.

For the Educator's Style

What does a *humanitas* anthropology suggest for teachers and parents by way of their teaching style—for their pedagogies? One summary proposal: *engage the whole person as active participant.* I elaborate, beginning from the end.

As Active Participant

Education there is, and lots of it, that treats people as passive recipients of knowledge, as if the whole enterprise is no more than a transfer of information from the knowledgeable heads of teachers to the empty heads of learners. The renowned Brazilian educator Paulo Freire (1927–97), likely the most prophetic voice on pedagogy of the twentieth century, claimed that such teaching is the dominant paradigm throughout the world. He named it "banking education" because teachers "deposit" information in waiting receptacles—and only for safekeeping; when asked—e.g., in exams—they should give back to the teacher exactly what was given to them, without even minimal "interest."

Whether Freire exaggerated or not—and there may be a little hyperbole to make his point—we can be confident that a *humanitas* anthropology calls for the antithesis of "banking education." It demands a pedagogy that engages people as active participants in the teaching/learning dynamic, that prompts and empowers them to become agents of their own learning rather than treating them as dependents and telling them what to know. A *humanitas* pedagogy should bring to full bloom what Maritain called "the inner vitality" of people for knowledge and creativity.

Maritain explained that "the vital and active principle of knowledge does exist in each of us" but that it can be enlivened or deadened by the mode of education. No naive romantic, Maritain insisted on a "cooperative" role for the educator—much as a doctor helps to heal by cooperating with nature, the latter being the primary healer. In this, Maritain recognized that there are "two dynamic factors at work in education . . . the inner vitality of the student's mind and the activity of the teacher." However, "any education which considers the teacher as the principal agent perverts the very nature of the educational task"; every pedagogy should reflect that the "primary dynamic factor . . . is the internal vital principle" in the learners.[30]

Maritain's sentiments find echo in all the great philosophers of education of the Western world. For example, John Dewey often lamented teachers who "ladle it out in doses";[31] Alfred North Whitehead insisted that "education is not a process of packing articles in a trunk";[32] and Maria Montessori championed the shift from "receptive" to "active" education, urging teachers to build upon and draw out what is "already within" students because of "the personal and universal force of life within the soul."[33] In fact, theologian Louis Dupre points out that the whole tradition of Western education has a maieutic emphasis, a midwifing to birth what is already there in potency, and notes that this points to "the primacy of nature."[34] Theologically, we could add that it also points to the primacy of grace, or better still, to a "graced nature"!

Democratic sentiments about pedagogy should not diminish the vital function of the educator. Although I have considered more liberal proposals, I remain convinced that teachers and parents have a crucial role in good education. But instead of working like "jug to mug," a *humanitas* anthropology calls the educator to "cooperate" as resource person and question raiser, as guide and coach, as companion and friend, and to see to it that learners have vital access to the knowledge, wisdom, and aesthetic of the sciences, humanities, and arts.

Rendering access to what Dewey called "the funded capital of civilization" is a constitutive responsibility of educators (a main theme of chapter 5). Within this, there will be occasions, topics, or contexts where effective access may be rendered by some method of didaction, e.g., a good lecture. But even when a teacher or parent is patently didactic, they can and should engage learners as active participants—addressing interests, suggesting connections, encouraging reflection, giving examples, using image-laden language, prompting personal appropriation, inviting decision, and more.

We can all tell an engaging lecture from a boring one when we experience either, but what is the functional difference between them? A colleague of mine at Boston College, the Rev. Michael Himes, is renowned as a most engaging lecturer in theology. I once asked a student in one of his classes why he found Michael so stimulating. He responded, "Fr. Himes gets me thinking for myself and gives me the resources to think with." As a lecturer, Michael has mastered the art of engaging people as active participants.

The Whole Person

A common Western fable, at least in academia, is that education is scholarly and thus "serious" only if marked by dispassionate rationality and disembodied ways of knowing. A *humanitas* anthropology recommends pedagogies that engage the whole person—head indeed, but heart and hands as well—if not on every occasion, at least across the educational spectrum. One thinks of the work of Maria Montessori as an eminent instance of such holistic education, but all good schooling strives to do as much, and the "domestic school" likely has the most opportunity for educating the whole person.

In prompting people to use their heads, educators do well to avoid the Enlightenment reduction of the mind to reason alone. Indeed, parents and teachers must engage learners' reason—intuitive, logical, and critical—but also their memory and imagination. Memory is needed to know oneself, to locate in time and place, to uncover the influences of past experience, to remember what should not be forgotten; identity requires memory. Imagination is necessary to perceive the consequences of choices, to imagine what should be or could be and to help create it; responsibility demands imagination. Reason, memory, and imagination are all essential to a humanizing pedagogy. All three are needed for processing information, for pushing beyond to understanding, and then onward to making informed judgments and responsible decisions.[35]

A *humanitas* anthropology recommends that educators engage people's hearts—their emotions and wills—in the teaching/learning dynamic. This, of course, must be done with care, caution, and sensitivity—yet how can humanizing education take place if it engages nothing but learners' heads? I suspect that pedagogies which do not engage and educate people's feelings and their ability to make choices are most likely to misinform their knowing and malform their character. Thoughts without emotion are lifeless, as emotions without thought can be dangerous. It is possible, of course, to instruct without tapping into learners' feelings or affecting their choices; a great deal of Western education does as much. But to touch their "being," to influence who they become and do so *for life for all*, requires teaching styles that engage people's emotions and wills.

In my own doctoral work in education at Columbia Teachers College, I had an advisor, Professor Dwayne Huebner, who would often ask students—in classes, seminars, and advisement—"How do you feel about that?" At first, I found such questioning strange in an academic setting; at most, I expected him to ask, "What do you think?" But the frequent invitation to look to my feelings about an issue or topic began to open up a whole "way of knowing" that previous education had neglected. Eventually, I became convinced that far from diminishing "academic rigor," such questioning is essential to it, that we "know" more truthfully and reflectively by looking to emotions as well as thoughts. Our best hope of any objectivity in our "thinking" is to become aware of how subjective we are, and this requires tending to the emotions.

People using their hands in education is most readily associated with trade schools—with training for manual labors, crafts and trades, and the skill of the artisan. In chapter 5, I propose that such "manual" education be viewed not as a lesser form but when done to enhance the art of living—*for life for all*—as a necessary aspect of a liberal arts curriculum. My focus here, however, is on a once vital but now neglected conviction of Western education, namely, that our bodies carry their own wisdom; and we need pedagogies which honor our corporeal ways of knowing.

There is nothing more obvious about us than that we are embodied beings. Our bodies are the space we occupy, and through our bodies we receive the "raw material" of everything we know. Our bodies carry the traces of past experiences and the wisdom we learned from them long after our minds may have forgotten. In a sense, the body "forgets" nothing but stores our biography for us—literally, what is written (*graphia*) on our living cells (*bios*). Pedagogies that actively engage people's bodies and tap into their bodily wisdom seem imperative for a humanistic education and are suggested by the positive attitude toward the whole person of a humanitas anthropology.

Corporeal knowing was a key insight of Montessori; she built her whole approach on the foundation that children learn best when the curriculum is organized so that they can see, touch, taste, smell, hear, and play with real things. She discovered that young children could advance rapidly in conceptual curricula, figuring out for themselves, for example, mathematical equations considered far beyond their cognitive readiness, when the "materials" of the curriculum were tactile and sensory. Her insight should not be confined to Montessori schools; every teacher and parent can imagine ways to engage learners' bodies in their pedagogy.

My spouse Dr. Colleen Griffith will often have graduate students reflect on where and how they are carrying in their bodies a particular opinion or experience. Although for most this is a new question, students soon learn to intentionally listen to their bodies for insight and wisdom—even in graduate theological education.

Engage

All the pedagogy suggested up to this point pertains to actively engaging learners in the teaching/learning dynamic. Here are some more specific suggestions to encourage engagement, and you will imagine others.

- *Arouse and create interest in learners.* This may entail beginning with people's personal interests, but should also include stimulating interests, encouraging them to broaden their interests, and develop new ones. I think of a friend who is a junior-high music teacher. With each new class in September, she inquires about and begins with the young people's own musical interests—pop-rock or whatever— but, by mid-semester, she has them listening to and enjoying classical music.

- *Build curriculum from and for learners' lives.* Encourage people to look at and reflect upon their own experiences, draw upon what they already know, teach with relevance to their lives, and help them "make connections."

- *Pose personally engaging questions and questioning activities.* The invitation to reflection can reach beyond recall and logic to engage people's souls—to elicit their feelings, their insights and understandings, their memories and imaginings, to encourage their judgments and decisions.

•*Challenge learners.* Perhaps teachers and parents affirm learners most effectively by challenging them to reach beyond present achievements, to excel according to their capacities, to quicken their own "inner vitality" for learning.

•*Imagine ways to arouse curiosity.* In an interview with a widely respected high-school science teacher, I asked him the secret of his success—he is renowned for getting young people excited about science. His simple response was, "I bring to everything I teach a sense that there is a great mystery here, something that would be wonderful and exciting to know, and they become curious enough to investigate it."

•*Have enthusiasm for what you are teaching.* This was an old insight of St. Augustine; writing in Latin, he said that the educator needs to have *hilaritas.*[36] The word is usually rendered as "enthusiasm," but it loses a little in translation; why not bring some hilarity to teaching? Likely the most engaging educators you have known were a bit hilarious.

•*Vary teaching methods.* Variety is certainly the spice of teaching. Favor methods that invite learners into partnership and conversation and that engage them as agent subjects in the teaching/learning dynamic (e.g., self-expression, listening to each other, reflection on experience, storytelling, creative projects, research assignments, artwork, forms of ritual, service to human need).

•*Assign varied "requirements," favoring, when possible, ones that demand their own generativity.* For example, in assigning a book report, do not settle for a summary of the book but insist upon the students' judgments and opinions about it; an essay should reflect learners' own outlook and sentiments; problem-posing should engage their problem-solving potential.

•*Help them to make meaning.* Teach always within the backdrop of people's need to make meaning out of their lives, to find purpose, to connect what they are learning with themselves as people and with their world. This may well be the surest key to eliciting and maintaining their active engagement.

For the Educational Space

Proposals for the educator's soul and style pertain as well to the educational space; indeed, these three categories overlap throughout the book, and it is often a toss-up as to where to place a particular proposal. So teachers' and parents' general attitudes of affirmation, anticipation, and love for learners should permeate the educational environment they help to create.

Likewise, relating with learners as "agent subjects," helping them to develop and integrate all their gifts, and nurturing them in authentic freedom, rights, and responsibilities should be reflected throughout the environment. And nothing is more decisive for an educational space than the style of its educators.

Yet, with this third category of space we can draw attention to aspects of the "implicit curriculum"—what is taught, ever so subtly, by the educational ethos—that might otherwise slide by. We will focus particularly on the moral climate, the values and virtues that are modeled and encouraged, and the way learners are treated and are expected to treat each other.

The moral climate is the touchstone for character education. With a bit of attention, every educator can be as deliberate about the implicit as the explicit curriculum. For parents, the educational space—the ethos that prevails in the family, the "domestic school"—is likely the most significant aspect of their responsibility. Nothing in a home teaches more effectively than its environment.

It would seem that a *humanitas* anthropology recommends an educational space marked by respect, challenge, and the practice of personal virtues; you will imagine other fitting emphases for the environment.

A Respectful Environment

We will return repeatedly to respect throughout *Educating for Life*, approaching it from different angles. Here I highlight that for the educational environment by way of the person, respect demands that all participants be heard and taken seriously.

First, this means encouraging people to value their own word, expressions, ideas, feelings, work, and creations—to have respect for themselves. Society has so many ways of devaluing people; educators should resolutely refuse to be agents of negative socialization and be countercultural as necessary, teaching people to respect and value themselves and doing so throughout the educational environment.

Second, respect requires learning to grant others the same, and one effective way of teaching as much is to create an environment where learners learn to listen and to respect the word and work of others as well as their own.

A particularly pernicious form of disrespect that has no place in any educational environment—classroom, parish program, or family—is ridicule. In a college Latin class, upon confusing an adverb with a participle, Frank was told by the professor, "You should sue your high school for the lousy education you received." Everyone laughed—except Frank. Forty years later, he still tells the story, vividly remembered, with a note of deep pain. On the other hand, to state this sensitivity in a positive way, a respectful environment helps people to respect themselves and others by giving encouragement. As Maritain wrote, "Encouragement is as fundamentally necessary as humiliation is harmful."[37]

A Challenging Environment

A "realistic optimism" about people calls for education that challenges them to excel—precisely because they are so capable. I proposed this above for the individual educator, but the whole environment can value excellence and challenge learners to excel—not in competition, but according to their own capacities and particular gifts. A school in New Haven, Connecticut, has designed a self-esteem program built around challenging students to excel and to develop their own talents; its success has brought national attention.

To place the program in context, some years ago this particular school joined the "self-esteem" movement, then catching fire throughout American schools and encouraging teachers to give students much unconditional affirmation. But like the example I cited earlier of Amy working with "problem" students, this school recognized that lasting self-esteem must be linked to challenge—that students need to say both, "I am special because I am me," and then add, "and I will work hard and do well at my studies."

The school's insight and revised program is supported by follow-up research across the country—that students' self-esteem is enhanced to the greatest degree by real accomplishments, when they are invited to rise to a challenge. The research is saying what every astute student has always known: if teachers offer praise too readily—when it is clearly unmerited—students suspect insincerity.

I recently asked a third-grade friend, "How was school today?" He said, sounding perplexed and a bit disappointed, "Oh, the teacher said that my homework was just wonderful . . . but I did it on the bus." The child knew that he was capable of much better. Teachers and parents should not be grudging with praise, but it is most effective when specific and believable—as when learners take the challenge to do their best!

Practice of Personal Virtues

A great debate began in the ancient world about how to teach virtue—if it can be taught at all—and the discussion has continued ever since. Plato, although reluctantly, and Aristotle both agreed that it can be taught but differed markedly as to method: for Plato, virtue is based on having the right knowledge—so its formation is a more cognitive process, whereas Aristotle said that a person becomes virtuous only through practice—more a formation of right habits. My own position, reflected throughout this book, is that each had a half-truth which should be combined—both knowledge and practice are needed for formation in virtue.

Subsequent chapters make proposals on how education can teach the knowledge needed for virtuous living; for example, reason should help people to know why certain behaviors are most desirable, thus nurturing people's autonomy rather than dependence on outside authority (chapter 6). Likewise, I will often propose giving learners the opportunity to practice virtues; for example, justice cannot become a habit unless learners have the opportunity to practice it (chapter 8). With a bit of intentionality, the educational environment—school, family, or parish—can strive to model, to expect, and to give opportunity to practice virtues.

In this chapter, let us focus on personal virtues; the more social ones will "fit" better further on. I propose that the whole environment, and especially its discipline—the expectations that participants rightly have of each other—should encourage and practice the following:

- *Integrity and reliability:* Model and expect truth telling, honesty, and fulfillment of commitments.

- *Personal hygiene and cleanliness:* I now remember gratefully my second-grade teacher who lined us up each morning for an "inspection" that included hands and nails, face, even behind the ears, and hair. Her great battle cry was: "No one is too poor to buy soap!" and we learned personal hygiene for life.

- *Care and compassion:* Schools can be among the cruelest institutions in the world; conversely, they can also be made places of care and compassion. Likely the same can be said of families—and maybe even of parish programs. I know a single mother who raised three children in the midst of great poverty and what anyone would call major social problems. But amazing was the spirit of care and compassion that prevailed in that home, for each other, and for others in need. In spite of the many "strikes against them," all three kids have grown up to become wonderful young people. I put it down to the care and compassion they "learned" by osmosis in their home.

- *Responsibility for the environment:* Every educational space can model commitment to the "three Rs" of "recycle, reuse, and reduce." For some reason that developmentalists have yet to explain, the hearts of younger children seem particularly ready for ecological concern. Every school, home, or parish can sponsor a variety of exciting projects to foster this increasingly urgent virtue!

- *A balanced life:* It seems that the "modern" world has taken us further away from an integrated and balanced lifestyle. Education must retrieve its ancient task of enabling learners to achieve integration, and every environment can be made to encourage it. Even simple things like providing recreational time and opportunities; imagining creative things to do for fun; taking time out to mark birthdays and special events with celebrations; encouraging Sabbath; recognizing nonacademic achievements as well as academic ones—all can help form learners in a balanced approach to life.

•*Forgiveness and mercy:* What educational environment cannot model and encourage these highest of human virtues, appealing to what is most generous about humankind? I had an experience in high school when I felt that the football team could have blamed me for a heartbreaking defeat, but the coach intervened and was the first to console me, urging my teammates to do the same. I remember it as a singular act of forgiveness and mercy, and perhaps so do they!

For Reflection

•Given how crucial an educator's anthropology is for one's educating, what new insights have emerged for you from this chapter? What would you add to its proposals?

•How do you describe the core consequences for education of a *humanitas* anthropology? What are you coming to see for yourself as asked of your soul, of your style, and of the educational space you help to create?

•Are there any particular decisions you feel drawn to by this chapter?

Notes

1. For this etymological note I am indebted to Dr. Anton Vrame.
2. Confucius, *The Analects,* Book II, Par 21, 66.
3. *The Catechism,* #1934.
4. Ibid, # 406.
5. This does not deny the possibility of psychopathic people who may have a particular proneness for destructive behaviors; the point is that we recognize psychopathic behavior not as "natural" but as a mental illness.
6. See *The Catechism,* # 1707 and 2566.
7. Note that scholars of the Hebrew Scriptures now claim that the Hebrew term *adam* is no longer well translated as "man" since *adam* is a gender inclusive term that literally means "person from the earth." For this insight I am indebted to the work of the biblical scholar Phyllis Trible, see *God and the Rhetoric of Sexuality,* chapter 4.
8. Emmanuel Levinas, "Revelation in the Jewish Tradition" in *The Levinas Reader,* 202.
9. St. Augustine, *The Confessions,* Book I, Par. 1. I have used the old and more familiar translation here.
10. This is Trible's insight; she notes that the Hebrew word *ezer* is best translated as "partner" or "companion." See *Rhetoric,* 91
11. For clarity on this rather Thomistic understanding of "person" and for the phrase "person-in-society" - I am indebted to the work of Jacques Maritain. See *The Person and the Common Good,* esp. chapter 3.
12. Ibid, 65 and 85.
13. See Pope John XXIII's encyclical *Pacem in Terris* in Joseph Gremillion, ed., *The Gospel of Peace and Justice,* 203-6.
14. St. Athanasius, *On the Incarnation,* chapter 54, 93.
15. *The Catechism,* # 406.
16. See "Catalogue of Errors on Grace and Original Sin" chapter 1 (circa 435), in *The Church Teaches,* 156-7.
17. For this nuance on Calvin's position, I am indebted to Stephen Minnema, Boston College Summer School, 1997.
18. See *The Church Teaches,* 159 and 242.
19. Stanley Harakas, *Toward Transfigured Life,* 232.
20. Quoted in Canfield and Hansen, *Chicken Soup for the Soul,* 129.
21. Adapted from Canfield and Hansen, *Chicken Soup for the Soul,* 3-4.
22. See Martin Buber, *I and Thou.*
23. Canfield and Hansen, *Chicken Soup for the Soul,* 124.
24. See St. Irenaeus, *Against the Heretics,* 4: 20, 7.
25. St. Augustine, *The First Catechetical Instruction,* 24.
26. See St. Augustine, *Confessions,* 13:9.
27. See Howard Gardner, *Frames of Mind: The Theory of Multiple Intelligences.*
28. See Daniel Goleman, *Emotional Intelligence.*
29. It is interesting to note that the legal code of Roman Catholicism, the *Code of Canon Law,* makes such education a mandate of the church's ministry: "A true education must strive for the integral formation of the human person"; people are to be educated to "develop harmoniously their physical, moral, and intellectual talents, . . . to acquire a more perfect sense of responsibility

and a correct use of freedom, . . . and be educated for active participation in social life" (Canon 795).

30. Jacques Maritain, *Education at the Crossroads,* 29-31.

31. John Dewey, *Experience and Education,* 82.

32. Alfred North Whitehead, *Aims of Education,* 33.

33. Maria Montessori, *The Montessori Method,* 73, 74, and 23.

34. Louis Dupre, "Catholic Education and the Predicament of Modern Culture," 295.

35. The activities of knowing data, understanding it, coming to judgment and making decisions is Bernard Lonergan's fourfold schema of authentic cognition; I return to this in some detail in chapter 6 on rationality and wisdom.

36. See St. Augustine, *The First Catechetical Instruction,* 17.

37. Maritain, *Education at the Crossroads,* 39.

◆

CHAPTER THREE

A Gracious Reality:
"Seeing God in All Things"

"I Give You That"

It was a lovely spring Sunday afternoon, but Colleen was in the doldrums. Mary Ann, with her maternal antennae, sensed it and said, "Let's take a walk." They took off round the Point—looping the little peninsula with the sea to their left.

Spring was breaking out all over, rising miraculously from the dead of New England winter. The little crocuses had heralded the grand march into bloom, and now daffodils were marshaling the parade and promising that cherry blossoms and dogwoods, azaleas and rhododendrons were not far behind. A warming sun erased the lingering chill of winter—except in Colleen's heart.

"Tell me about it," invited Mary Ann, and Colleen began. The boy she had a crazed crush on didn't know she existed. She was afraid she wouldn't get into the college of her choice and wasn't even sure she had chosen the right one. Two very different majors held equal attraction and maybe she would have to do both—but how? She was in charge of the senior concert and nothing was falling into place.

By now, they had reached the Point and stood looking southward into the mouth of Long Island Sound, both mesmerized by the tableau. The rippling gold of the afternoon sun was strewn across the tranquil water; the swath of land that framed it to the right had revived as an emerald green; the majestic wings of the gliding osprey looked like parentheses of peace around it all. Colleen had fallen silent, and Mary Ann hadn't said much. Then she put one arm around Colleen's waist. Gesturing with the other to the panorama before them, she said, "I give you that!"

And Colleen felt like it was all hers, the breathtaking beauty before her. She drank it in and made it her own. They remained a while in the awe of the moment and then turned for home, taking the other side of the peninsula and completing the loop. A spring came back into Colleen's step, her shoulders lifted, and her heart felt lighter, too.

Fifteen years later, Mary Ann had put up a courageous battle, but clearly the cancer had won. It had never been a fair fight. Colleen sat by her bed. Their eyes turned at the same time to look out the window. Again, it was a lovely spring day. Lo, the cherry blossoms had come into bloom that very morning. It was like a miracle—overnight. What were pregnant buds only yesterday were newborn flowers today.

They gazed together for a long time in quiet wonder. Eventually, Colleen took Mary Ann's hand and said, "Mom, I give you that." Likely, Mary Ann made it her own and brought it with her!

So Much Depends on How You Look at It!

A half-glass of water: is it half-full or half-empty? A whimsical old question that yet reflects a profound human issue—one's outlook on life. And all of us have a "worldview" that influences what we see, a "tint to the lenses" that colors everything we look at. In more dressed-up terms, all persons have perspectives that permeate their interpretation of life and the world around them. Truth is, all of us "have an attitude!" And so much depends on our "point of view."

Recently, I set down the penultimate manuscript of this book on the counter of a copy shop. The attendant, a young smiling man, looked at me with an inquisitive stare. I looked at him, with the relief of getting it this far beginning to well up in my heart and, presuming that he was as impressed with the stack of pages in front of him as I was, said philosophically, "Yeah—an awful lot of work!" He responded with diffidence, "Nah—we'll have it ready in about a half-hour." We had two very different perspectives on this manuscript!

The early philosophers recognized that how we view the world greatly influences how we live our lives in it. They created a branch of philosophy called cosmology, from the Greek *cosmos* meaning "ordered universe," with the intent of understanding the existence of the world and the best way of looking at it. Note that even their choice of term already reflected a perspective—that the world does make sense and has patterns of meaning, being ordered by some intelligent principles; *cosmos* is the opposite of *chaos.*

They must have been convinced, too, that human reason can uncover these guiding principles—not a foolish assumption, but an assumption nonetheless. Their approach was to treat "the world" as simply "out there," presuming that they could stand back and take a look at it objectively—another perspective already in place. Ah, but if they set out with such prior perspectives to find *the* perspective on the world was their quest not already skewed? Indeed! And so is ours. Where to begin to find the best view—if we always have a view already? Will we not simply meet ourselves coming around in circles?

The only difference between ancients and moderns on this question is that we may be a trifle more aware of our perspectives—how and what we bring to look at things. At least as we read them, with our biases, of course, the ancients seemed more intent on what to look at—the world—and less concerned about how they were looking. They focused in particular on what they thought were objective categories for describing everything that exists—like being and nonbeing, time and space, cause and effect, necessity and contingency, matter and form, potentiality and actuality.

Maybe there was wisdom in what they were up to. Present philosophers do not pay much attention to such categories, but perhaps we are missing out on some helpful ways of looking at the world. And "helpful" perspectives may be as much as we can hope for—infallible ones seem beyond our reach since "everywhere" we stand seems to have a "view."

Anyhow, after a couple of thousand years of reflecting on the world and trying to understand it, in and of itself and as if it were "out there," the modern approach is to turn to how people look at the world from their lives within it, concentrating more on the "lookers" and treating the "looked at" as our attitude toward life in the world. Contemporary philosophers also broaden the scope of cosmology beyond creation to include the world of culture and society—the "world of meaning," as they call it.

"World"—and this is how I use the term hereafter—refers to the created order *and* to what humans have created as well. And the fanciest name we can put on the theme of this chapter is cosmology; it focuses on the perspective that people bring to interpret and make their own meaning out of the physical, social, and cultural world around them—how they look at life. In short, I use *cosmology* to mean people's attitude toward their life in the world.[1]

Now, much as I proposed in chapter 2 that the operative anthropology of teachers and parents—what they really think of humankind—is a foundation of their vocation as educators, likewise I propose that their operative cosmology—how they really look at the world—has great educational import too. Note, of course, that these two issues go hand in hand; the distinction between them is subtle indeed. Yet the question of cosmology and the attempt to clarify our worldview is a worthy pursuit in itself and foundational for teachers and parents.

In the body of the chapter, I will propose a cosmology suggested by the depth structures of Catholic Christianity, an outlook that finds echo in many other traditions. It can encourage education *for life for all* if educators allow it to permeate their teaching. As an advance alert, and in theological terms, I will summarize it as a sacramental cosmology, captured well by the oft-quoted phrase of Ignatius of Loyola (1491–1556), founder of the Jesuits, "To see God in all things."

Philosophically, it amounts to a gracious outlook on the world that experiences life as gift, seeing the more in the midst of the ordinary. The exchange of "gifts" between Colleen and Mary Ann were intensified sacramental moments. The intent throughout, as always, is to engage the reader's own operative cosmology, inviting review and prompting adjustments if deemed wise in your vocation as teacher or parent.

Now, nonphilosophical types might protest, "But I don't have anything like an operative cosmology!" (Or, as my childhood mentor Joe Kane might say on hearing such a term, "Oh, I had one of them at home, but the legs fell off it.") Even those of us with proclivity to the philosophical usually stop short of questioning our own point of view; we are happy to present our "views" but reluctant to probe how or from where we are looking—the outlook that focuses what we "see."

And even if we venture to this second level of reflection—to thinking about our thinking—we are not likely to talk to friends about it as our "operative cosmology." Who needs that kind of reputation! Yet, the truth remains that we all have one; it is simply not possible to be "a human being in residence" without having a point of view on the world that influences how we engage in it.

Human encounter with the world begins through the senses, through our bodies; the first foundation of our cosmology is corporeal. As babies, we begin to discover an amazing new world through our seeing, touching, hearing, tasting, and smelling. Our innate curiosity leads us to wonder about this "raw data" from the senses; we begin by differentiating things and other people from ourselves and with first intuitions about what and who they might be. As infants, our world is limited to the immediate—what we physically encounter through our bodies.

As we grow up, however, we begin to realize that the data absorbed by our senses belong within "worlds" of meaning which humankind around us and before us have created. Even something as simple as that thing for sitting on belongs within a world of design, craft, and culture—"Why, that's a Queen Anne"—and the chair becomes a symbol that mediates a whole world of meaning to us.

And so we discover a "meaningful" world of language, culture, and society and, within these, the beliefs and traditions, customs and attitudes, relationships and roles, rules and laws, values and virtues, structures and expectations, artifacts and arts, tools and technologies, and everything else humans create in their effort to live with cosmos rather than chaos.

To be human makes it impossible to ignore "the world of meaning" around us. The rattle that simply felt good because it relieved sore gums also helped to bring forth new teeth which soon find themselves in a world of dental care—with toothpaste, floss, dentists. We cannot be indifferent to this "world of meaning"—we can lose those teeth through neglect of good brushing or go bankrupt without dental insurance; nor can we absorb ways of meaning by instinct alone.

Some creatures (e.g., ants in an anthill, bees in a beehive) can function in apparently meaningful ways by instinct rather than reflection and personal decision. Humans, however, have the amazing capacity—and thus need—to "make meaning" themselves, reflectively, by personally appropriating the world of meaning mediated to them and by figuring out and choosing for themselves "what it's all about?" and asking "What does it mean for me?"

In our efforts to make sense out of the world, we notice that all is not rosy! This is not a perfect place—far from it. The renowned philosopher and theologian Bernard Lonergan writes of the

> world of meaning . . . that is organized by intelligence, that is described by language, that is enriched by tradition. It is an enormous world far beyond the comprehension of the nursery. But it is also an insecure world, for besides fact there is fiction, besides truth there is error, besides science there is myth, besides honesty there is deceit.[2]

As this "mixed-bag" evidence sinks in, one wonders if this world is trustworthy or deceitful, gracious or threatening, worthwhile or purposeless, gift or burden, friend or foe? Is a person to embrace and welcome it or retreat and put up defenses? Does it really have meaning, with a backdrop of ultimate Meaning, or is it, finally, absurd, with nothing behind it but an abyss of absurdity? Such unavoidable questions land us knee-deep in constructing our operative cosmology.

Not that many people take an outlook on the world as either/or. Total pessimism and complete optimism are likely what are now called "personality dysfunctions." And yet, most of us adopt a stance on the major issues either positively or negatively and our cumulative position shunts us—however slightly—more one way than the other.

On a pessimism-to-optimism scale of 1 to 10, we might barely score a 4 or a 6, but that slight favor permeates our outlook on life, influencing how we interpret everything and thereby shaping the world that we "make" for ourselves. Because our way of interpreting the world is so crucial—in large part, what we see is what we get—the age-old questions that the ancient philosophers grappled with as cosmology are now approached more often under the banner of hermeneutics.

In the old Greek world, Hermes was, among other things, the messenger of the gods who interpreted and explained divine oracles to humankind. Hermeneutics, an ancient practice, has developed extensively in recent times as the combined art of interpretation and explanation, with these twin activities ever intertwined. So hermeneutics figures out the most reliable way to interpret the meaning of things and, further, how to help others understand the meaning for themselves. Clearly, hermeneutics is of great significance to educators. (Is not aiding interpretation and prompting understanding at the heart of our work?)

I will often draw insights from contemporary hermeneutics; here I focus briefly on one of its key insights to accent the significance of our operative cosmology. Originally, hermeneutics attended only to written texts; in fact, it began as the art of interpreting and translating the Bible. But more recently, it has been broadened to include the process of interpreting all of life, any "text of meaning" that comes our way—like an experience, a symbol, a sign, a spoken statement, a written passage. And since to be human means to comprehend one's world, to interpret and explain it—if only to ourselves—we recognize that all of us are inevitable hermeneutes.

Hans Gadamer, German philosopher and perhaps the greatest exponent of modern hermeneutics, has raised to awareness the general principle that what we bring to acts of interpreting/explaining has a major influence on what we find and take away from any "text." For Gadamer, all the meaning we make in day-to-day living is shaped by the "pre-understanding" that we bring to the world, and this "pre-understanding" is the effect that our personal history has had on us.

One's "effective history," as Gadamer calls it—the prior perspective we have from our life experiences—colors all our subsequent interpretations and explanations of the world around us. As elaborated in chapter 5, this does not bring Gadamer to skepticism but rather to encourage awareness of one's pre-understanding to avoid distorting "the texts" of life—reading into them what one wishes to find.[3] Chapter 6 highlights the role of education in helping people to question their preunderstandings—not to be held bound by their "prejudices."[4]

Gadamer's reflections highlight that perspective on the world which is a crucial educational issue. Are people's worldviews totally "hardened," immutable to change, impervious to adjustment? I am convinced not—why else this chapter? Good education can help change a person's worldview, but better by far that teachers and parents help learners to put in place a *for life for all* outlook from the beginning. Doing so depends largely on one's own. An educator who sees the world predominantly as threatening will, even unconsciously, encourage learners to live defensively. A teacher or parent who sees life as a gift will teach an outlook of gratitude toward the world. But you know this well already from your own experiences of teaching and being taught. Pause here and take the opportunity to recognize and name some of your own worldview.

For Reflection
- Take a few notes on "my basic outlook on life." List some of its dominant features and favors.

- Drawing its leading characteristics together and, on a scale of 1 to 10 (10 being most positive), give yourself an overall rating. Are you happy with your score? Why or why not?

- What are some biographical influences that have shaped your outlook on life? Take a few from your family background, from your culture, from your society. How do you feel about them? About the cosmology they formed in you?

A Catholic Christian Cosmology: One Proposal

As to be expected, Catholic Christianity recommends a worldview that is symbiotic with its understanding of the person—chapter 2. One can say that its anthropology and cosmology are two sides of the same coin: the attitude toward God's creation—of ourselves first—and then of the world and our life in it.

Reiterating that I use *world* to refer to both God's created order and to everything of human making, a Catholic Christian cosmology begins with the foundational claim that everything God creates, whether directly or in partnership with humankind, is essentially good. Like the person, the world is more graced than sinful—goodness more than evil is the generative force of human history. And why? For the same reason that the person is essentially good: because God the Creator is God of Love who creates out of love. Why is there anything and not nothing? Why does there exist what exists? The Christian response is "because of God's love," and to quote a popular poster phrase, "God does not make junk."

As with the person, such perspective should never fall into naiveté or romanticism. It is patently true that the dynamics and laws of nature can bring great suffering and misfortune to humankind, that we humans can bring as much to ourselves by our own bad choices or by perverting the purposes of our generativity. And yet, a Catholic Christian cosmology comes down on the side that nothing which God has made, makes, or causes to be made is essentially evil; instead, it is essentially good.

Such an outlook finds its highest expression in the theological principle of sacramentality. No greater claim can be made for the world than that it is the ordinary medium of God's outreach to humankind and of human response to God. A world so good as to be sacramental, pointing to it as gracious, meaningful, and worthwhile, is the core of a Catholic Christian attitude toward the world. I will call it a sacramental cosmology. To elaborate will require some forays into sacramental theology.

Richard McBrien writes, "No theological principle or focus is more characteristic of Catholicism or more central to its identity than the principle of sacramentality."[5] This principle reflects the conviction that *God mediates Godself to humankind, and we encounter and respond to God's grace and desire for us through the ordinary of life*—through nature and the created order; through human culture and society; through our minds and bodies, hearts and souls; through our labors and efforts, our creativity and generativity; in the depth of our own being and through our relationships with others; through the events and experiences that come our way; through what we are doing and what is "going on" around us; through everything and anything of our world.

Catholicism has a strong mystical tradition and spiritual practices that encourage personal experiences of God. But as chapter 7 will elaborate, Christian spirituality is profoundly communal; even one's mystical experiences of God take place in the context of life and community and are never for one's own benefit alone but to turn outward to the neighbor in love. Christianity recognizes, too, the possibility of people experiencing a theophany—a direct encounter with the divine. But such experiences are extraordinary and rare and, given the human condition compared to God's, always remain partial. Even the experience of Moses on Mount Sinai was partial because "no one can see the face of God and live" (Exodus 33:20); perhaps with a bit of irony, Moses saw only "the back side" of God (Exodus 33:23). And people who receive such a gift must rely on human words and symbols to reflect on it and share it with others. In other words, when Moses came down from the mountain, he had to communicate with the Israelites what had happened, and his message—e.g., the Ten Commandments—is still struggling to get through to humankind.

Such extraordinary possibilities notwithstanding, the ordinary human encounter with God is mediated rather than immediate, is realized through some ordinary media communicable with humankind. The *Catechism* states that precisely because we are "body and soul, [humanity] expresses and perceives spiritual realities through physical signs and symbols." It is in and through the world that we "read the traces of its Creator."[6] A central principle of Scholastic theology, the predominant voice of traditional Catholicism, is that God communicates with humankind "according to the mode of the receiver"—thus making God's self-communication available to all rather than only to rare mystics.

For humans, "the mode of the receiver" necessarily means through the ordinary and everyday things and experiences of life. Therefore, sacramentality means that we both encounter and respond to God through the medium of life in the world. To practice a sacramental consciousness—the epitome of living a Catholic Christian cosmology—is indeed "to see God in all things."

An old story I heard as a child was of a monk who came galloping into a village on his donkey at breakneck speed, skidding to a halt by a group of villagers. He panted, "I'm looking for my donkey. Have you see him?"

They laughed at him and he rode on. He galloped into another village and asked another knot of villagers, "Have you seen my donkey?" but they, too, laughed and he rode on.

In the third village, he inquired again if anyone had seen his donkey, and this group responded, "What a ridiculous monk you are—going looking for your donkey riding on your donkey." He thanked them for helping him find his donkey, and then said pensively, "But I am no more ridiculous than humans who go looking for God."

For all his silliness, the old monk had a sacramental consciousness— that it is God coming looking for us more than we going looking for

God, and typically God does so through the ordinary and everyday—the obvious—if we but allow ourselves to be found.[7]

Not only is it God's presence in grace and love that we encounter through the world, but also God's ongoing self-disclosure of God's desire—"will"—for us as persons in our day-to-day lives. We take up the theme of revelation in chapter 5 on Scripture and Tradition and the theme of discernment in chapter 7 on spirituality; but here an echo of both can be heard within the sacramentality of life. A strong sentiment runs through traditional Catholicism that God's Spirit moves through people's spirits, constantly drawing humankind to Godself, guiding and directing every person through ordinary signs and symbols to know God's will and giving them the needed grace—again, through ordinary means—to respond faithfully.

Thus, by looking at our lives, noticing what is unfolding there, "reading the signs of the times" (a favorite phrase of Pope John XXIII), praying and probing for the movements of God's Spirit, we can discern how to live as a person of God—what is God's desire for us personally as our lives unfold.

I was listening as a *soul friend* to a man in his late forties who found himself at a crossroads about what do with the rest of his life. He said, "If God would only tell me what I should do, I would do it happily!"

I inquired, "If one of your three children came to you and asked, 'Dad, what should I do with my life?' what would you say?"

With an air of "what a silly question," he said, "I'd ask them, 'What do you really want to do—what would make you happiest?'"

Then, I posed, "And what do you think God says when you ask—since God's love is so much like a parent's?" With this we moved to discerning and testing what were the deepest and most authentic desires of his own heart and looking to the realities of his life—talents and opportunities, responsibilities and support systems—at the ordinary—to discern "God's will" for his future.

That God's grace can be encountered and God's will discerned in the ordinary and everyday of life does not at all diminish reverence for the liturgical sacraments and for the Word of God through Sacred Scripture, professed by Christian faith to be the primordial media for encountering God's grace and revelation. Rather it is that the liturgical sacraments of the Church and the books of the Bible are the normative sources of God's grace and self-disclosure, but they are realized within the divine milieu of the world and represent high points—the epitome—of the sacramentality of life.

The faith of Catholic Christianity is that God's grace is mediated primarily through seven liturgical sacraments: baptism, confirmation, eucharist, reconciliation, anointing of the sick, marriage, and holy orders. Within the seven, there is a strong Catholic tradition of looking to the Eucharist as "the sacrament of sacraments" (Aquinas's phrase), as the most eminent instance of the divine/human encounter through sacrament.

The faith regarding all the sacraments, however, is that by the power of God's Holy Spirit working through a Christian community, they catalyze and are climactic celebrations of the grace-filled encounter between God and humankind that is ever taking place in the divine milieu of the world. God's presence and offer of grace reach out to all humanity through creation and history, through everything of their own existence in the world. As intensified and primordial symbols of faith, "The sacraments signify, celebrate, and effect what God is, in a sense, already doing everywhere and for all."[8]

And note that the mediating symbols in each of the liturgical sacraments are of the ordinary—bread, wine, water, oil, human love, words, gestures; they are celebrated by a community of faith and their grace is to be lived in the world. In other words, every liturgical sacrament celebrates and epitomizes an aspect of the sacramentality of life.

Regarding divine revelation all mainline Christians embrace the Bible as the primordial source; the biblical word is, to use another phrase of Aquinas, "the norm of norms beyond every other norm." And yet, though believing that the primary expression of God's revelation is through Sacred Scripture, the Catholic perspective insists that the texts of Scripture are written, as Vatican II reminded, "in human language."[9] Although the primary one, Scripture is no more than a medium of God's revelation, a symbol of revelation rather than an immediate divine transmission—a sentiment that helps to avoid biblical fundamentalism. And while recognizing the primacy of Sacred Scripture, Catholic Christianity also looks for God's ongoing self-disclosure through the traditions of the Christian community and in people's daily lives. As the *Catechism* states, God's revelation can also be encountered in "the great book of creation, and that of history—the page on which the 'today' of God is written."[10]

What the principle of sacramentality represents by way of its broader cosmology can be amplified by some traditional notions from sacramental theology. Augustine's time-honored definition of a sacrament is "a visible sign of invisible grace"—pithy and to the point. To it, Aquinas added the clarification that a sacrament not only "signifies" grace, but is an effective means of it, a medium through which God actually mediates grace to humankind. Thomas favored the definition "a sign that causes to happen what it signifies"—echoed later by the Council of Trent.

To appreciate these traditional definitions, it helps to understand their use of sign as what people today mean by symbol—something that points to a meaning beyond itself and can cause a sentiment or response in those who encounter it (e.g., a national flag stirring feelings of patriotism.)

To say that the sacraments are powerful symbols—causing what they symbolize—does not mean that they function like magic or that human response to them is unnecessary. On the contrary, they ask faith of participants, and human effort to live the grace of each sacrament is essential for its effectiveness, a point to which we return shortly. Yet, they function as more than signs of God's grace—more than reminders; as the Catechism states, "By the action of Christ and the power of the Holy Spirit the sacraments *make present efficaciously* the grace that they signify"[11] (emphasis added). Sacraments are effectively laden with the grace of God.

Extending this old theology of sacrament now to the broader principle of sacramentality, we can say that the world is not simply a reminder of God, but the medium through which God's grace is present to humankind. More than a sign of God's love, the world is the symbol and locus of the Divine/human encounter. Such understanding of the principle of sacramentality encourages in people who embrace it a "sacramental consciousness" about the world.

In spiritual terms, sacramental consciousness means becoming aware of and alert to God's presence as both the backdrop and the foreground of life. It looks at the world and then through it to see the Transcendent in the ordinary, the Creator in the created, the Supernatural in the natural, the Gift in the everyday, the Divine in what is very human—"the more in the midst." It experiences God's Spirit reaching out through the world and responds to God in like manner.

In the *experiences* of life—sunrise and sunset, birth and death, and all experiences in between; in *relationships*—with friends or strangers, within one's inner depths or in community with others; in the *generativity* of life—what we do and create, in the efforts and creativity of humankind—in all we find the media of encounter with God who reaches out to humanity with love and desire through the ordinary and everyday.

I refer to a sacramental outlook as a "consciousness" because it implies awareness, an alertness that intentionally looks at life ever expecting "to see more than meets the eye." Some would doubt if we even have much choice in our attitude toward life. I readily recognize that it is much influenced by our experiences, by our sociocultural context, and by genetics, but the anthropology outlined in chapter 2 would insist that our voluntariety is never permanently and totally erased, that the average person retains "a center that holds" (Yeats's imagery)—holds out for our own choosing.

The classic work by Viktor Frankl, *Man's Search for Meaning,* is persuasive on this point. From his experience of a Nazi concentration camp he became convinced that even a situation of such horror could not erase "The last of the human freedoms—to choose one's attitude in any given set of circumstances, to choose one's own way."[12]

Let us now return to the broader question of cosmology, asking what the principle of sacramentality might imply for one's entire outlook on life—beyond its spiritual practice and without using religious language. *I summarize a sacramental cosmology as the attitude that the world is gracious, meaningful, and worthwhile.*

The world is gracious—sharing the same root as grace—in that ultimately it is gift and can be embraced as generous and trustworthy. It is gracious, too, in that there is always "more" in the most ordinary, and the "more" is gift as well—without being earned.

The world is meaningful in that it reflects amazing design with patterns and probabilities, cosmos more than chaos, and likewise human imagination and generativity. It is coherently interwoven by its natural dynamics and human agency, with each aspect of the world and every experience of life reflecting a vitality and cause from beyond itself.

I use worthwhile of life in the world to stretch beyond meaningful and accent that we can find a sense of purpose in it all, that our lives are not useless but efficacious, that we can have a will to life even for its own sake and beyond that, to quote Yeats again, because "All things remain in God."[13]

The attitude that life in the world is gracious, meaningful, and worthwhile need not and should not ignore the facts that suffering and evil happen—by chance or choice; that not everything can be explained or made to make sense—mystery ever remains; and that the humdrum and banal abound—with the terror lurking that all may be finally absurd. But even the worst of circumstances can sustain hope, if only from the power of human spirit to transcend them—as in Frankl's instancing of the concentration camps. Despite evidence to the contrary, humankind can take a stand on the side of choosing life and embracing the world.

We can experience amazing gifts and extraordinary beauty—beginning with the gift of life itself; uncover enduring truth and deep meaning in it all—if only of our own making; be sustained by a worthy sense of purpose—ultimately to give glory to God. Particular moments and experiences can point beyond themselves to a greater vitality of which they are an expression.

Our own generativity and creativity can feel worthwhile and connected with a wider web than the immediate results. We can contribute to a world that is favorable to humankind, that can provide us a home rather than alienation and chaos. Certainly, it can bring experiences of suffering and evil, of the senseless and meaningless, of futility and disappointment. But the human outlook, however slightly in favor, can be to expect the good, the true, and the beautiful from an essentially gracious, meaningful, and worthwhile world.

What is the key to choosing a sacramental cosmology for one's life in the world, and what does it invite of people who so choose? We address these two questions because they are significant to what a sacramental cosmology might mean for education, teachers, and parents.

When Mary Ann and Colleen gave each other "the gift" of what was before them—sacramental moments surely—they were inviting each other to consciousness and, as I described above, to an alertness and awareness of what was "there." A sacramental consciousness engages the entire psyche of a person—their soul (the Greek *psyche* originally meant soul or spirit). But I suggest that the particular fulcrum of a sacramental cosmology is likely people's imaginations. Imagination is key for at least two reasons: first, to "see" the "more" in the midst of the ordinary; and, second, to perceive what ought to be and have motivation to act accordingly.

The stereotypical association with imagination is reverie or fantasy of a make-believe world. This is precisely why Plato and many ancient authors railed against imagination as unreliable (and why Plato excluded the poets from any voice in his ideal state), as misleading people into "shadows" rather than "substances" (Plato's terms).

But nothing could be further from the truth about it. The first function of imagination is to see beyond taken-for-granted appearances to the very substance of what is there—the opposite of Plato's caricature. This is precisely what its greatest exponents—the poets and artists—do with imagination. They "see" what is really "there" and help the rest of us to see it, too, by naming or expressing it for our attention.

Instead of fantasizing, imagination is recognizing what truly is and how things are; it is seeing what should be seen but could be easily missed. I think of Jesus' frequent benediction of "blessed are those who have the eyes to see" or "have the ears to hear" as a call to imagination. For him, it was key to becoming a disciple of the Reign of God.

Second, a sacramental cosmology requires active imagination for ethical reasons, that people may know what they ought to do and create in the world. Many contemporary moral philosophers are convinced that there is a crucial correlation between nurturing imagination and ethical formation.[14] This is true for both personal and social ethics, but I take the example of social to make the point.

The social ethics function of imagination also begins with "seeing" what is there but could be missed otherwise because society and our own myopia can blind us to it. We have innumerable ways of "hiding" the poor and oppressed in our societies, effective ways of ignoring injustice; we can even have a tinge of the "bad faith" that makes oppression seem like justice, evil seem good. A sacramental imagination cuts through such falsehood to "see" what should be seen and what ought not to be!

Beyond such perception, imagination helps to stimulate empathy for those less fortunate than ourselves. Although memory and reason may lend clarity to the will for decision making, imagination gives it the emotional incentive to make the choices it should make. Then, imagination invites onward to conceive what ought to be, to strategize on its behalf, and rouses human generativity to bring it to birth.

There is an old Christian tradition of imagining that one can see Christ in the poor and, thus being motivated, to respond to their needs. The sixth-century *Rule of St. Benedict* stated: "All guests at the monastery should be welcomed as Christ because he will say, 'I was a stranger and you took me in.'"[15] Benedict was only echoing Jesus' own description of the final judgment of humankind (see Matthew 25:31–46). The gospel story is that there will be sheep and goats, divided according to whether we gave food and drink to the hungry; clothing and shelter to those in need; care to the stranger, the sick, and imprisoned. Ironically, both sheep and goats will confess to God that "we did not see you"; but the sheep cared for the poor anyhow, whereas the goats did not. "We did not see" will be an insufficient defense.

The sacramental imagination, it seems, is not so much to see God first and then to act—who would not upon clearly seeing God?—but to see the poor and oppressed, and to respond to their needs for their own sakes, and then one can recognize the face of God. (I take up this theme again in chapter 8, but here note a deep correlation between a sacramental outlook and commitment to justice.)

There is, indeed, a long theological tradition of understanding sacraments as effective symbols—causing what they symbolize. What then does a sacramental cosmology effect in the lives of people who try to live with a sacramental consciousness? On this question, the themes of cosmology and anthropology clearly merge, for as the person has an attitude toward life in the world, that attitude, in turn, shapes the person's identity and is effective in their lives, greatly influencing who they become and how they live—their "being."

Let us begin with the generic response: a sacramental outlook will enable people to make the most out of life and to become fully alive human beings—as alive and as human as they can become in their divine vocation. But beyond this, our reflections on imagination and its ethical function point to a specific consequence of a sacramental consciousness for its participants: it will enliven their generativity.

Thus far, I have emphasized a sacramental cosmology as "seeing" what is "there" and then "the more" in the midst of the world, receiving the giftedness of life, expecting it to be gracious, meaningful, and worthwhile. I submit that such a perceptive and receptive stance is integral to a sacramental consciousness. In theological terms, the divine/human encounter is always by God's initiative, outreaching with grace toward us; the beginning of our response—by God's grace again—is awareness, alertness, becoming conscious of the gift that is ours. But then, and echoing the relationship of nature and grace proposed in chapter 2, God's grace always brings us, literally, response-ability, inviting but also giving us the wherewithal by which we can live the gift. In gist, a sacramental cosmology invites both sacramental consciousness about life and generativity for life.

By generativity I mean a perduring disposition to "choose life" for oneself and others, encouraging them to choose likewise. Essentially, it is looking at each new day as a gift and then making the most of it in life-giving ways. When Moses delivered his final exhortation to the Israelites, poised at the edge of the Promised Land but knowing that he would never enter it himself, he reviewed all that God had made known through him and the demands of the covenant in which they were enjoined. As if by way of a summary, he reached for these dramatic lines, "I have set before you life and death, the blessing and the curse. Choose life, then, that you and your descendants may live" (Deuteronomy 30:19). This is the invitation, too, of a sacramental cosmology: to choose life by embracing and initiating what gives hope and regeneration rather than what brings despair and destruction.

As the ancient philosophers made a choice for cosmos over chaos—and there was as much warrant then as now for either one— the choice remains as between life and death. We have, it seems, only two real options: between making and keeping life human for self and others—in spite of the odds against—or of choosing to be agents of death and decay. We could, of course, try not to choose at all, but that might be to choose poorly by default. Certainly, a sacramental cosmology recognizes the gift of life and responds with generativity, choosing life for self, others, and the world.

Historical Record, Theological Sources, and Perduring Questions

As for all of these depth structures, Catholic Christians must recognize that their record in living faithfully to a sacramental cosmology is a "mixed bag" at best. In the past and present, they often fail—myself included—to live and foster a positive attitude toward life in the world; here I echo the critique made in chapter 2 regarding a positive anthropology. And as I reiterate throughout, it is not enough simply to confess shortcomings—too easy an out; Catholics and all Christians must lament sins against their "creed," repent of them, and in this case, recommit to living a sacramental cosmology.

In particular around the theme of sacramentality, Catholicism can overemphasize the seven liturgical sacraments—what takes place in church—to the point of downplaying the sacramentality of life. The Catholic church, too, can at times give the impression that it functions more as a controller than a mediator of God's grace—deciding who does and does not receive it, exaggerating the importance of the church as institution.

Likewise, the Catholic church has a long history of exercising undue control of the sacramentality of God's word in Scripture, limiting its availability and confining its interpretation—one of the compelling reasons for the Protestant Reformation. In addition, the institutional church has often fallen into authoritarianism rather than encouraging "ordinary" members to look with discernment to their own lives for the movements of God's Spirit. And there have been instances when Catholicism's devotional practices have obscured the line between faith and magic—presuming to control God by some ritual or formula rather than worshipping with inner faith and openness to God's will.

Its shortcomings notwithstanding, the sacramentality of life may be among the depth structures to which Catholic Christianity has been most faithful in its pastoral practice. Its abiding sense of the goodness of the world and that everything can be a "channel" of God's grace encourages in people a healthy embrace of the world and a joyfulness about life. Its sacramental sentiments reflect the conviction that the sensual mediates the spiritual; celebrating this sacramentality—epitomized in its church liturgy but encouraged, too, in the "liturgy of life"—fosters an incarnational and holistic faith, a faith that engages the whole person, body and soul, mind and senses. Its sacramentality can also nurture an experienced sense of wonder and awe at the sacred in the midst, a feeling of the nearness of God in the everyday.

Catholicism celebrates the climax of its sacramental consciousness in the Eucharist. The deep conviction of the presence of the Risen

Christ in the assembly of people, in the Scriptures proclaimed, and "real presence" in the consecrated bread and wine, received as in a meal, all lend the experience of an incarnational moment of encounter between the divine and the human. And this eucharistic sentiment should flow out into all of life. There is something profoundly engaging and humanizing about such a "historical" and "tangible" faith.

Let us turn now to further theological warrant for a sacramental cosmology and to address some of its problematics—for example, the reality of evil and suffering. Is a sacramental outlook affordable only to those who are doing quite well?

Many people of different faith traditions—indeed, many devout Christians and many people of no particular tradition who are intelligent and of good will—reject anything like a sacramental cosmology, with or without the religious language. The most common and immovable stumbling block is the reality of all the suffering and evil in the world, some caused by natural disasters and frequently by human irresponsibility; oftentimes life in the world appears neither gracious, meaningful, nor worthwhile. I vividly remember a moment at the bedside of a dear friend who was dying of cancer. He looked at me and said, "Life is the pits." In that moment, I could only agree.

And, of course, across humankind, people maintain a positive outlook on life from many religious perspectives, and some from none at all. Catholic Christianity is certainly not the only source of a sacramental cosmology. Yet, that the rationale for a sacramental outlook may be coherent, at least within the discourse of Christian faith, we should elaborate its theological sources and then come back to some of the challenges that always remain.

The key theological foundation for a positive cosmology is, I propose, a particular image of God. Whatever we say about the world also reflects its Creator. As we focused on the human side of the covenant in the rationale of the previous chapter, here the appropriate focus is the Divine Partner, though it is never possible to say much about one without implicating the other.

A sacramental outlook on life in the world reflects at least two convictions in faith: (a) that God takes the initiative to reach out to humankind in the world and enters into partnership with us — enters into a covenant—and (b) that God's intentions toward humankind are gracious, God's sentiment for the world is abiding LOVE. Such an image of God is, of course, an act of faith. Many good women and men do not believe it, finding the evidence to the contrary insurmountable. Here we can only elaborate the warrant in the Hebrew/Christian tradition for imaging a God of covenant love.

In the ancient Western world, we find two contrasting images of God: that of Greek philosophy and of Hebrew faith. Although the Greek philosophers did not agree on one image of divinity, the predominant sentiment was that God is a Cosmic Reason who designed creation but is now totally removed from everyday life (Aristotle) or an Ideal Form with faint reflections in creation but not a personal God directly involved with humankind (Plato). Aristotle's God is the Unmoved Mover, the great First Cause who created everything, threw it out into eternity, and, as it were, "went home," leaving creation to its own devices. God is God of "another world," uninvolved with human history, inactive and above caring for the welfare of humankind, dwelling in unchanging stability of perfect "contemplation."[16]

The God of Hebrew faith is also Transcendent Other, God of the Heavens. As Moses learned before the burning bush when he asked for God's name, the divine name is beyond all names. The response Moses did hear constitutes the word *Yahweh,* based on the verb "to be" (Exodus 3:14). A favored translation is "I am who am." So, rather than a defining name for God, Yahweh is a statement of faith that "God is." Perhaps this is enough to know in order to take on the pharaohs of the world. And, in fact, knowing the complete name— essence—of God is impossible for humankind; to presume as much is to break the First Commandment against "graven images"—idolatry.

Although the Hebrew and Greek notions share a similar sense of mystery and ultimacy about God, by contrast and paradoxically, for Hebrew faith the Transcendent God of the Heavens is also Immanent God of the Earth, as near as our own heartbeat. God is the One by whose very breath we breathe, who is "with us" now and acting in our favor, who promises to be "ever present in your midst," and to "go with you wherever you go." (See Leviticus 26:11–13.)

The God of Hebrew faith—who is also the God of Jesus Christ and of Christian faith—has the best of intentions for creation and humankind: peace, justice, freedom, love, compassion, wholeness, holiness, and fullness of life for all. God acts within history and takes humankind into covenant on behalf of these intentions. This means that what God wills *to* humanity—fullness of life—becomes God's will *for* humanity as well—the law by which we should live. God desires peace for us—we should try to live peaceably; God desires us justice— we are to live justly, and so it goes. Clearly, this law is neither whimsical nor an arbitrary test—two common caricatures of God's law, even in religious education; rather it signposts what is best for humankind and creation; it can maintain us in freedom and bring shalom.

A parenthetical note: It is surely significant that both classic statements of the Ten Commandments in the Bible (Exodus 20 and Deuteronomy 6) are prefaced by "I am the Lord your God who brought you out of Egypt, a place of slavery." Then, there follows the Decalogue. The ancient rabbinical interpretation was that God is a God of Freedom, willing to intervene in human history to set free the oppressed and that God gives the commandments that people might continue to find freedom in life. It is God saying, "I set you free. Now, to continue in freedom, live this way . . . ." Think of each commandment; to erase any one could readily lead to slavery— especially as addiction or violence.

The God of Hebrew faith endows men and women with freedom even to reject God's covenant and desires for us, but then we also suffer the consequences of wrong choices. Here, we may have found one clue to the reality of human evil. It is as if God chooses to limit God's omnipotence—Godliness—in order to be in covenant with humankind. God chooses to wait upon our free cooperation that we might freely choose to do good, but this "requires" the possibility and risk of our choosing evil instead.

Likewise, because of our freedom and partnership with God, God allows judgment upon us by holding us responsible for our own agency—in a sense, we judge ourselves by our choices. Anything less would not honor us as human beings, suspending the reality of the covenant. Contrary to any image of a judgmental God, however, as if God rushes to judgment with a legal code, the God of Hebrew faith— and thus of Jesus—is One of great compassion and boundless mercy. A favorite description of God in the Hebrew Scriptures is *Hesed,* usually translated as "loving-kindness." In the Greek version of the Bible, the word is *karis,* which is the root of the English word "grace." God is Ultimate Graciousness!

God forever takes the initiative and reaches out to humankind with loving-kindness—graciousness. Since humankind are bona fide partners in covenant with God, God's outreach is "according to the mode of the receiver." Again, anything less would suspend the covenant. God mediates the divine outreach through creation and culture, through the experiences and events of history, through human hearts and relationships, generativity and creativity, through the ordinary and everyday of life.

For Christian faith, God's ultimate outreach was in Jesus, the Christ, fully human and Emmanuel, "which means God is with us" (Matthew 1:23). Jesus was the high point of God's seeking out humankind, coming as fully human, guaranteeing within his very person the covenant of "right relationship" between God and humanity, and revealing unequivocally that "God is love" (1 John 4:8).

For Christian faith, too, Jesus is God's primary sacrament to the world—the most effective symbol of God's grace and desire—of God's reign. After Jesus, everything has the possibility to be sacramental because the world is taken up into the Risen Christ to be saved and liberated, the Risen Christ is present "until the end of time" (Matthew 28: 20), and God's Holy Spirit continues to make humankind whole and holy. The world continues to mediate the divine/human encounter and is ever the locus of human partnership with God.

And, for Christian faith, the Trinity stands as the ultimate symbol of God as Loving Relationship, both within Godself and toward humankind. That God is Triune Relationship symbolizes the permanence of divine initiative to be in loving relationship with humanity and to draw us into divine love. With the world indwelt by the Trinity, an old Christian conviction, one can understand why Karl Rahner writes poetically, "The very commonness of everyday things harbors the eternal marvel and silent mystery of God and [God'] grace."[17] And likely the poets see most readily *the more in the midst,* what even scientists now seek as "the God particle" in creation. The English poet and Jesuit Gerard Manley Hopkins (1844–89) wrote, "The world is charged with the grandeur of God. It will flame out, like shining from shook foil."[18] And I love the line of the Irish poet Patrick Kavanagh (1905–67) that "God is in the bits and pieces of Everyday."[19] Kavanagh capitalizes "Everyday" because of his sacramental consciousness!

And now to some of the problematics of a sacramental cosmology. I address three, although there are likely more. I choose these because if left without caution or ignored, a sacramental consciousness could debilitate rather than enhance education.

The first is that a too-positive outlook on the world could encourage historical naiveté; within this, I include ignoring the reality of evil and suffering or of fatalistically accepting them or, worse still, making them sound like "God's will"—all lessening human responsibility to oppose and alleviate them. For example, I often wonder of myself and other Christians how we can celebrate Eucharist—the Bread of Life—and yet ignore or do so little to alleviate the various "hungers" of the world around us? Worse still, we can assuage consciences with a Scripture verse like "The poor you will always have with you" (see Mark 14:7)—as if poverty is God's will—or be content to only pray for the hungry of the world, again making them entirely God's responsibility.

The second problematic is the danger of sacramental practice becoming mechanical or worse, even verging into a kind of magic as if humans can control God with the correct formula or ritual. I will address these two in tangent since both are instances of false consciousness instead of a sacramental one.

The third problematic is simply the challenge that the reality of evil and suffering poses to the very possibility of faith: How can a good God in an essentially good world allow so much of both? This is a "problem" for all people of faith, but a sacramental outlook requires Christians to address it head-on.

Are claims of God's presence and mediation in the world as unambiguous and readily available as I have made it sound? Good Protestant theology has often warned Catholic Christians of not taking the reality of sin and evil seriously and the danger of sacraments becoming superstition. These are valid cautions; Catholic Christians ignore them to the peril of authentic sacramental practice.

One can take these cautions seriously, however, and with a sound theology of sacramentality avoid their pitfalls. This requires a brief exposé on a traditional aspect of Catholic theology—namely, the use of analogy. Commentators often note that in interpreting the relationship between God and the world, classic Catholic theology favors an analogical relationship, whereas Protestant theology tends to favor a dialectical one. Put plainly, Catholicism emphasizes the similarities and closeness between the human and divine, whereas classic Protestantism, with more accent on human sinfulness and the otherness of God, tends to emphasize the distance between them. The first encourages a positive attitude toward the world; the second, a healthy suspicion.

We are familiar with analogy as a figure of speech that highlights some resemblance between things that are otherwise dissimilar. So, "airplanes are *like* birds"—well, not really; they are very different in every way except that both fly. Thomas Aquinas championed the notion that all theological statements are analogical because they say something that is true, but they always fall far short of the whole truth. Analogy is the best we can do, however, because, unless we have direct divine illumination, the normal mode of expressing what we know of God—*theos logos,* theology—is to draw upon human experiences and use human modes of expression. Therefore, we *liken* God's activity to human activity. Of course, we must never claim to be speaking literally or as if our feeble efforts at "God-talk" correspond fully to the Reality they attempt to represent.

Analogically, then, we can say that "God is like a loving parent," and this expresses a profound truth—but then God is much more than a loving parent.[20] We can say that "God knows," and there is a faint similarity with human experiences of knowing but great difference too. God does not have to learn from experience and knows infinitely more than humans ever could.

The same applies to everything we say about God; our language and concepts are never more than analogous. In fact, Aquinas was adamant that God is such Infinite Mystery that whatever we say is literally more untrue than true in that the difference is always greater than the similarity. And the Fourth Lateran Council (1215)—an ecumenical council of the Church and thus a magisterial voice of its faith—stated unequivocally about theological language: "No similarity can be found so great but that the dissimilarity is even greater."[21]

So, to say that "God is present in the world" is indeed to make an analogous statement; it represents a profound truth and yet, literally, is more untrue than true. Catholic sentiment is that there is at least enough closeness between the Creator and creation to warrant such analogy, but the great distance also remains. David Tracy of the

University of Chicago Divinity School and a great theologian of our day says that Catholicism in general is marked by an "analogical imagination"[22]—the willingness to imagine "the more" behind the ordinary and everyday. Such an outlook certainly requires imagination and its expression is never more than analogous. Analogical imagination fuels a sacramental cosmology—imagining God present and mediating grace in and through the world.

But how can educators make such theological subtleties operative within their pedagogy? How can a teacher or a parent educate for a sacramental consciousness without encouraging a false one instead? A specific proposal is made later under educational style—encouraging learners to reflect both *critically and contemplatively* on their lives in the world. Here I note the theological conviction that grounds this proposal, namely, that while favoring a sacramental outlook on life in the world, Catholic Christians need to adopt as well the Protestant emphasis on a dialectical attitude.

A great blessing of the ecumenical movement is that all Christians have access to each other's heritage of theology and spirituality! A dialectical outlook requires bringing a healthy skepticism to the world, with special alert for sin and suffering. Such a "critical consciousness" seems theologically appropriate to Catholic tradition, given how much untruth is in every statement of faith; likewise, as noted already, sacramental imagination should "see" both what is "there" as gift and what should not be so at all and should conceive of creating what ought to be.

Maintaining a dialectical as well as a sacramental perspective should help avoid both romanticism and pessimism about the world. The tension that exists between life's graciousness and burdens may often highlight the paradox of faith, believing in spite of great contradiction and without adequate explanation. I have a friend, well trained in theology, who within one year suffered two great tragedies—the loss in an airplane crash of an only brother and then his beloved spouse through cancer, leaving him with three young children. Some months later when I ventured to ask, "How are you doing with it all?" he responded: "Well, it's amazing. These two tragedies—they make no sense; I can't even bear to think about them theologically because they are totally absurd. And yet, throughout all the suffering and loss, never have I felt so loved by God."

My friend's experience and way of naming it were both dialectical and sacramental—both needed to reflect what is so often the profound paradox of faith. A naive or magical sacramentality might resort to absurd statements—not unusual in pastoral practice, e.g., "God must have needed her more"—which imply, in fact, that God directly causes such tragedies.

Every Christian must be cautious to remember that though God is close to humankind, God is also ultimately Other, Mystery, Transcendent—"God beyond all names" as a popular spiritual sings. No human language or construct, event or experience, desire or relationship, culture or society, even church should be over identified with God. Surely, the First Commandment forbids as much when it warns against making "graven images" of God (Exodus 20:4). Humankind in the midst of the world can experience enough of God's love and know enough of God's desire in order to live as a loving people of God, but beyond this, to human ken, an Infinite Mystery remains.

Such sentiment, I believe, allows for a sacramental consciousness without ignoring the world's ambiguities; it also cautions against a facile or mechanical practice of sacramentality—no outcome is inevitable or within human control. In addition, and apropos the second problematic in particular, Catholic Christians avoid slipping from faith to magic if they remember their better sacramental theology—namely, that the sacraments never suspend the need for faith on the part of their participants nor of human responsibility in response to their grace.

In sum, good sacramental theology insists that there is nothing automatic or mechanical about the effectiveness of sacraments. Catholic tradition holds that although the seven liturgical sacraments are always effective from God's side, they demand a human response of personal faith and effort to live their grace. (Here again note the echo with the theology of nature and grace outlined in chapter 2.) As the *Catechism* summarizes well, from God's side we can say, "The sacraments confer the grace that they signify"—whereas, from the human side we must then add, "The fruits of the sacraments also depend on the disposition of the one who receives them."[23]

When applied to the overall principle of sacramentality, this dual emphasis in sacramental theology on both God's grace and human response in faith makes clear that God's presence and grace in the world empower rather than suspend human responsibility. To reiterate, a sacramental cosmology requires the kind of generativity that "makes God present" in the world. When persons do not cooperate with God's grace—when we do not live as a people of God—then, analogously, God is "absent." For example, to point to injustice as if God is approvingly "present" in the midst of it is blasphemy. How God is present amidst injustice is with the oppressed, helping them to survive with hope, but opposing and absent to the work of the oppressors. Here again, note the need for both dialectical and sacramental principles.

Another old sacramental principle is relevant here—that a sacrament needs to be "an effective sign." Among other things, this requires that the very sign of the sacrament itself be clear and point to the reality for which it stands. As the Council of Trent stated, "Sacraments cause grace insofar as they signify it."[24] Applying this to the sacramentality of the world, things or experiences that do not signify God or signify the opposite of God's intentions are not sacramental at all. Evil does not signify grace but evil. Injustice violates the covenant rather than signaling God's intentions. Suffering does not symbolize God's arbitrary will; God laments human suffering and sides with those who suffer.

This brings us finally to the stumbling block for claiming the sacramentality of life in the world—that it is gracious, meaningful, and worthwhile. Indeed, here we touch upon the ultimate challenge, not only to sacramentality but to the very possibility of religious faith at all: the problem of suffering and evil. Some of the most persuasive atheists of modern time, for example, the German philosopher Frederick Nietzsche (1844–1900) and the French author Albert Camus (1913–60), made the reality of evil and suffering their primary argument against a personal and loving God. It would be easy to say that this issue takes us too far afield. However, as the great German philosopher Hegel (1770–1831) insisted, any cosmology worth its salt must face squarely the issue of evil and suffering.

Here surely we are knee-deep in mystery, facing how little we know and how inadequate is all of our God-talk. Let us admit immediately that theists have no finally convincing explanation of evil and suffering, much as atheists can be baffled by human goodness and a gift like love. Even the Bible seems stumped by the mystery and recognizes that it transcends human understanding. Although Job remains forever our hero for "taking on God" around this ultimate mystery—claiming his innocence and challenging God to come up with evidence to the contrary (Job 29 and 30)—his final sentiments are: "I have dealt with great things that I do not understand; things too wonderful for me, which I cannot know" (Job 42:3). And who can be content with a God who takes a whimsical gamble with the devil that Job will remain faithful in the midst of suffering? (See Job 1:6–12.) Likewise, what parent who has lost a child can be satisfied with the final outcome—God rewarding Job with "twice as many" children as he had before? (See Job 42:10–15.)

No wonder Archibald MacLeish (1892–1982) in his poetic drama *J.B.*—a modern-day version of Job—is faithful to the old story until the end, which he changes to J.B. forgiving God for not making a more just world and then choosing to go on living anyhow.

Without any tradition offering a fully satisfying explanation, all the great world religions help people respond to the reality of evil, human suffering, and death. The *Catechism* states: "There is not a single aspect of the Christian message that is not in part an answer to the question of evil."[25] Thus, the "whole Story" of Christian faith—from creation to eternal life with God—is essential backdrop for a Christian response to what is often called "theodicy"—literally, the attempt to reconcile the notion of "God" (*theos*) and "justice" (*dike*) in the face of human suffering. Beyond this, we can make a few summary statements, all of them analogous and, therefore, leaving more unsaid than they say. These statements only allow the principle of sacramentality to seem not unreasonable, even in the face of sin and suffering—they certainly do not explain the latter.

First, the overall conviction that emerges from the Hebrew and Christian Scriptures is that God does not directly send suffering as a punishment for sin. It is clear that poor human choices may have negative consequences, but this comes from the natural course of events—cause and effect. If someone commits a crime and gets caught, there is no point in blaming God for the penalty. Or if someone makes the poor choice to smoke excessively and gets lung cancer, again it does not make sense to blame God. Or even when someone who never smoked gets cancer, it is because of the radon in the soil or radiation from the local power plant or the electromagnetic field caused by high power lines or whatever, but again—it happens naturally. Therefore, much human suffering is the consequence of human choice or happens by the laws of nature.

Second, God never directly causes either human evil or natural suffering. God laments both but permits them out of respect for human freedom and for the dynamics of nature. If men and women choose to do evil things, God regrets their choice but does not suspend their freedom. Likewise, natural processes like hurricanes and earthquakes can bring destruction, but these happen because of the "freedom" of nature and its built-in dynamics.

Third, no situation is so negative that God cannot draw some good out of it. The *Catechism* states,

> God is in no way, directly or indirectly, the cause of moral evil. [God] permits it, however, because [God] respects the freedom of [God's] creatures and, mysteriously, knows how to derive good from it.[26]

Once when doing spiritual counseling in a prison, I had an inmate who had rediscovered her relationship with God say to me, "I think God put me here to bring me back to my faith."

I said, "No, Mary (not her real name), you put yourself here when you committed armed robbery. But now that you are here, God is still with you and can draw you back to your faith." God can draw great good out of negative situations, and especially, it seems, when we feel weakest and most in need.

Fourth, believers in a personal and loving God are faced with one of three options: (a) to say that all suffering is somehow the result of sin or bad choices—the "solution" offered repeatedly by all of Job's comforters; (b) to say that God is not all-good and all-loving; (c) to say that God is not all-powerful nor fully in control of life in the world.

Option "a" may be an explanation when people suffer consequences from their own evil or unwise choices, but what of others who suffer innocently, e.g., victims of murder or when the suffering is caused by nature—e.g., an earthquake? Option "b" has been taken by some religious traditions, e.g., to say that there are good and evil gods or good and evil within God, but this does not seem consistent with Christian faith. This leaves option "c" —that God chooses not to act all-powerfully in the world.

Given the anthropology outlined in chapter 2, the cosmology proposed here, and the theology of nature and grace that runs throughout, "c" seems to be the only option. It means that God chooses to wait upon human cooperation and to respect the laws and processes which God has written into nature. To do otherwise would be to constantly suspend human freedom—forcing people to comply with God's desires for them—or to vitiate the "freedom" of nature, e.g., stepping in to prevent an earthquake that all the laws of nature make ready to happen. For God to whimsically intervene in human choice or nature's dynamics would be to void the partnership between God and creation.[27]

And yet great mystery remains. Fine to say that God honors the partnership with creation, but then, one may ask, "What of miracles?" From the point of view of rational explanation, miracles present us again with the paradox of faith, and lost for words, we fall back on the biblical witness that God's ways are not our ways. On the other hand, there is an equally strong biblical tradition of praying for miracles—as long as we remember that their prime cause is never our prayers.

Fifth, God is deeply sympathetic to human suffering— sympathetic in its root sense of "suffering along with." And God forever offers mercy to sinners who repent. In Christian faith, the effective sacrament to the world of God's compassion and mercy is Jesus Christ. Jesus offered no final explanation for sin and suffering, but taught disciples how to avoid the first and alleviate the latter.

Contra evil, Jesus urged the disciples to live as people of God—to resist sin's power, personally and socially; to repent of it when repentance is needed. Jesus assured that repentance will always bring God's mercy. (Unlike some traditions, Christianity has no unforgivable sin.)

As for suffering, Jesus healed the sick, fed the hungry, condemned injustice, defended victims, included the marginalized, showed great empathy for the poor and afflicted, and told disciples to do likewise. As often noted, humankind will be judged precisely on this issue— whether we helped to alleviate human suffering. (See Matthew 25: 31–46.) In his final agony and death, Jesus symbolized God's suffering in solidarity with all humankind, carrying the crosses of life with us. In his Resurrection, Jesus symbolized God's power to defeat evil and turn suffering into new life. Now, even death has lost its sting. (See 1 Corinthians 15:55–56.)

All of the previous, in fact the theological excursus of this section, amounts to no more than claiming that the principle of sacramentality is coherent to the core of Christian faith, even in the face of ambiguity, evil, and suffering.

A Philosophical Summary

Before moving on, it may help to draw together a more philosophical statement of a sacramental cosmology. Apart entirely from its warrant in Christian theology, such a worldview can ring true to a person's own experience or find support in many other systems of faith or thought. For some educators, too, a philosophical summary may facilitate the transition from "God-talk" to educational implications, helping with the correlation—since philosophy is closely related to both.

Note, too, that as the theological statements of each chapter are cumulative, so, too, the philosophical summaries need to be heard as a whole to get a sense of the "philosophy of life" being proposed throughout *Educating for Life*. Therefore, here I propose some specific attitudes toward life in the world suggested by a sacramental outlook. I will not repeat the proposals from chapter 2 nor anticipate chapter 4 and the following. That being said, a sacramental cosmology suggests that:

• *Much depends on our attitude, and, in spite of suffering and evil, we can afford a positive one.* Every person shares a common world with others, and yet each has their own attitude—a world of our own —shaped uniquely by our perspective. So much about life and what we make of it depends on the attitude we bring to it. Although greatly influenced by genes and culture, by nature and nurture, we retain some level of choice about our perspective on the world. It is not unreasonable to choose a positive outlook, and we live more humanly if we do.

• *We can see life and the world as essentially "good" for us.* We can readily experience our lives as threatened, the world as capable of doing us harm; we can even make destructive choices ourselves. But we can reasonably choose to see it as essentially good for us, embracing our lives in the world and living them with joy while avoiding naiveté about the possibility of evil—from within and without!

• *We can approach life as gift.* That we have life in the first place, a "good" world in which to live it, and the "present" of each new day—all is gratuity; the backdrop of our world is graciousness. Life calls us to responsibility, but originally it is gift.

• *It is always possible to find "the more."* There is always "more to life than meets the eye." We find it if we "look"! Ordinary experiences can be more than ordinary. The entire world—creation, relationships, culture, society, history—can point beyond itself or can be looked through to munificence that is inexhaustible. We need to be alert to notice "the more," however, to be attentive—the proverbial "stopping to smell the roses"—and to unleash imagination.

Waiting in an airport lounge for a bereavement flight to Ireland, a small boy—about two—ran up to me, took my hands in his and with the biggest smile possible said, "Hi!" My heavy heart could not but feel a little lighter. As his mother took him away, apologizing for his behavior, he looked back, smiled again, and said, "Bye!" As I said "Bye" after him, I knew he symbolized the hope that one can have, even in the face of death.

• *We can approach the world as meaningful.* There are good reasons for asking about life "Does it make any sense?" for there is ample evidence of "nonsense" in our world and, indeed, within ourselves. The ancient philosophers simply assumed that the world was designed and functions by rational and coherent principles, and they set out to find the great universal ideas—what is always and everywhere true—that are reflected in the cosmos. Now, serious philosophers reject the very notion of universal ideas, claiming that everything we perceive is our own construct, that all ideas are "ad hoc" to the situation. A sacramental cosmology suggests that we approach the world as meaningful, whether the meaning be of our own making or a given of the world, or a combination of both.

• *We can find life worthwhile.* Closely related to the human desire for meaning is concern for a sense of purpose—that our lives be worth bothering about. Humans can experience an ultimate kind of terror that maybe this whole thing is futile—that we and the world are purposeless. Shakespeare has Macbeth wonder if each of us is not but "a poor player that struts and frets his hour upon the stage and then is heard no more." But we can choose ultimate value rather than the absurd as the backdrop of our lives, and daily we can find purposes that are life-giving for self and others—that are worthwhile.

•*Life is no bed of roses—but we can plant some.* Suffering, sickness, and eventually death come to all of us, much of it by chance, some by our own or other people's choices; we should not and need not be naive about such "realities." On the other hand, our lives are not fatalistically determined (e.g., by the social context). Even in the midst of powerlessness, we always retain our agency, our responsibility, and our hope.

•*Life invites us to generativity.* If life be gift and what we make of it, then it invites us to make the most of the gift! By developing and using our native talents, by harnessing our imagination and creativity, we can ever choose life rather than death—for ourselves and others. Each person can "make a difference."

•*To live well requires an act of faith.* All of the aforementioned amounts to choosing to live in ways that make and keep life human— individuals who are responsible to the world and its welfare. But what motivates to so live—the attitude behind it? No feature of the philosophy just outlined could be "proved" empirically. Though each has a persuasive argument and none of it is irrational, there is always "evidence to the contrary." So, to embrace a sacramental outlook on the world is ultimately an act of faith.

For Teachers and Parents

From experience, you know well that educators' perspectives on the world make a great difference in their teaching and especially by way of the outlook they encourage in learners. If we investigate the origins of our own worldview, we will surely find the traces left by parents and teachers. If educators opt for something akin to a sacramental cosmology—to favor, by whatever margin, that life in the world is good and gracious, meaningful and worthwhile, calling to generativity—what might this ask of their souls, indicate for a teaching style, recommend for educational space? I make a few suggestions, only to stimulate your own imaginings. First, pause to note your initial intuitions about the educational implications of a sacramental outlook.

For Reflection
- Review and summarize your general responses to a sacramental cosmology. What do you agree with, disagree with, or add as a recommendation by way of worldview?

- What do you imagine are some implications for education? For the educator's own soul? For style of teaching? For the educational space a teacher or a parent helps to create?

For the Educator's Soul
A sacramental outlook for educators' souls? I think immediately of one general commitment for their personal lives and a few more pertaining to what they encourage in learners; you will add to or adjust my list!

First, for their own lives as persons—since much of their educating depends on who they are—a sacramental cosmology invites educators *to develop and constantly nurture their own sacramental consciousness.* The old Scholastic philosophers had a dictum that is apt here: *"Nemo dat quod not habet"*—the colloquial translation being, "You can't give what you haven't got." When educators live their own lives as gift and gracious, as meaningful and worthwhile, with imagination and generativity, such cosmology inevitably permeates their teaching and encourages a similar outlook in learners.

No teacher or parent ever perfectly possesses and practices such a positive outlook all the time. It is a lifelong conversion process—with highs and lows. We can never be "finished" growing in a sacramental consciousness because our ultimate horizon is Mystery. And yet as a consciousness, we can be alert about it; we can be intentional about it; we can choose—and from a faith perspective can ask for God's help in the effort—to look at life in the world in a sacramental way.

The more we practice such an attitude, the more it grows on us, becoming a habit—and this is the counsel of both ancient philosophers and modern psychologists. We do need to make a choice for it, though, and then try to maintain the alertness of a sacramental outlook, reflecting on how well we are doing. Surely, it is worthwhile for teacher and parent to pause often to review their own perspectives on life and the world and thus the attitudes they are encouraging—by osmosis—in learners.

What educator is there who does not experience dismal times? I find it easy to have a very positive outlook in early September; then, by mid-February, the fervor can easily wilt. But we can pull back from a negative outlook and refocus; we have choice. Personal attitude is influenced by many factors, but it is not determined—not by genetics, personality type, cultural context, nor even by a New England winter.

Are there spiritual practices that can nurture a sacramental consciousness in educators' souls? For nurturing sacramental consciousness, it seems wise to highlight the practice of contemplation. At first blush, this may sound a bit pretentious. Contemplation is often associated with the higher reaches of the spiritual life, reserved to men and women in monasteries. But there are many kinds of contemplation. All the great religions have a tradition of it, and every person has a contemplative side to them. We live more humanly and nurture a sacramental outlook if we exercise it.

The contemplation I have in mind is the practice of *taking deliberate moments when we pay attention to the gift that is there, allowing ourselves to receive it and to be absorbed by it to the depths of our soul.* Thus, its core aspects are attention, gift, receiving, and being absorbed to our very souls.[28] Note well that contemplation is more receiving than working at something, giving oneself over to the largess of life rather than earning it, like the moments of gift that Mary Ann and Colleen helped each other to experience. In more colloquial terms, contemplation is "taking time to smell the roses"—to receive "the more" that we can miss from busyness and distraction, abandoning ourselves to the gift offered and allowing it to refresh our souls.

Just this morning, I paused for a moment of prayer before beginning the day. I intended to use a text of Scripture for meditation, but instead found myself looking out upon a small bird in the process of feeding some baby birds in the nest, coming with food, delivering it into their open beaks, and departing to collect more—to return again. Clearly, it was breakfast time. I was mesmerized by this drama of nature, losing for a while all sense of time, gazing upon it. Rather than having profound thoughts about the scene, I delighted in it. When I finally moved on, I knew this moment—a total gift—had touched my soul and, somehow, would permeate my day with a "different" outlook, hopefully a sacramental one.

There are many descriptions of contemplation throughout Christian tradition. In general, it refers to becoming aware of the presence of God. The intent is to reach loving union, a sense of being "at one with." St. Teresa of Avila (1515–82) likened contemplation to a "close sharing between friends"[29]—she had the person and God in mind and described the sharing as a commingling of spirits, a gazing upon, a quiet presence with, more than a wordy conversation. (The latter, at least in Christian tradition, is more meditation than contemplation.)

From a sacramental perspective, that which is "gazed upon" for the presence of God can include any aspect of life in the world. The *Catechism* says that "contemplation is a gaze of faith," adding that "the book of the world"[30] is especially fitting for contemplative wonder.

I have heard the mother of a small baby describe as contemplative the time at the end of breast-feeding when the baby falls asleep at her breast and she can gaze down with great love on the contented little face. At the other end of life, I remember being amazed as a small boy how my grandparents could spend long hours in the evening time sitting by the fire, not doing much and saying very little, and yet seeming very content in each other's presence and being terribly lonely if either one was not there. Looking back on it now, perhaps they had long moments of contemplation.

I know a university professor who spends the half-hour before class "centering down," sitting quietly, not reviewing her notes but, as she describes it, becoming aware of the gift before her and readying her heart to receive it. I do not seem to have such spiritual maturity myself—I am lucky to make it to class on time. But, hopefully, every teacher and parent can find some quiet moments in every day to "center down" and be contemplative.

Pause to recognize the gift of a new day each morning—we only have so many. Appreciate that quiet moment before falling asleep and be grateful for the day gone by. Pause for contemplative moments—however brief—in between. They will nurture a sacramental consciousness as well as a humanizing education.

Then, specifically for one's vocation as teacher or parent, a sacramental cosmology may ask the following commitments of the educator's soul in order to nurture a sense of sacramentality in the hearts of learners.

Commitment #1: Encourage People's Aesthetic and Sense of Celebration
This may seem a strange commitment with which to begin, but it permeates all my other proposals. A sacramental consciousness correlates closely with a person's sense of the aesthetic—appreciation for what is beautiful and pleasing, what is fitting and appropriate. An educator seems strategically positioned to foster the aesthetic of learners by encouraging them to appreciate the world as charged with grandeur and meaning; to enjoy its beauty—especially in creation; to treasure its knowledge and wisdom—especially in the sciences and humanities; to appreciate and contribute to human creativity—especially through the arts.

Educators can also foster the aesthetic of learners by encouraging them to bring a sense of celebration to life: to relish and love it; to be passionate about living it well and wisely; to appreciate the mystery and miracle of the human body; to cherish the gift of the human mind—beginning with their own; to delight in simple as well as extraordinary pleasures; to find moments to celebrate its goodness and giftedness.

Philosophies like pragmatism or puritanism might see merriment as a waste of time, even forbidden, but a sacramental outlook insists that celebration is necessary for a balanced life. It also suggests—as pedagogically wise—that the teacher or parent sponsor an occasional good party, even within the teaching/learning event itself. Might it not be integral to the curriculum?

Fostering the aesthetic of learners can be done in myriad ways, but surely a privileged mode is to help them develop their artistic capacities. I think again of Mary Ann; she made developing the artistic talents of her three children a priority and intentionally set up a home-schooling situation around the arts. In addition to teaching or having them taught dancing, singing, music and other performing arts, and often providing opportunities for family concerts, she encouraged them to develop in the visual arts. Colleen tells of coming home from school to find that her mom had set up the porch with paints, sketch pads, and all they might need for drawing and painting. An "art hour" was a frequent feature of their home education.

Commitment #2:
Encourage the Sense That Life Is Meaningful and Worthwhile
Parents and teachers can maintain an attitude that life has meaning, that it is worthwhile, and likely have this rub off on learners. Such an attitude is more "caught" than "taught" and, like the common cold, from someone who has it already. Whatever we teach, we can teach with a bias toward meaning and purpose—beyond strategic advantage or utilitarian end. The educator's decisive passion must be that learners come to live more humanly, and this can be done only by helping them to find life meaningful and worthwhile.

A friend, Fred, tells fondly of a weeklong cabdriving course he took in New York when he was between writing novels. The particular instructor was justly famous, and new cabbies vied to get into his course. He would begin by stating his intent, not only to teach them the regulations and skills of being a New York cabdriver—"to make a living"—but also how to "have a life" as a cabby.

They learned—in addition to being successful and safe cabdrivers—how to get along with and help each other, how to enjoy conversation with "fares," the best places to eat and rest, the radio stations to tune in to, which art galleries and museums had inexpensive admission, and the low-cost movie houses for the downtimes. In short, he was a true educator in the humanities (chapter 5) because he helped them make meaningful and worthwhile lives as New York cabdrivers. Any teacher or parent can have such a bias toward meaning and purpose—to educate *for life for all.*

It is easy and tempting for educators to fall into the glib assumption that learners are best taught to master reality, to control it, to exploit it for production or personal advantage alone. But such "meaning" is shallow and insufficient for human hearts. Better to help them enter into a gracious relationship with the world, to experience it as meaningful and worthwhile, to respect and protect it—with a sense of sacred ground.

The meaning that humanizes encourages people to reciprocate with the world—to receive and give, to look out for others as well as self, to critique as necessary but not with pessimism. This is not an illusory attitude; it can include preparing for a career, getting a job, being effective in society. But its guiding intent is humanization—the liberation of learners as human beings. And educators have a choice in what attitude to hold and inculcate.

A literature teacher can teach students to dissect texts, imparting a mastery of the technicalities of style and adding to their accumulated data and information. By contrast, teachers with a bias for meaning and purpose include attention to the technicalities as helpful but, reaching far beyond them, approach literature as a great mirror of life that reflects humankind's perennial questions, with wisdom to be gleaned from how others have grappled with living humanly. The meaningful and worthwhile approach is not simply to learn about texts of literature, but to learn from them for life.

Likewise, history can be reduced to memorizing dates, battles, names and places, or it can be taught so that students learn more from history than about it, and perhaps to avoid mistakes made before.

Geography can be reduced to technical knowledge, the kind that might be useful if one gets on a quiz show, or it can expose students to alternative worlds of meaning, thereby enriching and expanding their own.

Even a religious faith can be taught for the purpose of mastering its technical content—that people learn about it. But better by far to teach it for meaning and purpose—that people learn from it in humanizing ways and perhaps that they consider living it as personal identity.

Commitment #3: Alert Learners to "The More in the Midst"

Teachers and parents can enable learners to see for themselves that there is more to the world than meets the eye, that life has munificence and largess. The "more" is ultimately the mystery of it— not mystery as something we cannot explain but as a grace that allures us, brings us to awe, to reverence, that makes life gracious. Educators can invite learners to look at life carefully, contemplatively, intelligently, with curiosity and intuition, and then—reaching further—to look through life, to recognize and appreciate what is beyond the obvious and ordinary. We can help them notice design, pattern, consistency, and beauty, and to look through these phenomena to the larger order of which they are expressions, and perhaps even to their Creator.

I know of a high-school science teacher who urges students to notice the design, pattern, intricacies, and innate beauty of what they are studying—to see everything as a whole first and then as part of a larger reality that is equally fascinating. Perhaps science teachers are ideally situated to foster a sacramental consciousness. They can enable students to "discover," in the words of Vatican II, how "the whole of creation, from the distant celestial bodies and the immeasurable cosmic forces down to the infinitesimal particles and waves of matter and energy, all bear the imprint of the Creator's wisdom and power."[31]

Likewise, social science teachers can enable students to look beyond social data to the deep relationality of humankind, to recognize their own relatedness within the web of humanity, to discover that we are "made for each other."

Good math teachers encourage students to look beyond numbers to what they mean, to presume and be challenged by the notion of "infinity." Every science or topic can be taught in a way that points people toward "the more in the midst." Teachers not allowed to use explicit religious language can still encourage learners "to see" for themselves the mystery, beauty, and wonder of their world. (The science teacher just cited teaches in a public high school.)

Surely, parents have ample opportunity to help learners to look beyond the obvious and, with imagination, to see what is "there" and what it means. Mary Ann had a favorite game she would play with her family over evening dinner. She would have each tell of "something fun" that happened to them that day or "the best thing," or "something sad," and so on—sensing what seemed called for—and then invite each one to reflect on their story and what it meant for them. It was a way of forming them to stop, name, and reflect on the events of their lives and then to find "the more" and the meaning that might not have been noticed otherwise.

Commitment #4: Enliven—Give Rein To—Learners' Imaginations
Fulfilling the first three suggestions—to attend to the aesthetic, the meaning, and "the more" of the world—requires educators to engage and enliven the imaginations of learners.

Philosopher Immanuel Kant described imagination as "the power of shaping into one."[32] Imagination is what "brings it all together," enabling us to even have an attitude in the first place, to weave together a coherent view of the world. Imagination prompts generativity and ongoing human effort. As previously noted, it is needed for ethical discernment—to anticipate consequences, to see what might be and should be, and to move the will to respond. The more teachers and parents encourage use of imaginations, the more likely are learners to live humanly and join with gusto in the festival of life in the world.

My friend Sister Gervasie is one of the most creative religion teachers I know. Few would be more artful in getting children to use their imaginations, and after more than fifty years in Catholic schools and parish programs, she has a thousand stories to tell. One of my favorites: Her third-grade students had been studying the parable of the Prodigal Son, and finally she assigned them to create their own modern drama based on the story and to act it out. The agreement was that they would make up the characters and parts, without her intervention, and she left them to the task. When she returned for the production, she found that they had assigned all the extra boys as "the Prodigal's Pals" and the girls as "loose women." Later, Gervasie's phone rang off the hook with parents looking for an explanation of what she was teaching in her parish program.

Every teacher or parent can engage learners' imaginations. We can ask questions that cannot be responded to except by activating imagination, give assignments that require creativity, applaud imaginative efforts. Even in sciences we might think of as purely empirical, creative teachers can stimulate imagination. My senior-year math class was a daily exercise in discovering what we could imagine and create mathematically.

Art educators of all kinds are in a privileged position to stimulate imagination. For what artists and poets do is the quintessence of sacramental consciousness. What are the arts but "reflections of divine beauty in tangible form"?[33] As students are introduced to the arts, when they engage their own creativity and aesthetic ability, they are most likely to discover the sacramentality of the world, finding in it and themselves the work of the Creator.

Commitment #5: Encourage Generativity

The giftedness and graciousness of life bring responsibilities. Education should encourage and prepare people to fulfill them. But fulfilling responsibilities can sound minimal, though a necessary starting point. Teachers and parents can encourage learners to reach beyond the minimum required to get by, toward generating more life-giving possibilities for self and others, to achieve all that they can achieve with their lives—to make things happen *for life for all*. One thinks of "Mr. Keating" (played brilliantly by Robin Williams), in that wonderful movie *Dead Poets Society,* taking his students out of the classroom to the pictures of the "old boys" on the corridors and reminding them that, "Now they are all pushing up daisies. How many of them really lived out their dreams?" Then he urges the boys to "seize the day" (*carpe diem*), to "make your lives extraordinary," to "let them count for something," not by success as the world measures it—wealth and power, or becoming doctors, lawyers, and bankers as parents might have programmed for them—but to "look at things a different way," to remember that "poetry is why we live." What an exhortation to a sacramental consciousness!

Here, for a change of pace, let me cite a few egregiously negative examples of how teachers tried to diminish rather than enhance people's generativity. What of: the professor who failed William Butler Yeats on his final English exam at Trinity College Dublin; Beethoven's music teacher telling him that he was hopeless as a composer; the "Great" Caruso, perhaps the finest tenor of his time, being told by a music teacher that he had no voice and would never become a singer; Karl Rahner, one of the greatest theologians of the twentieth century, having his first dissertation rejected by a doctoral committee.

The list could go on and each of us could add personal examples. Think, too, of the many forms of social diminishment perpetuated by educators, robbing countless people of their generativity—women, people of color, and others discriminated against for whatever reason. That so many have risen above the diminishment put upon them by educators proves, happily, that the latter do not have determinacy over learners and that the human spirit of generativity is resilient. But, surely, it is better by far that teachers and parents encourage and challenge learners to become all that they can be—not, as in the human potential movement by their own self-definition, but by God's invitation through the gift of life.

Commitment #6: Encourage an Ecological Consciousness

I noted earlier that a sacramental consciousness encourages commitment to justice and, especially, to social justice. To develop this theme in any detail here would diminish from chapter 8—in any philosophy of education, justice deserves to be a chapter in its own right. It seems imperative, however, to at least mention one aspect of the call to justice: human responsibility to be good stewards of our shared environment. It surely warrants mention under sacramentality! The ancient philosophers who addressed cosmology focused on the created order; every cosmology should still include this concern.

Commitment to a sacramental cosmology can engender a deep reverence for creation, to appreciate its beauty and to care for its well-being. Encouraging learners to look at their natural environment with a sacramental consciousness may be the most persuasive way to encourage their good stewardship and opposition to its abuse. To nurture a sacramental consciousness is surely to nurture an ecological one.

The psalmists were women and men who knew well the sacramentality of creation. They encountered the Creator coming to meet them through the created order and responded by inviting creation itself to help them worship God. Psalm 148 calls on the "sun and moon and shining stars," on "fire and hail, snow and mist, storm winds . . . mountains and hills . . . fruit trees and cedars" and all the creatures of creation to praise God. All creation should be cherished and cared for as gift of God whom it praises. With or without religious language, every teacher and parent who embraces a sacramental cosmology is called to practice environmental responsibility and to foster the same in learners.

For the Educator's Style

Of the many suggestions that could be made for a teaching style in response to a sacramental cosmology, some will also "fit" in later chapters, so here I limit myself to two: as reader, of course, you should add your own. The two are closely related and may often unfold sequentially:

1. Turn people to look at and express their lives in the world—what is "there," what they are up to, and what is going on around them.

2. Get people to reflect on their life in the world—to contemplate it, interpret it, question it, imagine new possibilities for it, and even to probe their own reflections on it all, discerning why they think or feel or perceive the way they do.

These two suggestions amount to making learners' own lives in the world and their contemplations/reflections on them constitutive aspects of the curriculum—regardless of what science, humanity, or art is being taught.

Encourage learners to "look at" and contemplate their lives in the world, inviting their own expressions of them. To say that the world is sacramental—gift and gracious, meaningful and worthwhile, encouraging imagination and generativity—suggests a pedagogical response of turning persons to their encounter with it, to notice and even to contemplate their life world. Contemporary literature refers to people's "lives in the world" as their *praxis*. In ancient Greek philosophy, this term meant "reflection on action" or what we might intend by "learning from experience."

However, the dual moments in praxis—action and reflection—make it more suggestive for educators than the term *experience*.[34] Praxis highlights two things: that people's experiences include both what comes their way and what they initiate—"present action"—and that they must look at, express, and reflect on their lives in the world in order to learn from them.

Thus, turning learners to the "action" aspect of their praxis means encouraging them to notice and look at "the world" around them, which includes the following: noticing what is "there" in the created order and in the order created by humankind—culture, society, and human history; noticing what they themselves are doing—which includes any human activity of their own initiative; and then noticing what is happening to them and what is going on in the social and political world as it impinges on their lives. A favorite colloquial question today is "What's happenin'?" A full response would require looking at present praxis and bringing it to expression.

The recommended teaching style is first to draw learners attention to "what is there," to what one is doing, to what is "happening," inviting them to notice it and then to express—somehow—their consciousness of this "action." In the words of Brazilian educator Paulo Freire, such pedagogy is inviting people "to name their present praxis."[35]

Reiterating what was said already, the highest instance of "looking at" life is contemplation—"really noticing" with attention and absorption that touches one's soul. Contemplation is such an intense "looking at" the world that we begin to "look through" it, to see "the more in the midst." At whatever level, noticing and naming present praxis are the first moments in learning from one's life in the world.

A kindergarten teacher named Jan teaches in a rural area. Most days, weather permitting, she takes her class on a "field trip." Each has a focus, and over the year the children learn firsthand about birds, flowers, plants, insects, and a hundred other marvelous things of nature. She is helping them to notice, name, and know their world of creation—and surely nurturing a sacramental consciousness as well!

In expressing "present praxis," learners can signify their sentiments or feelings, attitudes or beliefs, overt activities or efforts—anything of which they are conscious. Their modes of expression can take any form of human communication—speaking or writing, actions or gestures, drawing or making artifacts, mime or dance. Getting persons to express their lives in the world gives limitless opportunity to the educator's creativity since learners can do this in myriad ways.

Encourage learners to reflect on their life in the world. In a sense, having people "look at" their world and bring it to "expression" already entails substantive reflection; one cannot express experience without reflecting on it. And surely contemplation is already a deep reflection on what is "there." But it is not a discursive nor a critical one, and there is need for both in education. While these two moments overlap, and especially in the dynamics of teaching, yet it can help the teacher or parent to know that both emphases are needed: "looking" and "reflecting."

John Dewey was adamant that we learn nothing from experience unless we reflect on it. ("Reconstruct" it was the term he preferred.) For Dewey, this meant to probe life-experience, to analyze it, to interpret its meaning, to ask the why and the wherefore of it, the reasons behind it and the consequences of it. Freire is even stronger than Dewey in emphasizing "*critical* reflection."

For Freire, the meaning we make of our world is much influenced by our social context. We are under powerful pressures to see and think as society does. But society has its vested interests, its blinding ideologies. Thinking what our society thinks is not necessarily thinking for ourselves—as persons. For Freire, humanization requires critical reflection—getting learners to truly think for themselves.

Critical reflection moves beyond noticing and even beyond contemplating one's life in the world to probing its depths, uncovering its meaning. The word *critical* does not intend to convey a negative activity. Rather, the educational intent is to encourage learners to be truly discerning in how they interpret their lives in the world, to see and make sense out of it for themselves, to remember what should not be forgotten, to imagine what might be and act to create it.

A sacramental consciousness sees the world as "revelatory," and "to reveal" literally means "to pull back the curtains." Critical reflection is pulling back the curtains to enable people to see better for themselves. In this first sense, critical reflection is, in keeping with a sacramental cosmology, a very positive outlook on life in the world.

Then, appreciating Protestant skepticism about the sacramentality of life in the world, its ambiguities call for a dialectical as well as a positive attitude. Critical reflection should ever entail a healthy suspicion toward the world. Besides "pulling back the curtains" to see the gift that is there, one must also see what is there but should not be so—even though society may favor it. In theological terms, it is becoming realistic about sin and evil in the world and about our own ability to make sinful choices.

Even in contexts where such religious language is excluded, there must be opportunity for critique as well as appreciation—for calling one's world into question. Without this aspect of critical reflection, a sacramental perspective can be naive, encouraging false consciousness. Toward one's social context, for example, critical reflection means questioning how society tells us to think in order to think for ourselves. It means probing who is benefiting from the way things are and who is suffering because of it.

To deepen the reflective aspect of critical reflection further, it even entails questioning one's own perspective on the world. Such "thinking about our thinking" is similar to Gadamer's advice about hermeneutics, referred to at the beginning of this chapter. All of us interpret the meaning of our lives, but we should also be aware of the preunderstanding we bring to interpreting in the first place. If we do not question ourselves critically, we may settle for personal biases or social prejudices. If we do not probe our own outlook, the nature and sources of it, we can be held bound by it. Uncovering and probing our own cosmology—our attitude toward life in the world, where it comes from, and what it leads to—is essential for personal freedom and authentic choice.

The depth of critical reflection will depend, of course, on many factors—the most obvious being developmental readiness of learners and likely of educators as well. Small children may not do critical analysis of their social world nor think about their own thinking, but they can begin to reflect for themselves at any age. Surely, good education—and from the beginning—encourages learners to really think for themselves.

I will return to critical reflection repeatedly in this book, looking at it from differing angles. For now, to summarize from the perspective of sacramentality, *critical reflection entails critical reason, analytical memory, and creative imagination.* They are, of course, always intertwined, but we can set them out for clarity.

- Critical reason reviews what is "there" in the world, both the positive and negative, asking the meaning of and reasons for both.

- Analytical memory uncovers the social and personal origins of how things got to be the way they are and the genesis of our own perspective.

- Creative imagination invites seeing the consequences of present praxis, perceiving what might or should be changed, and stimulating our own generativity.

Questions and questioning activities are likely the key pedagogy to encouraging learners in critical reflection, though, of course, provocative statements and social data can help as well.

Critical reason questions take such forms as:

> What do we think this means, and why?
> What is life-giving here and why?
> What is not life-giving and why not?
> Whose interest is being served?
> Who is suffering?
> What are some of the reasons for this present state of affairs?
> Can you explain some of your own attitudes?

Analytical memory is encouraged by such questions as:

> Where did this come from?
> How did this present situation arise?
> What is the history—personal or social—behind it?
> Whose interests brought things to be this way?
> What memories does this hold for you?
> What are some of the roots of your own attitude?
> Can you share some of the story behind what you're saying (or feeling, or doing, etc.)?

Creative imagination is encouraged by such questions as:

> What are the likely consequences of this?
> What should be the outcome here?
> What can we do on behalf of what is best for all?
> What changes can we make that are fitting?
> What consequences would we prefer and how do we help to shape them?
> How do you feel called to respond?
> What would it mean to act *for life for all*?

For the Educational Space

Much of what is proposed for the educator's soul and style impinges on the educational space as well, but again, space deserves its own attention—it has such significance for educating character. To encourage a sacramental outlook on life, teachers and parents can create an aesthetic and symbolically rich space that nurtures imagination and creativity.

Many school, home, and parish program spaces are drab, and the further along the educational continuum one moves, it seems, the drabber they get. I am thinking especially of my own typical teaching context of a university classroom. First-grade classrooms are festivals of pleasing color, gentle texture, and engaging symbols compared to doctoral seminar rooms. For colleges with desks nailed to the floor and facing the professor's lectern or for the parish catechetical program that meets in a church basement with terrazzo floor and tubular-steel chairs, my proposal may sound far-fetched. But I have been in both and am convinced that every physical space can be improved aesthetically and symbolically, made more likely to encourage imagination and creativity.

Much progress has been made in attending to the physical educational environment. Many schools and parish programs create environments that are tactile and sensory, congenial in color scheme and appointment, that can incorporate symbols and allow rituals that reflect students' lives and nurture their sacramental outlook. The consciousness of parents has also been greatly heightened in this regard, with a great variety of educational toys now available, especially for younger children. Creating educationally rich physical space for the older ones may require more intentionality.

Teachers with a homeroom in grade school or high school have the most scope for creating and maintaining aesthetically pleasing and symbolically rich space. It is also wise to enlist students to care for and contribute to the aesthetic of their environment. Even in my university lecture hall, I begin by inviting students to "tend to the aesthetic of our pedagogical space." Since most graduate classes meet later in the day, by the time we arrive cans, papers, and other debris are scattered around; we clean up before beginning. I usually ask for a volunteer each week to bring a "symbol" for our space, something that reflects themselves and their world and is also suggestive of our curriculum together. We begin the class with the volunteer placing his or her symbol for all to see and saying a few words about it.

Every teacher and parent can imagine ways to further enhance the aesthetic of the physical environment. I know of a fifth-grade teacher who plays classical music softly as background during work periods. She tells children what is playing and its composer. By year's end, they can distinguish a Bach piece from one by Beethoven and have grown in appreciating good music. This teacher rarely has discipline problems, although she works in what is considered a very "tough" school. Perhaps the music has something to do with the respectful environment of her classroom.

The pedagogies that teachers and parents use can also help to foster learners' aesthetic and symbolic sense. This is eminently true in education in the arts—music, drawing and painting, drama and poetry. If art education does not engage persons' own aesthetic creativity, it is unlikely to achieve its proper intent in the curriculum—that students not only grow to appreciate the arts but also develop the artist in themselves.

But beyond art education, teaching itself can be approached as an art. It is indeed a "fine art": creating a welcoming environment where learners feel at home; imagining how to actively engage them in the teaching/learning dynamic; facilitating conversation and participation; giving access in engaging ways to traditions of wisdom and knowledge. Every pedagogical move and moment can reflect its own artistry. To practice the art of teaching—and I am finding that it takes lifelong practice—is also likely to nurture the aesthetic sense and imagination of learners and thus their sacramental consciousness.

The concluding observation is that an environment that encourages creativity and imagination is particularly effective for moral formation—in nurturing virtuous character. Some fascinating initiatives have been taken, many inspired by Montessori education, which indicate that disruptive behavior in younger children decreases as their imaginations and creativity are engaged. Similarly, some penal systems are finding that prisoners who are allowed to engage in creative projects, and especially to cultivate a garden and grow things, have a much lower recidivism rate than others. It seems that an aesthetic environment that encourages creativity can abet the formation and rehabilitation of character. A sacramental cosmology suggests such educational space.

For Reflection

- Note a few of your overall responses to this chapter. What do they help you to understand about your attitude toward life in the world?

- What insights have you gleaned, either through agreement or disagreement, for your own soul? For your style as educator? For the educational space you help to create?

- If you were allowed only one decision in response to your dialogue with this chapter (you can, of course, have as many as you wish), what would it be? Why? How would you begin to implement it the next time you find yourself in an educational moment?

Notes

1. This was how Alfred North Whitehead used the term in his classic work *Process and Reality*, the subtitle of which was *An Essay in Cosmology*. He stated the purpose of the book as to provide a category of general ideas "in terms of which every element of our experience can be interpreted." 4.
2. Bernard Lonergan, "The Origins of Christian Realism," in *A Second Collection,* 241.
3. Hans-Georg Gadamer's best known work is *Truth and Method.* I cite from the Second Revised Edition.
4. Gadamer uses this term, but not with the negative connotation that it has in English. For Gadamer, "all understanding inevitably involves some prejudice" and "prejudice . . . can have either a positive or a negative value." Ibid., 270.
5. Ibid., 1196.
6. *The Catechism,* # 1146 and 1147.
7. There are many different cultural versions of this story; I suspect mine is an Irish one. For another see John Shea, *The Legend of the Bells: Stories of the Human Spirit,* 111-112.
8. McBrien, *Catholicism,* 794.
9. "Dogmatic Constitution on Divine Revelation" # 13, Abbott, Documents 121.
10. *The Catechism,* #2705.
11. Ibid., #1084.
12. Viktor Frankl, *Man's Search for Meaning,* 75.
13. *The Collected Poems of W. B. Yeats,* 253-54.
14. See, for example, Richard Kearney, *The Wake of Imagination.*
15. *Rule of St. Benedict,* Chapter 53.
16. See Aristotle, *The Nicomachean Ethics,* Book X, chapter 8: 6-8.
17. Karl Rahner, *Belief Today,* 4.
18. Gerard Manley Hopkins, *Poems and Prose,* 27.
19. Patrick Kavanagh, *Collected Poems,* "The Great Hunger," 22.
20. There is surely an important point for the current debate about religious language and the effort to move beyond using exclusively male imagery for God. On this issue, see my *Language for a "Catholic" Church.*
21. *Encyclopedia of Catholicism,* 43.
22. See David Tracy, *The Analogical Imagination: Christian Theology and the Culture of Pluralism.*
23. *The Catechism,* # 1127 and 1128.
24. See McBrien, *Catholicism,* 790
25. *The Catechism,* #309.
26. Ibid., #311.
27. Some of my reflections in the previous paragraphs have been influenced by the work of Rabbi Harold Kushner, see especially, *When Bad Things Happen to Good People.*
28. Some of my thinking here has been stimulated by the doctoral dissertation work of Barry Meehan, SJ, *The Child as Contemplative;* Boston College, 1998.
29. Quoted in *The Catechism,* #2709.
30. Ibid., #2715.

31. Vatican Congregation for Catholic Education, Religious Dimensions of Education in a Catholic School, #54.
32. I first came upon this insight in the work of Sharon Parks, see The Critical Years, 113.
33. Vatican Congregation for Catholic Education, *Religious Dimensions of Education in a Catholic School*, # 61.
34. Although I have in mind what educational literature typically means by "learning from experience" I prefer the less familiar "praxis" over "experience" because the latter can have a too passive connotation. We tend to think of experience as something we undergo rather than initiate ourselves. John Dewey struggled against this shortcoming of the term throughout his career, but people often missed his expansion of it to include personal initiative. This old Greek term *praxis,* now well revived, includes both what we undergo and what we do, what is going on around us, to us, and what we initiate ourselves. Praxis is reflection on our human encounter with the world. For further elaboration, see Groome, *Sharing Faith,* especially chapter 4.
35. In my opinion Paulo Freire, Maria Montessori, and John Dewey are three of the greatest educators of the twentieth century—or of any time—at least in the Western world. I will draw upon them frequently throughout *Educating for Life.*

CHAPTER FOUR

❖

A Community for Life:
"Made for Each Other"

An Unlikely Crew

There were fourteen of us in the course on television production at New York University the summer of 1973. The professor explained that everyone was responsible for producing a half-hour program, which a public-access channel had agreed to air in the fall. We were to work as one team, with everyone helping to produce each other's program.

He said we would rotate on camera, lighting, audio, direction, production, set design, and scriptwriting. By the end of this immersion—eight weeks, five days a week, at least ten hours a day—everyone would have had firsthand experience in every aspect of TV production. As an afterthought, he mentioned that there was no budget.

The task didn't seem possible. We were such a diverse group—women and men; gay and straight; black, brown, and white; a feisty Italian, a lost Irishman, two Brooklyn Jews; and more. Some had extensive TV experience, others were neophytes. How could we work as a team?

Amazingly, everyone contributed to every program as if it were their own and seemed to be reaching beyond self-interest—though the latter likely remained. We finished them on time, they were aired, and while causing no bumps on the Nielsen ratings, didn't embarrass either.

After the course ended, Ron, my best buddy in the group, and his wife, Roberta, came to Ireland with me for a much-needed vacation. My sister, Peg, and her husband, Kevin, put on a great dinner to welcome us the first night. It was a wonderful celebration, with the best of Irish hospitality.

After sumptuous hors d'oeuvres, Peg served the entree—a kaleidoscope of fresh homegrown vegetables and an aromatic meat. Ron oohed and aahed with the rest, but then, scrutinizing his plate and sounding apprehensive, asked, "What kind of meat is this?" Oh God, I had forgotten to tell Peg that Ron and Roberta were Jewish and kept kosher. The look of consternation on Peg's face indicated that she had now surmised as much—and yes, had served pork.

Everyone froze in panic. Then Roberta spoke up, quite firmly, "Ron, it's chicken." Slowly, Ron cut a piece, tasted it, and said, "Ah, the best of chicken! Peg, you must give me the recipe." All roared that laughter of relief.

We maintained our conspiracy throughout the evening— everyone knowing what everyone knew, and yet suspending it for something greater between us. It became a memorable story in our family, and perhaps in Ron's.

Looking back on it all now, I realize that the dinner incident epitomized what had happened with the whole group, and I still marvel at what emerged among that motley crew in the TV studio at NYU, the summer of '73. It stands as one of my most intense experiences of a "community"—if only for a few weeks. And I still wonder about what it takes to "build" community and the magnanimity needed to function for the common good—including but reaching far beyond self-interest.

Are We Each Other's Keeper?

The first question raised in the Bible about human relationship is when Cain asks defensively, "Am I my brother's keeper?" (Genesis 4:9). Since he had already killed Abel, we can presume that Cain asked rhetorically. Yet he posed an ultimate question for humankind ever after. The nub of Cain's issue—and ours—would seem to be "Must I care for others as well as myself?"

It is interesting to note that the two politicoeconomic systems with which the world is currently most familiar tend to favor either self or others in the extreme. Capitalism functions on private property for personal profit—to care for the self as individual; communism functions as a totalitarian collective—exalting the group to the denial of individual rights.

But individualism honors only a part of persons—their individuality, and collectivism treats persons only as a part—as cog in a wheel. Surely, it is possible to answer Cain's question not as either/or, but as both/and; that we are to care for ourselves and each other in a "community-of-persons." Such is the sociology proposed in this chapter.

Sociology as a science is the study of social relationships; of people's assimilation into groups; and of the expectations people can have of each other, of their communities and social institutions. However, beneath the science of sociology and of crucial import for how we live our lives is the fundamental issue of how we understand our relatedness in the world—how we are to live our companionship with others (the Latin *socius*). As for anthropology and cosmology, everyone has an operative sociology—a functioning outlook on their relationships with self, others, and society; a view on how members are to relate to each other and as a whole society. The focus in this chapter, then, is our perspective on "living together."

Clearly, the theme of sociology is closely related to the previous two and continues to explore our understanding of ourselves and what it means to live humanly. The difference is one only of emphasis or perspective. As chapter 2 focused on "persons-in-community," we can say that our theme here is "community-of-persons"—the other side of the same coin.

Again, we address a foundational issue for teachers and parents. Citing extremes to make my point, if their operative sociology favors rugged individualism, they will educate learners to "take care of Number One" with as little investment as possible in common welfare. By contrast, totalitarian regimes invariably co-opt their educators to socialize learners into making the state their "god"—at the expense of their personhood. Think back over some of the educators you have experienced and see if you can detect what their operative sociology might have been.

The social outlook proposed by Catholic Christianity must surely reflect its anthropology and cosmology. Its emphasis on the person as person-in-community rather than as an individual highlights that we are relational by nature; its emphasis on our essential goodness implies that we are capable of being responsible in relationship. Its sacramental outlook on life in the world encourages the attitude that society is more good than evil, that it is a medium of God's love for human well-being. Going further now and, as I elaborate presently, for its own faith life, Catholic Christianity has a substantial characteristic of communalism. It places more emphasis on the formal institution of Church than Protestantism typically does. This communal emphasis in its ecclesiology—understanding of itself as a church—reflects and encourages a similar attitude toward society—the conviction that we live most humanly as a "community-of-persons." We are our own and each other's keeper, bonded together for the common good—both spiritual and temporal; as humankind we are "made for each other"!

Before we venture on, pause to become more aware of your own operative sociology.

For Reflection

- How do you understand the relationship between the person and society? What are some responsibilities of each to the other?

- To what extent do you think society shapes the character and identity of its individual members? Rate social influence on a scale of 1 (very low) to 10. Then explain your rating. What are some consequences for teachers and parents?

- Try to figure out where your responses to these questions come from. Review especially the "sociology" of them, i.e., how has your own social context influenced your social perspective?

A Catholic Christian Sociology: One Proposal

The communal core of Catholicism is reflected in its appreciation for both church and society. Its ecclesiology and sociology go hand in hand. To ask which came first would be a "chicken-and-egg" question. In both, it radically affirms the well-being of the individual person and the common good of the whole community—a phrase that summarizes the purpose of society and its defining value.

With dual emphasis on personal and social, Catholic Christianity affirms the dignity and rights of the person and, at the same time, insists that humankind has an essentially communal nature—that we form societies by "nature" rather than by convenience or contract—and underscores people's responsibilities to society and society's responsibilities to all its members. Without choosing to favor either the personal or the social, Catholic sociology tries to balance both as a "community-of-persons."

A community-of-persons sociology can be amplified with three cumulative points. Since each pertains to both church and society, I blend theological and philosophical reflections.

Point #1: *Community is the primary context for "being saved" and "becoming human."* The core point—claimed ecclesially and socially—is that humankind is essentially communal, and both humanly and spiritually, we have our best possibilities in community. This proposal could sound a bit self-evident, but it cannot be taken for granted, neither theologically nor philosophically.

Many of the great religions of humankind do not emphasize a communal process of salvation, putting emphasis on the individual quest and paying little heed to the social realm. Within Christianity, the Reformers downplayed the role of the Church—in understandable reaction at the time to its manifest corruption and self-exaggeration—with the more strident calling it "the whore of Babylon."

Most of the Reformation traditions embraced Augustine's portrayal of society as a "city of sin"—over against the "city of God"—and beyond the pale of significant Christian influence. Catholic Christianity, even in its worst of times, clung to a more positive understanding of both church and society.

Few philosophers would dismiss the need for society, except perhaps the more extreme anarchists. But in the mainstream social philosophy that came to dominance in Western democracies, the scales were weighted heavily to favor "individual rights." The English philosopher John Locke (1632–1704), so influential on the framers of the United States Constitution, championed the "rights of the individual," insisting upon the "absolute liberty" of the citizen. Rather than being an essential disposition of human nature, society comes about by "social contract" negotiated and freely entered into by individuals. Within the social contract, nothing should violate individual rights—the only restriction being that one's exercise of rights not infringe upon those of another.[1]

And Locke's focus on personal and property rights reflected the broader Enlightenment mentality—the philosophy of our "modern" world—which championed the ideal of the autonomous self, the person as self-determining subject who exists independent of community. By contrast, Catholic sociology insisted then and now on a dual and equal emphasis on person and community—that we cannot become persons apart from society and the well-being of both is cooperative rather than competitive.

First, the theological point. Catholicism places a striking emphasis, some would say to a fault, on the role of the Church in "the work of human salvation" (Philippians 2:12). It agrees that everyone is to have their own personal relationship with God (elaborated in chapter 7 on spirituality), but insists that the primary context of divine/human encounter is through the faith community. While all of life in the world is sacramental, there is a primacy to God's outreach to humankind as a people, and individuals respond best as "a people of God"—from solidarity with a community of faith. In a word, for good or ill, Catholic Christians tend to take the Church more seriously than most.

The Hebrew Scriptures highlight the communal aspect of living the covenant, that the Israelites were called as a people and to become "the people of God." In this communal function, they were to be a source of blessing for all humankind and the human paradigm of how to live in "right relationship" with each other and with God. And yet, along with this communal emphasis, the Hebrew Scriptures make amply clear that each individual is to be respected and cared for— with special favor for the weakest and most in need (the poor, the widow, the orphan, and the "foreigner" in the land).

The Bible leaves no doubt that each person has nonnegotiable responsibilities to live the covenant faithfully and thus contribute to the faithfulness of the whole people. Every good done is considered both personal and communal, and, likewise, every sin.

Raised in this Hebrew covenant tradition, Jesus invited people into a "community of disciples." The New Testament offers little blueprint for how they were to organize themselves (one finds great diversity among the first Christian communities), yet there is ample evidence that Jesus intended his disciples to enter into a deep bond of union as his community in order to continue his mission and ministries.[2] At the same time, the New Testament leaves no doubt that the decision for discipleship is a radically personal one, bringing significant rights and responsibilities to each person. To cite Paul, every disciple is to become "another Christ" (see Galatians 3:27). What could be more affirming and demanding of each Christian? Of course, the ultimate demand on the individual Christian is to turn toward the neighbor—even enemies—in love, intertwining the personal and social at the very core of Christianity.

Even when beset with great abuses and corruptions, Catholicism clung tenaciously to the conviction that the Church is crucial to the faith of Christians and their spiritual well-being. As one contemporary theologian summarizes this tradition, Jesus is God's primordial sacrament to the world, and then the Church is the sacrament of Jesus.[3] Jesus is the primary means by which God reaches out to Christians and how they respond to God—together! Ever wonder, for example, why Catholics put so much emphasis on going to mass on Sunday? The theological rationale is its emphasis on being a community of faith, on approaching God together. Thus, the Sabbath mandate includes publicly worshipping God in community. Likewise, Catholic Christians usually do not make claims about their personal salvation—"I am saved" or "accepting Jesus Christ as my Lord and Savior." The undergirding theology is that Christians cannot be content with individual salvation alone, but must commit to living as a people of God in the world—a daily challenge as a community rather than a fait accompli of personal achievement.

Incensed at the corruptions so evident in the institution of the Church at the time, the Reformers tended to downplay its role in the work of salvation, emphasizing instead people's immediate relationship with God—rather than mediated through the Church— and the call to personal salvation. Although they rendered a crucial service to all Christianity by reclaiming the rights and responsibilities of the individual Christian—the priesthood of all believers, from a Catholic Christian perspective, the Reformers so favored the personal as to diminish the communal.

Catholicism remained convinced that, for all its sins and shortcomings, the Church is still the primary way that God comes looking for its members and through which they go looking for God. Although always an imperfect instrument, the Holy Spirit uses the Church as the first sacrament of Jesus to the world in mediating the divine/human encounter for Christians.

When brought into the social realm, Catholicism's communal emphasis encourages the outlook that human nature is essentially social and is so by the design of God, that instead of society being a "city of sin," it is how God intends us to be together. We become human beings only through social relationships, through interaction with and life in community. Society, while far from perfect and, like the Church, ever in need of reform, is the only context in which we can hope to realize our human vocation.

Apart from any theological warrant, the social sciences share a similar conviction. They describe the process of taking on human identity as socialization. As we enter into our social world, our social world literally enters into us. As we live in a context, we tend to interiorize—make our own—its perspectives and values. It is, then, through social interaction that our sense of self-identity emerges.

Sociologists debate the extent to which the social context shapes who we become and how much is the product of our own "nature"— genetics or whatever—the nature/nurture debate. Some sociologists (like Emile Durkheim) claim that we are in large part determined by our social context, while others (like Max Weber) grant us more autonomy. But none doubt that people are essentially social.

The classic Catholic Christian position on nature/nurture, autonomy/socialization would be to hold the two in balance, that our social context exerts considerable influence, but need not and should not determine who we become. Although we are social beings, we are ever persons—capable of freedom and personal choice. And yet, becoming persons is impossible apart from a social context. Society and ourselves are well-described together as a community-of-persons.

Point #2: *The Church is to serve the reign of God in the world, and Society the common good.* Here again is a parallel emphasis regarding the essential purpose of church and society. Both exist for the welfare of one and all.

The Church never exists for its own sake, but to be a sacrament of the reign of God in the world. Note that "reign of God" throughout the Hebrew Scriptures and in the New Testament is a profoundly social symbol or, perhaps more accurately, a spiritual symbol that demands social engagement and responsibilities of its members. Likewise, and echoing the classic definition of sacrament favored in chapter 3, to be a sacrament of God's reign demands that the Church be "an effective sign that causes to happen what it signifies."

This requires the Christian community to work in the world for God's intentions of holiness and justice, love and compassion, peace and fullness of life for all, and the integrity of God's creation. The Church's purpose is always first and foremost spiritual, with its mission rooted deeply in its faith. And yet, it is precisely its spiritual mission and faith motivation that give it a social purpose as well.

Again, the instance of the great commandment of love—the ultimate law of God's reign—makes the spiritual-cum-social point convincingly. It requires love of God and self, which cannot be realized apart from love of neighbor, and love of neighbor is a social action. As if in response to Cain's question at the beginning of the Bible, toward the end St. John declares bluntly, "The one who says, 'I love God,' but hates the brother or sister is a liar" (1 John 4:20).

As with the mandate of love, throughout the Bible all the values of God's reign are both spiritual and social—none is ever exclusively private or "otherworldly." This is why the *Catechism* states, "The Church's first purpose is to be the sacrament of the inner union of (people) with God." And then it immediately adds, "Because [people's] communion with one another is rooted in that union with God, the Church is also the sacrament of the unity of the human race."[4] So, the Church's spiritual mission gives it a profoundly social purpose as well. It exists, as Vatican II reiterated out of a long tradition, "for the salvation of the whole world."[5]

The symbol of God's reign, deeply rooted in Hebrew consciousness and the central purpose of Jesus' life, is perhaps captured best by the poets. It is what William Butler Yeats called "The Land of Heart's Desire." By noting the deepest and most authentic longings of the human heart, one gets some inkling of what God intends and desires for humankind, such as: holiness and goodness, love and compassion, peace and justice, inclusion and equality, hope and mercy, respect and responsibility, enjoyment and delight.

In the Hebrew Scriptures the word *shalom*—so rich in meaning that no English term fully captures its import—symbolizes both the spiritual and the social values of God's reign. *Wholeness* seems to come close to its meaning or *right relationship* with God, self, others, and creation. Perhaps the New Testament term that best summarizes the intent of God's reign in Jesus is "fullness of life" (see John 10:10).

Although rarely lived well and often taught poorly, Catholic Christianity has maintained a strong sense that God's reign is not simply for souls later but should begin now as human welfare—for individuals and communities—with God's desire of shalom for all being realized "on earth as it is in heaven."[6] The distinction between salvation history and human history is one only of perspective. The spiritual-cum-social values of God's reign are to permeate every level of human existence—personal, interpersonal, and sociopolitical. Christians should work to realize the peace and justice of shalom in every nook and cranny of life. The Church, as sacrament of God's reign, is under mandate to reflect such spiritual/social values within its own structures.

Of course, as human instrument, it never does—at least not perfectly! But rather than abandoning or bypassing the Church, better to see its sins and shortcomings as highlighting its need of reform and the responsibility of every Christian to live for God's reign in the world, thus enabling the Church to become more adequately the sacrament it should be. Every time Christians say "church" they should mean themselves, not something "over there" and apart from them. Church reform is always their own *metanoia*—change of heart—as well.

When such a perspective on the Church's mission is turned toward society and stated in philosophical terms, society is understood as a community-of-persons that is to function for the common good. Society must be valued and respected; it is not inevitably corrupt—a "city of sin"—but has an essential and beneficial role to play in human well-being. When a social structure is corrupt or unjust, the Christian response should not be fatalism nor withdrawal as if we can expect no better, but commitment to social transformation.

That society exists for the sake of the "common good" is emblematic of a Catholic Christian sociology. This conviction is certainly not unique nor original to Catholicism. It was a central conviction of many of the ancient Greek philosophers, most eminently Aristotle. Thomas Aquinas made the common good the ultimate measure of justice and the purpose of society. And his notion of it, again, is both personal and communal. The common good includes caring for the well-being of individual citizens and structuring the public realm to serve the welfare of the community as a social entity. In this Thomist tradition, Pope John Paul II has stated the common good succinctly as, "the good of all and of each individual."[7]

The *Catechism* says that "those who exercise authority in the political community" must care for the common good. Then it notes that this "consists of three essential elements: First, respect for the person as such . . . to respect the fundamental and inalienable rights of the human person. Second, the social well-being and development of the group itself. Finally, the common good requires peace, that is, the stability and security of a just order."[8]

Notice the dual emphasis on personal and communal well-being and then the need for peace overall. So rather than posing a conflict or a choice between personal and social welfare, both must be affirmed and society is responsible to serve both. Jacques Maritain, interpreting Aquinas, explained that "the common good . . . is neither the mere collection of private goods, nor the proper good of a whole . . . It is common to both the whole and the parts."[9]

Point #3: *In Church and Society, the proper relationship among persons and between individual persons and community is mutual reciprocity.* This point builds upon and makes explicit an aspect of the previous two. My emphasis here, however, is the responsibility that every member has to each other and to the group, and, conversely, the responsibility that the community has to enhance the life of each individual member. Parenthetically, I note that the Catholic church is not readily recognized for promoting mutuality and a democratic spirit. In fact, its history clearly reflects the kind of hierarchical style in its own ministry that encourages dependency among laity. In society, also, it has often favored monarchies and oligarchies. Yet, neither top-down totalitarianism nor individualized anarchy is consistent with its faith traditions. And, as I review in the next section, there are signs that Catholicism is coming to deeper commitment to a "discipleship of equals" in its ecclesiology, and to democracy in its sociology. Such sentiments are more consistent with its own substantial characteristic of communalism.

Probably nothing from Christian faith better captures the essentially mutual relationship that should exist between individual

Christian and the faith community than the image of Church as Body of Christ. As the historical Jesus was present in his physical body, St. Paul was convinced that the Body of Christ continues in the world through the community-of-persons called Church. He wrote to the Christians at Corinth and to all Christians thereafter, "You are Christ's body, and individually parts of it" (1 Corinthians 12:27).

But Paul's understanding of this body and how it functions places equal stress on the personal and communal. In the Body of Christ, each individual is valued, cherished, needed, and has a unique function—a role that no one else can play. And yet each part needs the whole for its own functioning. A hand or foot by itself would be simply dead, or "If the whole body were an eye, where would the hearing be?" (1 Corinthians 12:17). So, the well-being of the whole is crucial to the well-being of individual members, and vice versa. "As a body is one though it has many parts, and all the parts of the body, though many, are one body, so also Christ" (1 Corinthians 12:12).

Beyond such mutuality among "the parts" and between the whole and parts, Paul proposed an amazingly egalitarian spirit for this Body of Christ. It was to have a deep and abiding equality. "For in one Spirit we were all baptized into one body, whether Jew or Greek, slave or free person, and we were all given to drink of one Spirit" (1 Corinthians 12:13). Baptism, then, is the key to the equality of Christians and no one is any more baptized than anyone else.

With God's Holy Spirit animating the Body of Christ, the Christian communitarian spirit must be "all for one, and one for all." Or, as Paul put it, "There should be no division in the body, but the parts should have the same concern for one another. If one part suffers, all the parts suffer with it; if one part is honored, all the parts share its joy" (1 Corinthians 12:25–26).

Reflection on our own bodiliness confirms that we naturally care for each member, and yet our overall well-being is found in the health of the total body. When one small part is sick or injured—even a little toe—it brings down the health of the whole, and yet the well-being of the body and caring for all its members cannot be neglected to care exclusively for a little toe. Each member and the entire body must have their own care and emphasis, and these individual and corporate claims are not in competition but mutual reciprocity.

The Church's self-understanding as the Body of Christ closely correlates with the celebration of Eucharist, of the body of Christ in

Holy Communion. I noted in chapter 3 the centrality of Eucharist to Catholic Christian spirituality, claiming strongly, as it does, that the bread and wine of Eucharist is the real presence of the Risen Christ. But all mainline Christians celebrate this community meal as symbol and source of their bondedness as Body of Christ in the world.

As St. Augustine often challenged his congregation at the end of celebrating Eucharist, "Go and become what you have received—the Body of Christ." Again, Paul was the first to correlate celebrating Eucharist and becoming Body of Christ. "The cup of blessing that we bless, is it not a participation in the blood of Christ? The bread that we break, is it not a participation in the body of Christ? Because the loaf of bread is one, we, though many, are one body, for we all partake of the one loaf" (1 Corinthians 10:16–17).

If Catholicism keeps Eucharist at the heart of its identity (not a rhetorical question since it faces a dire shortage of celibate priests), it may better resist patriarchal hierarchism within its own institution and prophetically encourage mutuality in the social realm.

Looking from church to society and in more philosophical terms, mutual reciprocity entails responsibility of individual citizens to each other and to society and of society to its individual citizens. Here again I am amplifying points already made; I approach it first from the person's side and then from society's.

Each member has abiding personal rights that society must honor and, likewise, significant responsibilities to contribute to the well-being of the whole society. As noted in chapter 2, our essential human rights bring with them corresponding responsibilities. So, our right to life and to a worthy manner of living, to respect as persons, to education and the pursuit of truth, to worship God freely and to choose a state of life, to decent work and just compensation, to organize and participate in public affairs—all must be exercised in ways that promote the same rights for others. As rights, they are responsibilities. How apt it seems that in ancient Greek political parlance *idiotes* meant someone who cared only for themselves and with no sense of responsibility to others; perhaps social isolationism is still best described by the word *idiot*.

Then, society's function is to see to it that the rights and responsibilities of its members are protected and fulfilled and in ways that contribute to the common good. The Catholic tradition of differentiating "basic justice" into three emphases helps clarify society's role in promoting social reciprocity. (I return to this in more detail in chapter 8 on justice.) Basic justice entails: *commutative justice,* requiring society to promote fundamental fairness in all exchanges between individuals; *distributive justice,* requiring society to distribute resources so that all may have what is needed for a decent quality of life; and *social justice,* requiring society to honor the rights of all to participate fully in its social life and to contribute to the common good.

In summary, for a community-of-persons sociology the resounding response to Cain's question is, "You're darn right—we are our brothers' and sisters' keepers, as well as our own."

Some of the Theological and Historical Story

Catholic Christianity finds the roots of a community-of-persons sociology in its traditional theology and interpretation of Scripture. However, as evident, all three of the previous points translate readily into a social outlook that could be embraced on philosophical grounds. In fact, as ever, Catholicism's interpretation of both Scripture and Tradition is greatly influenced by its sense of a natural law within the human condition that is the design of God.

It may be clarifying, however, to further elaborate a community-of-persons sociology from a theological perspective. I do so by focusing on contemporary ecclesiology—an understanding of the nature and the mission of the Church. Renewed emphasis on the Church's own communal nature and mission encourages a community-of-persons understanding of society as well.

In Hebrew faith, God called Abraham and Sarah to become "a great nation" in whom "all the communities of the earth shall find blessing" (Genesis 12:2–3). Ever after, the Hebrews were convinced that their identity was to be "the people of God"—that they were to live in covenant with God and with each other. Instead of being abolished by Jesus, this original covenant between God and the Hebrew people is "irrevocable"[10] the first covenant has never been revoked.

The Hebrews knew that their well-being—salvation—depended upon faithfulness to their communal covenant. While each member retained personal responsibility, they were held accountable as a people. Their blessings were for all; their sins were to the detriment of all; their repentance was as a community. Each individual member saw themselves as crucial to the community's keeping of the covenant with God, with every member of ultimate importance. A Hebrew person would have understood themselves as both individually and communally accountable. It was from these Hebrew roots that Christianity learned to appreciate both person and people.

New Testament scholarship has deepened the appreciation that Jesus called his followers into a community of disciples, into what the great Scripture scholar Elisabeth Schussler Fiorenza calls "a communal discipleship of equals."[11] Jesus reached out not only to mainstream people but to the excluded of society, welcoming all into a community that accentuated the equality and importance of each member.

Scholars point especially to the inclusiveness of Jesus' table fellowship—how he welcomed the socially marginalized and public sinners to eat with him. This action, in a culture for which eating together symbolized a profound bond of fellowship, became a parable in action of Jesus' commitment to an inclusive community, of his deep respect for every person, and of the modus operandi he intended among disciples.

The hallmark of Jesus' community was to be radical love—with love of God, self, and neighbor intertwined and neighbor as person-next-door and everyone else besides, including enemies. Contemporary theology has also come to keener awareness that this love command is at once a personal and social mandate—that it cannot be limited to one-on-one relationships but demands love that does justice in the public realm as well.

As cited already, the first Christian communities reflect much diversity in style and structure, but what is notable is their bondedness as disciples of Jesus. Never did they understand Christianity as an individual following of a great guru unto personal salvation. They knew that they were to be "church." Even this term that they chose to describe themselves reflects their self-understanding as community-of-persons.

When Christians began to distinguish themselves from the Jewish community of the synagogue, they choose the term *ekklesia*—which becomes the English word *church*—as their self-description. Its etymology is from *ek-kalein*, meaning "to call people together." Apparently, it was a term used in Greek politics of the time and referred to "a community of equal citizens." It would seem that the first Christians chose intentionally to emphasize the communal and personal nature of their new movement—with each member of equal "count."

The first Christians used "church" with three levels of meaning: (1) to designate an assembly of disciples for worship, as we might intend by "going to church"; (2) for the Christian community in a local place—as Paul wrote, "to the church of God that is in Corinth" (1 Corinthians 1:2); and (3) most generically, for "the whole universal community of believers."[12] Note that all three of its meanings— assembly, local, and universal—have the communal emphasis.

When the early Christians began to reflect on the nature of their Church, they resorted to images—again, choosing all communal ones. I already highlighted Paul's beautiful image of Church as the Body of Christ. Another early favorite was "Temple of the Holy Spirit." Taking the metaphor of temple as the special dwelling place of God, the Christian community realized that it was like an edifice indwelt by God's Holy Spirit, with each member being a stone upon another. A favorite, too, was "new people of God." They borrowed this communal image from the Hebrew Scriptures, with "new" signaling awareness that the covenant with Israel had not been revoked. In fact, all the great images of the Christian Church throughout history have been communal ones.[13]

The Church claims that there is a divine dimension to its nature (e.g., Body of Christ)—that it is "of God." But at least in its better moments, Catholicism avoids "church-idolatry"—as if it is an end in itself, without human limitations or need of reform. Augustine wrote eloquently of the Church as the "corpus Christi" but also recognized it as a "corpus mixtum"—a "mixed body" of saints and sinner.

Augustine, too, distinguished between the "visible" and the "invisible" church—one the official public structure; the other, the spiritual communion of faithful people. He said that oftentimes the "visible" church is a poor expression of the "true church" of faithful Christians who live for the reign of God. The Church does best when it maintains such a balanced attitude toward itself and avoids inflating its own importance. Often, it has not been so wise nor so honest.

The Protestant Reformers, led by Martin Luther and John Calvin (sixteenth century), had eminent good cause to revolt. Apart from doctrinal differences, the Church was dreadfully in need of institutional reform. They rightly challenged its corruption, authoritarianism, and exaggerated sense of its own importance—for acting as if it were replacing rather than representing Jesus Christ, as if it controlled rather than mediated God's grace, as if it could tell the Holy Spirit where to blow, whereas, like the wind, God's Spirit "blows where she will." (See John 3:8.)

Understandably, then, the Reformers de-emphasized the role of the Church as mediator between God and people. They championed the rights of individual Christians to read and interpret Scripture for themselves and to bypass Church control in their pieties and go directly to God. In this, they did an extraordinary service to the emerging human consciousness of the Western world. The "modern era" would not have been possible without the Reformation's advance of personal responsibility and the rights of the individual person—values that the Church should have been championing.

When Catholicism regrouped at the Council of Trent (1545–63), it was sobered by the challenge of the Reformers and determined to put its own reforms in place. Trent reiterated the original Christian conviction that everyone should have a personal relationship with God. But rejecting the tendency toward individualism it perceived in the Reformers, Trent strongly reaffirmed the centrality of the Church for living in Christian faith. Though sometimes more honored in the breach than in the observance, Catholic Christianity has continued since then to emphasize both personal discipleship and Christian community, instead of an either/or stance choosing both/and.

A rather extraordinary symbol of Catholicism's insistence upon a community-of-persons ecclesiology—and thus sociology—was its reiteration at the Council of Trent of the "communion of saints and sinners," representing the somewhat radical notion that the community of faith reaches beyond the grave, that even death cannot break the bond of baptism.

Since the early Church, Christians had had the belief and various pious practices attendant to it that the living can pray to the saints and for the souls. The saints—who are in God's presence and with Mary having pride of place as the mother of Jesus—can pray to God for particular people, much as living people might pray for each other. Then, for departed "souls" who need preparation before entering

God's eternal presence, the living can pray or do a work of mercy or love or justice on their behalf, and somehow it can pertain to their benefit.

Practices associated with the communion of saints and sinners have led to many abuses, including at times the appearance of the Church buying and selling salvation. In general, the Reformers rejected the whole practice. The scandal of taking money for "indulgences"—benefit to the dead—was the last straw for Luther, causing him to put a match to the powder keg that became the Reformation.

Although challenged to reform the pastoral abuses associated with this piety, Catholicism continued in the conviction that the bond of baptism and of Christian community transcends even the grave. Perhaps the sentiment that underlies remembering the dead in prayer strikes a deep cord in the heart of the living for more than half of humankind has some such practice. It remains a striking symbol of the communalism of Catholic Christianity.

After the Council of Trent and feeling under siege, the Catholic church took on a defensive posture about its institutional structure. It put new emphasis on the "hierarchical" nature of the church, with the great theologian of the Counter-Reformation era, Robert Bellarmine (1542–1621), proposing that it is a "perfect society"—thus beyond questioning or need of reform. The aftermath of Trent also saw far greater emphasis than ever before on the church's clerical leaders, on their sacramental power and their authority to teach and rule. *The Catechism of the Council of Trent*—typically called *The Roman Catechism*—stated that, "Priests and bishops are, as it were, the interpreters and messengers of God, commissioned in his name to teach men [sic] the divine law. They act in this world as the very person of God. Rightly have they been called angels (Micah 2:7), even gods (Exodus 22:28) . . . ."[14] One may understand this exaggerated clericalism as an over-reaction to the Reformers' revival of the "priesthood of all believers," yet it threatened the communal nature of the church, encouraging an all-male oligarchy more than a "community of equal disciples."

Despite the threats from patriarchy and hierarchism, Catholicism's communal emphasis survived in the ethnic churches of the common people. Perhaps it was the blend of culture and faith—a theme we take up in the next chapter—that gave Catholic Christians a sense of bondedness as community. Whatever it was, the role of the Church in the work of salvation and its essential social nature as a community-of-persons has survived some mighty tests.

Scholars are unanimous that the Second Vatican Council brought renewed commitment to a communal ecclesiology. Even the sequence of chapters in its "Dogmatic Constitution on the Church" signals the Council's overall championing of Church as community. The document offers the primary description of Church as "The People of God" (chapter 2), and only then moves to consider its "hierarchical structure" (chapter 3).

This sequence was hotly debated because the intent was precisely to emphasize the Church as community, with the hierarchy serving the people, and to lay to rest the hierarchism that defines the Church as its leaders and the people as their dependents. Further, the Council insisted that the hierarchy should function with collegiality—communally—rather than by chain of command.

Note, too, that Vatican II was strongly ecumenical in its understanding of the Church, insisting that all baptized Christians—Catholic and Protestant—form a community of the one Body of Christ in the world. "All those justified by faith through baptism are incorporated into Christ."[15] The Council reaffirmed that the Holy Spirit guides and sanctifies through this whole Christian Church—not just through the Catholic expression of it.

In addition, the Council reclaimed the significance of baptism for all Christians, making clear once again that by baptism, and according to charism and state of life, each disciple is to participate fully in the ministry and mission of the Church in the world. The Christian community is every Christian's business, rather than a "service station" of a few providers and many dependents. The council declared:

> Incorporated into Christ's Mystical Body through baptism and strengthened by the power of the Holy Spirit through confirmation, the laity are assigned to the apostolate by the Lord himself. They are consecrated into a royal priesthood and a holy people in order that they may offer spiritual sacrifices through everything they do, and may witness to Christ throughout the world.[16]

It would seem that both the nature and the purpose of the Church is to be a bonded community of Jesus' disciples that live for the reign of God in the world.

Let us now review more precisely how the Church as community-of-persons is to fulfill its mission—its purpose in the world. I summarize this briefly since it will be relevant to a philosophy of education.

Within the overarching purpose of God's reign, the early Christians saw the Church as having specific tasks or ministries. Their categorizing has endured the test of time. Though variously listed from three to six, I offer a fivefold schema, using the ancient Greek terms by which they were first named. The Church has the ministries of:

- *Koinonia* (a *welcoming* community): to be an inclusive community of faith, hope, and love; a truly "catholic" community that welcomes all with a fundamental equality and mutuality, and invites each one's gifts into shared mission as members of the Body of Christ.

- *Kerygma* (a *word*-of-God community): to preach and evangelize, and to teach (*didache*) God's word in Jesus and about Jesus recounted in the New Testament; the word of God encountered through the Hebrew Scriptures; and the "word of God" mediated through Christian tradition.

- *Leitourgia* (a *worshipping* community): to publicly worship God as an assembly of Christian faith, celebrating God's covenant with humanity through Jesus Christ and the universal hope of salvation for all humankind.

- *Diakonia* (a community of *welfare*): to care for human needs—spiritual, psychological, and physical—helping to build God's reign of peace and justice at every level of human existence, personal and social, with a special favor for "the poor" and the disadvantaged.

- *Marturia* (a *witnessing* community): to bear credible public witness to Christian faith through lifestyle and example, living as a sacrament—as an effective sign—of its own preaching, even to the point of suffering and death if necessary.

When such understanding of the Church's nature and mission is translated into a sociological statement—without theological language—it calls for a community of persons that serves both personal and common good as one, that welcomes the gifts of all, that offers life-giving word in its language world, that ritualizes its identity in empowering ways, that works for the welfare of each one and everyone, and that gives credible witness to core values that humanize. While no school, parish program, nor family will ever be "perfect" in its communal life, every educational venture can allow such a community-of-persons sociology to permeate its curriculum, and especially its quality of shared life.

For Teachers and Parents

What does a community-of-persons sociology mean for the educational work of teachers and parents? What does it ask of their souls, recommend for their teaching style, and suggest for their crafting of educational space? I make a few proposals; you will add insights from and for your own social context. First, take time to reflect on some of your responses to a community-of-persons sociology.

For Reflection

- What has clarified about your own operative sociology from dialogue with the preceding reflections? What agreements or disagreements stand out? Any need for adjustments emerging?

- If an educator is committed to educating for a community-of-persons, what might this mean for one's soul? For teaching style? For the educational environment of home, school, or parish?

- In your social context, what adjustments would a common-good perspective recommend?

For the Educator's Soul

A community-of-persons sociology suggests one general commitment for the souls of teachers and parents, and one that pertains more directly to their educating.

In general, *teachers and parents need to commit themselves to the "common good" as integral with the personal good of their learners.*

Surely, every teacher and parent intends the personal well-being of their learners—that they may fulfill basic needs for food and shelter, for safety and security, for worthwhile work and sustaining relationships, and beyond needs to become fully alive human beings. But a community-of-persons sociology requires educators to see such eminently appropriate intentions as integral with the common good of society.

Fulfilled human beings are also good citizens, for there is a symbiosis between the personal and the communal. This represents a profound shift in consciousness for educators in societies that have weighed the scales to heavily favor individual rights, competition, and taking care of oneself alone. Intertwining personal and social good is in contrast to the philosophy of modernism, which champions the ideal of the autonomous self—the person as self-determining subject who exists independent of community.

There is an ancient tradition in both East and West of officially classifying teachers as "public servants," highlighting the sociopolitical nature of their vocation. Regretfully, Western society has ceased to have this expectation of its teachers and, likewise, no longer appreciates the social significance—the political nature—of what they do.

For teachers to recenter their purpose in the common good could have a transforming effect on Western society—permeating what, how, why, and where they teach. No one captured more forcefully the vocation of teacher as public servant than John Dewey. As a rousing finale to his "Pedagogical Creed"—the summary of his entire educational philosophy—Dewey wrote,

> I believe, finally, that the teacher is engaged, not simply in the training of individuals, but in the formation of the proper social life. I believe that every teacher should realize the dignity of [her or his] calling; that [he or she] is a social servant set apart for the maintenance of proper social order and the securing of the right social growth. I believe that in this way the teacher always is the prophet

of the true God, and the usherer in of the true kingdom of God.[17]

Note well Dewey's merging from social purpose into Transcendent ground for it—and some claim he was an agnostic!

Even more neglected now in the West is the ancient notion that parents serve the common good precisely by how they raise their children. A spate of Enlightenment philosophers, prominently the Frenchman Jean-Jacques Rousseau, proposed that the public and private spheres should be kept separate, with the citizen belonging to the public state and the individual to the private family—forgetting that the citizen and individual are but aspects of one person. However, their proposal found acceptance and permeated social thought.

Now, contemporary thinkers, most notably feminists, are trying to undo such naiveté, insisting that "the private is political" in the sense that the quality of people's private lives always impinges upon the common good of all.

In contrast, the East never lost the correlation of private and public realms. Confucius saw education as primarily the responsibility of parents and as an eminently sociopolitical process precisely because the quality of education is the touchstone of the public life of society. For Confucius, the most effective service parents can render to the common good is to raise their children well. Asian cultures, in general, have never lost this social understanding of parental responsibility. The West must relearn it!

Teachers and parents need to become keenly conscious again of the "civic" aspect of their vocation and intentional about educating for the common good. This means educating learners to contribute to society rather than simply to receive its services, to fulfill their civic duties with generosity rather than with legal minimum. It means educating in ways likely to form character in the personal-cum-social values of honesty, loyalty, and integrity, in seeking justice and making peace; in democratic values like the rule of law and respect for government, equality of opportunity and due process for all, in exercising franchise as an informed citizen, to appreciate public discourse and reasoned argument. Teachers and parents committed to the common good will develop in learners compassion for the poor and opposition to all forms of social oppression and discrimination.

Education for the common good also includes nurturing in learners a critical social consciousness. It is indeed possible for educators to be co-opted by social interests that would reduce education for citizenship to preparing learners to simply "fit" into the socioeconomic status quo, to maintain the sociocultural milieu as is. But this is social domestication rather than education for the common good. The latter encourages learners to become agents of social transformation—precisely as good citizens. This requires teachers and parents to encourage learners in thinking critically about their social context, to be alert to detect injustice, discrimination, and oppression and committed to oppose such social evils.

Teachers in schools can certainly educate for the common good, but parents may be even more influential in this regard. When I trace the genesis of whatever level of commitment to the common good I actually live by and the modicum of social consciousness reflected in my life, the influence of my father looms large. He spent most of his public career in professional politics, and his life reflected passionate commitment to the common good.

In conversations around the dinner table or by a winter's night fire, he was the first person I heard speak against—and vehemently— every form of discrimination or sectarianism, to defend the rights of workers, to question industrialization that threatened the environment, and to raise many other social issues. He was a parent educator deeply committed to the common good—and at least a little rubbed off!

Given the symbiosis in Catholicism between sociology and ecclesiology, we should raise here what commitment to the common good might mean for *religious educators* apropos the life of the Church itself. (That they must be committed to the good of society will be emphasized again in chapter 8 under justice.) Whether in parish catechetical programs or religiously sponsored schools, Christian religious educators are to serve the common good of the Church itself in at least three ways.

First, they are to nurture learners in ecclesial identity—in a sense of belonging to and being responsible for the life of the Church. Such particular identity must be achieved without encouraging sectarianism—teaching the universality of God's love and that God's family is all humankind.

Second, the common good of the Church requires religious educators to prepare and encourage learners to contribute their gifts to the mission of the Christian community—welcome, witness, word, worship, and welfare—to be active and contributing members according to their charisms and circumstances.

And third, religious educators should foster social consciousness about the life of the Church itself, encouraging learners to be both appreciative of its assets and critical of its shortcomings, to commit themselves to its constant reformation to be a more adequate sacrament of God's reign in the world. For religious educators to encourage learners to tolerate sinfulness within the structures of the Church—e.g., sexism or racism—would be treasonous to their ministry.

Shifting now to a commitment for the educator's soul focused specifically on curriculum, *let educators proceed in ways that foster cooperation and partnership among learners—that form them for "right relationship" in every context of life.*

This proposal could certainly be dismissed as naive, as the antithesis of what predominates in Western education. A substantial literature portrays contemporary schooling as marked by rampant individualism and competition, as focused on serving the interests of unbridled capitalism[18] and creating what the prophetic educator Jonathan Kozol has portrayed—the title of one of his books—as *Savage Inequalities* throughout society.

In general I am sympathetic to this critique of much of Western education, but I remain optimistic and can find significant signs of hope. Some of the most promising literature in contemporary education is on collaborative and cooperative approaches to teaching—getting people to learn together in partnership and so being formed in "right relationship" for life.[19] Surprisingly, such educational shift is finding supporting sentiment within the commercial, industrial, and military establishments. All the best literature on business leadership, for example, emphasizes getting people to work in partnership, encouraging employees to contribute their gifts more than fulfill a function, to work as a team.[20] Even the U.S. military has begun to encourage "total quality management"—the code term in leadership literature for cooperation and partnership.

As societies become more diverse and specialized, people learning to work together becomes even more imperative. There is a pragmatism to a cooperative mode of educating in modern societies. Educators need to foster partnership among learners by their very way of teaching. How else can they form them as citizens for the common good, to live in "right relationship" wherever they find themselves? Every teacher and parent can invite learners to work together and help each other out, can discourage isolationism and avoid setting up competition for its own sake.

I know of a high-school religion teacher who enters into learning contracts with her class. One of the conditions for successful completion is that every class member clearly understand and be able to take an informed position on a variety of religious teachings and practices. As long as anyone in the class fails the test, the class has not fulfilled its learning contract. The result is that everyone takes on responsibility to help everyone else until the class contract is fulfilled. She says that the process encourages an amazing level of partnership, making the method integral to the content being taught.

For the Educator's Style

Turning now more specifically to teaching style, a community-of-persons sociology recommends that educators *adopt a general approach of conversation.*

This proposal, too, is counter-cultural to the expected language pattern of teaching and, perhaps, parenting. There is an enduring stereotype that "teaching is telling," with teachers talking "at" students rather than "with" them or they with each other. A commonplace finding of social researchers is that the quantity and quality of conversation in Western families is abysmally low. Whether the deterrents be television, busy lives, or generation gap, there is little conversation happening in our homes, and the consequences can be grave.

There are warning signs, for example, that the lack of communication with and among teenagers contributes to drug and alcohol abuse, heightened crime rate, and destructive behavior— toward others and self. Conversely, there is growing evidence that young people learn best through conversation some of the most important social habits and lessons of life—the ability to cope with stress and fear, to handle rejection or failure, to let go of hurts and anger, to handle freedom and express affection appropriately.

Teachers and parents committed to a community-of-persons sociology have pragmatic as well as philosophical reasons for adopting conversation as their general educational style—thus forming learners in the practice of conversation themselves.

First note that all teaching is essentially a "language event"—a crafted discourse with language patterns that reflect and mediate a "world of meaning." This is especially true in the humanities, but education in the sciences, the arts, and even in trades and manual skills creates its own "language worlds"—to an outsider or neophyte, sounding like a code—with numerous technical terms used to communicate information, exchange, explanation, critique, and encouragement. Typically, the educator has the most influence on the pattern of language within any educational event and, therefore, has the most responsibility for its quality.

Second, contemporary thought is marked by keen awareness of the power of language, not only to express ourselves, but to shape our very selves as well. Truth is that language is the primary means of socialization. We make our own the world around us, taking in its perspectives and values, as we learn its language and the patterns of it. The German philosopher Martin Heidegger (1889–1976) summarized this insight with the incisive phrase, "Language is the house of Being," meaning that the language world in which we dwell shapes who we become and how we live.[21]

It would seem imperative, then, that educators take great care about the language world they create by their teaching. With words their "tool-of-trade," likely nothing has more influence on learners than the language educators use, the language patterns and exchanges they encourage. At a minimum, this requires teachers and parents to use language that affirms the dignity, equality, and value of all people. They should avoid words and language patterns that disvalue or degrade; that shame or demean; that are chauvinistic, oppressive, or exclusive on any basis; that are mechanistic, controlling, or manipulative.[22] Beyond this, given the formative power of language and what would seem called for by a community-of-persons sociology, I propose that educators consider a general language style of conversation.

I deliberately use the word *conversation* instead of *discussion* because the latter, regretfully, has become associated as a fad of the

'60s for rambling free-for-alls, endless chitchats, sitting and shooting the breeze—something that "just happens" without language rules, structure, or intentionality.

Another debilitating stereotype is discussion as *everyone talking*— usually "off-the-top-of-their-heads"—as if listening, intuiting, reflecting, probing, testing, researching, and reading are not integral to good conversation. A participant once approached me as I was about to begin a day-long seminar with religious educators and said, sounding apprehensive, "I hope we won't be having a lot of discussion—I'm here to hear you!" I responded, "Well, I will do lots of talking and listening, but I hope the entire event will be a conversation for all of us." He seemed relieved, at least enough to stay on. Then my responsibility was to structure the event to encourage conversation throughout and that requires as much intentionality and craft as any other style of teaching.

Conversation

Conversation in its most precise sense is people having face-to-face personal exchanges with each other, but note that the underlying dynamic can include any kind of reflective expression and reception. Let us begin with the specific and then move to the broader sense of conversation.

Conversation is not easy to describe, much less to define. Yet we always know when we have been in a good one. It engages us personally, we feel listened to and we listen ourselves, we are stimulated by its "to-and-fro," enriched by its "give-and-take." We can get "caught up" in a really good conversation—loose track of time, have a sense of adventure—risking the possible outcome.

Jurgen Habermas, a German philosopher who writes extensively on communication, says that true conversation requires at least four commitments of participants: (1) to pursue the truth; (2) to be honest in what they share; (3) to avoid attempts to manipulate, dominate, or control the outcome; and (4) never to force agreement other than by genuine persuasion.[23] Habermas admits that these conditions are never realized perfectly, but they remain the defining ideal for every conversation.

Can such conversation be even remotely approximated in a typical classroom or around a family meal or in the religious education of a faith community? Yes, and teachers and parents, with a bit of intentionality, can help it happen. At the beginning of my own courses, I invite participants into a mode of conversation and often share a handout with suggestions for "practicing" it—the only way to learn any art. These include:

- Be "out there" making things happen rather than sitting back and letting others carry the ball.

- Welcome the opportunity to work in partnership with others.

- Be open to share your thoughts and, as comfortable, your feelings.

- Recognize everyone as a resource and welcome the contributions of all.

- Be willing to truly listen to people—more than just hearing them but listening "between the lines" and with empathy—even if their perspective is very different from your own.

- Try not to dominate or to talk too much.

- Help to draw out other people, enabling them to express what they know or want to share.

- Practice speaking clearly, concisely, and without repetition.

- Appreciate all contributions and let people know that they are being heard.

- When you disagree, as you must when that is your sentiment, do it respectfully.

- Don't try to control how the conversation turns out.

- Be faithful to your own point of view, but open to change your mind as well.

One could respond to such a list as suited to graduate courses but impossible in a grade-school classroom or for the language pattern of a family. But surely every educator can find ways to encourage conversation; each must stop to imagine what might be effective in their own context. This seems more feasible, too, if we broaden beyond face-to-face exchange and recognize that conversation begins with oneself, in the ruminations of our own minds and hearts—a point also emphasized by Habermas.

It is significant that the Greek *dialogismos*—the same root as *dialogos* (conversation)—means one's own thoughts. When our own thinking process starts rolling, are we not literally "talking to ourselves"? Oh, to really know what we think needs the testing and clarifying of sharing with others and hearing what they are thinking. But anything that encourages learners to think for themselves and bring their reflections to expression falls within the ambit of a conversational style of teaching.

Now the possibilities broaden to include methods like the following:

- asking questions that "draw out" (*e-ducare*—educate) what learners know, feel, and do;

- inviting people to share their work and their reflections on it;

- encouraging students to "carry on a conversation" with what they are reading or finding in their research— their own figuring out of what things mean;

- fostering genuine listening to other people—trying to really hear what they are saying;

- testing out with others what one is "coming to see" and the decisions one is making.

I know a high-school religion teacher who was committed to a conversational style but, not unusual, met great resistance from reticent teenagers—especially about matters religious. Before giving up the effort, he introduced a fairly formal program of having them keep a journal of their participation in the course—with an explanation of its possibilities, how and what to write about—and giving them the option of submitting their journal as a course assignment. At least, they began to ruminate about their lives and express themselves somehow, and, by his account, with some heartening outcomes. And you can add to the list of "conversation starters" from your own experience. The key is for educators to take on the mind-set of conversation and then to imagine how to get learners to at least be in conversation with themselves and to bring their reflections to some kind of expression.

Let us now take two "hard cases" in which it could be difficult for educators to imagine proceeding by a conversation style of teaching: events of direct instruction or lecturing and the process of reading a textbook.

Conversation through a Disclosure Presentation

Research on teaching indicates that lecturing and didaction are good for some educational purposes and poor for others. In high-school and college teaching, for example, lecturing is not good for personal appropriation or formation or for bringing people to their own positions. Yet it can be effective for giving an overview of something, for lending a sense of the "big picture." Lecturing can give ready access to research findings, to general principles, and to basic information on which students can build their own research and reflections.[24]

Far from ruling out lecture or didaction, a conversational style requires that when teachers think "presentation" they also imagine how to craft it as a conversation. From experience I am convinced that the best of lecturing is done by talking with rather than at people—by crossing over into their mind-set, ever engaging them as active participants, albeit without their talking much.

Regarding lecturing, it may be helpful to distinguish between a *closure* and a *disclosure* mode of presentation.[25] The closure style tries to say it all and definitively, telling people what to think and how to think it, delivering rather than revealing. The disclosure mode is more suggestive than definitive, opening things up and inviting people to think for themselves.

Disclosure helps people to discover what they already know, to notice what may have been hidden or only implicit. It reveals in the etymological sense of "pulling back the curtain." It stimulates people to think, remember, and imagine, to understand, judge, and decide. A disclosure style of presentation is a form of conversation. If you remember an effective lecture you heard recently, one that really "got you thinking," I will wager that you experienced it as a kind of conversation.

Disclosure style lecturers tend to use lots of images and examples, metaphors and analogies, stories and parables—whatever literary forms help to personally engage people, to get them to think for themselves. Their statements are more suggestive than exhaustive, they invite our own thoughts more than acceptance of theirs, they avoid pronouncements "from on high" and make proposals for consideration instead.

In my own style of presentation, I usually begin by trying to engage participants with the core theme of the occasion. Before proceeding with my reflections, I pause and invite people to first note their own and—if time permits—to express their sentiments to a neighbor (allowing some quiet time for writing their thoughts can alleviate anxiety about sharing).

Next, I encourage participants to bring these initial thoughts and reflections into dialogue with what I have to propose. As I proceed and attempt to make a disclosure-type presentation, I find that an occasional phrase like "I'm wondering what you're thinking, and we'll pause soon to hear" encourages people to "keep the conversation going" throughout. If time permits, pausing often to hear some of their reflections is ideal. At the end of such a lecture, instead of "inviting questions," I ask, in some form, "What are you thinking now?" On my better days, at least, participants usually experience such a presentational event as a kind of conversation.

Conversation with a Textbook

And what of reading textbooks; so much curriculum in Western education is focused on assigned readings. Here again, it is possible to encourage a conversation-like exchange with written texts, or with other symbolic expressions, e.g., art pieces. Hans Gadamer, the great philosopher of hermeneutics whom I introduced in chapter 1, argues that the most appropriate way to approach a text of any kind is as a "conversation."[26] He counsels against the belligerent approach of trying to "master" the text and recommends entering into a relationship with it, setting up a "to-and-fro" in which one brings one's own life to the text and the wisdom of the text to one's own life.

Gadamer says that conversation between reader and text is stimulated best by good questions—along the lines of asking "What am I bringing to this text?" "What do I find in it?" and "What does it mean for my/our life?" In this exchange, the reader questions the text and is questioned by it. "The essence of the question," writes Gadamer, "is to open up possibilities and keep them open."[27] The broader point implied here is that learners can have access by a mode of conversation to traditions of knowledge, wisdom, and aesthetic in the sciences, humanities, and arts—which I elaborate in the next chapter.

In summary, every teacher and parent can take on the general mind-set of a style of conversation—of talking *with* rather than *at* learners. How this unfolds will undoubtedly vary greatly from first grade to a doctoral seminar, between an undergraduate math class and an adult Bible study in a parish. But every teacher and parent can make the paradigm shift from "teaching as telling" toward "creating conversation."

For the Teaching Space

By way of educational environment, a community-of-persons sociology self-evidently recommends *that every teaching/learning context—school, family, and parish program—strive to be a life-giving community, fostering personal growth and the common good.* Given the differences between school, parish, and family contexts, it seems wise to separate out the reflections on each. Without trying to be exhaustive and for the sake of brevity I focus primarily on the school—and the public school—environment. I begin with a general note about Catholic schools.

Catholic schools should be communities that form students to be citizens who care for the common good and people of faith identity committed to the reign of God in the world—the two functioning as one social commitment enlivened by faith. The Second Vatican Council stated that a Catholic school should teach students "to take their part in social life . . . and be willing to act energetically on behalf of the common good." Regarding faith formation, the Council said that the "school community" must be "an atmosphere enlivened by the gospel spirit of freedom and love" that nurtures the Christian identity of its students.[28]

Whether or not Catholic schools fulfill these formation responsibilities to society and church, depends, first and foremost, on whether or not they create real community—of citizenship and of faith—within the school environment. And, it should be noted, there is indeed some empirical evidence that Catholic schools generally achieve a high level of civic and faith community.[29]

But there is exigency on every school to build up community, because the "implicit" curriculum of school life as well as the "explicit" one taught in the classroom is significant for formation. In the United States, there is mounting evidence that creating civic and humane community within public schools has fallen on hard times to the detriment of their social effectiveness. Writing in 1894, John Dewey sounded the clarion call that schools must be democratic communities in order to educate citizens for a democratic society.[30] But sadly, one hundred years later, and summarizing much empirical evidence, the educational researchers Bryk, Lee, and Holland write, "The public schools have become increasingly private, turning away from the basic social and political purposes that once lent them the title of 'common school.'"[31]

Regardless of the sociocultural reasons for this state of affairs, public schools must redouble efforts to create community within their environment in order to prepare citizens who serve the common good of society.

I noted previously that the mission of a Christian faith community entails the functions of word, welcome, witness, welfare, and worship. A Catholic school cannot and should not try to be the equivalent of a parish, yet in its own way—as a school—it can approximate these five functions. Perhaps these functions, too, reflect the purposes of every bonded community, and fulfilling them can encourage community life in any school. So, instead of elaborating around religiously based schools, I will focus on schools in general, and especially American public schools. It may be stretching a bit, but let us see how any school might fulfill the equivalent of these five functions to the enhancement of its community life. If we find *word, welcome, witness, welfare* and *worship* relevant to the life of public schools, they apply self-evidently to religiously sponsored ones.

Word

Every school is a "language world" and its quality as a "house of being" (Heidegger's phrase) greatly affects the "being" of participants.

Beyond this, much of a school's educating is focused on "the word," beginning with learning the rudiments and then practicing the basic arts of the word—reading, writing, and rhetoric.

I earlier accented the responsibility of teachers and parents to take great care with their personal language because of its formative power on learners. This proposal can be pushed to the total school environment. schools must try to create a community of discourse *for life for all.* Every school should be a language world that teaches the dignity and equality of each person; that nurtures the holistic growth of students and heightens their self-esteem; that encourages respect for society, stewardship of creation, and care for the common good.

The primary purpose of a school's curriculum of reading, writing, and rhetoric should be to humanize the person and advance the common good. Such life-giving intent can be reflected throughout the curriculum, even in the way that schools teach and practice the arts of the word. Let us take reading as an example or, more precisely, teaching basic literacy.

The great Brazilian educator Paulo Freire heightened awareness that literacy can be taught in a humanizing or domesticating way, to enhance or diminish the person and the common good. His point was that literacy can be taught as a nonreflective technical skill, enabling people to recognize the correct words for the corresponding markings and thus readying them to consume written texts; this he saw as domesticating. On the other hand, literacy can be taught in ways that encourage people to think for themselves, to read and interpret not only the phonics of written words, but also the life and world represented by the words; this Freire saw as humanizing.

If there is a "politics" to the methods of basic literacy—a central theme of Freire's—then surely every aspect of a school's language world deserves to be scrutinized often for its life-giving and community-building quality. A teacher friend tells of coming to realize that his language pattern implied that students were machines—like giving "input," inviting "feedback," "cranking it out," "being on the right track," "cracking" the problem, and more. He ceased and switched to humanizing language instead—"sharing ideas," "inviting reflection," and so on. His shift and what it implies for education should be reflected throughout the language world—the word—of every school.

Welcome

Every school should be a hospitable community for its students, faculty, and staff, one where everyone can feel at home. No one should be excluded or discriminated against on any basis—race or ethnic background, sex or sexual orientation, religious affiliation, physical condition, social class, or economic bracket. A school that practices social bias or promotes sectarianism defeats its very purpose of the common good.

When available, a school should welcome the opportunity offered by cultural diversity among its population. How enriching it is for students to encounter firsthand expressions of culture—arts, traditions, and ways of making meaning—other than their own. It encourages the mutual respect and conversation needed for the "global village."

With a bit of imagination and initiative, a school can build up a supporting community around itself, with parents and families of students, with alumni/ae and neighbors. This is "social capital" that could be of great value to schools but is often not developed or left untapped. For instance: schools can encourage and help families to become partners in the educational process; they can provide opportunities for continuing education in the neighborhood; they can lend facilities for worthwhile neighborhood events. As the teacher is a "public servant," the school as an institution can be likewise, beginning with its local community.

Witness

The witness asked of schools is that they practice what they preach. In its explicit curriculum, a school may teach students to live by great personal and social values like honesty, truth-telling, civility, justice, respect, and compassion, but if these values do not permeate the life of the school itself and how it functions daily, it will be ineffective— perhaps even counterproductive—in character formation. Thomas Lickona, an insightful author on "character education," writes, "The way a school is run . . . is the most important kind of character education it provides."[32] He adds,

> Schools, if they wish to develop character . . . must
> provide a moral environment that accents good values
> and keeps them in the forefront of everyone's

consciousness. It takes a long time for a value to become a virtue. . . . The whole school environment, the moral culture of the school, has to support that growth.[33]

Every school should look regularly at its whole environment and review its many aspects for integrity with the values the school intends to teach. I suspect, however, that the touchstone of the moral culture of a school is how it administers discipline. This measures the school's integrity and effectiveness in forming students in a host of the great virtues, including justice and nonviolence, respect and responsibility, mercy and compassion.

A. worked at D. Boys' Home, an orphanage school in a poor country. Its boys come from the streets or are referred by the courts and social agencies. For five years he protested the school's use of corporal punishment, that it lacked integrity to the school's Catholic identity. Finally, more as a way to silence him, the school allowed him to take on responsibility for discipline.

A. announced an end to all physical punishment and set up a "dare-to-be-your-best" challenge program. He found ways to reward every boy—for completing homework, trying hard at band practice, taking care of personal hygiene, looking out for someone in need. Discipline infringements dropped dramatically and a great community spirit emerged. The program transformed the school—for a while. It was dropped when A. left, and the school returned to violence and fear as means of discipline. How sad!

The moral environment of a school, of course, is built up from that of its classrooms—so crucial to moral formation. Drawing upon extensive research, Lickona writes that it is simple enough to create a moral community in the classroom—the three basic conditions being:

> (1) Students know each other . . . (2) respect, affirm, and care about each other . . . (3) feel membership in, and responsibility to, the group.[34]

Surely, every teacher can help students in the same class to know each other, to be respectful and caring, and to actively participate. And as in the school environment, discipline is likely the measure of the moral culture of a classroom. The French sociologist Émile Durkheim wrote insightfully, "Discipline is not a simple device for securing superficial peace in the classroom; it is the morality of the classroom as a small society."[35] How true!

My friend Sr. Mary Gervasie has an extraordinary reputation as a grade-school teacher, having taught at every grade level during her fifty-year career. I once asked her about discipline. She responded, "Never a problem," and explained: "At the beginning of every year, I welcomed them to 'Sunshine Valley.' Then I invited them to make up the rules that would keep it a sunshine place all year. They would begin—no laughing at other people's mistakes, wait to take turns, listen to each other, try to work well together. When they had agreed upon the list, I would post them where all could see. Then I put them in charge of enforcing their own rules." What an ingenious strategy—nurturing their moral formation by putting them in charge of classroom discipline!

Welfare

Essentially, every school exists to care for human welfare—through education. This is an obvious point worth restating: to educate is an eminent human service. From a Christian perspective, education can well be named a social ministry. I once had a young Jesuit tell me he was "getting out of education to get into social ministry."

I cautioned, "Why not say you're changing your form of social ministry?"

He thought about it and agreed. In this light, a school is a "welfare agency"—educating precisely to care for personal and social welfare.

The school must be a community of consistent care for all its students and staff, and for the neighborhood and world outside of it—the most effective way to turn students into caring people. There has been some debate among educators whether becoming too concerned about students' welfare can distract a school from its primary purpose—academics. But showing care is necessary to nurturing character, which is integral to good education.

There is no conflict here, for good academics and character formation support each other. Lickona reports a survey of elementary and secondary schools which shows that good schools "excel in fostering both student character and academic excellence"; and the top ones have many things in common, among them "a stress on conduct that is considerate of the welfare of others."[36]

Through service programs, schools can form students to care for the common good and render a service to their surrounding community as well. Such programs have been a standard aspect of parish programs and Catholic schools for some time. Now more and more public schools are developing programs of outreach into the local community—of compassion, charity, and justice.

I know of first graders who have partnered themselves with residents of a local retirement home, fifth graders who have an elaborate system for collecting and distributing clothing to the poor, adolescents who have a big brother/sister program with younger children who need it, and university students who spend their vacations helping build houses in poor areas. With a bit of imagination and organization, every school can have service programs—as much for the formation of its own students as for helping those in need.

Worship or Ritual

Of all functions in my fivefold schema—borrowed from the listing of Christian ministries—I admit that this one, at first blush, invites the biggest "stretch" apropos public schools. First, let me make a parenthetical point about worship in religiously sponsored schools. No one would question that Catholic and all religiously sponsored schools should be places of word (God's Word as well as human ones), welcome, witness, and welfare. But their function as places of worship cannot be taken for granted, with some sentiment that worship is better kept to the parish or congregation.

I propose that every Catholic and religiously sponsored school should have a vibrant worship life, with ample opportunities for student liturgies, times of prayer and reflection (e.g., retreats), and be suffused with religious symbols that nurture the faith identity of students. To provide opportunities for worship would seem integral to the raison d'être of such schools as places of spiritual and faith formation. Beyond offering opportunity for worship within its own life, a religiously sponsored school should also help to form students, in the words of Vatican II, for "full, conscious and active participation" in the liturgical life of their parish or congregation.

Apropos public schools and worship, instead of digressing into the quagmire politics of "school prayer" I draw attention to the symbols and rituals that permeate the life of every school. Some of these border on the religious in that they provide an anchor (*re-ligare*) for the vision and ethos of the school. From orientation to graduation and at many ritualized moments in between, every school has its communal rituals and distinctive ways of observing them. And just walk down the corridor of any school and notice its identifying symbols that are displayed, some of them enshrined. These will reveal much about the life of the school and what it teaches to be of value.

I once visited two high schools in the same vicinity on the same day. Upon entering the first, a renowned sports powerhouse, I was arrested by the huge trophy display case that dominates the lobby. There could be no doubt about the altar at which this school worships. Along the first corridor were photos of former coaches, graduates who became famous athletes, current team captains—the school's pantheon of sports heroes, or might we say "communion of saints"?

The lobby of the second school had no trophy case (although it, too, has a fine athletic program) but, instead, two artistically beautiful inscriptions—one was President John F. Kennedy's "Ask not what your country can do for you, but what you can do for your country"; the second, a lengthy excerpt from Reverend Martin Luther King's "I have a dream" speech. As I walked on, the corridor was festooned with posters advertising the upcoming school musical, with photos of the leading players.

I discovered that the community life in these two schools is as different as the contrast between the "sacred" symbols in their lobby. Do the communal symbols and rituals form the "soul" of the school, or vice versa? It probably works both ways. The point is that no school can be exempt from scrutinizing its symbols and rituals for how they affect the school environment and, thus, the character of its students.

Epilogue on Parish Program and Family

The fivefold schema I have used to reflect on the communal life of a public school—and surely, by implication, of a religiously sponsored school—can be as fruitful for helping to build community within parish religious education programs and Christian families. At the end of an already long chapter, brevity is in order.

A parish program should strive to be a Christian community that does the following:

- gives people access to the Word of God through Scripture and Christian tradition;

- welcomes all into a community of faith, hope, and love, with openness to diversity and respect for everyone;

- gives witness by its ethos to Christian faith and values;

- offers opportunity to participants to care for human welfare;

- and provides opportunities for prayer and Christian worship.

In short, parish programs should stop thinking of themselves as confined to *informing* people in Christian faith and expand their horizon to become communities of *formation* and *transformation* in Christian living as well.

Regarding the Christian family, the Second Vatican Council revived a rich notion from early Christianity by referring to the family as "the domestic Church."[37] This implies that the family is to take on all five functions of Christian ministry, with far-reaching implications for the kind of community it tries to become together.

As domestic Church, the Christian family has the vision of becoming: *a community of God's Word*—that studies and shares its faith around the Scriptures and Christian tradition; *a welcoming community* of equality and mutuality that nurtures the gifts and participation of all; *a witnessing community* of faith, hope, and love, that is an effective sign—a sacrament—of Christian faith to its own members and to the world; *a community that promotes human welfare*—spiritual and temporal—within itself and toward the broader society; and a *worshipping community* that has its own ways and traditions for ritualizing Christian faith together.

For Reflection
- Note some of the most significant insights that have emerged for you from your conversation with this chapter on sociology and ecclesiology.

- What are some disagreements you have with it? Additions you would make to its proposals?

- Write a fresh articulation of the social perspective that undergirds your own work as educator. Are there some particular decisions to which your summary invites you as teacher or parent?

Notes

1. See John Locke, especially his book *Two Treatises of Government,* which was first published 1690.
2. For an excellent review of the diversity in the first Christian communities see Raymond Brown, *The Churches the Apostles Left Behind.*
3. See Edward Schillebeeckx, *Christ the Sacrament of Encounter with God.*
4. *The Catechism,* #775.
5. "Constitution on the Liturgy," #83 Abbott, *Documents,* 163.
6. For a scholarly review of how the term has been understood over time, see Benedict Viviano, *The Kingdom of God in History.*
7. See John Paul II, "On Social Concern," 1992, in O'Brien and Shannon, eds., *Catholic Social Thought.*
8. *The Catechism,* #1906, 1907, 1908, 1909, and see 1925 for a summary.
9. Maritain, *The Person and the Common Good,* 51.
10. *The Catechism,* # 839.
11. See Elisabeth Schussler Fiorenza, *In Memory of Her.*
12. See *The Catechism,* # 752.
13. For a rich reflection on the three metaphors of Church as People of God, Body of Christ, and Temple of Holy Spirit see *The Catechism,* #781 -810.
14. *Catechism of the Council of Trent,* first published 1566, 313-14.
15. "Decree on Ecumenism," #3, Abbott, *Documents,* 345.
16. "Decree on the Laity," #3, Abbott, *Documents,* 493
17. John Dewey, "My Pedagogic Creed," in Dworkin, *Dewey on Education,* 32.
18. See any of the writings of Henry Giroux (e.g., *Theory and Resistance in Education*) or of Ira Shor (e.g., *Empowering Education*).
19. Again, this is a vast literature, but I have found particularly helpful and inspiring the work of KennethBruffee for college age and adults. See for example, *Collaborative Learning.* For younger children, the work of Mary Hamm and Dennis Adams offers very practical guidance for implementing a collaborative approach. See for example, *The Collaborative Dimensions of Learning.* For cooperative learning, the work of Johnson and Johnson is particularly significant. See for example, *Cooperation and Competition: Theory and Research.* See also Dennis Adams, *Cooperative Learning: Critical Thinking and Collaboration across the Curriculum.*
20. This literature is huge, but Senge's *The Fifth Discipline* seems to be a defining piece.
21. See Heidegger, *Basic Writings,* 213.
22. For some practical help with the issue of inclusive language, see my small book *Language for a Catholic Church.*
23. See Habermas, *Theory of Communicative Action,* vol. 1, 285 ff.
24. See, for example, Marjorie Powell, *Teacher Effectiveness: An Annotated Bibliography.*
25. I first came upon this helpful distinction in Ian Ramsey, *Models and Mystery.*
26. See Gadamer, *Truth and Method,* 367 ff.
27. Ibid., 299.
28. "Declaration on Christian Education," #1 and 8, Abbott, *Documents,* 639 and 648. Later Church documents, interpreting these sentiments of Vatican II, noted that emphasis on the school as community was encouraged by the

reaffirmed community understanding of the Church that the council had championed. See *The Religious Dimension of Education in a Catholic School,* #15.

29. This is a consistent report of empirical researchers, at least in North American Catholic schools. See for example Covey's *Catholic Schools Make a Difference.* Drawing upon significant research in schools, sociologists James Coleman and Thomas Hoffer report that community within Catholic schools is fostered by the broader community of support that surrounds them, made up of parents, alumns, and the local church. They claim further that community within the schools and surrounding them is explained, in part, by a sense of shared vision and values—grounded in religious ideology—and that this "social capital" of Catholic schools explains much of their success. See James Coleman and Thomas Hoffer, *Public and Private High Schools: The Impact of Communities,* especially chapter 1.
30. See Dewey's "My Pedagogic Creed" in Dworkin.
31. Bryk, Lee, and Holland, *Catholic Schools and the Common Good,* 16.
32. Lickona, *Educating for Character,* 24.
33. Ibid., 63.
34. Ibid., 91C.
35. Émile Durkheim, *Moral Education,* 148, quoted in Lickona, *Education for Character,* 109.
36. Ibid., 24
37. "Constitution on the Church," #11, Abbott, *Documents,* 29.

❖

CHAPTER FIVE

A Tradition to Inherit:
"Our Family Heirloom"

Youngest in the House

I remember my grandmother explaining one of her favorite old traditions. "Yeh see, the Christchild often comes again, specially 'round Christmas time. We should be ready to give a welcome. But we never know how Christchild will come. Could be an old woman or man or a little child, but poor—yeh can be sure o' that! So we light a Christmas candle and put it in the window to bid the stranger welcome. A hundred thousand welcomes! That's the tradition."

She would go on to tell stories of Christmases when she was young. It wasn't too long after "The Great Famine" in Ireland (1845–47), and many poor people still walked the roads begging for food and shelter. For a week before Christmas and throughout all twelve days of the season, her parents would fix up places for guests to sleep in the hay barn, put on a big pot of stew, and then light the Christmas candle. Soon the barn would be full of poor people with a warm bed for the night and a good meal. "And before long," she'd say with a smile in her eye, "someone would strike up a tune, and we'd have a siamsa" (an Irish party with music, song, dance, poetry, and storytelling).

"When we could take in no more people, we had to blow out the candle. Couldn't stay lit and then refuse a welcome." To emphasize the point, she'd whisper with awe, "Could be the Christchild."

And we would nod, without a doubt, "Yeah, could be the Christchild!"

Then she'd conclude—and this was my favorite part of all— "'Course 'twas always the youngest in the house who lit the Christmas candle." And she would tousle my hair.

As the youngest of ten children, it wasn't easy to stand out in the crowd. But the Christmas candle was my moment at center stage. They couldn't light it without me! I remember deliberately coming home a bit late, after nightfall when it should have been lit already, and finding delightfully that the whole family had been brought to a standstill. Siblings waiting for supper would ask angrily, "Where were you—didn't yeh know we were all waitin' to light the Christmas candle?" Of course I did—that's why I came home late.

Years later, I read in liberation theology about God's special presence among the poor, but it didn't sound new at all. Throughout the Christmas season we still light the Christmas candle in my home. Being no longer the youngest in the house, I don't get to do the lighting anymore, and I'd never want anyone but the youngest to do it. As Granny would say, "That's the tradition."

"The Time of Our Lives"

"What then is time?" St. Augustine queried—about sixteen hundred years ago—and responded himself, "If no one asks me, I know; if I want to explain it . . . I do not know."[1] How right he was! We dwell in time—like fish in water—and yet find it so difficult to conceptualize and understand. And we are equally if not more vague about time-over-time—what we familiarly know as history.

Each person has their own operative understanding of time—and of history—but some colloquial sayings may signal the predominant attitude in modern culture (note the "timely" phrase). We say that "time flies," especially as hairs grow grayer or fewer. We may advise each other, "Have a good time," or "Have a nice day." We say that we go through "good times" and "bad times," "fun times" and "sad times." We often "check the time" or wonder, "Is this the right time?" or try to "enjoy our time." We can refer to former events as "all behind us" or "past and gone." About the future, we can talk of something as "coming soon" or ask, "When will it ever arrive?"

As such phrases reflect, we tend to talk about time/history more as a "thing" outside of us—a wheel of fate that grinds by from future to past, serving us, buffet-style, with what to have. But could there be a more holistic understanding of time/history, one more likely to enhance our sense of agency within it, one that encourages us to dwell in and shape this "time of our lives" rather than simply *being had* by it?

That the notion of time held by teachers and parents is significant for education becomes self-evident when we shift beyond conceptualizing it to focusing on the bequest of time-over-time—the legacy of history that we call "tradition." Suddenly we are faced with a pressing social and political issue. A flash point in every society is its citizens' attitudes toward tradition. Likewise for educators: perspectives on tradition are a touchstone of their curriculum—for what, how, why, and where they teach.

In modern society, e.g., in North America, two diametrically opposed social attitudes coalesce around tradition—often, though misleadingly, called "liberal" and "conservative." The first reflects a modernist bias against tradition, assuming that the new is always an improvement over the previous, that things ought to become obsolete (the sooner the better for sales), that the people before us were not as "enlightened" as we are, that the young and the beautiful clad in this year's styles are the norm for everyone else.

The second attitude, often more an antiquarian than a truly conserving sentiment, romanticizes tradition as if the old ways and days were always best, canonizing a static version of it as the norm for how things ought to be done now—with the present a rerun of the past.

That tradition is something from which to be ever drawing new life, rather than rejected or repeated, is not the dominant social attitude and is often absent from educational practice as well.

Lurking behind both liberal and conservative social attitudes—to the first, inspiration; to the second, a menace—is the philosophy of modernism and, more recently, postmodernism. Disparaging of tradition, modernism champions the ideal of an autonomous self, the person as a self-determining subject who follows the dictates of reason alone, independent of tradition and from every semblance of its "authority."

As Hans Gadamer has pointed out, and we return to his rebuttal presently, the whole Enlightenment movement had a bias against tradition, insisting that people "think for themselves" instead. Then postmodernism—the cutting edge of contemporary philosophy—on the issue of tradition could be called a hypermodernism. It robs even the present of its "realness," seeing nothing as stable and "present" but everything as ad hoc and virtual. Whatever emerges is particular to each social age and context and is soon superseded by another "virtual reality" with nothing remaining to be called a tradition.

There is a countervoice to both modernism and postmodernism—a third option, as it were—which appreciates their insights but refuses their bias against tradition, insisting that it can be reclaimed in reflective and life-giving ways—with critical appreciation. Such sentiment will be our leaning here!

For almost 2,500 years, the West has favored Aristotle's philosophy of time as a measure of motion along an imaginary line of history. This linear sense of temporality still flourishes, as is evident in the colloquialisms cited at the beginning. But a linear perspective treats past, present, and future as distinct and separate, as if the past is finished and gone, the present is what we have in the immediate moment, and the future is not yet here but coming—fatalistically.

If we push such a concept of time to its logical conclusion, however, the "present" ceases to exist because time present becomes time past as soon as it comes into existence. Any given point on the line of time can be subdivided so minutely into past and future that the present disappears into "nontime" between them. And it would seem that Aristotle's linear notion of time has been taken on with a vengeance by postmodernism with its bias against tradition and the present disappearing—or needing "update"—as soon as it arrives, like this summer's fashions or my new computer. Such objectifying of time—something that flows by us—encourages fatalism rather than active participation in its outcome. It robs us of "the time of our lives."

A trichotimized understanding of time—as separated past, present, and future—predominates in the theory and practice of education. A brief excursus into curriculum theory will illustrate my point. When it comes to deciding what and how to teach, curriculum theory divides itself into three schools of thought, with each reflecting a heavy favor for past, present, or future.

Some theorists accentuate the "Disciplines of Learning" and give priority to the traditions of knowledge—what has arisen from past human experience and experimentation. Pedagogically, the emphasis is on didactic teaching of academic content.

Other theorists argue that curriculum should give priority to the "Experience of Learners"—encouraging students to discover knowledge through their own present activities, interests, and aptitudes. Pedagogically, the emphasis is on experiential process.

The third position makes curriculum decisions according to the "Needs of Society," either what students need in order to have a future in society or to help construct a better future according to "some conception of . . . the good society."[2] Pedagogically the emphasis is on socialization—preparing people to fit into or reform society.

All three curriculum emphases—the disciplines of learning, the experiences of learners, and the needs of society—seem valid. But to neglect any one or to give undue emphasis is to opt for a linear notion of time, and, I submit, to be less likely to educate *for life for all*. To over accentuate the disciplines of learning can give too much power to the past—neglecting people's own present lives and the future needs of society. Too much emphasis on learners' experiences canonizes the present, neglecting the wisdom of the ages and each generation's responsibility for the future. Undue concern to prepare persons to fit into or reform society can tilt the balance toward the future—neglecting people's need to live humanly now, to enjoy and draw upon the legacy of tradition.

Curriculum with balanced attention to *experience, disciplines,* and *society* requires educators to move beyond separating time out into three disconnected things, weaving them together instead as an integrated unity. Better by far that educators and their curricula honor people's "whole time"—past, present, and future—as a unity. If teachers and parents maintain a more integrated sense of time, they will also teach its legacy—tradition—in ways that enrich the present rather than determine it and that encourage agency rather than fatalism toward the future.

Throughout Western philosophy there has been a significant subtradition that resisted Aristotle's philosophy of time. When Augustine responded to his own question, "What is time?" he proceeded to reject Aristotle's understanding and proposed a more integrated one. This subtradition—echoed now, for example, by Gadamer and the third option referred to previously—can be a better foundation for the vocation of educators and for humanizing education. The overall proposal I make in this chapter runs along these lines.

A recent spokesperson for an integrated sense of time is the philosopher Martin Heidegger. To get a "feel" for the alternative, let us use Heidegger's "existentialist" method for a moment. I invite you to look into your own consciousness of time. How do you experience it? When you think about time, what is your felt sense of it? I wager you will find that your past is not past and gone at all. It is very much with you, shaping who you are and how you respond to everything now. Likewise, your future is not just "not yet." You have a sense of shaping it in the present time—what you are doing now has a bearing on your future.

So we really do not experience time as three separate things outside of ourselves, but as something within us and in which we dwell, with a felt sense that our present is influenced by our past and is shaping our future. In Heidegger's memorable phrase, we are "beings in time"—both shaped by it and taking part in forging its outcomes. We can integrate our three times into our own time, consciously bringing the past with us into the present and engaging the present in ways that affect the future.

This is true of individuals and communities alike. Our sociocultural present is the product of our communal past, and our shared future is not simply a fate coming to meet us—present generations participate in its direction and outcome. A more holistic notion of time lends a better sense of our own historical agency than the linear understanding of Aristotle or the postmodernists. As persons and societies, we can consciously appropriate our past, fully participate in the present, and take a hand in shaping our future.

Teachers and parents can enhance learners' lives by placing an integrated sense of time at the foundation of their educating and curriculum choices. At least, I propose as much in this chapter, and it is the perspective on history and tradition recommended by Catholic Christianity.

But, pray tell, by dwelling on tradition, do we not fall again into an undue emphasis on one aspect of time—the past and its legacy? No, unless one insists upon a linear notion of time. With an integrated sense of time, tradition becomes the past, present, and future combined, representing our whole time over time—that in which we dwell—lending continuity and new direction. And while our focus here is on tradition as the legacy of history—what John Dewey called "the funded capital of civilization"—the present has been the focus, timewise, in chapter 3 on engaging people's present experience and the future in chapter 4 on educating for the common good of society. All three concerns will permeate subsequent chapters as well, neglecting or over emphasizing neither one.

So to honor a holistic sense of time, let teachers and parents adopt an attitude toward tradition of critical appreciation that would encourage learners to personally and discerningly appropriate its legacy as their own in the present—rather than passively inheriting or naively canonizing tradition—with each generation creatively renewing and amplifying its wisdom into the future. If grounded in an integrated philosophy of time, tradition becomes a living experience rather than a dead letter, a stream of vitality rather than stagnant water. With critical appreciation and creative appropriation, tradition need neither be forgotten nor repeated, but can be constantly and creatively renewed.

Before proceeding, let me clarify the terms I use to name the "educational content" of tradition. Without pretending to settle age-old debates, I will use three generic terms—*humanities, sciences,* and *the arts.* By <u>humanities,</u> I mean disciplines like philosophy and theology, history and literature, that carry the wisdom and culture of the ages; they are so named because for thousands of years they have been recognized as humanizing. By <u>sciences,</u> I mean the more empirical traditions of knowledge like the natural sciences (biology, physics, chemistry) and the social sciences (sociology, psychology, anthropology). By <u>the arts,</u> I mean expressions of human creativity— aesthetic arts, performing arts, applied arts, and—note well for I am taking liberties—what have traditionally been called the liberal arts.

Aesthetic arts include the fine arts like painting and sculpture; the performing arts include music, dance, opera, theater, and film. Under applied arts, I include the arts of artisans and craftspersons, and professional arts like medicine and law that are based on both scientific knowledge and practiced expertise. Lastly, stretching the "arts" category beyond its tradition—always possible—I include the liberal arts on the grounds that at least three of the old four R's— reading, 'riting, and rhetoric—are best learned and practiced as arts to do them well. And good 'rithmetic, as any worthy math teacher will aver, requires creativity and imagination.

As you look at your own educating, and especially at how you make curriculum choices, how do you understand your responsibility to tradition—this cultural heritage assembled as the humanities of wisdom, the sciences of knowledge, and the arts of aesthetic? Many educators neglect tradition entirely or draw from it, cafeteria-style, only what seems "useful" for some technical or productive purpose. Other educators can make the tradition so sacrosanct that, instead of encouraging its critical and creative appropriation, they try to passively transmit it, intending learners to recall and repeat. But surely there are possibilities in between. Pause to note some of your sentiments about time, history, and tradition.

For Reflection

- How would you describe your own philosophy of time? Of history? What might be some implications for your work as educator?

- On a scale of 1 (liability) to 10 (asset), how do you rate the value of tradition? Recall and review some of the "history"—personal or communal—behind your response.

- With the poles being "traditionalist" and "iconoclast," where do you place yourself? Why?

A Catholic Christian Notion of History and Tradition: One Proposal

A prior note! As set out in chapter 1, I wrote this book for any educator who might be inspired by the depth structures of Catholic Christianity—from the devout catechist in a parish program to the agnostic scientist in a university laboratory. Thus, I am concerned with at least two "traditions" here—that of the wisdom, knowledge, and aesthetic gathered into the humanities, sciences, and arts and then the heritage of Christian faith over time, often referred to generically as "Scripture and Tradition." NOTE: I will use capital *T* for Christian Tradition: (a) to signal it as a comprehensive term and (b) to distinguish it from the general phenomena of tradition—the broader focus of this chapter.

I offer parallel reflections on each instance in the following sections. As in all the chapters of this book, we will find that the theological and philosophical emulate each other. It would be tempting to refer to "secular" and "sacred" traditions, but I refrain because Catholic conviction is that the distinction between general history and salvation history is only one of perspective. So I refer to the human and the explicitly religious traditions of education.

Typically for Catholic Christians, tradition tends to be a lived experience, something that permeates their identity. For "cradle Catholics" especially, their religious tradition seeps into their "marrowbone," is felt deeply, shapes who they are. Langdon Gilkey says that Catholicism epitomizes "the reality, importance, and 'weight' of tradition and history." He cautions wisely that if made absolute or given too much weight—as has often been the case—tradition for Catholics can be "stifling and corrupt," but if critically appropriated, it "can be a source of vast strength."[3] To appreciate what Gilkey is saying, we should first get a feeling for tradition as a substantial characteristic of Catholicism.

"Steeped in tradition" may be an apt phrase for Catholic Christians. Steeped has the connotation of having something soak in—permeate, marinate through and through. Catholicism is such a strong marinade, capable of steeping its members and permeating their identity. It shapes their self-understanding and worldview, as well as their statements of religious belief.

There are other religious traditions still capable of such in-depth formation, yet for much of modern society—at least in the United States—religion is not such a marrowbone affair but more of a "preference," the assumption being that one's choice could readily change without undue adjustment of identity. This is why Gilkey highlights Catholicism's affinity for tradition as a distinctive if not unique feature. Even when "cradle Catholics" reject the traditional professions of faith or move away from the institutional church, the traces remain in their character—like an indelible mark. An atheist friend who grew up in a tradition-laden Catholic home always refers to himself as a "Catholic atheist"—and knowing him, rightly so!

Anthropologists advise that people are most likely to become "steeped" in a religious tradition when the religion is integrated with a culture or, more accurately, as it becomes a culture—a way of life.

Judaism is a prime example of religious inculturation, and Gilkey claims that Catholicism has inner dynamics that encourage a similar intermingling. Some characteristics already cited explain Catholicism's ability to inculturate—the contemporary term for uniting faith and culture.

All Christians take a strong position on the reality of the Incarnation—the central doctrine that God in Jesus became fully human, "became flesh, and dwelt among us" (John 1:14). It condemns as heresy any position which claims less than a full and real union of the human and divine in the one person of Jesus. The conviction that God in Jesus took on the language, mores, and ethos of a particular culture—that of a first-century Palestinian Jew—encourages making Christian faith indigenous among every people. In other words, the union of divine and human in Jesus encourages the integration of faith and culture in history.

The sentiment to inculturate Christian faith is supported by a positive anthropology, the principle of sacramentality, and emphasis on community. The innate goodness of people and God's coming to meet them in the ordinary of their lives, especially through their relationships, suggest that God is always present in every culture.

Just as there is never a cultureless Christian faith—it is always mediated through particular human symbols—so there is never a Godless culture. God is present among every people. The universal divine presence in love makes every culture a fitting medium for expressing Christian faith. Conversely, for Christian faith to become vital, it ought to become indigenous to each culture. As Pope John Paul II stated well,

> The synthesis between culture and faith is not just a demand of culture, but also of faith. A faith which does not become culture is a faith which has not been . . . thoroughly received, not fully lived out.[4]

Surely, all human beings need to express their relationship with God in ways native to them. Catholic Christianity, however, has a strong sentiment that the community of Christian faith which gathers as Church is not to stand *over-against* or *above* the world, but should be a catalyst of God's reign in the midst of its cultural context. To be Church that, in the words of the Third Eucharistic Prayer of the

Roman Rite Sacramentary, helps to "advance the peace and salvation of all the world" requires a blending of faith and culture—a faith that is historical in the sense that it is realized in the ordinary and everyday context of history. And in saying that Catholic Christianity is a historical religion, we already intimate its attitude toward history and tradition.

With a strong disposition, then, for inculturation, Catholic Christianity became a mosaic of diverse expressions, bonded in faith, yet each unique to its culture—Catholicism that is Italian, Hispanic, French, Polish, Irish, German, American, and then Anglican, Greek, Russian, and much more. Probably no religion in history has had more diverse cultural expressions and yet retained its identity as a distinct tradition. This has been part of Catholicism's genius—an ability to maintain a basic unity of faith and to be realized through diverse cultural expressions—to be both universal and local at the same time.

Regretfully, it transpired that Catholic missionaries in their evangelizing often imposed their cultural expressions of Christianity on other contexts, confusing what was very Irish or Italian with what was essential to the Christian Gospel. Of late, the Church has become more determined to avoid such cultural invasion and advocates authentic inculturation of Christianity in every context. Vatican II said that each people should come to "express Christ's message in its own way," and that the Church must foster "a living exchange" between Christianity and culture which enriches the local context and, likewise, the universal Christian community.[5]

I digressed around inculturation because anthropologists suggest that the deeper the blending of faith and culture, the more powerful the tradition that emerges to "steep" people in its identity. Catholicism is an eminent instance of such a marinating tradition, and the blending of faith and culture has been a feature of its educating throughout history.

With some felt sense of the power of tradition in Catholic consciousness, let us continue with the primary focus of this chapter—the relevance of this depth structure for education. Already we can anticipate that Catholic Christianity fosters appreciation for and commitment to tradition and thus accents the sacred responsibility of educators to teach the traditions of wisdom, knowledge, and art—the explicitly religious and the simply human.

Education that respects tradition should have a strong core curriculum.

Catholicism's appreciation for tradition needs careful nuance, however, if it is to be reclaimed as a source of new life rather than a deadening burden. Much of human and, indeed, Catholic Christian tradition has not been life-giving. In fact, some of it has been destructive and at times deadly. One has only to think of something like slave ships or the oppression of women to realize that no tradition—general or religious—can be glibly canonized.

Catholic Christianity has often been unfaithful to the life-giving spirit of its own tradition, adopting an antiquarian attitude which insisted that anything not in its past could not be in the present or future either. Later, in the pedagogical section, I propose how tradition might be appropriated critically and creatively—with each generation and context bringing its own life to interpret it as a vital resource, rather than passively inheriting it as a museum piece or repeating as "the tradition" what is not life-giving at all.

History as Revelatory

Catholicism's appreciation for tradition reflects its theology of revelation and particularly its conviction that human history is a medium of revelation—of religious knowing. For what else is tradition but the legacy of history? We can tease out three theological convictions about history-as-revelatory. They overlap and combine to encourage appreciation for religious tradition and, philosophically, for simply human traditions.

Because our interest is educational, it seems wise to focus on tradition as source of religious and human knowing. I state the theological point as it pertains to religious knowing first, and then note its resonance for human knowing through the humanities, sciences, and arts. To each, too, I add a caution, accenting the sensitivity with which educators must teach tradition if it is to be life-giving rather than deadening, if people are to have a critical rather than a naive appreciation of it. In the subsequent sections, I offer further caveats and clarifications—all needed for a harmonizing understanding of history and tradition, and for what that might mean for a philosophy of education.

Theological Conviction #1 about History-As-Revelatory

For Religious Knowing: God mediates revelation through human history.

Although remaining always Mystery, God has taken and continues to take the initiative to reveal God's Self and will to humankind and does so through the medium of history.[6] Encouraged by its theology of the person and creation, of sacramentality and community, Catholicism can readily claim, as it did at Vatican II, that history is the standard medium through which "God . . . uninterruptedly converses" with humanity.[7]

So Divine Truth comes through the great and small happenings of human life, through our own hearts and other people, through the ordinary and extraordinary events in the history of faith communities. Echoing the sacramental outlook proposed in chapter 3 and, as always, only humanly speaking, God has no other way of reaching out to humankind except through our history—personal and communal.

To reiterate the caveat of chapter 3, however, every historical event, experience, and movement should not be glibly accepted as reflecting God's will. Every instance and aspect of history must be scrutinized—reflected on critically—to discern what is of God's reign and what is not. Humankind can and often chooses to do what is not God's will at all—to sin—and some sinfulness gets established as a tradition. Nature has its own "freedom" and its dynamics can cause disaster and great suffering. To presume that everything in history reveals God's presence and will would deny the freedom of humankind and of nature.

For Human Knowing: People's own history and the history of communities over time are sources of truth and wisdom, of knowledge and creativity.

Simply put, we "learn from life"—our own and, as highlighted in the third point that follows, from the wisdom, knowledge, and arts bequeathed as legacy by the lives of those before us. As in John Dewey's "one great proposal" for education, the fundamental source of human knowing is encounter with the world and its history through experience. Our own time in history is our first teacher—we learn from what is going on and from what we are experiencing, from what has transpired before us and what other people learned from their experience and experimentation over time.

History is a "given" of our lives; shall we say "gift"? We find it here—willy-nilly—and it invites us to appropriate and make meaning out of it, to investigate it with curiosity, to use our creativity in response. As we do so, we come to know as human beings!

The similar caveat here is that history—personal and communal—should be critically reflected upon, thoughtfully engaged. Dewey was adamant that we learn nothing from experience unless we reflect upon it—"reconstruct" it was his term. And the great Swiss developmental psychologist Jean Piaget (1896–1980) insisted that even what is wise, true, and beautiful must be "reinvented" by each person if it is to become their own. We have to "come to see things for ourselves" in order to truly appreciate and integrate them into our identity.[8] And because history can present us with the foolish, the false, and the ugly, we always need to "keep our wits about us"—be discerning—rather than passively soaking in what comes our way.

Theological Conviction #2 about History-As-Revelatory

For Religious Knowing: By God's grace, humankind is capable of knowing, appropriating, and responding to God's revelation through history.

This also reflects the theology of nature and grace from chapter 2 and again echoes the sacramental consciousness of chapter 3. By an original grace that God implants in human "nature," we have an innate capacity and even affinity for recognizing God's revelation in our lives and in the life of our communities over time. And God's actual grace—daily help—enables us to appropriate and respond to this historical revelation in our day-to-day living.

Although we need to become explicitly aware of "God's word" in our own consciousness, we have an aptitude that readies us to receive and live it in covenant as God's people. Thomas Aquinas helped establish this conviction—human affinity to recognize God's revelation—but it long predates Aquinas.[9] As Moses taught the Israelites, God's word is "not too mysterious and remote" but "something very near to you, already in your mouths and in your hearts; you have only to carry it out" (Deuteronomy 30:11 and 14).

Here again, the previous caution lingers: there is nothing inevitable about God's revelation through history being recognized and believed. God never imposes revelation, but communicates with us according to the mode of the receiver—as noted, an old Thomist maxim. Instead of faxing people the truth from on high, God's revelation through history demands our personal openness and recognition, interpretation and appropriation. As always in the divine/human partnership, God's revelation comes as gift, but we have the responsibility to be open to God's self-disclosure, to discern its meaning, and to choose to live accordingly.

For Human Knowing: People have an "inner vitality" for wisdom, knowledge, and creativity.

Humans have an insatiable capacity and disposition to "know" their world. And we reach beyond its immediate data to make meaning, to know it in ways that enable us to live humanly. Viktor Frankl called the human drive to make sense of our world and lives—out of history—"the will to meaning." He said that its outcome is not our personal fabrication, but the will to meaning causes us to reach for universal truths, for transcendent values. For Frankl, we "detect" meaning as much as we "make" it—it comes to meet us as gift in the midst of our questing.[10]

Jacques Maritain used the phrase "inner vitality" to describe people's innate disposition to know the world—to uncover its wisdom and truth, to appreciate and create what is beautiful, to use and produce what is useful and thus to make meaning out of life. In chapter 7, I propose that the source of inner vitality is "the soul"—also Maritain's sentiment!

But by whatever name, humankind has a dynamic spirit that compels us to know our world and to create a home here. We cannot be passive and indifferent to our history. As humans, we simply must engage in life, reflect upon and wonder about our own history, learn from it—come to know in humanizing ways.

Theological Conviction #3 about History-As-Revelatory
For Religious Knowing: In Christian faith, the original and cumulative symbols of God's self-disclosure over time are its Scripture and Tradition.

God's revelation through history is continuous. For Christian faith, divine revelation began in a primordial way with the Israelites, reached its high point in the event of Jesus Christ, and has continued over time as a living tradition in the community of Jesus' disciples, the Church in the world. The primary and unsurpassed symbol of this primordial divine revelation over time is the Scriptures. Again to cite Aquinas's phrase, the Bible is "the norm of norms" of Christian faith.

Catholic Christianity emphasizes, however, that biblical faith must continue to "develop" (Vatican II's term) as a living tradition. As Christians have lived their faith in different times and places, their understanding and appropriation of it has grown and developed, and guided by God's Holy Spirit working through the faith community, this living tradition gives rise, after time, testing, and consensus, to revered Tradition—with a capital *T*. This Tradition functions as a partner with Scripture, and together they provide the primary Christian symbols through which God mediates revelation to people's lives from one generation to the next.

The caution here is that mainstream Christianity does not view Scripture and Tradition as direct equivalents of "God's word." Never embracing a fundamentalist position—in which primordial symbols of revelation would be taken literally—Catholicism insists that Scripture and Tradition, as media of communication, reflect the historical context in which they emerged—its mores, language, and culture.

Even when a Hebrew prophet claimed to preach the divine message of a "theophany"—a vision—it was subsumed and interpreted within a great variety of other more historical literatures that reflected the hard-won wisdom of the everyday. Unlike Islam, for example, which believes that Mohammed received the Koran as direct divine communication, mainstream Christian faith approaches its Scripture and Tradition as symbols of revelation rather than the equivalents—as Vatican II stated, "the word of God in human language."[11] These symbols must be constantly reread and reinterpreted in every age from the perspective of what God is revealing now in people's lives and consciousness, and their reception must be guided and tested by the living faith of contemporary Christian communities.

For Human Knowing: The disciplines of wisdom, sciences of knowledge, and arts of life carry the cumulative legacy of history—"the funded capital of civilization." They are the entitlement of every person in the present.

Throughout history, our ancestors have learned much wisdom and knowledge from their lives in the world, have created an amazing bequest of things beautiful and useful. They leave a rich heritage to which their progeny now are entitled and which we need for living humanly. The curriculum of all education should reflect some aspect of this legacy and give people ready access to it. Teachers and parents have a defining responsibility to teach tradition. Tradition is like a great conversation that has been going on across the generations of humankind—since the beginning of history. For educators not to teach it to rising generations would be to leave them out of the conversation and so to live less humanly.

And a familiar caution must be echoed here too. History's legacy must be critically appropriated and creatively renewed instead of passively received and repeated. Pedagogically, traditions of wisdom, of knowledge, and of aesthetic should never be imposed, but should be taught in ways that demand and stimulate people's own agency—to appropriate it as living tradition and to make their own unique contribution. Sometimes a present generation can improve upon the legacy of the past. (Think of the advances made by recent generations in communications technology or in medical science.) In other instances, the present inherits the past and makes its own unique contribution to the legacy, but could scarcely claim an "improvement." Perhaps there will never be better compositions than Beethoven's, nor better plays than Shakespeare's, nor better paintings than Da Vinci's, but we can create more lovely music, more powerful drama, and more beautiful art that reflect the experience of other times and cultures.

Being Careful of Tradition:
Some of the Historical and Theological Story

The pages of history attest that Catholic Christians have often experienced tradition as burdening baggage more than as a great treasury of new life. Likewise, there have been Christian as well as human traditions that have been more death-dealing than life-giving. This suggests a keen alert on the part of educators, who have a crucial function as care-full stewards and mediators of tradition.

Turning to some of the strengths and weaknesses of Roman Catholicism in regard to tradition, a little of the historical and theological story can add further nuance and caveat that may help teachers and parents to approach tradition with critical appreciation and to encourage its critical and creative appropriation—*for life for all.* I gather my reflections around three headings: (1) A Humanist Tradition, (2) Scripture and Tradition As Partners, and (3) Tradition As Life-giving Authority.

A Humanist Tradition

Although Catholicism has often failed to live up to its own depth structure of a humanizing tradition, yet it must be noted that Catholic education has been a prime carrier of the humanist tradition of Western culture. It would be unfair to its history not to recognize this—and learn from it for education today. Catholic education has reflected a strong humanizing sentiment in at least two ways: a partnership between faith and culture and a humanizing curriculum in purpose, content, and pedagogy.

Partnership of Faith and Culture: I previously noted the theological disposition of Catholic Christianity to inculturate itself. Here I review briefly how the blending of faith and culture has, in fact, been a consistent aspect of Catholic education.

Related to Catholicism's sense of history-as-revelatory is the conviction that God is the Author of all truth—"secular" and "sacred," a distinction of perspective instead of kind—and of all that is life-giving and worthwhile in human creativity, of culture in all its manifestations. Clement of Alexandria (circa 150–215) wrote "The river of truth is one, though fed by many streams."[12] About seventeen hundred years later, John Henry Cardinal Newman (1801–90) resounded: "All branches of knowledge are connected together, because the subject-matter of knowledge is intimately united in itself, as being the acts and the work of the Creator."[13]

Both authors reflect the enduring conviction that all truth reflects divine truth, all creativity divine creativity. (Remember, we are speaking analogously.) In consequence, Catholic education has continually reflected a deep bond and exchange between sacred and secular learning, between faith and culture.

The partnership between faith and culture finds echo, too, in the partnership between revelation and reason, between faith and understanding—convictions likewise present throughout the history of Catholic education. The First Vatican Council (1869–70) summarized an ancient sentiment when it declared: "Faith and reason . . . are . . . *mutually advantageous* . . . right reason demonstrates the foundations of faith, and *faith sets reason free . . .*"[14] (emphasis added).

Secular and sacred traditions of learning enrich each other. Christian faith, far from closing off the humanities, sciences, and arts, should encourage their embrace—with a faith perspective lending the means of their integration. Faith should open people up to all expressions of wisdom, knowledge, and creativity—to all instances of culture.

There have been voices of opposition to the marriage of faith and culture. I noted previously the battle cry of Tertullian, "Jerusalem has no need of Athens." With God's word revealed in Scripture, why turn to pagan authors? But Tertullian's sentiment did not prevail. His contemporary, Clement, around the year 200 C.E., founded a great school at Alexandria to teach both Christian faith and the best of classic literature. He initiated an enduring practice of marrying Christianity and culture into a Christian humanism.

Basil the Great (circa 330–79), bishop of Caesarea and the leading theologian of his day, wrote a treatise on "How to Derive Profit from Pagan Literature." He eloquently praised Hellenistic culture, urging Christian students to be like the bee who collects honey from many different flowers—an analogy repeated by many Christian authors.

St. Augustine, equally convinced of the partnership of faith and culture, used the analogy that as the Israelites took booty from Egypt, so Christians should make their own the best of pagan learning. Though always challenged by pietists like Tertullian, Catholic education has remained deeply committed to a core curriculum in the humanities and sciences of knowledge, convinced that to teach as much is "a work of salvation."

Catholic Christianity has a similar appreciation for the arts. It includes them in its educational curriculum and has often been their patron, cherishing them for expressing the human reach for the transcendent. Vatican II summarized well this sentiment toward artistic traditions: "Very rightly the fine arts are considered to rank among the noblest expression of human genius." They "are related to God's boundless beauty" and can "turn [human] thoughts to God persuasively and devoutly." For this reason, Catholicism "has always been the friend of the fine arts."[15]

A Humanizing Curriculum: From the beginning of the Middle Ages (circa 500 C.E.) when the Church began to evangelize the invading tribes that had overrun the Roman Empire—affectionately known as "Barbarians"—it recognized that civilizing and Christianizing must go hand in hand, that all education should have a humanizing effect. The great Celtic monastic schools (like Clonard, Clonmacnoise, Durrow, Iona, Lindisfarne) and the great Benedictine monasteries (like Monte Cassino in Italy, Tours in France, Jarrow in England, Fulda in Germany) all taught the classic humanist traditions of Greece and Rome, as well as Christian faith, with the purpose of promoting wisdom and humane living.

Not that early Catholic education neglected knowledge and science, the trades and professions, or eschewed pragmatic interest—the monasteries taught the medieval world the art of farming and fostered guilds for artisans. But the defining intent of the monastic schools in teaching all tradition—religious and secular—was wisdom and living wisely. *Wisdom for life* was emblematic of the curriculum of the Middle Ages.

The great monk-educator Alcuin of York (circa 730–804), himself a product of Celtic monastic education, convinced Emperor Charlemagne to launch the momentous Carolingian Renaissance (circa 800)—the turning point in the revival of Western culture after the "Dark Ages." Alcuin's argument was that the Empire needed education if it was to live peaceably and "to flourish in the beauty of wisdom." With a proclamation often called "the first decree of universal education" (issued 787), Charlemagne required all monastery and cathedral schools not only to teach their monks and future priests, but "all people who by the grace of God are able to learn" and to instruct every citizen—boys and girls—in "wisdom."[16]

Under Alcuin's leadership, the "wisdom curriculum" of all schools in the Empire revolved around the seven liberal arts—called "liberal" because of their capacity to liberate people to more humane living. Alcuin was the first to organize the liberal arts as the curriculum of an entire school system. The seven were made up of the *trivium* of grammar (what we mean by literacy), rhetoric (public speaking), and dialectic (the ability for good conversation), and the *quadrivium* of music, arithmetic, geometry, and astronomy—all seven, in one way or another, likely to enhance the person qua person. People were to develop the liberal arts through studying the humanizing legacy of antiquity—the philosophers and poets, musicians and mathematicians, the Scriptures, and patristic writings (works of early Christian theologians).

The liberal arts and humanistic curriculum was enhanced at the great universities that emerged from the monastic and cathedral schools. Even students in the premier professions—then law and medicine—were required to study the humanities and liberal arts as necessary foundation for living humanly. The arts of reading and writing, of presentation and conversation, of calculating, measuring, and music, with scholarship in literature and languages, in philosophy and theology, history and ethics—all intending to educate the person in wisdom and to enhance human development—is the traditional core curriculum of Catholic education.

Curriculum in the humanities reached a high point during the Renaissance—their triumph. Thereafter, as the natural and social sciences developed, they were welcomed into the curriculum but on the foundation of the liberal arts and humanities—ever directed to enhancing the human spirit and "the art of living well." Perhaps the *Ratio Studiorum* of St. Ignatius of Loyola, founder of the Jesuits (1540), is the epitome of this humanistic curriculum—grounded in faith, built on the humanities and liberal arts, subsuming the emerging sciences, and directed toward wisdom and living wisely. (I develop the theme of wisdom in chapter 6).

One could also make a strong case that the predominant pedagogy throughout the history of Catholic education was a humanistic one, favoring active student participation in the teaching/learning dynamic. The style of the old monastic schools was Socratic, engaging students in conversation and teaching them to think for themselves.

Later, the Scholastic "*quaestio* method" at the great universities was built around taking a controversial question and having students debate its outcome. The more lively classes at the University of Paris led to riots among the students. From the time of their founding, the Augustinians, Dominicans, and Franciscans were renowned for their humane approach to teaching. The Brothers of the Common Life, founded in 1376 by Geert De Groote—the first order of vowed religious brothers dedicated specifically to education and who included girls in their schools—had a passion for teaching the common people in ways respectful of their dignity. Later, the Jesuits made students' personal development their central concern, and Jesuit education became synonymous with learners being taught to think for themselves.

Thereafter, the male religious orders were joined by the great teaching orders of vowed religious women that emerged after the Council of Trent (1545–63). These women educators had a profoundly humanizing influence on Catholic education. The Council of Trent had explicitly discouraged women's orders from participating in the educational ministry of the Church. But the faith and persistence of many great women—who often knowingly functioned contrary to the expressed directives of their church authorities (e.g., the Roman Curia had Mary Ward imprisoned to prevent her from opening schools)—prevailed over papal opposition and led gradually to the approval of women to be educated and to become educators.

The Ursulines, founded in 1535 by St. Angela de Merici, began this women's movement in Catholic education. Some of the notable women's teaching orders which immediately followed include: the Congregation of Notre Dame, cofounded in 1598 by Blessed Alix le Clerc; the Visitation Sisters, cofounded in 1610 by St. Jane Francis de Chantal; the Institute of the Blessed Virgin Mary (also Loretto Sisters), founded circa 1615 by Mary Ward; the Daughters of Charity, cofounded circa 1633 by Louise de Marillac; and the Sisters of St. Joseph, founded in 1650 by John Peter Medaille.

These pathfinders were followed by a countless host of other religious communities of women dedicated to the humanistic tradition of education. Most had an amazingly "progressive" pedagogy. For instance, Mary Ward (1585–1645)—original founder of IBVMs and Lorettos—forbade her Sisters to use physical punishment and encouraged them to teach in ways marked by gentleness and respect for each student, with lots of engaging and fun-filled activities, singing and art.[17] This was in marked contrast to what her contemporary John Amos Comenius (1592–1670), the grandfather of modern education, aptly called "the slaughterhouse pedagogy" of their day.

Scripture and Tradition as Partners

At first blush, this clarification has more relevance for Christian religious education than for education in general, but it enhances the nuance that every form of education should teach tradition of any kind as evolving, vital, and life-giving. Let me recognize, too, at the outset that a real partnership between Scripture and Tradition within Catholic Christianity—with the possible exception of Anglicanism—is more a contemporary promise than a past achievement.

Though claiming commitment to "Scripture and Tradition" as the primordial media of God's revelation, for over four hundred years Catholic Christians neglected the Scriptures and unduly favored Tradition. This imbalance was a legacy of Reformation-era polemics that ill-served Catholicism and perhaps Protestantism as well.

When the Reformers rightly called the Church back to the Word of God in Scripture, demanding that the Bible be recentered at the core of Christian faith, the Catholic reaction was to downplay Scripture and increase its emphasis on Tradition. And the more one side exaggerated its position, the more the other took the opposite, so that Catholics ended up neglecting Scripture, as perhaps Protestants did Tradition—with the cry of *scriptura sola*—"scripture alone."

Even into this era, the curriculum of Protestant Sunday schools is heavily biblical, whereas, up until Vatican II, Catholic catechesis was primarily a doctrinal catechism. A similar imbalance was reflected in each community's Sunday worship. There, the issue was "word" or "sacrament," with, until recently, Protestants having little but "word" and Catholics little but "sacrament."

A blessing from contemporary ecumenism is the effort to find balance beyond Reformation polemics. Although late—perhaps better than never—on the 500th anniversary of Luther's birth (1983), Pope John Paul II, speaking on behalf of Catholicism, publicly thanked Luther and the Reformers for maintaining Christian faithfulness to the Word of God in Scripture. As Protestantism retaught Catholicism to value individual conscience and personal rights in the previous era, so too, in our own time, it is helping Catholic Christians to reposition the Bible where it belongs—at the heart of Christian faith.

Vatican II decreed that "easy access to sacred Scripture should be provided for all the Christian faithful."[18] Probably nothing has created more renewal in Catholicism than the implementation of this mandate.[19] The Council also helped to move beyond Reformation polemics by proposing a true partnership between Scripture and Tradition, as if there is one revelation with two manifestations: "Sacred tradition and sacred Scripture form one sacred deposit of the word of God." For this reason, "both sacred tradition and sacred Scripture are to be accepted and venerated with the same sense of devotion and reverence." And the two must be interpreted within a faith community. Scripture, Tradition, and Church "are so linked and joined together that one cannot stand without the others." They "all work together . . . under the action of the one Holy Spirit" for "the salvation of souls."[20]

From a religious education perspective, repartnering Tradition with Scripture provides the former the guidance of an original identity to which it must be faithful. Tradition lends vitality to Scripture as the community of faith continues to mine the "surplus of meaning" in God's original revelation and to live a biblical faith in each new generation. Far from being a dead letter, the Scriptures themselves encourage their own reinterpretation from age to age.

The Israelites told the story of Exodus very differently when they were doing well during the monarchy than when they were exiles in Babylon. And surely Jesus was encouraging such a vital approach to the "treasury of faith" when he counseled, "Every scribe who is learned in the reign of God is like the head of a household who takes from the storeroom both the new and the old" (Matthew 13:52).

As Scripture is reinterpreted to bring new life to Tradition, Tradition must likewise be reinterpreted according to contemporary understanding and living of biblical faith. Contrary to conservative sentiment, Vatican II was adamant that Tradition not be static and unchanging, but should ever remain vital and evolving—continuing to unfold as a "living" tradition. The Council first reiterated that "the Christian dispensation . . . as the new and definitive covenant, will never pass away, and we now await no further new public revelation." In the primordial sense, the original expression of Christian revelation was complete with the death of the last apostle. However, people's life-centered appropriation and living of Christian revelation remains an ongoing project that continues throughout history. The Council stated:

The tradition which comes from the apostles develops in the Church with the help of the Holy Spirit. For *there is growth* in the understanding of the realities and the words which have been handed down.

Rather than already possessing a fixed or final Tradition,

As the centuries succeed one another, the Church constantly *moves forward toward the fullness of divine truth* until the words of God reach their complete fulfillment in her.[21] (emphases added)

The function that Scripture should play within Catholic Christianity and education—as a source of vitality to evolving tradition—has an analogy in the function that the classics should play within education in general—here again, the theological having a philosophical resonance. Every expression of education has responsibility to teach some traditions of wisdom, knowledge, or art. Note, too, that every community of meaning or discipline of learning has its "classics." By *classic,* I mean symbols, texts, or practices that: (a) have withstood the test of time; (b) continue to be a source of new life, giving vitality to succeeding generations; and (c) are so rich in meaning that they lend themselves to reinterpretation, to being built upon as times and circumstances change.

Leading American theologian David Tracy writes, "Classics are those texts that bear an excess and permanence of meaning, yet always resist definitive interpretation."[22] He continues, "A classic, by definition, will always be in need of further interpretation in view of its need for renewed application to a particular situation"[23]—which is why the classics of any tradition can help to sustain its vitality. Educationally, the classics epitomize how the whole tradition should function—never forcing people to repeat the past, but serving as a treasury from which people can draw new possibilities as well as the tried and true.

Tradition as Life-giving Authority

I have already "qualified" the authority of tradition by emphasizing that it must remain vital, living, and evolving—never allowing it to exercise a stranglehold on the present, never presenting it as a mold for reproduction. The question remains, however, what precisely is the authority of tradition as a depth structure of Catholic Christianity? What "weight" does it have?

Though it takes us a bit afield, the issue must be weighed within a broader one—the strong Catholic Christian sentiment that the Church has "teaching authority." This is surely of significance for Catholic education—an eminent instance of how the Church teaches. But all instances of education have an interest here. The very function of teachers and parents invests them with a kind of authority. "'Cause the teacher says" is a magisterial voice that echoes throughout all cultures.

And surely some of the educator's authority should be personal. The best of educators have passion for what they teach and teach it with integrity; but passion and integrity lend authority to any teacher or parent. Since Jesus had no official designation as "teacher" in his culture, it must have been his passion and integrity of life that brought people to say of him, "He teaches with authority" (Matthew 7:9).

So, though at first blush tradition and the "teaching authority" of the Church pose a distinctive issue for Catholic education, perhaps a proper understanding of the authority of tradition within Catholicism may be insightful for all educators. In Roman Catholic consciousness, the most recognized symbol of Church authority is the papacy—the pope. The pope has primacy of leadership and teaching authority in succession to St. Peter, considered the first among the apostles. As Richard McBrien points out, its emphasis on the Petrine office is the "one characteristic . . . which sets the Catholic Church apart from all other churches."[24]

The sense of papal authority is summarized in the Latin term *magisterium*—literally, "authoritative teacher." In mainstream Catholic understanding of papal magisterium, however, the pope, as bishop of Rome, must teach in consultation and collegiality with the bishops of the world and represent the consensus faith of the whole Church, in fidelity to Scripture and Tradition.[25] But even with such important nuance, the magisterium of the institutional church, symbolized in the papacy, functions as "authoritative teacher" for Roman Catholics.

Catholic Christianity has always cast a strong image of being an entire system of meaning and ethic, a comprehensive worldview reflecting the conviction that there are universal truths and moral norms—things that are always true and ever normative. Even when not teaching its own religious faith, Catholicism would encourage educators to teach scholarly traditions in ways that help learners to develop their own sense of meaning and ethic. So both as institution and tradition, "authority" is a Catholic issue—a substantial characteristic. As such, it seems best to first address the theological issue of the Church's teaching authority and then return to a "Catholic" philosophy of the authority of tradition in general. Again, we will find parallel points.

Teaching Authority of the Church: That the Church has the right and responsibility to carry on Jesus' teaching mission has been a central conviction of Christianity since the first communities. (See, e.g., Matthew 28:16–20.) The Church's teaching mandate is to interpret and teach with faithfulness the Scripture and Tradition of Christian faith in every age and context. But, as a good scholastic philosopher might rejoin, "Much depends on what you mean by '*Church.*'"

If we remember that the Church is the whole community of the Body of Christ, including all baptized Christians and not just its leaders, then we recognize that the Church's "teaching authority" cannot be limited to the institutional magisterium.

At least since Aquinas, the Church has understood itself to have three cooperative sources of teaching and learning: (a) the research of scholars; (b) the discernment of ordinary people of faith, often called the *sensus fidelium* ("sense of the faithful"); and (c) the official magisterium of the papacy/episcopacy.[26] One can imagine this as a triangle, with Scripture and Tradition at the center and each agency functioning in concert with the other two. All three should reflect and guide each other as they take from "the storeroom" both old and new.

The official magisterium should act as consensus builder, articulating positions that reflect the faith of the community over time, witnessing to its shared faith as a guiding perspective for all. It should be informed, however, by the research of its scholars and listen attentively to the sense of the faithful. Likewise, as ordinary Christians try to understand and live their faith, they are guided by the consensus of the magisterium and informed by the research of scholars. Similarly, theological scholars should be in constant dialogue with the sense of the faithful and draw guidance from the consensus of belief and practice taught by the magisterium as the faith of the community. When it works—with all three functioning in partnership—it is a great system of checks and balances. At its best, it should prevent Catholic Christianity from falling into authoritarianism.

So, contrary to the stereotype shared by many—that the pope can arbitrarily create teachings or laws and require blind obedience in faith—the papacy is meant to be a witness to what is already the faith of Catholic people. And remember that freedom of the individual conscience has been a teaching of Catholic Christianity since the beginning of the Church. Reflecting this ancient tradition, Vatican II referred to conscience as "the most secret core and sanctuary of a [person]" where we are "alone with God, whose voice echoes in [our] depths"—conscience is always the last court of appeal! The Council went on to say that not only may a Catholic follow her or his conscience, but "in all . . . activity . . . is *bound* to follow . . . conscience faithfully, in order [to] come to God"[27] (emphasis added). However as one describes the authority of tradition within Catholicism, it must always leave room for freedom of conscience—or it is not faithful to Tradition.

Authority of Tradition: When one brings together a communal understanding of the Church—all as teachers and learners together—with the conviction that Scripture and Tradition are to be continually reinterpreted in light of changing circumstances and contemporary consciousness—and add in the note of freedom of conscience—then Catholicism has no place for fundamentalism or dogmatism in the authority it grants to tradition. Instead, it is called, as is every human community regarding its tradition, to a critical and creative appropriation of "the faith handed down."

Forging consensus among its magisterium, people, and scholars, Catholicism can critically and creatively appropriate its Tradition by following at least three guidelines: (a) trying to discern the original spirit of some text or symbol of its faith—considering its context and what it might have meant "back then"; (b) reviewing what it has meant over time and the "fruits" throughout history—again considering the contexts; and (c) discerning how the whole faith community receives and perceives it today and how contemporary consciousness can draw new life from it for the present context.

Thus, the authority of tradition for Catholicism is analogous to what it might be in any community that respects its tradition. Philosophically, Catholic Christians are no different from other people who face the question of how best to go about interpreting tradition—to make it come alive and give life in different times and places. In other words, and as these three guidelines suggest, the authority of tradition becomes an issue of hermeneutics—of interpretation—a recurring theme throughout this work.

For a long time, the Western world granted absolute authority to tradition, accepting it without question as dictating norms of meaning and ethic. But people often experienced its authority as authoritarian, as preventing them from thinking for themselves, from imagining new possibilities. As noted already, tradition as authoritarian was vigorously challenged by the Enlightenment, a "free-thinking" movement that began in the seventeenth century among European intellectuals.

They were surely correct in their challenge to authoritarianism, but it would seem that they "threw the baby out with the bath water." Hans Gadamer, perhaps the greatest contemporary philosopher of tradition, argues that the Enlightenment "had a prejudice against tradition." It saw tradition as the enemy of critical reason, as needing to be overthrown if people were to "dare to think" (Kant) for themselves. At least among "enlightened" people—mostly scholars—this led to wholesale rejection of tradition as an irrational and authoritarian burden.

No one has done more than Gadamer to rehabilitate tradition while avoiding the pitfall of authoritarianism. He proposes that the Enlightenment's mistake was to presume "an exclusive antithesis between authority and reason" when they are not mutually exclusive at all. When one recognizes that tradition represents the hard-won wisdom of countless ancestors who have gone before us, it seems eminently reasonable to grant it significant weight as a resource for living humanly in the present.

We can also presume that what others have discovered and bequeathed as tradition "is not irrational and arbitrary but can, in principle, be discovered to be true." So rather than being an exercise in "blind obedience," "acknowledgment" of the value of tradition is "an act of reason and freedom." In fact, to grant such "authority" to tradition may be the most reasonable thing to do.[28]

For Gadamer, to save tradition from authoritarianism requires that its "texts" (i.e., however it is carried or expressed) be constantly reinterpreted—with critique and creatively. Here I reiterate a few points presented in previous chapters.

Rather than naively presuming to take and simply "apply" tradition to the present, Gadamer proposes a hermeneutical approach—constantly reinterpreting tradition in light of what we bring to it from the present. He compares this to setting up a "conversation" between tradition and ourselves. In the "give-and-take," we bring our lives to a text of tradition and the text to our lives; we question the text and are questioned by it; we ask what it meant in its original context and the possible meaning for ours; we become aware of our own history that we bring to the conversation and how this influences and contributes to what we take away. The best hope, says Gadamer, is that a "fusion of horizons" emerges between tradition and our present perspective—a melding of the "the world of the text" with our own, in which "the new and the old combine into something of living value."[29]

For Gadamer, every authentic act of interpreting tradition, far from being a repeat of the past or a blind submission to its authority, should offer a new moment of understanding. And this moment adds to the tradition, helping to maintain its dynamic and humanizing power. It is within this vibrant, critical, and creative approach to interpreting tradition that educators can appreciate it, teach it, and teach others to appreciate it, and yet not make it an authoritarian limit to people's lives.

Catholic Christianity understands tradition as a reliable source of wisdom, but far from stymieing reason, invites it; far from asking blind obedience, requires critical appropriation; far from arresting investigation, encourages it; far from posing anything as final, offers signposts and benchmarks of achievement to stimulate creativity and new life along the pilgrim way.

For Teachers and Parents

Such a perspective on history encourages an abiding appreciation for its legacy of tradition. As the culture of humankind before us, tradition can be humanizing, lending us both roots and branches reaching to the sky—much depending upon how it is taught. Educationally, tradition is mediated through the humanities, sciences, and arts. Together, they offer parables of enduring truth and value that lend wisdom to life in any age, human achievements in knowledge that help us to know our world and make a home here, and aesthetic creativity for appreciation and to stimulate our own. As one might expect, "Catholic" education reflects a strong commitment to teaching this "funded capital of civilization."

By way of educational proposals, for this chapter it seems advisable to first insert a new category on curriculum, with emphasis on "content"—what to teach from tradition. Then we will move back to our pattern of what appreciation of tradition might mean for the teacher's soul, style, and space. First, name some of your own pedagogical insights and convictions around the theme of tradition.

For Reflection
- Drawing together your reflections thus far, restate your own attitude toward "tradition."

- Whatever your attitude may be, what does it imply for an educational curriculum?

- What do you think tradition asks of the educator's heart? For the teaching style? For the educational environment?

What to Teach from Tradition

Given the endless possibilities for educational curricula, I can offer only a few guidelines here for selecting from tradition the "content" to be taught. You will add suggestions for your own situation. I begin with the curriculum of general education and then address Christian religious education curricula—for parish programs or family catechesis or for Catholic or other religiously sponsored schools where religious education is integral to the curriculum.[30]

For General Curriculum

Guideline #1 for General Curriculum: The guiding intent for all curricula is humanization—to educate people to become fully alive and free human beings.

Regardless of which of the humanities, sciences, or arts is being taught, the intended outcome is that persons fulfill their human vocation, that they continue to realize their potential as human beings, that they become wise and integrated persons. All curricula should help learners to make and keep life human—for themselves and others. The defining character of education should be what is traditionally called liberal education or, as Maritain prefers, education for freedom. Maritain offered an inspiring definition:

> Education directed toward wisdom, centered on the humanities, aiming to develop in people the capacity to think correctly and to enjoy truth and beauty, is education for freedom, or liberal education.[31]

Maritain had a rich and balanced understanding of freedom. His classic Thomist approach is that human freedom is analogous to God's freedom, because God is the ground of true freedom. As such, human freedom is freedom to love, to choose truth, to do good, to create the beautiful.

Far from being a license, freedom brings responsibility, especially to love one's neighbor. Although the realization of freedom demands every human effort and responsibility—echoing chapter 2—freedom also comes as a gift or, as Maritain prefers, as "the work of love"— God's love for humankind. Because we are like our God, we can recognize what is good and true and, moved by God's grace, freely choose it. For Maritain, the raison d'être of liberal education is responsible human freedom.[32] Right on, say I; so, let human liberation be the first guideline for every educator in choosing curriculum. In other words, let parents and teachers see to it that learners have access to that of tradition most likely to liberate and humanize.

Guideline #2 for General Curriculum: A humanizing and liberating education is the entitlement of every person, regardless of what their particular vocation may be.

The history of Western education is fraught with social biases and class distinctions, with "liberal education" itself having an aristocratic aura. Though some of its exclusivity and elitism has been eroded by democracy, much still lingers, slotting some learners for a humanistic education, others for a technical one—preparing for trades or manual labor and, tragically, excluding a huge number from any effective education at all. Witness the virtual breakdown of learning in many inner-city American schools and the continued practice of child labor throughout the world.

Although people's formal education should prepare them for and nurture their particular vocations, the first education deserved by all—and the foundation needed for every vocation—is a humanizing one. After describing education for freedom, Maritain adds:

> Whatever [their] particular vocation may be, and whatever special training [their] vocation may require, every human being is entitled to receive such a properly human and humanistic education.[33]

Guideline #3 for General Curriculum: Not only the humanities and liberal arts, but all disciplines of learning—including manual and professional trades—can and should be taught in ways that contribute to a humanizing education.

Everything that humankind has learned and everything we need to know in order to live humanly and to fulfill our particular vocation in life is worth including in some curriculum of education. As far back as the manual labor of the first monasteries, there is strong Christian sentiment that all human labor has equal dignity and can be done "for the honor and glory of God."

Maritain writes, "Manual work and intellectual work are equally human in the truest sense and [are] directed toward helping [humanity] to achieve freedom."[34] Every vocation should be able to find its foundations in liberal education. Further, everything can be taught in ways that humanize—to engage learners as human beings, and to inform, form, and transform them in living humanly. All curriculum content can become "education for freedom," argues Maritain, if it engages "the activity of the human spirit."[35]

I know an instructor in an automobile mechanics program. I have watched him interact with apprentices and have heard him tell stories of his teaching. He has a wonderful way of engaging apprentices as human beings, of inviting them to think and figure things out for themselves. He urges them to do work they can be proud of, to be attentive to and scrupulously honest with customers, to recognize the importance of their service in people's lives. There is even an aesthetic aspect to his curriculum as he urges them to appreciate the beauty and details of a fine car. He is a liberal educator—teaching mechanics. And what a service he renders to the common good! Who does not appreciate finding a mechanic like one of his graduates?

Guideline #4 for General Curriculum: A society's schools need a core curriculum of humanizing education that lays the intellectual, moral, and aesthetic foundations needed by everyone for their human and particular vocations.

I restate: the content of all the humanities, sciences, and arts—including trades and crafts—can be taught with the style and intent of liberating education by engaging and nurturing the human spirit of learners in the process. Yet, the long history of Western education attests to the fact that there are some basic intellectual abilities and virtues, some wisdom and general knowledge, that provide an adequate basis for the human vocation—*for life for all.*

Traditionally, this core curriculum has been provided by the liberal arts and the humanities. Nowhere, however, could I find an agreed-upon listing of what is currently meant by either. They have certainly been expanded beyond the traditional *trivium* (grammar, rhetoric, dialectic) and *quadrivium* (arithmetic, geometry, music, astronomy) of Alcuin—as liberal arts, and beyond the culture of ancient Greece and Rome as humanities. But what should they now include?[36]

Maritain called for "a more comprehensive concept of the humanities, and to recast and enlarge the list of liberal arts."[37] He defined the humanities (excuse his dated language) as

> those disciplines which make man more human, or
> nurture in man his nature as specifically human, because
> they convey to him the spiritual fruit and achievements
> of the labor of generations, and deal with things which
> are worth being known for their own sake, for the sake
> of truth or the sake of beauty.[38]

The humanities, therefore, are humanizing ways of inheriting the legacy of those before us—for our well-being as persons.

Maritain went on to define the liberal arts as "those matters the knowledge of which refers directly to the creative or perceptive activity of the intellect and to its thirst for seeing and understanding."[39] These, then, are the "arts"—we might say competencies—which enable us to interpret and appropriate our culture (e.g., reading), to think and express ourselves (e.g., writing and rhetoric), and to measure and correlate things and time (e.g., mathematics).

A Proposal for the Core Curriculum

Many attempts have been made to reconfigure the core curriculum of Western education, including a creative proposal by Maritain.[40] Without presuming to complete such a complex task here, I propose five foundational intellectual competencies—"arts"—that people need for their wisdom and work as human beings. Reflecting a critical appreciation for tradition, I include the liberal arts familiarly known as the four R's—reading, 'riting, 'rithmetic, and rhetoric—with each one recast for our time. Then I add a fifth—reflection. Alcuin might claim with good reason that it is implied in the other four, but I mention reflection explicitly as often as possible because I see it as central to all education worthy of the name—general and religious.

Then I suggest four configurations of humanities for core curriculum: literature and languages, the natural sciences, the social sciences, and the aesthetic arts. Together, they can give learners ready access to the legacy most likely to enhance their freedom and growth into fullness of life.

These arts and humanities overlap and intermingle. Although the arts focus on abilities to perform intellectual exercises of inquiry and creativity and the humanities on the legacy of culture over time, they necessarily contribute to each other. In learning literature, one is developing the arts of reading, writing, and rhetoric. In learning the social sciences, one is developing the art of reflection on one's reality. For "liberal arts," I propose:

- *Reading*—including the ability to read literature with comprehension, insight, and exchange; to "read" one's own reality in the world, recognizing what is "going on" in the surrounding society and what one is "up to"—becoming aware of one's own ideas, feelings, and activities; and the capacity to "read" critically and to creatively appropriate the various media and symbols of communication in the contemporary world. With the average American child spending thirty hours per week watching television, such media literacy is imperative.

- *'Riting*—including the ability to express oneself in writing and do so accurately and engagingly; to use both traditional and contemporary media of expression to record and communicate one's sentiments. The vast horizons being opened up by the World Wide Web highlight the imperative of being able to use modern methods of communication.

- *'Rithmetic*—including the ability to accurately measure and correlate things and time, volume and quantity, through the use of numbers and symbols; to reason logically and by intuition from what one can measure in the world; to figure out unknown data and hypotheses and to imagine new possibilities in the correlation of things to each other. Just the challenge of driving an automobile highlights the contemporary imperative of developing one's capacities for 'rithmetic.

- *Rhetoric*—including the ability for conversation and dialogue; to develop the capacity for self-expression and being a good listener; to speak with clarity and to listen with empathy; to be able to engage the interests of others and to express one's perspective persuasively; to see what should be seen and to name it imaginatively—as in the gift of the poet or novelist.

The pluralism and complexity of modern society highlights our contemporary need of the ability to handle the "to-and-fro" of conversation and respectful exchange. I know of a high-school program in a high-crime neighborhood that has been effective in defusing gang violence. Essentially, it teaches young people the ancient art of rhetoric—to be able to express themselves and listen to each other, to stop, think, and negotiate.

- *Reflection*—including the ability to think for oneself, using to the full one's own reason, memory, and imagination; to question and probe the world for understanding and meaning, for error and evil; to question and probe one's own assumptions, perspectives, and ideologies; to be able to make balanced judgments and wise decisions. A key to living humanly in any age is the art of reflection.

  Any one instance within my fourfold grouping of the humanities that follow could be a lifetime study, and then some. Clearly, there needs to be a scope and sequence within the humanities curriculum that introduces children to a broad spectrum at an early age and provides a foundation on which to build throughout their lives. The intent of teaching the humanities, as Maritain insisted, is not "useless memorization or piecemeal information," but rather enabling students to learn early the essential structures of the human disciplines, being readied to continue building on this foundation.[41]

- *Literature and Languages*—including all the genres of writing (prose, drama, and poetry) with emphasis on literature that addresses the human condition, its nature and destiny, its meaning and ethic (like history, philosophy, and theology); study of languages, beginning with one's own to learn it well and to become an artist of it and then expanding one's horizons of consciousness and communication by knowing other languages, both classical and modern.

- *Natural Sciences*—including all the research sciences that help people understand and appreciate the natural world, their own physicality, and the functioning of "life" (like physics and chemistry, biology and anatomy, geophysics and astronomy, and more).

- *Social Sciences*—including all the research sciences that help us understand our human condition: our own interior and exterior estate within the human world (like sociology, psychology, anthropology, political science, and economics).

- Aesthetic Heritage—including the ability to appreciate aesthetic expression, whatever its artistic form, and opportunity to develop one's own artistic talents across a broad spectrum of the arts: the *fine arts* (like painting and sculpture); the *performing arts* (like dance, drama, film, music, and singing); the *applied arts* (like medicine and therapy, architecture and engineering, furniture making and interior design).

Religious Curriculum

The question of what to teach in Christian religious education curricula is a vast one, and a detailed treatment would take us too far afield.[42] Again, I propose only a few guidelines suggested by Christian faith itself for curriculum choices. They likely have resonance for the curricula of Sunday schools and parochial schools of all mainstream denominations.

Guideline #1 for Religious Curriculum: In choosing what to teach in the curriculum of Christian religious education, it is imperative to keep purpose in mind—what one is educating for.

The tradition itself bears witness that the "intended learning outcome" of Christian religious education is *nurturing disciples of Jesus Christ, people who follow his "way" through a community of disciples— the Church—in the midst of the world.* Such purpose reminds us that the defining content of Christian religious education is neither creed nor dogma, Scripture nor Tradition, important as all these are, but a person—the person of Jesus, whom Christians believe to be the Risen Christ, the Savior and Liberator.

Coming to "know" Jesus is much more than knowing about him and his teachings; it entails the "knowing" of relationship with him, becoming a disciple in the midst of a community of disciples that carries on his mission of God's reign of holiness and justice in the world. The Greek word for disciple—*mathetes*—also means "apprentice." The content of Christian catechesis should be chosen to mentor people as apprentices to Jesus, with all that this entails.

Guideline #2 for Religious Curriculum: In deciding what to teach in Christian religious education, it is imperative to keep in mind the kind of faith one is educating for.

Catholic Christian tradition reflects the conviction that Christian faith is to be *lived and living, whole and wholesome.* Lived in that it is realized—made flesh; living in that it ever remains vibrant, growing, ongoing; whole in that it engages the total person—mind, heart and strength, and should permeate every level of existence: personal, interpersonal, and social/political; and wholesome in that it should be life-affirming and celebrating, promoting "fullness of life" (John 10:10) for self, others, and God's creation.[43]

Guideline #3 for Religious Curriculum: The full scope of Christian religious education is to *inform, form,* and *transform* people in such lived and living, whole and wholesome Christian faith.

By inform I mean more than "information" in the sense of knowing data, but in the etymological sense (Latin, *in-formare*) of molding minds and hearts in the wisdom of Christian faith. Christian religious education is also to form people in Christian identity—a special responsibility of the faith community and the family. This was our central focus in chapter 4, but here I highlight that content can also be chosen and taught in ways that form as well as inform. And Christian religious curricula should encourage lifelong conversion and social transformation, inviting persons to commit themselves to the realization of God's reign of peace and justice in their own lives and in their society.

Story and Vision as Symbols of Christian Religious Curriculum

Beyond these general guidelines, I have found the metaphors of Story and Vision helpful in evoking the content to be taught in Christian religious curricula.[44] They can symbolize the whole reality of Christian faith (Story) and how it is to be lived (Vision). The metaphor "Story" points to a historicized faith—one that people make happen. Story is also likely to engage learners in a personal way, to lead to their own stories and draw them into dialogue, giving a sense of something unfolding and unfinished.

"Vision" suggests an open horizon. It reflects both the invitation and demand of Christian Story and suggests that Christians are to live with hope. Ultimately, the Christian Vision is the reign of God—the ongoing coming to fulfillment of God's intentions of shalom and fullness of life for humanity and creation.

More immediately, Vision refers to the meaning and ethic, the hopes and responsibilities, the promises and demands that every aspect of Christian Story symbolizes for adherents. Christian Vision is Christian living. It would seem imperative that Christian religious curricula teach Christian Story and propose the Vision of Christian faith.

Within the Story/Vision of Christian faith, Catholic religious educators need to give special emphasis to the study of Scripture—both the Hebrew Scriptures and the New Testament. Catholics need a kind of "affirmative action" regarding the Bible. Unlike Protestant brothers and sisters, the Bible is still far from the core of Catholic consciousness. And let Scripture be recentered without a new imbalance of neglecting Tradition.

Regarding Scripture and Tradition, Christian religious education should give people access to the many ways in which Christian Story is symbolized and carried, including liturgies, sacraments, and symbols; creeds, dogmas, and doctrines; myths and theologies; gestures and religious language; virtues and values, ethics and laws; spiritualities, expected lifestyles, and models of holy people; songs, music, dance, and drama; art, artifacts, and architecture; ways of sanctifying time, celebrating festivals, and appreciating holy places; community structures and forms of governance.

Not all of this, of course, can be taught by any one program. Curriculum across the life span recommends a crafted scope and sequence that teaches the entire breadth and depth of the rich storehouse that is Christian faith, suited to age and background, context and interest. The curriculum-content imperative is that Christian religious education offers people access to the "whole Story" and proposes the "full Vision" of Christian faith.

The "whole Story" and "full Vision" of Christian faith could sound overwhelming for religious education. How could the content of any curriculum include all of this vast tradition with its multiplicity of acceptable positions and practices, its dominant and subversive traditions? It is important to remember an old Catholic conviction—that Christian faith reflects what Vatican II called a "hierarchy of truths."[45] Every aspect is not equally important. Some beliefs, values, and practices are "constitutive" of Christian identity; others, more a distant ripple from those central convictions. A relative few aspects of Christian faith are Tradition with a capital *T* whereas the rest is tradition with a small *t*. The catechist's primary responsibility is to the former. I have two particular suggestions for the religion curricula of religiously sponsored schools. First, recognize that deeply religious questions can be engaged through any of the humanities, sciences, or arts. What teacher does not have ample opportunity to converse about ultimate issues, to raise questions of meaning and ethics, especially if she or he teaches in a humanizing way?

Looking back on my high-school days, I remember a literature teacher who often raised what were ultimate questions. In some ways, he was more effective in having us address religious issues than the designated religion teacher. Even in government schools that exclude explicit religious education from the curriculum, alert teachers can find artful ways to raise what are in fact spiritual issues and to share what is, in essence, spiritual wisdom.

Second, all religiously sponsored schools should avoid proselytizing students from other religious traditions. Any kind of proselytizing seems antithetical to authentic education. Of Catholic schools in particular, I am convinced that wherever possible and if warranted by numbers, they should provide curriculum in the religious traditions represented in their student body. If non-Catholic students participate in Catholic religious curriculum, it should be presented in ways respectful of their traditions and likely to enrich their own religious identity.

In an undergraduate course entitled *Catholicism,* I invite non-Catholic students who choose to take it, to allow the course to be an opportunity to reclaim their own religious identity, whether Jewish or Buddhist, Baptist or Methodist. Then I try to teach in a way that invites them to look at their own religious traditions in dialogue with this rich tradition for being human, religious, and Christian called Catholicism.

For the Educator's Soul

Let us return now to our pattern of proposing what this depth structure—commitment to a humanizing tradition—might mean for the soul, style, and space of the educator. For the soul of teacher or parent, I can think of one personal commitment and three pertaining specifically to their teaching.

Teachers and parents need to cultivate their own personal appreciation for tradition, that they reflect in their person some of the refinement carried in the arts, sciences, and humanities. That educators themselves be cultured people is a traditional expectation and, it would seem, a reasonable one. It is equivalent to expecting our doctors to care for their own health, our accountants not to be arrested for tax evasion. Think about it; a boorish teacher is not likely to educate in any holistic sense of the term, regardless of their competence in a specialized field.

And surely parent educators need at least an appreciation for learning and culture in order to motivate their offspring to pursue a humanizing education. The social research on learning indicates that children who do well in school predominantly come from homes where education is highly valued—even if the parents have not had privileged access to as much themselves.

Apropos encouraging in learners a critically appreciative attitude toward tradition and enabling them to creatively appropriate it, I can think of three commitments asked of educators' souls: conservation, liberation, and celebration.

Conservation: Teachers and parents should help learners to cherish tradition as the wisdom of the ages, to appreciate it as the legacy of their forebears in this human pilgrimage through time. To conserve tradition amounts to maintaining a "radical democracy" by including the legacy of those gone before us—something analogous to "the communion of saints"—as if they still have voice and vote. Teachers and parents should encourage each generation of learners to become reliable trustees of their heritage, to conserve and pass it on, as they would any valuable inheritance.

Liberation: Each generation must be readied to build upon tradition, to question it, to add to it, to appropriate it creatively in order to bring new life and freedom. If taught and learned in humanizing ways, if critically appreciated and creatively appropriated, tradition brings human liberation.

Teachers can provide access to it as a great communal wellspring into which each generation can plunge deeply to draw up fresh water—life-giving images and new possibilities or (continuing the water imagery) as a great river of vitality at which they can constantly refresh themselves. Whichever image one favors, teachers and parents must maintain tradition as living water; otherwise it becomes a deadening influence—reduced to a stagnant traditionalism.

Celebration: Sociologists point to a deep insecurity marking contemporary society and a pervasive lack of self-esteem besetting a high percentage of "modern" people. Whatever the cause, all the social sciences attest that being rooted in tradition seems to be a powerful antidote to such anomie, that tradition provides those "steeped" in it with a strong sense of identity, purpose, and meaning.

If this sense of security is grounded in life-giving traditions, they encourage persons and communities to embrace life, to find joy in it, to celebrate the gift that it is. Teachers and parents need to teach the kinds of traditions and in ways that ready learners for the celebration of life, to find happiness as human beings—*for life for all.*

For the Educator's Style

A number of proposals for style made in previous and subsequent chapters could be repeated here too. I accent especially the need for critical reflection apropos tradition. But that emphasis is present in almost every chapter, so it need not be our focus here. I reiterate, however, that without critical reflection on tradition learners will never really know it for themselves, and, more urgently, will miss out on the negative and death-dealing aspects of tradition—and all traditions have the latter.

Beyond this, I have three specific proposals for the style of teachers and parents by way of their commitment to tradition: (a) provide access; (b) encourage relationship with its "texts"; and (c) invite its critical and creative appropriation to life.

Provide Access to Tradition

One function of an educator is to ensure that learners have access to the symbols and texts of tradition. Professional teachers do this more obviously, but parents can do it in more subtle ways. The phrase "providing access" implies a gentle and mentoring style of teaching— not imposing upon but making available, not a doctrinaire delivery but facilitating an encounter in which learners and tradition are the primary actors, with the educator simply seeing to it that they "get together."

This does not mean an insipid "take-it-or-leave-it" attitude on the educator's part. Providing access implies dynamic engagement by learners; it can even entail rhetoric and persuasion on the teacher's or parent's part, and yet it always encourages people's active encounter with the tradition being taught.

Religious educator Mary Boys, who has developed "making accessible" as the preferred style for teaching tradition, captures its gentling dynamic as well as its variety:

> Access is given in numerous ways. To provide access means to erect bridges, to make metaphors, to build highways, to provide introductions and commentaries, to translate foreign terms, to remove barriers, to make maps, to demolish blockages, to demonstrate effects, to energize and sustain participation, and to be hospitable.[46]

The more direct access students can have the better—a suggestion that is age-related and not readily possible in all circumstances. "Direct access" means people getting directly into the texts and symbols of tradition themselves, going to the "original" rather than receiving someone else's mediation of it. Far better to read Shakespeare's play *Macbeth* than a commentary or to hear a lecture about it. Better to encounter an original piece of art or a good reproduction than to be told about it. And in the context of religious education, better for students to go directly to Scripture and study it themselves than have someone tell them about a text and what it means for them.

Encourage a Relationship between "Text" and Learner

In the subhead above, *text* is in quotes because, as noted in chapter 1, contemporary hermeneutics broadens beyond written texts to include any symbol of tradition—written or oral, art or artifact, sign or gesture. Earlier, too, I proposed hermeneutics as a conversation between interpreters and text. Here I echo the implications for teaching.

Pedagogically, there are two much-favored approaches to texts of tradition—one tries to apply them directly to the present as if they are to be repeated; the other approaches them as objects to be conquered, to be dissected by critical tools as if learners are to "master the text."

The first approach encourages traditionalism, whereas the second is violent toward tradition and encourages studying texts without being personally enriched by them, to use them without touching one's own "being."

Between these extremes is the hermeneutical approach recommended by Gadamer and others whereby people enter into a relationship with a text of tradition, are open to being questioned and changed by it, and consciously bring their own life and world to interpreting it.

This "to-and-fro" between person and text is akin to a relationship. Interpreters bring their lives to a text of tradition to make it come alive again with a fresh interpretation, and conversely, the text brings new life to the interpreters, enriching them as persons. In my own teaching, I often pose a reading assignment along these lines: What do you hear this text saying to your life? What do you say in response? What are you coming to "see for yourself" from this encounter? This is a hermeneutical approach!

Encourage Personal Appropriation of Tradition

The third point follows from the previous two and, pedagogically, is the typical dynamic as people "come away from" their encounter with texts of tradition. Imagine it as the moment when learners come to see for themselves what the tradition means for their lives, when they critically and creatively appropriate its legacy and make choices informed by their encounter.

This can be a dialectical moment in which learners judge and make some aspects of tradition their own, might question other aspects (refusing to repeat what is destructive and deadening), and create a new moment for tradition as living and vital. Appropriation requires an honest exchange—honest in that the person may be changed but so too may be the tradition—a new moment for both.

Key to an educator encouraging a personal and creative appropriation by learners is activities that ask them, in one way or another, questions like:

What do you really think about this?

What are you coming to see for yourself?

What does this mean for you, for us, for now?

What do you agree with or disagree with?

What new insights do you find here?

What new wisdom is emerging for you?

The intent is that learners come to "know for themselves" the wisdom, or knowledge, or beauty of the tradition. It can often be an exciting moment—as when we say that we "get it." Piaget says that the dynamic of personal appropriation is more of "recognition" than "cognition" and, as noted before, likens it to learners "re-inventing" something for themselves.[47]

Teachers and parents must allow learners the freedom they need for authentic appropriation. Without freedom to think for themselves, they are less likely to make tradition their own. Let me highlight that such freedom should prevail as well in appropriating religious tradition. People must be granted the religious freedom which is their human right.

The Second Vatican Council's *Declaration on Religious Freedom* is testimony to a hard-won struggle by Catholic scholars, led by American Jesuit John Courtney Murray (1904–67), who pushed back against a long tradition of religious coercion. After much debate, the Council stated unequivocally,

> In spreading religious faith and in introducing religious practices, everyone ought at all times to refrain from any manner of action which might seem to carry a kind of coercion or of a kind of persuasion that would be dishonorable or unworthy.[48]

A later church document applied this principle of religious freedom specifically to religious education, stating:

> A Catholic school cannot relinquish its own freedom to proclaim the Gospel and to offer a formation based on the values to be found in a Christian education; this is its right and duty. To proclaim or to offer is not to impose, however; the latter suggests a moral violence which is strictly forbidden, both by the Gospel and by Church law.[49]

The reference to Church law is to Canon 748 #2, which states:

> "Persons cannot ever be forced by anyone to embrace the Catholic faith against their conscience." Such a strict mandate against indoctrination requires Catholic teachers and parents to encourage learners to act freely in their appropriation—or rejection—of Christian faith.

For the Educational Space

At the end of a long chapter, and with much said already, I make only one proposal: *Let commitment to tradition pervade the ethos of school, home, and parish so that they become communities of moral discourse and formation.*

This proposal directly counters Immanuel Kant's separating of theoretical knowledge and moral reasoning as different pursuits. For education, Kant's legacy was either the neglect of moral formation entirely or its separation from general curricula into a particular class or course of studies—e.g., values education. Such a dichotomy—between theoretical and practical reasoning, as Kant stated it—should not be never be practiced in a school committed to humanizing education. The curriculum of tradition should provide the occasion for moral discourse and formation. My point may be more apropos a school environment, but families and faith communities can imagine how to honor it as well.

The proposal here is not new but revives a neglected emphasis. There is a long tradition in humanistic education of making the liberal arts and humanities a basis for moral formation. The liberal arts give people the ability to think and reflect—essential to ethical discernment—and the humanities should raise the great moral issues of life and suggest models for responding to them, with examples of virtues and vices, of saints and sinners.

Maritain reflects this ancient understanding of humanistic education when he proposes that "the great ethical ideas conveyed by civilization" should be taught "not as a subject of special courses" but "be embodied in the humanities and liberal arts, especially as an integral part of the teaching of literature, poetry, fine arts, and history."[50] Maritain is not naive about the limits here. He writes, "Virtue is not a by-product of knowledge" (as a good Thomist, he insists that moral formation requires practice as well), and then adds, "but true moral knowledge is a condition for virtue."[51]

Thomas Lickona, a contemporary author, persuasively proposes that all Western education return to integrating moral formation throughout the curriculum. He says that every teacher must ask, "What are the ethical issues and values in the subject I teach? How can I make those issues and values more salient to my students?" Intentionality is needed on the teacher's part—to look for ethical issues that can be raised and to attend to them in an appropriate way. According to Lickona, "There is a new awareness that the academic curriculum has been a sleeping giant in values education."[52]

I agree, for surely reflecting on and making choices about what is good, true, and beautiful is integral to teaching our traditions of wisdom, knowledge, and art.

Teachers should be intentional about bringing the core curriculum of humanities, sciences, and arts to moral discourse. Otherwise, it does not happen or only rarely by chance. Surely every educator in every religiously sponsored school, regardless of her or his discipline of learning, should be committed to integrating moral formation throughout the curriculum.

But every humanistic educator can and should engage the curriculum and especially the teaching of tradition—of whatever kind—as an opportunity for moral discourse and virtue formation. In addition, not only the explicit humanities, but any topic taught in a humanizing way can encourage moral formation. My friend the auto-mechanics instructor raises issues of honesty with his apprentices and explains to them that they will live happier lives and also do better business in the long run if they are honest with customers.

For Reflection
- What are some of your best insights from your conversation with this chapter?

- Do you have disagreements with it or adjustments to suggest?

- Apropos tradition, are you coming to some decisions for your own vocation as teacher or parent?

Notes

1. St. Augustine, *The Confessions,* Book 11, Par. 14, 287.
2. See Michael Schiro, *Curriculum for Better Schools,* 9–12, for a fine review of these emphases in the curriculum field. Schiro, in fact, has a fourfold schema, but I stay with the more traditional threefold division, combining Schiro's third and fourth categories into "Needs of Society"—be that to fit into society or to contribute to its reconstruction.
3. Gilkey, Catholicism Confronts Modernity, 17.
4. Pope John Paul II, quoted in Robert Schreiter, "Faith and Cultures: Challenges to a World Church." 752.
5. "Pastoral Constitution," #42 and 44, Abbott, *Documents,* 242 and 246.
6. "Revelation as history" now seems to be the dominant understanding in the Church and among its theologians of how revelation occurs. Avery Dulles explains that "some theologians of the nineteenth century, followed by a great throng of twentieth-century theologians," became convinced "that revelation occurs primarily through deeds, rather than words."

   For this "model" of revelation, "the content is the great deeds of God in history. . . . The form of revelation is primarily that of deeds or events, especially the climactic events of the death and Resurrection of Jesus. . . ." (See *Models of Revelation,* 53 and 60.)

   Although this is only one of five models of revelation outlined by Dulles, it has wide support among scholars and ready resonance among Catholic ones. In fact, Catholic commitment to Tradition as well as to Scripture as a medium of revelation encourages Catholics to add that God's presence and self-disclosure is not just in great past events. Existentially, it continues in the lives of people and communities as history unfolds.
7. See "Constitution on Revelation," #8, Abbott, *Documents,* 116.
8. See, especially, Piaget's text, *To Understand Is to Invent.*
9. Aquinas used the term "conaturality" to describe the human readiness to recognize and receive God's word. He saw it as a gift of God's grace, guided by the Holy Spirit, and functioning especially in our capacity for judgment. See *Summa Theologica,* II–II, 45, 2, vol. 3, 1374.
10. See Viktor E. Frankl, *Man's Search for Meaning.*
11. "Constitution on Revelation," #13, Abbott, *Documents,* 121.
12. Clement of Alexandria, *The Stromata,* 1.5.
13. Newman, *Idea of a University,* 88.
14. Vatican I, "Constitution on Faith," *The Church Teaches,* 34.
15. "Constitution on the Liturgy," #122, Abbott, *Documents,* 174.
16. For both Alcuin's statement and Charlemagne's decree, see Cully, *Basic Writings in Christian Education,* 85–92.
17. See *Till God Will: Mary Ward through Her Writings,* M. Emmanuel Orchard, ed.
18. "Constitution on Divine Revelation," #22, Abbott, *Documents,* 125.
19. Just to mention one instance: the "base Christian community" movement throughout Latin America has been a source of ecclesial and social transformation simply by having people meet around the word of God in Scripture, bring the struggles of their lives to the text, listen to what it means for their lives, and share their faith together. These communities are living

testimony that the Reformers were right: "direct access" to the Scriptures can be transforming.

20. "Constitution on Revelation," #9 and 10, Abbott, *Documents*, 117–118.
21. "Constitution on Revelation," #8, Abbott, *Documents*, 116.
22. Tracy, *Plurality and Ambiguity*, 12.
23. Tracy, *Naming the Present*, 115. Note that Tracy's own central statement about the classic is found in *The Analogical Imagination*, 99–153.
24. McBrien, *Catholicism*, 1189.
25. See "Constitution on the Church," #25, Abbott, *Documents*, 47ff.
26. See the classic essay by the great Yves Congar, "The Magisterium and Theologians."
27. "Church in Modern World," #16, and "Religious Freedom," #3, Abbott, *Documents*, 213 and 681.
28. See Gadamer, *Truth and Method*, 277–80.
29. Ibid., 306.
30. Throughout this section I find Maritain a most helpful companion; he gave concerted though to a "Catholic" perspective on curriculum content.
31. Maritain, *The Education of Man*, 69.
32. See ibid., chapter 8.
33. Ibid., 69.
34. Ibid., 150.
35. See ibid., 69.
36. The wide scope given to the term "humanities" can be seen in the language used by the United States Congress in the law establishing the National Endowment for the Humanities: "The term 'humanities' includes, but is not limited to, the study of the following: language, both modern and classic; linguistics; literature; history; jurisprudence; philosophy; archeology; the history, criticism, theory and practice of the arts; and those aspect of the social sciences which have humanistic content and employ humanistic methods" *Encyclopedia Britannica*, vol. 8, 1983, 1179.
37. Maritain, *The Education of Man*, 90.
38. Ibid., 84.
39. Ibid., 84, 85 ,and 92.
40. See ibid., 90–93.
41. Ibid., 139.
42. My sense of the content to be included in the curriculum of Catholic religious education is most obviously reflected in the three children's religion curricula of which I am primary author: *God with Us* (K to 8, 1984), *Coming to Faith* (K to 8, 1989), and *Revised Coming to Faith* (K to 6, 1995) series from William H. Sadlier.
43. For a more complete statement of this summary, see Groome, "Looking Back on Twenty-five Years: A Personal Reflection."
44. See my *Sharing Faith* chapter 4 for a more detailed review of these terms and my reasons for favoring them.
45. "Decree on Ecumenism," #11, Abbott, *Documents*, 354.
46. Boys, *Educating in Faith*, 209.
47. See Piaget, *To Understand Is to Invent*.
48. "Declaration on Religious Freedom," #4, Abbott, *Documents*, 682.

49. Vatican Congregation for Catholic Education, *The Religious Dimension of Education in a Catholic School*, # 6.
50. Maritain, *Education at the Crossroads*, 68.
51. Maritain, *The Education of Man*, 122.
52. Lickona, *Educating for Character*, 167 and 162.

CHAPTER SIX

A Reasonable Wisdom:
"Thinking for Life"

"Never Trouble Trouble"

On the farm we worked in pairs, and I loved to partner with Joe Kane. Workers assembled early morning to get our day's assignment, and I hoped my grandfather would pair me with Joe. He usually did—except when he saw us "doin' more talkin' than work" the previous day. Working alongside Joe was the highlight of my long summer holidays from high school and, later, from college.

Joe had a well-earned reputation as the best and handiest farm worker for miles around, although now he was "slowin' down a bit," as he would say wistfully. I knew I was apprenticed to a master, yet he made me feel like his partner. Not a decision was made about our work together without consultation between us.

Joe knew farming better than most and had great wisdom about life as well. He was a gentle teacher, and I wanted to learn everything—like how to grow the best potatoes; care for a motherless calf; fatten a lean pig; thatch a cow barn; build a reek of straw; catch eels; know the names for local plants, weeds, and birds; and a thousand other important things.

And Joe had stories, oh, did he have stories! They were often funny and always had some wisdom about life. Even ones I'd heard ten times before, I'd say "not lately" when he'd ask, "Have I told you the one about . . ." just to hear Joe tell it again.

There was nothing I couldn't discuss with Joe, even real personal stuff. After listening intently, he would usually say, "Well . . . you have to make up your own mind about somethin' like that," and then would ask a few questions. Thinking back, Joe seldom gave advice, but asked the best of questions—ones that encouraged my own wisdom. On rare occasions, though—and they were memorable—he would give a bit of direct counsel, often as a proverb.

Late one Saturday afternoon, a local farmer came to borrow hay for his cows—he had run out. Everyone made themselves scarce—just about to quit, pay in our pockets, ready to clean up for a night in the village. I hated it when my grandfather gave Joe and me the assignment and griped all the way through. Joe said nothing.

We loaded the hay in a hurry—too much of a hurry—and set off with it pitched precariously on the tractor and trailer. We had to go up and down a very steep hill called Mullahanna to deliver it. As we approached Mullahanna, I panicked; the hay would surely slip, and then what? We'd spend our Saturday night collecting it from the four winds. I fretfully told Joe what was surely about to happen.

He was perched comfortably on the passenger seat of the tractor, smoking his pipe; I was driving. He reached over, put his hand on my arm and said gently, "Tom, 'y'er a young man, and now's a great time to learn a lesson." Joe had a kind of solemnity, his style in such moments, as if he knew he was representing the wisdom of the ages. He continued, "Never trouble trouble 'til trouble troubles you."

We made it with the hay and still got to the village that night. To this day, when I look to the horizon and see an array of problems coming to meet me, instead of struggling to solve them before they arrive, I try to remember Joe—and have a mental picture of him perched on the back of the tractor, serious but with that twinkle in his eye: "Never trouble trouble . . ." And in moments of reverie, I think of how much else Joe taught me and can only imagine how he came by so much wisdom about life. It is time I gave him a footnote.

Forbidden Fruit?

Every moment of our conscious life entails an act of knowing and is shaped by our knowledge. "Knower" is an apt metaphor for humankind. To begin with, our bodies have a vast reservoir of instinctive and experiential knowledge, from the sensory motor skills needed to get around to the wisdom that bodies can remember when minds forget.

Just putting one foot past the other and instinctively avoiding placing either one in the fire—or in our mouth—reflect complex kinds of knowing. Moving beyond the corporeal to consciousness, we gather immediate knowledge by noticing the data that comes to us through the senses from the world around. We can know a lot just by "taking a look" or "having a listen."

Then, beyond body knowledge and immediate sense data, every person knows endless volumes of information. Just pause and notice the quantity of information that you possess—and often with a feeling of certainty. Some of it you learned from experience, more from your education or personal study, or you just picked it up along the way. I have an acquaintance who for years has been reading encyclopedias in training for TV quiz shows. He retains more facts than anyone I have ever met—lists of presidents, politicians, and popes, capitals, countries, and climates, and a million others. Even without being able to win jackpots, every person possesses a vast amount of information.

Building upon but reaching beyond body knowing, data, and information, we are capable of personal knowledge by which we make meaning out of life and even come to "know"—in the relational sense—ourselves and other people. We are able to know as "making sense" because of our specifically human capacities for intuition and understanding, for judgment and evaluation, for decision and commitment.

Through these capacities, too, we come to know for ourselves a portion of the legacy of civilization—the communal world of meaning around us and some of what those before us came to know. We can even turn our cognitional capacities upon ourselves, to think about our own thinking, enabling us to know ourselves—in a self-conscious way—though mystery ever remains.

When mixed with our capacity for relationship, our cognitional ability prompts us to reach for "knowing" other people, as when I say that "I know Colleen well"—even as I recognize how much she is still mystery to me. And pressing on in this realm of mystery, I can even reach to know the Transcendent—not just know "about" but in the personal and relational sense of "knowing" God. So beginning with knowing how to open our eyes and take a look, ultimately we can reach to "know" Mystery as an open vista.

Apropos Mystery, I put "know" in quotes because surely there is a qualitative transition between knowing how to tie my shoelaces and begin walking; knowing the neighborhood I walk through and the things I notice along the way; knowing that a walk is good for me after being so long at my desk; knowing my own thoughts as I walk along and what might make sense to write next; knowing the neighbors I recognize upon the way and, eventually, noticing the beauty of nature that turns my mind and heart to "knowing" God. Can the terms *knowledge* and *knowing* be used across this continuum of cognitional possibilities? Is there one common activity of knowing—albeit at different levels—that can be described? If so, what would be its dynamics—the things a human being "does" in order to know anything?

Going further, when I reflect a while on my personal knowledge of the world of meaning around me, I begin to wonder about the reliability of it—especially after being palpably wrong many times about something I "knew for sure." Can we be certain—really—about anything other than verifiable data or mathematics—like the capital of India or two plus two make four? Given the human capacity for delusion—of self and others—are any of our personal convictions beyond doubt or our commitments beyond question?

So, ironically, our cognitional capacities leave us with perplexing questions about their very functioning and dependability: What does it mean to know or to "have" knowledge? How do we come by it? Can we know the things that matter most with any reliability?

The philosophers, as we would expect, have struggled mightily with questions about knowledge—what it is, how we come by it, if it is credible. They call such study epistemology. From the Greek *episteme* for "knowledge," it inquires about the nature, sources, and reliability of human knowing.[1] Epistemology goes back to the dawn of Western thought with the pre-Socratic philosophers (circa 600 B.C.E.)— the first to begin to reflect systematically on the meaning of life. Soon, some smart alecks put a cat among the philosophical pigeons by questioning whether humans can know profound human matters by their own efforts—without direct messages from the gods. Of ourselves, can we know issues of meaning, purpose, and ethic—reliably?

With the gauntlet of skepticism thrown down to the whole philosophical enterprise, bedlam broke loose and the philosophers divided into various epistemological camps. There were among them absolutists and relativists, idealists and realists, rationalists and empiricists—with cynics and skeptics continuing to worry the rest. All were convinced, however, that decisions about the nature, sources, and reliability of knowledge are of fundamental importance. Epistemology pertains to the very ground of the human enterprise.

The Athenian scholar Plato, star student of Socrates (circa 470–399 B.C.E.), was the first philosopher to recognize that epistemology is of central concern to educators. Teachers' understanding of knowledge and how people come to know undoubtedly shapes how they educate—a rather obvious thesis. Whether or not they have given it as much thought as Plato, all teachers and parents have their own "operative epistemology"—a working sense of *what it means to know and how to promote knowledge.* It greatly influences how they educate.

"Old Charlie" McGowan, my high-school English teacher, had a game he played with us on a slow day. He would simply ask, "What's a button?" and invite us to write down our definition. No matter what we said, Charlie would have a rebuttal like: "But that's its use—what's a button?" or "That's what it's made of—what's a button?"

His most demanding probes, usually when someone started talking about "buttonness," were "How do you know?" and "Can you be sure of that?" We never did come up with an agreed-upon definition of a button, and failing to define so simple an item, we were left wondering about much more we thought was "obvious" or that we knew for certain.

At the time, we saw the game as a bit of fun—for when even "Old Charlie" did not feel like working. Years later, I recognized that it epitomized his whole style of teaching—ever trying to get us to think for ourselves and to probe our own thinking. And when I read in graduate school that all knowledge is perspectival and constructed, I had a new appreciation for what "Old Charlie" was up to.

It is surely significant that the Bible presents the will to know as the root of humankind's original sin. The actual sin, indeed, is represented as disobedience, but what pushed our first parents over the brink was not the lusciousness of the fruit but the temptation to be "like God, *knowing* good and evil" (Genesis 3:5).

Contrary to God's forewarning, having eaten from the "tree of knowledge," Adam and Eve did not die "that very day" (Genesis 2:17). Was it only an idle threat—God hoping to deter them—and they called God's bluff? Maybe, but as Irish poet Patrick Kavanagh wrote of the forbidden fruit, "It had death the germ within it." And there are critics who claim that much of our knowledge and ways of knowing have served injustice and death.

Yet, though we have been banished from the "garden of Eden," we should remember the dual potential of that tree. Can people come to know in ways more likely to encourage good than evil, life than death? I am convinced that we can, but, far from being inevitable, such knowing demands intentionality and great care, especially on the part of educators.

In the Celtic mythology that was part of my childhood, the salmon rather than the serpent is associated with knowledge. In all the ancient stories, to catch the *bradán feasa*—literally, "salmon of wisdom"—is the most worthwhile pursuit in life for everyone. However, the exalted piscine must be caught by hand—imagine—and burns to the bone anyone who touches it. Becoming wise requires much effort and getting your fingers burned. And the wisdom gained from catching the salmon always makes the proprietor accountable for the well-being of others and for sharing wisdom. Both the biblical and the Celtic myths infer that there is risk and responsibility in coming to "know"—not a venture to be taken lightly!

As Langdon Gilkey points out, Catholic Christianity reflects an enduring appreciation for knowledge and for the role of the mind in knowing, even in knowing the affairs of faith.

> There has been throughout Catholic history a drive toward rationality, the insistence that the divine mystery . . . insofar as possible be penetrated, defended, and explicated by the most acute rational reflection.[2]

This mirrors a deep conviction that the mind is a gift of God. Like the human condition and world, it is essentially good and to be put to worthwhile purposes. From a Catholic Christian perspective, reason and revelation are partners, theology is "faith seeking understanding."

Historically, there has been a strong leaning in Catholic theology to identify God with "Reason," and to claim that it is by the intellect that humankind most resembles God. St. Thomas Aquinas wrote that "the Divine intellect is the Essence of God," adding that "man . . . is most perfectly like God according to . . . his intellectual nature"[3]—an unfortunate exaggeration. For Christian faith, surely the essence of God is love. (See 1 John 4:8.) The human ability to love is our closest reflection to God. Yet, Aquinas epitomizes the Catholic (over-) appreciation for the mind and human rationality.

Although Gilkey commends this appreciation of the mind, even in matters of faith, he wonders if Catholicism is comfortable with speculative reason only—figuring things out logically from accepted premises, but closed to the full force of critical rationality; questioning one's own assumptions and vested interests; and uncovering the influence of the social context on our knowledge. A "recovering Catholic" friend of mine is fond of saying, "Catholicism is a very reasonable system—so long as you don't question the system." Which is to say, from within its faith perspective, Catholicism can be made to seem coherent, but does it bear critical review from other reasonable perspectives?

Aquinas's *Summa Theologica* is an impressive example of speculative reason in theology: providing definitions, distinctions, and logical arguments; establishing foundational principles; drawing out implications and elaborations; explaining and defending faith; making explicit what was implicit. But this was not yet the critical rationality of the later Enlightenment era that emphasized "free thinking"—reasoning without commitment to any system, without authority other than reason itself. In fact, the Catholic church clashed mightily at first with the Enlightenment's critical rationality, insisting on the primary authority of Scripture and Tradition. In his famous *Syllabus of Errors* (1864), Pope Pius IX condemned as heresy the notion that "human reason . . . is autonomous," rejecting reason alone as "the principle norm" of "all truth."[4]

Catholicism retains a fair amount of skepticism about the "free thinking" of modernity. It rejects the Enlightenment's bias against tradition and sees unbounded confidence in reason to solve all human problems as naive—even dangerous. Although some of its skepticism has proved to be well-founded, nonetheless, Gilkey rightly wonders if

Catholicism can move beyond the speculative reason of Scholasticism to embrace a truly critical rationality. At the end of the day, can Catholics really think for themselves—critically appropriating their traditions and questioning their own and their church's thinking or may they think only what their church tells them to think, repeating their traditions?

I am convinced that Catholicism can embrace—and is doing so— a truly critical rationality. And yet it may prove wise in hesitating about the Enlightenment's version of rationality—as if reduced to the mind alone—resonating, ironically, with a similar critique of modernity by the postmodernists. The latter group of contemporary critics, although mentored by the Enlightenment, have turned with a vengeance against its rationality as deeply flawed and inimical to humanization.

A common sentiment among postmodernists is that Enlightenment rationality, now the dominant epistemology of the West, (1) can be violent toward the world and divisive of peoples; (2) is elitist, being controlled by academics and scientists; (3) is blind to the influences of social context and self-interest on what we know; (4) is obsessed with "what works"—for power and production; (5) has no sense of ethics or commitment to what ought to be; (6) makes farcical claims to objective and value-free knowledge; (7) supports some of the West's worst oppressions and most destructive powers. Whether for right or wrong reasons, Catholicism's skepticism about Enlightenment epistemology may prove wise after all.

Postmodernist critics have brought epistemology to center stage in contemporary thought or, more accurately, have placed it in the eye of a storm. Beyond their charge that Enlightenment rationality threatens human well-being, bringing us eventually to the brink of nuclear destruction, they propose a more holistic way of knowing in the interest of humanization—*for life for all*. Since the body of this chapter joins the effort to weave a humanizing epistemology as a foundation for education, I will situate the postmodernist critique of the ruling epistemology with a brief historical sketch.

As a force for humanization, Western epistemology has gone downhill since its early days.[5] Plato insisted passionately that all knowing should serve human well-being and that knowledge ought to promote happiness by helping people realize what is true, choose what is good, and create what is beautiful. He insisted on unity

274

between "being" and "knowing"—that people's lives should inform their knowledge and what they know should shape how they live. For Plato, as noted, the teacher's function is to "turn the soul" of students—to touch and shape the very depths of people's "being" through knowledge.[6]

Aristotle, star pupil of Plato, also insisted that knowledge should enhance the human condition and bring happiness. Although he preferred the sequence of doing the good in order to know it—in contrast to Plato who favored the reverse, putting knowledge first— Aristotle agreed with his teacher on the symbiosis between being and knowing. What people know should shape their identity and how they live, and their lives in the world should be a primary source of what they know. For Aristotle, knowledge should enhance people as human beings and be realized in their lives as wisdom.

Maintaining unity between people's knowledge and how they live continued, at least tenuously, throughout subsequent centuries but eventually ran aground on the Enlightenment's "triumph of reason." The Enlightenment pulled back from the unity of knowing and being and, thus, from a life-giving epistemology in at least three significant ways.

First, the human desire for truth and wisdom, which prompts us to seek knowledge in the first place, was diminished to a quest for rational certainty—for finding the correct intellectual ideas and being sure of their veracity. This narrow rationalism placed trust only in the mind, excluding feelings and experiences, and even limited the mind to reason alone, disparaging memory and imagination as untrustworthy.

Such rationalism was epitomized in the work of the French philosopher René Descartes (1596–1650) with his famous slogan "I think, therefore I am." He proposed this syllogism as the ultimate "certain idea" on which to build all reliable knowledge and succeeded in convincing Enlightenment philosophers to swallow it—hook, line, and sinker.

Thereafter, reason standing alone—separating itself from memory and imagination, from the body and feelings, from experiences and real-life situations, from tradition and community, and claiming to be objective and without bias—became the "god" of knowledge. Knowing became a quest for "clear and certain ideas" (Descartes' phrase)—a far cry from the wisdom, happiness, and integrity of life sought by ancient philosophers.

Second, German philosopher Immanuel Kant convinced the Enlightenment movement that theoretical and practical reason are two different activities with no correlation between them. The first is concerned with understanding data and making judgments to lead to scientific knowledge; practical reason is concerned with morality, with faith and religion. Although Kant thought he was defending a place for ethics and faith alongside the "modern" sciences, he tragically separated them and, thus, knowledge from life.

Science without an ethic has brought humankind to the brink of ecological disaster and nuclear destruction. Scientists who were there tell that when the Manhattan Project began in 1942, commissioned to create the first atomic bomb, no one present ever asked, "Should we be doing this?" or "Who will suffer?" but only "How will we do it?" Scientific knowledge, if devoid of ethic, will eventually destroy us.

Third, rationally certain knowledge—considered the only "real knowledge" by Enlightenment proponents—was now ruled by the sciences and their scholars. This discouraged ordinary people from trusting their common sense, their experiences of life or the wisdom of tradition and, instead, encouraged them to depend entirely on the opinions of experts who have scientific knowledge and enjoy epistemic privilege over nonscholars. To this Enlightenment perspective, my friend Joe Kane was an uneducated peasant who knew nothing of any value. How absurd!

The exclusion of ordinary people as agents of knowing and from what counts as knowledge was directed against everyone outside of the sciences, but aimed with a vengeance against women—excluded from academia throughout the history of Western civilization. As feminist scholar Sandra Harding observes, the history of Western epistemology is marked by "an androcentric ideology" that associates "the rational mind" with "men and masculinity" and "women and femininity" with "the pre-rational body and irrational emotions and values."[7] The so-called Enlightenment did little to challenge this misogyny, which, though claiming to be reasonable, was eminently irrational in its bias.

Within postmodernism, the most devastating critique of Enlightenment rationality is mounted by philosophers called "deconstructionists." As the name implies, their intent is to dismantle the whole edifice of what passes for knowledge and knowing in

Western culture. Trying to be faithful to their own principles, they propose no overarching schema in its place.

Yet beyond their great diversity, deconstructionists reflect three central epistemic convictions relevant to educators—teachers and parents: (1) there is no one privileged group or starting point for knowledge—anyone can know from anywhere; (2) all knowledge is perspectival and no one view can explain everything—mystery remains and every perspective is partial; and (3) no perspective is "innocent" in that all knowledge is intertwined with systems of power and serves some interests to the neglect of others. The deconstructionists could keep awake at night anyone still concerned with rational certainty!

The deconstructionists are good at their job—taking apart—but now the task is "reconstruction," to gather up the positive legacy of the Enlightenment and reweave a "way of knowing" that is humanizing and encourages education *for life for all*. I am convinced that there is a Christian perspective on knowing that can make a significant contribution to this reconstructive project. In fact, the technical rationality now so dominant lacks precisely a faith perspective. Given its traditional appreciation for the mind as gift of God and its trust in the world and history as reliable sources of knowledge, Catholic Christianity can embrace critical rationality—an instance of the Enlightenment's positive legacy. Then, blending this with its ancient commitment to a wisdom way of knowing, it can help to forge a humanizing epistemic for education.

For Reflection

- From your own experience, what does it entail to really "know" something?

- Outline how we come by such knowing and the steps we take. In other words, how do you describe what philosophers call "the dynamics of cognition?"

- When you teach, what is the most complete kind of "knowing" you intend people to reach? What difference do you hope such "knowing" will make in their lives?

Sources for Holistic Knowing

In this chapter, it seems wise to alter the sequence a bit. Instead of summarizing a Christian epistemology and then reviewing its sources, it will be more constructive to reverse the order. I outline three building-blocks for constructing a holistic epistemology: (1) the biblical tradition of wisdom—which defined the first millennium of Church education; (2) the enduring commitment of Christianity to keep theory and practice united—even in the aftermath of the Enlightenment; and (3) the work of feminist scholars in epistemology—so promising for holistic knowing and, to the surprise of many, most congenial to a "Catholic" way of wisdom.

The Biblical Tradition of Wisdom

Wisdom and becoming wise are now understood more holistically than knowledge and knowing—at least as the latter terms have come to be identified in Western consciousness. There is, of course, an ancient tradition that was holistic in its understanding of knowledge and knowing, but this epistemology was lost in the reductionisms of the Enlightenment era and is absent entirely from the now dominant technical rationality—concerned primarily with knowing "what works."

Although knowing and knowledge should never be left behind, it seems that a more holistic connotation is now conveyed by reaching beyond them to wisdom and becoming wise. The latter are still heard as pertaining to who and how people are, to their whole identity and agency in the world. Although wise people indeed have knowledge of one kind or another, they are wise in their very being—in their thoughts, desires, and actions. Joe Kane was a wise person and a teacher of wisdom. He might not have been able to quote chapter and verse, but he was the Solomon of my youth.

Wisdom is a complex notion in the Hebrew tradition and is referred to most often by the word *hokmah*. The Septuagint—the Greek Old Testament—uses the term *sophia*. Wisdom evolved in meaning over the span of biblical tradition. Originally described as a craft or skill (Exodus 31:6) or a cleverness (2 Samuel 14:2), soon it emerged as a practical wisdom of life that brings success, respect, and personal well-being. Wisdom comes from reflection on life experience (Job 12:12), but is also learned from tradition (Proverbs 19:20) and from other persons of wisdom (Isaiah 19:11).

After the beginning of the monarchy in ancient Israel (circa 1020 B.C.E.), a special class of wise women and men emerged around the royal court, dedicated to the study of wisdom (2 Samuel 14:2). By the time of Jeremiah (eighth century B.C.E.), they had taken their place alongside the prophets and priests as a major religious and social influence (Jeremiah 18:18). While these scholars added a specifically intellectual aspect to Hebrew wisdom, it never lost its practical and life-oriented meaning. The Bible locates wisdom in the *leb,* a term typically translated as heart and meaning the very core of a person (Ecclesiastes 10:2). The *leb* is the intellectual source of thought and reflection (Isaiah 6:10), the center of affections (Psalm 4:8), and the seat of volition and conscience (1 Samuel 24:5). It is clear that biblical wisdom, situated in the *leb,* pertains to a person's head, heart, and hands.

In the period after the Exile of the Israelites in Babylon (return in 539 B.C.E.), the emphasis shifts to wisdom as an ethical response to God's revelation and law. For humankind, the beginning of wisdom is respect for God, manifested by faithfulness to the covenant (Job 28:28). Wise people do God's will, and this especially means living with justice, compassion, and peace (Proverbs 2). The sinner is the real fool (Psalm 14:1). God's wisdom is experienced in God's saving deeds for the people (Isaiah 1:3) and is reflected in nature (Proverbs 3:19)—the work of God's hands.

Eventually in the Bible, Wisdom is personified as the Craftsperson whom God employs in the work of creation (Proverbs 8:30). She (always feminine) is the giver of life (Proverbs 4:13) and the One who saves the people (Wisdom 9:18). She creates and renews the earth (Psalm 104:30). Wisdom takes the initiative and comes looking for those who love Her. She seeks out those who desire Her; they allow themselves to be found as much as they find Her (Wisdom 6:12–16). The promised Messiah will have God's "spirit of wisdom" (Isaiah 11:2). In summary, and as Wisdom says of Herself in the Book of Proverbs, "Whoever finds me, finds life" (8:35).

Scholars now propose that the biblical tradition of Wisdom/Sophia reaches its peak as the personification of God. Leading American theologian Elizabeth Johnson proposes that Sophia "is the most developed personification of God's presence and activity in the Hebrew Scriptures."[8] Furthermore, contemporary scholars emphasize that Wisdom is a feminine figure. Not only are *hokmah* in Hebrew, sophia in Greek, and *sapientia* in Latin of the feminine-grammatical gender, but adds Johnson,

> The biblical depiction of Wisdom is itself consistently female, casting her as sister, mother, female beloved, chef and hostess . . . and a myriad of other female roles wherein she symbolizes transcendent power ordering and delighting in the world.

Because of "the functional equivalence between the deeds of Sophia and those of the biblical God,"[9] Wisdom points to both the femininity of God and to the divinizing aspect of becoming wise. God is like a Wise Woman and wise people are like their God.

In the New Testament, Luke has Jesus present himself as wiser than Solomon (Luke 11:31). For Matthew, Jesus is wisdom made flesh. For John, Jesus is Wisdom personified, and Paul portrays Christ as "the wisdom of God" (I Corinthians 1:24).[10] The scripture scholar Marcus Borg summarizes, "According to the synoptics, Paul, and John, that which was present in Jesus was the Sophia of God."[11] For James, Jesus-like wisdom is realized in doing the works of peace, mercy, kindness, and justice. (See James 3:17–18.) Disciples of Jesus are called to live as wisely as he lived.

It would appear that the Hebrew and Christian Scriptures recommend wisdom as the highest purpose of education. Such wisdom is profoundly holistic, engaging the total person—head, heart, and hands—consciously located in the world. It requires commitment and a thorough awareness of the context of one's responsibilities, willingness to work in partnership, and dedication to seek what is true and choose what is good—to live the wisdom one knows. Surely, education could have no higher "intended learning outcome" than biblical wisdom and becoming so wise.

Unity of Theory and Practice

The Christian intellectual tradition reflects enduring commitment to knowing that unites the theoretical with the practical, knowledge with life, cognition with ethics. For the first thousand years of Christian education, this unity was warranted by the biblical tradition of wisdom. Although threatened by the advent of the universities and Scholasticism, and even more so by the Enlightenment, Christianity continued to propose that what people know ought to shape who they are and how they live. There are many spokespersons for this integrated sense of knowing; I cite Augustine, Aquinas, and Bernard Lonergan.

Augustine and Monasticism

Although St. Augustine lived a monastic life for only a short time after his conversion to Christian faith (circa 387), he was imbued with the monastic conviction that all knowledge should lead to wisdom for life. For Augustine, this meant living a life of love. Essentially, Augustine's way of knowing reflected the monastic method of prayerful contemplation.

For Augustine, the soul is the agent of knowing and has three capacities—reason, memory, and will. The three work together and are as united in function as is the Triune God. The soul is reason as source of understanding, the soul is memory of what the person already knows, the soul is will that initiates action by desire and choice. Reason and memory, prompted by the will, pursue truth and offer back to the will the knowledge required to make informed decisions, to choose what is true and good.[12]

The will, for Augustine, can choose according to *caritas* (love), opting for truth and goodness, or can follow *cupiditas* (concupiscence), which leads to sin and destruction. But the cohesion of the three capacities—reason, memory, and will—maintains a unity of theory and practice, or, as Augustine preferred, of contemplation and action.[13]

The monastic wisdom tradition lost pride of place to the university-based and more rational Scholasticism of the early second millennium, and yet it remained an important subtradition within Christian understanding of knowledge and the process of knowing. Christian education never entirely lost the monastic emphasis on education for wisdom. It maintained a humanizing purpose for all study of the humanities, arts, and sciences. As a way of knowing, the monastery preferred contemplation over rational analysis, personally engaging the student to appreciate and enjoy what is, to imagine and choose what ought to be.

Monastic epistemology was most eminently reflected in its theological method. Monasticism, which included the abbeys of vowed religious women as well as monasteries of men, was convinced that "talk about God" (*theos logia*) should originate from "talking with God"—prayer. Thus, the monastic way of doing theology—its theological method—was, essentially, a prayerful contemplation of life and of the *sacra pagina* (the sacred pages of Scripture), engaging the whole person—mind, heart, and will. This "spiritual reading" of sacred texts and of life—*lectio divina* as it was called—had the defining purpose of spiritual wisdom, of holy living and an ever deepening relationship with God. For monasticism, to know is to become wise—for life.[14]

Thomas Aquinas and Scholasticism

Scholastic philosophy and theology emerged around the beginning of the second millennium and has remained the dominant conceptual system of Roman Catholicism ever since. With the founding of the first universities (circa twelfth century), theology moved beyond the monastery and went off to school (*schola*).

Responding to its new context, theology became a "science" in quest of rational knowledge instead of prayerful contemplation seeking spiritual wisdom. Yet the wiser exponents of Scholasticism continued to maintain a unity between theory and practice, between knowing and living. Such was the intent of Aquinas as evident in his understanding of the workings of the mind and his attempt to correlate knowing the true with choosing the good. How well he succeeded is a debated question, but his honorable intentions were to keep theory and practice united.

For Aquinas, citing Aristotle, "Nothing is ever in the mind that is not first in the senses." All knowing begins with sense perception, with the data presented through our senses from experience. The mind then works on this data to produce knowledge. Within the mind, Thomas made two distinctions—one between the active and the passive intellect, the other between theoretical and practical knowing. Although he made such distinctions, Thomas never separated these functions, seeing them instead as working cumulatively and in partnership.

The passive intellect receives the data presented from sense perception, and then the active intellect turns the images from the passive intellect into thought, understanding, and judgment. The theoretical activity of intellect seeks the truth, and its findings inform the practical intellect and move it to choice.

The whole intellect—active and passive, theoretical and practical—functions to provide the will with the knowledge and moral principles necessary to make free choices concerning truth and goodness. In sum, Aquinas proposed that our entire capacity for thinking should work in concert with our capacity for doing—we should do what we think and think what we do. At least conceptually, Thomas succeeded in keeping united what people know and how they live.

Bernard Lonergan and the Dynamics of Knowing

As with Augustine and Aquinas, I summarize in a few paragraphs an intellectual giant. But it is worth the risk of reductionism to highlight Lonergan's efforts to maintain the unity of theory and practice. Canadian-born Jesuit Bernard Lonergan (1904–84), one of the leading theologians of the twentieth century, is especially helpful for his description of the dynamics of cognition—the activities we perform in the process of knowing. Lonergan effectively challenged the separation of theoretical and practical reason bequeathed by Kant.

Lonergan proposed that all persons have "a dynamic structure of . . . cognitional and moral being"—a pattern of activities we perform when we know or make choices. There are four such activities, and the "eros of the human spirit" for the true and the good prompts us to follow them.[15] Lonergan encouraged people to recognize them in their own consciousness. In other words, stop and think about it, and you recognize for yourself these four sequential activities in coming to know anything: (1) We notice and attend to the data of experience. (2) We try to understand what the data mean. (3) We make judgment about the truth or falsehood of what we understand. And (4) we finally come to a decision.[16]

Although these activities may be performed in the wink of an eye and all be rolled together, yet we can pull apart the act of knowing anything well and notice these functions at work: we notice things first, think about them to figure out what is going on, evaluate or make judgments about the adequacy of our understanding, and finally make up our own minds about what to do in their regard. Whatever comes my way in life, I know it for myself when I take a good look, try to understand, weigh my opinion carefully, and then make up my mind.

These four activities of knowing give rise to what Lonergan called the four "transcendental imperatives"— what everyone ought to do in order to really know something, namely: *be attentive, be intelligent, be reasonable,* and *be responsible.*[17] As we honor these four activities, we can intentionally and self-consciously move from attending to the data of experience, to understanding what is intelligible, to judging what is true, to choosing what is good—to knowing.

Beyond appreciating his helpful description of the dynamics of cognition, I highlight from Lonergan that authentic knowing entails the fourth activity of decision making and taking responsibility. He would say it is indeed possible for a person to stop at understanding something (the second activity) or to cease with judgment (the third), and judgment is indeed where Kant concluded the activity of "pure" reason. But to become an authentic person in everyday life—for what Lonergan called the "existential subject"—our knowing must push on to the fourth activity of decision making and being responsible. We must make decisions in order to "know" as human beings.

A friend and professor of humanities once told me that his only interest was in getting students to understand things. What they personally discern or decide was beyond his job description as a professor. My response was, "But then, you are not really helping them to know—not in any human and full sense of knowing." We argued awhile, with my claiming that not to encourage students to make judgments and decisions is to allow them to stop short of really "knowing." He objected that inviting them to reach decisions would violate the "objective norms of academia." I agreed! I am confident that Lonergan would take my side; he proposed an epistemology—a way of knowing—that unites "theory" and "practice."

The Constructive Project of Feminist Epistemology
The contemporary scholars I find most constructive in humanizing our ways of knowing—*for life for all*—are feminist epistemologists. In general, feminist epistemology focuses on the gender bias in the dominant "ways of knowing"—how men are favored—and proposes a more inclusive and humanizing alternative from the perspective of women's experience. It also subsumes many nongender-related assets of postmodern epistemology and thus can serve to summarize contemporary proposals for an alternative to Enlightenment rationality.[18] In brief, *feminist epistemology proposes a wisdom way of knowing!*

There is a vast spectrum of opinion among feminist theorists and certainly no one position on epistemology. Yet, mainstream feminist thought seems to share the following five features that are assets for a humanizing way of knowing.

To Know, Engage the Whole Person and All People

Knowing should engage the whole person and all people. Instead of reducing our capacity for knowing to "reason alone"—the narrow-minded legacy of Descartes—feminist epistemology insists on engaging the whole person in the act of knowing. Human feelings and emotions, productivity and creativity, the personal and social, the individual and relational, the spiritual and ethical, corporeality and sexuality, memory and imagination as well as reason—every aspect of human being—should be honored as a valued way of knowing and source of knowledge.

Likewise, the knowledge enterprise of humankind should welcome the participation of every person—not just an elite few who "know" and instruct the rest—encouraging everyone to learn from their lives in the world. There should be "democracy in the production of knowledge"[19] because, in a favorite phrase of feminist epistemology, "experience counts"—everyone's, especially for reaching wisdom. Feminists highlight that women have traditionally been excluded from constructing what counts for knowledge and insist that they become full participants instead. The whole person and all people should participate in knowing and constructing knowledge.

To Know, Engage in Conversation and Partnership—In Community

The best way to know is in conversation and partnership with others—in community. Feminist scholars stress the need for partnership, dialogue, and relationship in knowing. This especially requires expressing one's own word to others in order to know it better and listening to their responses and personal contributions. Such conversation counters the individualized way of knowing so favored by modernism—people making up their own minds not only for themselves but by themselves. The dominant epistemology goes so far as to encourage admiration for "rugged" individualists who "dare to think" (Kant) without consulting anything—community or tradition—except their own thought process. From the perspective of traditional social-gender roles, feminists see such individualism as a male way of knowing.

To Know, Reflect on, and Value Your Own Perspective; Be Open to Others'

Knowledge is always influenced by people's social and cultural context. Feminist epistemologists insist that our own perspective becomes an asset if we are self-reflective about it and open to that of others. There is strong consensus among postmodernist scholars that our personal situation and social context have a profound affect on how and what we know. These scholars unmask the mythical claim of modernism that "knowing" can be and should be "objective"—as if it were possible to prevent our perspective from influencing our knowledge.

Feminist scholars whimsically call this "a view from nowhere" pretense. Their own positive proposal for "remapping the epistemic terrain . . . abandons the search for and denies the possibility of the disinterested and dislocated view from nowhere . . ."[20] They favor instead what Sandra Harding calls "a standpoint epistemology." (See footnote 18.)

A "standpoint epistemology" means: (a) recognizing one's own social perspective and its influence on one's knowing; (b) appreciating one's perspective as an asset—as highlighting what might not be "seen" otherwise; (c) questioning it for distortions or biases rather than canonizing it; and (d) being willing to share with, listen to, and be enlightened by perspectives different from one's own. Simply, it is having an opinion, knowing that it is both valid and limited, and being open to other opinions. Better by far than a "view from nowhere" is to welcome "views from many wheres."[21] In fact, argues Harding, such "standpoint epistemology" is even more scientific and reliable than the feigned objectivity of Enlightenment rationality.[22]

To Know, Accept Responsibility, and Favor Relationships in Ethical Decision Making

Feminist epistemology emphasizes the responsibility of knowledge, favoring an ethic of care grounded in relationship. Postmodernist thought is intent on repairing the damage done by Kant in separating science from ethics and theory from practice, insisting instead that humans should maintain integrity between what we know and how we live. The aspect that feminists add to reuniting theory and practice is to make relationships the primary consideration in ethical decision making. Further, they propose care—for self, others, and world—as the normative value of a relational ethic.[23] Our ways of knowing should deepen our commitment to care.

To Know, Think Beyond Dualisms

Feminist epistemology helps to overcome destructive dualisms. The dominant Western epistemology is rampant with dualisms of all kinds, separating out, for example: male/female, mind/body, subject/object, thought/emotion, acceptable/marginal, theoretical/practical, scientific/common sense. All are hierarchically arranged to favor the first over the second. All fail to recognize that each always depends on the other. As feminist author Jane Flax summarizes, these dualisms produce "distorted forms of knowledge" that are destructive even of those they favor and of the environment as well.[24]

With their commitment to inclusion and integration, to dialogue and relationship, to welcoming diverse perspectives, and to uniting knowing with responsibility, feminist theorists help to transcend debilitating dualisms and to encourage a holistic way of knowing.

In effect, feminist scholars are trying to forge "a utopian epistemology in which no discrimination exists."[25] While this can be readily dismissed as impossible to realize in full, it is no more naive than the biblical ideal for how and what people should come to know. Given its emphasis on wisdom, the Bible's epistemology is holistic—engaging the whole person and all people—and is done best in a covenant community, with knowledge realized through responsible living, leading to wisdom of life. There is a patent resonance between biblical and feminist epistemology!

Biblically, the foundational sources of human knowing are everyday experiences, relationships, and efforts to live the covenant—to do God's will. The ultimate way to know is to love and be loved. How significant it is that the Hebrew verb for knowing—*yada*—is also used for lovemaking. The New Testament Greek verb—*ginoskein*—is similarly used.

Some older translations of the Scriptures were quite literal about this, as in "and Adam had *knowledge* of Eve" (Genesis 4:1) or Mary asking, "How can this be since I *know not* man" (Luke 1:34). When the Psalmist prays, "O God, you probe me and you know me" (Psalm 139:1), she or he was really saying, "You love me as I am." As God knows us, God loves us, and the eutopian hope for human knowing is stated by St. Paul as "to know as we are known." (See 1 Corinthians 13:12.) Would that all our knowing and knowledge be ultimately directed to enabling us to love God, self, and others—as God first loves us. Indeed, a eutopian ideal, but I propose that educators should settle for no less.

A Christian Epistemology: One Proposal

Biblically and philosophically, wisdom engages the whole person, is located in time and place (in tradition and community), and encourages integrity between knower and knowledge, to become wise. At least until the term can be reclaimed with holistic connotation, knowledge does not seem sufficient to name the highest intent of humanizing education. Wisdom would seem to be a more adequate term.[26]

Wisdom includes knowledge, but goes beyond it to unite what is known with the "being" of the knower. *Wisdom is the realization of knowledge in life-giving ways—for self, others, and the world.* Becoming wise is eminently reasonable but goes beyond reason to engage the whole person—head, heart, and hands, and all the capacities thereof, in activities of cognition, affection, and volition.

Wisdom maintains congruence between knowing and doing. Being wise means living with integrity. In the biblical tradition, in all the great philosophical and religious traditions, and in contemporary feminist thought, *wisdom is knowing with an ethic*. We often speak of wisdom as a possession, but it really refers to a way of being—responsible. Joe Kane not only had wisdom but was wise.

Wisdom presents educators the task of not only informing, but of forming and transforming learners in who they are and how they live—in their character. Although the many expressions of education will promote it in different ways and to varying degrees, the overarching epistemological purpose of education is best stated as wisdom. Jacques Maritain wrote,

> Education and teaching can only achieve their internal unity if the manifold parts of their whole work are organized and quickened by a vision of wisdom as the supreme goal.[27]

I agree!

How, then, can teachers and parents educate for wisdom? What are the ways of knowing that encourage becoming wise? From the resources just reviewed, and echoing the work of previous chapters, I can think of fifteen "ways" that educators can weave together a wisdom epistemology. The reader's own wisdom will add to my list.

None of these ways can stand alone. Many overlap each other, but together they may amount to a "wisdom way of knowing." As elaborated in the final section of this chapter, each educator must consider taking them on as intentional commitments, trying to realize them within the teaching/learning dynamic, and promoting them throughout the ethos of a school or parish program, or in the environment of a family.

What follows is always more an ideal than ever fully achieved. Besides the intentionality of the educator, much depends on the age and background of the participants, the context and purpose of the curriculum, and many other factors. Yet, why should any teacher or parent intend less than a wisdom way of knowing?

- *Establish persons as "the subjects" of knowing.* Notice that we typically refer to the "thing" being taught as "the subject"— as in asking a teacher, "What subjects do you teach?" Referring to the topic taught as the subject could imply that students are the "objects" of education—things to be worked on—and much education proceeds this way.[28] In contrast, wisdom educators treat people as the real subjects of education by insisting that they become the primary agents of their own knowing.

  Whether learners are originating knowledge for themselves or inheriting the legacy of tradition through the humanities, sciences, and arts, they need to reinvent it in the sense of making something their own as personal knowledge.[29] Whatever teachers or parents can do to get learners to "see for themselves"—to be active agents rather than passive recipients of knowledge—contributes to a wisdom way of knowing.

- *Prompt people to use all their human capacities.* The more of learners' gifts that are actively employed, the more likely education is to encourage wisdom—ever a holistic affair.

Teachers should teach in ways that dispose participants to use their minds, and their whole minds: reason indeed—its intuitive, logical, and critical capacities—but also the depths of memory and the heights of imagination.

As elaborated below, good questions are the catalysts par excellence for engaging the whole mind. And beyond the mind, educators can imagine ways to fittingly invite persons (without invading privacy) to draw upon their affections and desires, their volition and will, their aesthetic and creative capacities, and all the wisdom and ways of knowing of the human body.

• *Help people to learn from their own lives in the world.* Wisdom educators insist that "experience counts," and they include learners' own lives—their historical praxis—as an integral aspect of any curriculum. Wisdom requires experience and reflection—even to appropriate as one's own the "wisdom of the ages." When teachers and parents invite learners to look at their lives in the world and to reflect on and express their own perceptions of what is going on, they encourage them to reach toward wisdom for life.

• *In giving access to tradition—the humanities, arts, and sciences—favor wisdom.* Teachers spend much of their time giving students access to the traditions congealed in the humanities, arts, and sciences. My encouragement is to allow a wisdom interest to permeate how and what they teach from tradition—to influence all their curriculum choices. Highlight what humanizes and teach in humanizing ways. Be convinced that even the most mundane data— learned appropriately—hold the possibility of wisdom.

• *Welcome everyone.* Wisdom educators welcome every person to participate fully in the teaching/learning process. They try to create a democracy wherein all have equal entitlement to the resources and are expected to contribute their own word and wisdom to the curriculum. Democracy in education does not exclude the function of the educator as instructor, enabler, and learning resource—not a false liberalism. It does mean giving no one a "godlike" status as controller and dispenser of knowledge, but welcoming everyone to participate and contribute according to their learning style.

I know a single-parent family where all five children, even from their earliest years, have been consulted about all decisions affecting their lives. The parent takes the time to listen to their positions, invites them to reflect on their perspectives, and gradually moves toward what emerges as the wisest way to proceed. If it is a decision that affects the whole family, her mode is one of consensus building—often slow and painstaking. Those children, some now young adults, clearly have a positive self-image, respect for the opinions of others, and know how to negotiate and build consensus. They have learned well from the inclusive modus operandi of their family.

Beyond avoiding blatant violations such as showing favoritism to some or victimizing others, wisdom educators scrupulously eschew the more subtle practices of exclusion—like sexism, racism, classism. Wisdom is the antithesis of injustice. After participating in a teacher's conference on negative gender roles in the classroom, a seventh-grade teacher friend commented: "I began to notice that I prompt the boys to respond about twice as often as the girls. And most often I say to the boys something encouraging—'good point'—whereas to the girls, I'm more critical. I had no idea I was doing this." And according to classroom research, my friend's old pattern is typical rather than unique to her.

- *Engage the very "soul" of people.* Wisdom educators encourage persons to reach deep into themselves, to draw upon the resources at the core of their own being. We can absorb much information and learn a lot "about" things without being so personally engaged, but if something is to touch our personhood, lead to wisdom, then our souls must be employed. While being careful not to violate privacy, teachers and parents can imagine activities and issues that turn learners to their own depths. Even a simple question like "What do you really think (or feel, or do, etc.) about that?" can prompt drawing upon the core of people's being.

- *Encourage relational ways of knowing.* As a wisdom epistemology invites persons to draw upon their own resources, it also invites them out of themselves into reciprocal relationships with other knowers and even with what is to be known. Instead of a rugged individualism that works alone to analyze things "objectively," a wisdom mode is one of partnership with others in the learning process. Wisdom is more likely when teachers and parents encourage working in partnerships so as to cooperate or collaborate with each other. Similarly, encouraging learners to approach whatever is to be learned with a style of conversation and exchange, as something to be befriended rather than conquered, fosters them in wisdom.

- *Create a community of conversation.* Echoing the previous point, a humanizing way of knowing is most likely to emerge in a "wisdom community"[30] that is marked by conversation and dialogue. Again, it is possible to know "about" things by oneself alone and to tell others "about" things through monologue, but wisdom and becoming wise is fostered by a community of discourse. Whatever teachers and parents can do to build community within their school, program, or family and to encourage conversation promotes a wisdom way of knowing.

- *Mentor learners in critical reflection.* As noted in chapter 3, "critical" in this context does not have its colloquial meaning of criticizing—usually negative. I use it with its root sense from the Greek *krinein* meaning to discern or judge. Teachers and parents foster critical reflection when they get learners to really think for themselves and then to think about their thinking in order to personally understand their lives and traditions; to discern what is true and false, good and evil, beautiful and ugly; to weigh what should be done or avoided and why; to consciously make responsible decisions.

  The reflective aspect of critical reflection engages all three capacities of mind—reason, memory, and imagination—while interweaving the intentional activities of attending, understanding, judging, and deciding. Educators can help people to critically reflect about their own lives in the world and to discerningly appropriate the legacy of tradition—the humanities, sciences and arts.

In sum, teachers can encourage critical thinking about the "texts" of life and about the "texts" of tradition. And critical reflection has both *personal* and *social* emphases.

Educators foster personal critical reflection as they help people to use their reason to take in the data of life or tradition, to interpret and comprehend their meaning, to make judgments, and arrive at decisions. Likewise, they get people to use their memory to draw upon previous experience and knowledge and to remember their sources, to have a perspective from which to interpret, evaluate, and make decisions. They can encourage imagination to fashion data into images for understanding and to judge them and make decisions according to likely or desired consequences.

As suggested often already, critical reflection essentially encourages persons to think for themselves, to "have a mind of their own." The emphasis to reiterate here is that critical reflection invites us beyond thinking to thinking about our thinking. At this "second level" of reflection, we not only think for ourselves but probe the quality, the undergirding perspectives, the biases, and the influences upon our thinking.

By such testing of our own thinking, we engage in truly critical reflection; undoubtedly, its depth depends on age and developmental readiness. And yet, we can ask children, "What do you think?" (or feel, or do, etc.) and then inquire, in one way or another (and the more concrete the better for younger children): "Why do think (or feel, or do, etc.) that way?" or "What do you know about this already, and why?" or "What do you imagine this might lead to?" However rudimentary a form, such critical reflection contributes to a wisdom way of knowing.

My friend Sr. Florence tells a story of a Christmas card she received from a woman many years after Florence had been her teacher, thanking her for the difference she had made in this woman's life. She wrote:

> Above all, you taught me to think for myself, to address
> my own problems, to question even my own ideas, and

to look at things differently than I was used to. At first I was hesitant, but then I began to trust you because you were so kind to me as I went through . . . [Here she recounts a difficult experience—as if Florence should remember.] After that, I really began to think for myself.

Florence acknowledged that try as she might, she failed to even place the name with a face, much less remember the experiences to which her former student referred. She represents the countless number of people whom Florence—an extraordinary educator and soul friend—has taught to think for themselves. Observe, too, the power of supportive presence on the teacher's part—as well as of good questions—to encourage people to think for themselves.

Now, the social aspect of critical reflection deserves its own emphasis—the next "way" of knowing.

• *Encourage social analysis.* Like our very persons, what we know and how we know is profoundly influenced by our context—by where we are and whom we are with. For wisdom's-sake, social analysis means becoming aware of how our culture and history, race and ethnic background, sex and social gender roles, religious tradition, economic conditions, and political structures all have profound influence on our knowledge. Instead of simply relativizing everything we know, however, social analysis should enable us to embrace and cherish the gift and truth of our own perspectives. Then, beyond affirmation, social analysis should encourage us to question our cultural context and worldview, to recognize sins as well as graces, to be open to perspectives other than our own.

I once had a group of young men in a theology course who offered stout resistance when I introduced readings in feminist theology. When their resistance continued, I assured them I respected their right to their positions, but suggested for their next essay assignment that they write on how their perspective was being shaped by the fact that they were men in this culture and that they reflect on how their families and societies might have socialized them into male gender roles and patriarchal attitudes toward women. They saw this as a worthwhile topic and good-humoredly agreed to take it on.

Their essays were some of the most honest, probing, and critically reflective I have ever read. Though there were no catalytic conversions, all arrived at more openness to a feminist perspective. Simple as it may sound, I believe the pedagogical key was that I invited them to think about their thinking.

- *Nurture the contemplative.* Aristotle was convinced that the highest mode of knowing is contemplation, that it leads to godlike wisdom and to the happiest life. We noted, too, that the favored way of knowing in Christian monastic tradition is contemplation. Maritain defines contemplation as "simply to see and to enjoy seeing" and then claims that the "highest achievement of education" is "to develop the contemplative capacity of the human mind."[31]

  Teachers and parents can encourage contemplation by inviting learners to truly gaze upon something of life or tradition, to dwell on it, to enjoy and relish it, to give it time and real attention. And then imaginative questions can prompt them to reach beyond the obvious to the "more" that is there, to "see through" to what is "behind" it all. As emphasized in chapter 3, contemplation is crucial for nurturing a sacramental consciousness—and now, I add wisdom.

- *Promote responsibility and commitment.* A refrain throughout this work is that our knowledge should influence our "being"—who we are and how we live. Here I highlight that educators need to help learners to know in ways that promote responsibility, that encourage commitment to what is true, good, and beautiful. As in the biblical view, knowledge is realized in doing what is right, and the biggest fool is one who knows better but does wrong. To know wisely is to become responsible to self and others.

  There are, indeed, ways of teaching that bring learners only to understanding and no further. However, as Lonergan argues persuasively, to really know as a person in the everyday—as "an existential subject" is his term—one must push on to judgment and decision. This is most likely to foster wisdom. Educators should not limit concern for responsibility to moments of applying knowledge, but let it be a concern throughout their teaching.

Bob is a remedial teacher in an inner-city grade school. Students sent to him for help have often become "discipline problems" as well. Bob's reputation for success in turning their lives around is legendary, not only helping them academically but changing their behavior. I asked him why he is so successful, and one comment was, "Usually when they begin to learn for themselves, to read or do math or whatever they hadn't been able to do, their behavior problems also recede." To "know for oneself" can change behavior. Teach as if it ought to.

• *Be intentionally political—for freedom.* That power and knowledge, politics and education are deeply intertwined are old insights. I earlier cited the Chinese sage Confucius for this insight, writing twenty-five hundred years ago, and Plato recognized the same about a hundred years later in the West. In contemporary literature, the lifework of the notable French philosopher Michel Foucault (1926–84) highlights the "politics" of all knowledge—that it is "produced" by networks of power within its social context.[32]

Jurgen Habermas emphasizes the "cognitive interest" of all ways of knowing. As we can recognize from our own experience, the very motivation to know anything depends on our level of interest, and our particular interest "tints the lens" of our knowing. Beyond this, Habermas offers a powerful argument that the dominant ways of knowing in modern society are shaped by the interest of social control or commodity production, whereas for humanization, we need ways of knowing grounded in an emancipatory interest—one that sets free.[33]

Educators must recognize that they can instigate knowledge and knowing that stymie and control learners, that indoctrinate and limit their possibilities or that they can encourage ways of knowing that set persons free from needless constraints—internal and external—and encourage them to become transformers of their context rather than creatures that "fit" into it. And surely wisdom educators should choose the latter—helping learners to know in ways emancipatory for themselves and their society.

As I expand upon in the next section, the key to teachers and parents practicing such politics of freedom is to be deeply committed to "the truth"—wherever and however it can be found. As Jesus preached and witnessed with his life, the truth sets people free. (See John 8:32.)

• *Foster lifelong learning.* A wisdom way of knowing is antithetical to closed-mindedness or personal stagnation. John Dewey was fond of repeating that education must promote growth, and once when asked, "Growth for what?" is reported to have answered, "For more growth." He certainly wrote in his "Pedagogic Creed" (1894)—the platform statement of his whole career—that the best education "gives people the courage to change their minds."[34] Dewey's key suggestion was to form students in the habit of reflecting on their experience—"reconstructing" was his term. Then they will remain learners all their lives and their knowledge will remain ever vibrant. I agree!

Building on Dewey's suggestion, the clue to educators fostering lifelong learning is to help people to learn how to learn—analogous to the old maxim, "Better to teach a hungry person how to fish than to give them a fish for dinner." Every teacher and parent should help kindle an ongoing curiosity and excitement about learning and should help learners develop the habits and the arts needed to continue as agents of their own knowing.

In teaching undergraduate theology, my constant intent is to educate students to think theologically for themselves, to begin to do their own theology, rather than simply teaching them what theologian X said about Y. What I have found most effective in educating "theologians" is: (a) to arouse curiosity with generative themes and topics—engagement with personal interest; (b) to give students the tools to investigate the topic, e.g., how to find relevant authors and texts, to read them critically, to discern their own positions in conversation with the texts of tradition, and to develop foundational principles that can guide reflection on related topics; and (c) to constantly ask questions of relevance—the "so what"—for their own and others' lives.

Good math teachers have methods of helping students to think mathematically rather than simply to know about math, and similarly for other academic disciplines.

* *Unite theory and practice.* This last commitment reflects and gathers up all the previous ones. Surely the most debilitating dualism of Western epistemology is the separation—even antagonism—contrived between theory and practice. This encourages separating knowing from life, science from ethics, knowledge from experience, head from heart, academia from the world. Further, such dualism is hierarchically arranged, with the theoretical favored as real knowing and the practical reduced to skill or the application of theory. A wisdom education must transcend this destructive separation.

  Although there are appropriate emphases according to context or program, there is no knowledge that is purely theoretical and no wise practice that does not reflect knowing of some kind. All theoretical knowledge should be permeated with the interest of humanization, and the practical should reflect sound principles and informed conviction.

  Even skills are most humanizing when people know the principles behind them as well as the art of doing them well. A way of knowing that unites theory and practice seems imperative to education for wisdom, for wisdom is achieved when knowledge and life come together. The questioning schema I suggest under "style" below is one approach for educators to encourage the unity of theory and practice— and, thus, wisdom.

Historical Epilogue

As with all the substantial characteristics of Catholicism, its community of faith has never faithfully lived a wisdom epistemology and, like myself, has offended against every aspect. In fairness, of course, I have outlined an ideal, and no educational agency has practiced or even come close to such a vision. But as with all these depth structures, lack of faithful practice should not alleviate efforts now but redouble them. Such recommitment is what it means to be in covenant with God—always confident of God's grace in spite of past failures and, by grace, ever turning to repentance and renewal. The only good reason to point out shortcomings is to encourage such *metanoia.* This chapter proposes a "reasonable wisdom" epistemology, a critical rationality that leads to wisdom of life. In brief, Catholicism has sinned boldly against both rationality and wisdom.

I noted in chapter 1 that many would be surprised by Gilkey listing "the rationality of the traditional faith" as a depth structure of Catholicism, because for most this has not been their experience. Indeed, the partnership of revelation and reason, faith and understanding was practiced by its great scholars and reflected in official church teachings. But for the vast majority, undue emphasis on the church's authority amounted to "the church has already done the thinking for you—and now you must think as it thinks." In fact, any kind of questioning or critical inquiry about magisterial teachings was considered a "lack of faith."

Nor was this attitude simply the piety of unlettered peasants—it was often encouraged by the teaching style and attitude of the church itself. *The Catechism of the Council of Trent* (first issued 1566) taught that true faith is "free from an inquisitive curiosity" and "must exclude not only doubt, but all desire for demonstration."[35] Nor is this "don't think about it" attitude entirely past and gone. Certain controversial issues now seem to be off limits for discussion, even by the church's theologians—surely an "un-Catholic" sentiment!

Second, in the history of the Church one can say that a wisdom epistemology reigned when its intellectual life was centered in the monasteries. But, as hinted above, a profound shift took place (circa twelfth century) when the intellectual locus shifted from monastery to university. It was understandable in its new academic context that theology would attempt to become a science. But in the process, it tended to lose its primary focus on wisdom, opting for rational knowledge instead. And although the great scholastics like Aquinas intended to maintain the unity of theory and practice, their interpreters were not so wise.

It is true that Catholicism maintained a healthy skepticism about rationality—e.g. it never joined the Enlightenment's "worship" of reason—yet, at least in how it educated in faith, it often seemed more concerned about certainty of ideas (ironically, an Enlightenment quest) than about wisdom of life. Now, in a new moment, would it not be possible to carry forward the best of both monastery and university, favoring critical rationality for wisdom of life?

For Teachers and Parents

What does it mean for educators—in schools or parishes, homes or programs—to commit themselves to educate for wisdom, to encourage a holistic way of knowing? It would surely permeate one's whole vocation as teacher or parent, asking deep commitments of one's soul, with suggestions for style, and for the quality of educational space. First, pause and observe some of your own intuitions of what a wisdom epistemology asks of educators.

For Reflection

- Has your own sense of "knowledge" and of the "ways of knowing"—your own epistemology—clarified any from the previous reflections? In what ways? Why?

- What do you imagine a wisdom epistemology asks of an educator's heart? Of how he or she teaches? Of the educational environment?

- If you had one piece of advice to give young teachers or parents about their epistemology—how and what they want learners to know—what might you say?

For the Educator's Soul

The whole previous section points to commitments that a wisdom epistemology asks of the educator's soul—so much has already been said. Now, as a summary commitment, a humanizing epistemology asks of teachers and parents *a deep passion for truth—for knowing and doing what is true—and for fostering others in this way.* As Maritain states—somewhat dramatically to make his point—the defining purpose of the educator's life must be "for the sake of truth." This requires bringing students to their own "deep-rooted convictions" and "taking pleasure" in their making their own choices about truth, even if they are contrary "to the teacher's personal convictions."[36] How true, but how painful as well—especially for parents.

I once went by the office of one of my professors in graduate school for an appointment and found him in tears. When I inquired if I could help, he said "no" and explained that his daughter had just informed him of an important life decision that was contrary to what he had hoped for. Eventually, he smiled and said, "Her mother and I raised her since she was a little girl to think for herself, but, oh how painful it can be when she doesn't think as we do."

From the conversation between Jesus and Pilate in the Gospel of John, we get an inkling of how Jesus, in continuity with his Hebrew tradition, understood "the truth." Jesus had referred to himself in his public ministry as "the way, the truth, and the life." (See John 14:6.) Now, at his trial before Pilate, he stated boldly, "The reason I was born is to testify to the truth. Anyone committed to the truth hears my voice" (John 18:37). Clearly, Jesus was placing "the truth" at the core of his "being"— as central to his identity and life's purpose, requiring commitment of disciples in order to know it. I wonder what went on in Pilate's heart as he reflected on Jesus' statement. Perhaps to escape the reflection, Pilate asked, likely in cynical jest, "Truth, what is that?" (John 18:38). Alas, we have no report of how Jesus responded, if he did at all.

But we must at least try to describe this passion that belongs at the heart of every teacher and parent. Without it, educators are less likely to awaken and mentor the quest for truth in learners. I propose that educators commit themselves to truth as having a *cognitive*, a *relational*, and a *moral* aspect.

The Cognitive Aspect of Truth

"Reason alone" is the great battle cry of Enlightenment epistemology. Yet in pushing beyond the cognitive to a more integrated notion of "truth," it would not be wise to leave it behind. Surely, truth has a cognitive aspect—something to be known. Although always more than reasonable, the truth is not irrational. I had a philosophy professor in college who often repeated the patent, but helpful, adage,

"If it sounds crazy, doubt it." If something does not make sense, the wise become skeptical. In the tradition of Western philosophy, this cognitive aspect has itself had three distinct emphases, each with its own "truth."

The Correspondence Theory of Cognitive Truth: This theory proposes that an idea or statement is "true" if it corresponds to the facts of life. As Aquinas stated, "Truth is the correspondence of the mind to reality."[37] I know it is true that the refrigerator contains enough food to make dinner because I put it there. Although this theory is roundly critiqued (e.g., presumes that words and ideas can precisely correspond to reality; ignores the knower's perspective—my sense of "enough" is different from others; and someone may have raided the fridge), yet it rightly insists that a claim should "ring true" for persons in that it resonates with the evidence from their own experience.

If a claim does not correspond to people's observations of life, they are not likely to embrace it as true or allow it to affect their commitments. So it is wise for teachers and parents to invite learners to probe what they know with the criterion—however they ask the question—"Does this ring true to your own experiences?" And "Why?"

The Coherence Theory of Cognitive Truth: This theory proposes that a claim is true if it makes sense within our schema for making sense—fits within our rational system. Since we do a major grocery shopping every Monday and today is only Wednesday, I just know that there is enough food for dinner. Or, to let Socrates take a bow, I know that persons are mortal, I know that I am a person, so it would be nonsense to think that I am not mortal.

While this theory has its limitations (e.g., confines people within their perspective, does not question "the system," etc.), it also reflects a truth about truth. We need truth to make sense for us. Otherwise, we are unlikely to have a personal commitment to it. So it is wise for teachers and parents to invite learners to probe what they know with the criterion—however they ask the question—"Does this make sense to your way of thinking?" And "Why?"

The Pragmatic Theory of Cognitive Truth: This theory emphasizes that truth is measured by its usefulness. My grandfather had an ultimate criterion to which he submitted all proposals and opinions, "Will it put bread on the table?" He and American philosopher William James (1842–1910), the leading exponent of pragmatism, would have been soul brothers. What is true helps to stock the refrigerator.

This theory, too, has serious limitations (the truth should be "useful" but to whose advantage or disadvantage? It leaves no room for contemplation, for the poetic, for smelling the roses) and, yet, it reflects a truth about truth. Truth must be realized—move beyond concept and get done—in life-giving ways. So, it is wise for teachers and parents to invite learners to probe what they know with the criterion—however they ask the question—"What are the likely consequences of this?" "Will they be humanizing?" "For whom?"

In summary, the cognitive emphases about truth point to what "rings true" to experience, "makes sense" to one's way of thinking, and "works" for life. But all three theories, even the pragmatic, presuppose that "truth" is what we know cognitively, with our minds and can state in propositions. Wisdom truth includes as much and then is more holistic. Yes, teachers and parents should help people learn and discern what rings true, makes sense, and is useful, but then should invite them onward to truth as relational and as moral imperative.

The Relational Aspect of Truth

When we speak of a person as truthful or as a true friend or when we promise to be true to someone, to our word, or to a commitment, we are making fiducial statements—referring to truth that is realized as faithfulness in relationship. Fiduciality is the core biblical notion of truth—to be steadfast, loyal, faithful in commitments. When the Psalmist says, "Guide me in your truth, O God, teach me your ways" (25:5), the prayer is for truth as faithfulness to the covenant, for truth as "right relationship" with God, self, others, and creation.

The relational sense of truth, with emphasis on faithfulness and being trustworthy, was carried in the old English word for truth—*troth*—as in "I pledge my troth," but was marginalized by the Enlightenment emphasis on truth as "sure and certain ideas" (Descartes' phrase). Educators can play a key role in bringing it to the fore again, especially by attending to character formation as an aspect of their commitment to truth. Every teacher and parent can find opportunity to nurture learners to be true to themselves and to each other, to be honest and reliable, to make and keep commitments, to be persons of their word.

The Moral Aspect of Truth

The relational aspect has already moved us toward the moral imperative of "living the truth," yet the moral aspect deserves its own emphasis. Truth must be one's way of life. The First Epistle of John urges "not to love in word only, but in deed and in truth" (1 John 3:18), and First Peter urges Christians to "be obedient to the truth with sincere love" (1 Peter 1:22).

The ancient Greek philosophers also held together as a unity knowing the truth and doing the good. Later, their distinction became a separation, and the Enlightenment era made them seem completely unrelated—as if different modes of reasoning. But knowing truth and doing good become symbiotic again with a wisdom epistemology. Wisdom truth is being in truth and acting morally, realizing the truth we know *for life for all.*

Reclaiming the relational and moral aspects of truth, without neglecting cognitive aspects, makes it imperative for educators to address character formation. If teachers and parents make a soul commitment to holistic truth, they must be concerned for learners' characters—not just for their heads. The educator's vocation as servant of truth demands that he or she commit to inform and form people to *know, desire,* and *do* "the truly good."

Attention to character education, woven throughout this book, is emphasized in each chapter section on the educational space. Character is ever so influenced by the social environment. Here seems like the best place to take on, however briefly, the question of what values teachers and parents should inculcate. That truth is relational and carries a moral imperative requires educators to be clear about the central values that should guide their efforts at character formation.

As a Christian, I embrace the *for-life-for-all* ethic of the Bible and the "seamless garment" of life-affirming values and norms taught by Jesus through his example and preaching. Biblical ethic stands radically *for life for all* in that it champions the well-being of self, others, and creation. This is spelled out in the Hebrew Scriptures through a plethora of values and laws and summarized in the Decalogue—the Ten Commandments. Biblical ethic is gathered up and summarized as the eutopian value of *shalom*—God's vision for human history and the fruits of living the covenant. Shalom is the realization of fullness of life for all, of mutuality and solidarity among humankind, of its good stewardship of creation, of a "peaceable kingdom" of full justice and contented peace.

In continuity with his Hebrew faith, Jesus incarnated a *for-life-for-all* ethic, symbolized in his preaching of the Reign of God and its radical law of love. In teaching the Great Commandment, Jesus explicitly united love of God, neighbor, and self—lived with all one's mind, heart, and strength—and with no limits as to who is neighbor.

As noted in chapter 2 under anthropology, Catholic Christian ethics is based as much on natural law as on the Bible, with the two sources clarifying and confirming each other. Catholicism strongly embraces the "natural law" moral tradition, which claims that God has implanted in humankind a sense of God's own divine law, lending us the capacity to know right from wrong, good from evil, and a disposition to choose what is morally correct.

Because of our creation in God's own image, the conviction is that the "natural" law—in fact a gift of God's original grace—proposes universal moral values that all can know by their own reflection on life. The asset of a natural law perspective is that moral norms and values can be presented in the public forum and argued persuasively without appeal to special revelation—e.g., the Bible—even without using religious language.

The significant asset of a natural law tradition for educators is that they can choose and inculcate moral values in contexts where a Christian or religion-based morality is excluded. They can move beyond "values clarification," which refuses to propose particular content for learners' values, and suggest core values warranted by reason and humankind's native sense of morality.

Even without using religious language, educators can invite learners to reach beyond self actualization—beyond "the self" as the measure of morality—toward universal ideals and values that are grounded in transcendence. I propose three great moral values that are "naturally" so persuasive, generic enough to suggest other more specific values, and powerful enough to lend real substance to character formation. The first two are companions, *respect* and *responsibility*,[38] and then I add *compassion* to permeate the first two.

305

Renowned moral educator Thomas Lickona writes,

> Respect means showing regard for the worth of someone or something. It takes three major forms: respect for oneself, respect for other people, and respect for all forms of life and the environment that sustains them.

He goes on to explain that "*Respect* is the restraining side of morality; it keeps us from hurting what we ought to value."[39] With a bit of intentionality, every educator can find ample opportunity to teach people respect—for themselves, for others, for creation. Perhaps parents have the greatest opportunity in this regard, beginning with the respect they show for each other and for their children.

I have an old Jesuit friend whose burning passion throughout life has been to oppose racial discrimination. I once asked him how he came by the depth of his commitment to respect for all, and he told me a story. His father had come to America from County Kerry in Ireland and would often regale his family with stories about the beauty of Kerry and the distinction of its people. In his Irish-American ghetto, the young lad grew up thinking that Kerry people were God's own chosen race. One day, at about age seven, his father took him downtown to buy some new clothes—he was about to receive his First Holy Communion. While they were in the store, an African-American man entered—it was the boy's first personal experience of seeing someone of another race.

He ran to his dad and said with excitement, "Daddy, Daddy, look at the black man!" His father took him in his arms, and said, "Joe, I want you to learn something today and never forget it. That black man is as good as any man who ever came out of Kerry." The boy spent his life living and teaching the lesson of respect and equality he learned that day.

Lickona describes *responsibility* as "an extension of respect," as "the active side of morality. It includes taking care of self and others, fulfilling our obligations, contributing to our communities, alleviating suffering, and building a better world."[40] What *respect* demands that we avoid—e.g., discrimination—*responsibility* mandates us to do the opposite—to treat all humanity with equal dignity and work to realize social equality. Every teacher and parent, if on the alert, can find opportunities to help form character in responsibility.

Within the generic categories of respect and responsibility, Lickona extrapolates other moral values to be taught, "such as honesty, fairness, tolerance, prudence, self-discipline, helpfulness, compassion, cooperation, courage, and a host of democratic values." He lists democratic values as "rule of law, equality of opportunity, due process, reasoned argument, representative government, checks and balances, democratic decision making." All of these specific values, in one way or another, "are forms of respect and/or responsibility or aids to acting respectfully and responsibly."[41] Every educational setting has opportunity to teach them!

Compassion is the third universal value I propose to lend substance to character education for what is "truly good." The Latin root of the word means "to feel at one with" someone. Compassion is a deep crossing over into the sufferings and needs of others. It engenders an empathy that moves one to act with love and mercy. Compassion can permeate respect and responsibility with a spirit of largess and generosity. It prompts one to "go the extra mile."

In the Hebrew Scriptures, God is often described as "full of compassion" (especially in the Psalms). As a core attribute of God, compassion is often interchanged with *tender mercies, loving kindness,* and *true holiness.* In the great "holiness code" of the Book of Leviticus (see Leviticus 19), God's people are urged, "Be holy, for I the Lord your God am holy"—and then the mandates that follow reflect the highest value of compassion. And as always with the covenant, God's way of relating to humankind is the model for how we are to relate to each other.

As noted, many propose that compassion is the summary value in the life of the historical Jesus and that Jesus also understood compassion as epitomizing God's way of relating to humankind. Scripture scholar Marcus Borg writes, "For Jesus, compassion was the central quality of God and the central moral quality of a life centered in God."[42] The Bible and the life of Jesus clarify, too, that compassion is not only for others, but should be directed toward oneself as well—with authentic self-love.

In addition to the Hebrew/Jewish and Christian traditions, in Karen Armstrong's best-selling book *A History of God,* she proposes that many of the major religions share this commitment to compassion—that it is the most universal religious value.[43] And pushing beyond faith traditions into the great philosophical and ethical codes, one likewise finds central emphasis on compassion.

In Confucianism, for example, benevolence (*jen*) is the supreme value—the highest ideal that is to permeate all ethical living. In *The Analects of Confucius,* we read that of all the virtues, "benevolence is the most beautiful . . . it cannot be surpassed."[44] As the text goes on to describe benevolence, it clearly echoes the biblical sense of compassion. Note, too, that in all great traditions, compassion is not only a personal and interpersonal virtue, but also a profoundly social one. It demands justice with mercy in society. The "common good," at its best, reflects deep compassion for all.

So, although suggested by the Bible, compassion can engage people as a human universal. It appeals to the highest sentiments of humankind, to what is most generous about us, and invites us to become most like ourselves—truly human beings. For teachers and parents to make compassion a central value in forming character, it must be ingrained in their own souls, riven into their hearts. Then it will permeate their whole way of "being with" learners, what and how they teach, the environment they help create, thus inculcating compassion as a character trait in others.

For the Educator's Style

The ways of knowing and wisdom commitments proposed in the two previous sections of this chapter have implied much for educators' style—their approach to intentional educational moments. Now, focused specifically on style, I begin with a summary proposal: a wisdom epistemology recommends that teachers and parents be catalysts who mentor learners (a) *to think for themselves*, (b) *in dialogue with others*, (c) *about meaning for life.*

Learners *think for themselves* as they become agents in the knowing process, as they use all their capacities of mind and heart and think critically in and about their own lives and social context. The most supportive setting for a wisdom way of knowing is *a community of partnership and conversation* in which all experience "equal regard." And although a wisdom epistemology is capable of the best of theory and abstraction, its thinking is never only theoretical or metaphysical. It has a humanizing interest in what this—whatever is being learned—*might mean for life,* leading on to wisdom that encourages responsibility. Every educator, school, program, or family can help people to think for themselves, in dialogue with others, about meaning for life.

Beyond this, teachers can surely give students access to the humanities, sciences, and arts in ways that foster wisdom. What else is this legacy of tradition but "the wisdom of the ages?" (our major theme in chapter 5). In rendering such access, there are styles of didaction that can help students think for themselves, in conversation with others, and with relevance for life. Which one of us has not come away from a stimulating lecture with our "heads spinning" and valuable insights to take into our lives? But surely the teaching process for fostering wisdom is to draw upon learner's own inner vitality with reflective questioning and activities that encourage them to *reflect together for life.*

Recall the biblical portrayal of wisdom as One who comes looking for us, She who seeks us out, and we as much allow ourselves to be found as we search for Her. (See Wisdom 6:13–14.) This insinuates that wisdom is not so much imparted as uncovered, not so much communicated as drawn out—that an educator will often simply help to "draw back the curtains" (*revelare*) to enable learners to see more clearly what is "already there" coming to meet them.

One key catalyst to such revelation is surely the quality of an educator's questioning and reflective activities. In a community of conversation—school, parish program, or family, and with adaptation to such factors as age, discipline, and topic—a teacher or parent may find the following six kinds of questioning activities helpful to encourage a wisdom way of knowing. As usual, they often overlap, and I urge the reader to add to my proposal.

Questions to Engage

Pose questions or reflective activities that personally engage people, that arouse their present interests or encourage new ones, that make them aware that this topic (whatever the theme) could be relevant to their lives, interesting to know, helpful to learn. Engaging questions and activities can appeal to any and all of persons' capacities—mind, will, or body—but most effective for wisdom are activities that engage their "souls"—their very core as human beings. Any question or reflective activity that stimulates learners' personal interest in what they are to learn, that taps into their hearts and gets them to draw upon their own intuiting, thinking, and feeling is effective for wisdom. By way of such a reflective activity, who has not experienced the power of a good story or example to personally engage us?

Questions for Looking At and Contemplating Life, and Inviting Expression

Pose questions or reflective activities that get people to notice, to pay attention to the data of life or tradition, and then to express somehow what they think or feel is going on. Getting learners to "pay attention" is a standard educational concern, but here I mean much more than listening to a pedagogue. At its deepest point, attending to life merges into contemplation when one really notices and personally appreciates what is there. Even an invitation like "Let us take a closer look at this" or "What do *you* think is going on here?" or "How do *you* feel about that?" can invite attention and expression.

My friend Jan teaches first grade. At the beginning of the school year she introduces her students to a favorite activity that they will do regularly—"going exploring" outside as a class. She alerts them that when they return from their "walk about," she will ask them what they saw and heard. On the first few occasions, this elicits few and obvious responses, but as the children learn the habit of "looking at life," they begin to find the "details," especially in nature, and their curiosity prompts them to investigate further.

By the end of the year, they know the names of every bird and insect, flower and weed, tree and bush in the neighborhood and what happens to each as the New England seasons unfold. While teaching appreciation for nature, Jan is also helping to form their powers of observation and contemplation—great gifts for life.

Questions for Critical Reflection about Life

Pose questions and reflective activities that invite people to use their reason, memory, and imagination to think about and examine their lives in the world and then even to "think about their thinking" by probing its sources and consequences, by unveiling the influences of their social context. Questions like the following can encourage critical reflection:

What do you really think about that?

Why do you think or feel this way?

What might this mean?

How did you arrive at your position?

What are some possibilities here?

What needs to be changed?

Do you have any reason to question your own perspective?

I once had a graduate student who stood out among her colleagues as truly having the habit of critical reflection; it seemed to come naturally to her. When other people were still getting ready to think about something, Celine would not only know what she thought or felt but wonder about why she thought or felt as she did, what was influencing her opinion and sentiments, where she really stood on the issue, probing the authenticity and reliability of her position. I once asked her in private, "Celine, who taught you to think?"

Her immediate response was "My dad," and she proceeded with the story. He was an Iowa farmer who taught all his children how to farm—daughters as well as sons. The key to his pedagogy was to get them to "really think" for themselves, to figure out why to do things a certain way, and then to test the validity of their own thinking—since in farming, there are always many ways to do things. My guess is that, like Celine, her siblings all became virtuosos of critical reflection. What a gift that dad gave his children!

Questions to Reflect on Tradition
Pose questions and activities that encourage learners to reflect critically and creatively on the symbols and texts of tradition, keeping the focus on learning its wisdom for life. This means enabling them to encounter the legacy of the humanities, arts, and sciences as active agents rather than as passive recipients; to appreciate, question, and create out of this "funded capital of civilization"; to recognize its assets, liabilities, and new possibilities, ever searching out not only what it meant but what it means now and to forge new meaning out of it. Questions like the following can encourage a wisdom way of knowing tradition:

What is this teaching and why?

What can we learn from this for our lives?

What does this mean for us today?

What new possibilities do you find here?

Questions for Personal Appropriation

Pose questions and activities that encourage people to see things for themselves, to make their own judgments, to personally appropriate what they are learning into their own schema of knowledge and wisdom. Appropriation-type questions are most often posed to invite learners' responses to some aspect of tradition or new experience. Personal appropriation is a crucial step in uniting theory and practice. Questions like the following can encourage personal appropriation:

What are you coming to see for yourself?

What is your considered judgment about this?

What do you agree with or disagree with?

What do you learn from this for your life?

What new learning is emerging for you?

A friend, Sharon, was teaching her Sunday-school first-grade class the parable of the prodigal son—or, as she preferred, "the forgiving father." She told the story, had the children act it out, invited them to think about what they could learn from it, catechized them about God's great love for us—no matter what, and more. Finally, almost as an afterthought and toward the end, she asked them, "What do you really think about the daddy in the story."

One little girl immediately blurted out, "He was a mean daddy."

Sharon, although dumbfounded and presuming that the child had missed the whole point of the parable, had the good sense to ask, "Why do you think that?"

The little girl proceeded to explain that if she asked her daddy for a lot of money to run away from home, he would never give it to her because he loves her. At her age, she was thinking literally about the parable.

"Ever since that little girl," says Sharon, "I always check out what they really heard."

Everyone has their own way of making things their own. Consciously encouraging them to do so makes appropriation an important aspect of the curriculum.

Questions for Decision and Choice

Pose questions and activities that invite people to make decisions and to act on them. In educating for wisdom, decisions can be: cognitive (choices about what and how one knows) or affective (about one's feelings and relationships) or behavioral (about what to do, what commitments to make). But decision questions seem essential to a wisdom pedagogy in order to unite theory and practice. Even questions like the following can encourage people to move beyond knowledge to wisdom:

What is your own conviction now?

What are your own best hopes?

What are you going to do with this?

What decision do you need to make?

For the Educational Environment

Education in wisdom should permeate the ethos of every school and program, parish and family. Just to take one instance: how educationally important it is that discipline be administered with wisdom.

My nephew Austin tells of a wise high-school principal who taught him wisdom for life. (Many such stories are told about this particular principal.) One day during his senior year of high school, Austin and a friend skipped out at lunchtime—strictly forbidden—and went downtown. There they met a beautiful young woman on whom both had heavy crushes. They lost track of time until it was too late.

The teacher in their first period after lunch showed no mercy: "You're fifteen minutes late—you've been off-campus. Go to the principal's office." This was a serious violation. Along the way, they searched urgently for a likely story as an excuse. Eventually, Austin suggested, "Why don't we tell him the truth?" And they did.

The principal listened, paused, and first said, "Gentlemen, I appreciate your candor." Then, wistfully, as if remembering a youth gone by, he said, "At times like that, it's easy to lose track of time. Dismissed!"

Austin concluded the story, "And I have never lied to cover up anything since then." Eddy Lynch was a wise principal who taught wisdom, even in how he administered discipline.

A reporter who attended the Nuremberg trials of Nazi war criminals commented later that what seemed most striking about those accused of heinous crimes against humanity was not their patent evil but their "thoughtlessness"—they committed terrible deeds without thinking. In a deep sense, doing evil is thoughtless, and moral living is thoughtful. Not that morality and the practice of values which becomes virtue and good character are realized by reflection alone—it takes practice as well. Yet thoughtfulness is integral to acting morally and to moral formation.

As indicated, the natural law tradition emphasizes that we can discover and discern our innate sense of morality by use of reason— by being "thoughtful." Maritain makes the claim that "Morality is steeped in intelligence; the goal is to awaken moral intelligence in the pupil."[45] There can be no doubt that moral discernment and decision making is self-reflective, that it demands thoughtfulness. Crucial for younger children especially is that teachers and parents share the reasons for their moral expectations, so that children can interiorize the rationale as their own, thus forming their moral autonomy.

To Maritain's call for intelligence, I make explicit that this entails engaging memory and imagination as well as reason. Holistic reflection is even more likely to nurture moral formation. Likewise, the habit of moral thinking is fostered by posing moral dilemmas for learners and encouraging their ethical reflection.

American ethicist James Rest has outlined a helpful schema of the self-reflection involved in moral decision making. It has four sequential activities. I propose that teachers and parents can create a "thoughtful" environment which encourages learners to engage in activities of:

- *Moral awareness:* Heighten people's consciousness to be alert to moral issues, to be sensitive to ethical questions, to bring a moral framework to the situations and experiences of life.

- *Moral reflection:* Encourage thinking about the morality of a situation or issue, getting learners to analyze the details from a moral perspective, to recognize the moral issues involved, to weigh possible options.

314

- *Moral commitment:* Prompt learners to choose and apply moral principles to the issues of their lives, to reach well-considered moral decisions, guided by what will be *for life for all.*

- *Moral action:* Encourage people to act on the moral decisions they make, to overcome impediments to moral action, to find support for their moral behavior.[46]

All educators can adjust these reflective activities to their particular situation, according to age, context, background, and moral issue. As they encourage learners to be morally reflective, they provide a "thoughtful" environment—the kind that nurtures moral character.

For Reflection
- What do you take away from this chapter on epistemology for your own educating? List three aspects that seem most significant to you.

- Is there a concrete decision you want to make about "ways of knowing" and your own approach as a teacher or parent?

- What adjustments would be needed to implement a wisdom epistemology in your school, parish program, or family?

Notes

1. The word *epistemology* is of more recent coinage. The first person usually credited with using the term "epistemology" is the Scottish philosopher J. F. Ferrier (1808–1864) in his *Institutes of Metaphysics,* first published in 1854. Ferrier distinguished two branches of philosophy, ontology and epistemology, thus formalizing a dichotomy that had long been operative in Western philosophy.
2. Gilkey, *Catholicism Confronts Modernity,* 22.
3. Thomas Aquinas, *Summa Theologica,* Pt 1, Q. 79, Art 2, and Pt. 1, Q. 93, Art 4. I leave the exclusive language here because, regretfully, Aquinas was ambivalent about whether or not one could say that women are in the full image and likeness of God. see remainder of Article 4.
4. Pope Pius IX, "Syllabus of Errors," # 3 and 4, in *The Church Teaches,* 26.
5. See my *Sharing Faith,* especially chapter 2 for a brief review of the history of Western epistemology from the interest of religious education. There I raise up some of its assets as well as the liabilities.
6. See Plato, *The Republic,* 518 B–D.
7. Harding, The Science Question in Feminism, 136.
8. Johnson, *She Who Is,* 86–87.
9. Ibid., 91.
10. See ibid., 95.
11. Borg, *Meeting Jesus Again,* 109.
12. See Augustine, *The Enchiridion on Faith, Hope, and Love,* 124–125.
13. See Augustine, *City of God,* book 19, chapter 19, 467.
14. For a fine review of this monastic epistemology see Jean Leclercq, *The Love of Learning and the Desire for God.*
15. Lonergan, *Method in Theology,* XII and 13.
16. See ibid., 11.
17. Ibid., 20 and passim.
18. A question often raised is whether a feminist epistemology does not itself become another narrow perspective that limits, one more time, who gets to know and what passes for knowledge. One response is that this is a real danger if the perspective becomes absolutist, elitist, and naive about its own interests. I'm convinced, however, that the general run of feminist theory avoids blind bias. But then, in doing so, some query if it falls into subjective relativism—as if everything depends entirely on one's perspective?

    The most satisfying response to both concerns—absolutism or relativism—and one reason I have found these theorists so helpful is that, in general, feminist epistemology is self-consciously a "standpoint epistemology." This means that it is critically conscious of its own perspective. Sandra Harding explains that a "standpoint epistemology" begins with the recognition that all knowing is from some perspective, from a particular context, interest, and politics—from a "standpoint." Then it engages critical reflection to uncover and name its own perspective—*where* one is "standing" in constructing knowledge—and to recognize how and why this standpoint shapes what one known. (See especially, Harding, "Rethinking Standpoint Epistemology" in Alcoff and Potter's *Feminist Epistemologies,* 49–82.)

Rather than *relativizing* or *absolutizing* one's particular perspective, a "standpoint epistemology" cherishes the truth that its perspective highlights, appreciates it as good for reaching some kinds of knowledge, but recognizes its dependence on other perspectives for other kinds of knowledge. In fact, a multiplicity of perspectives is far more reliable and "scientific" than a single one that dominates or excludes the rest. And if people are well aware of their own perspective—and know that it is limited—then rather than allowing it to become a tunnel vision, it should encourage openness to other people's point of view.

19. Linda Alcoff and Elizabeth Potter, "When Feminisms Intersect Epistemologies" in *Feminist Epistemologies,* 3.
20. Ibid., 13.
21. Helen Longino, "Subjects, Power, and Knowledge," in Alcoff and Potter's *Feminist Epistemologies,* 113.
22. See Sandra Harding, "Rethinking Standpoint Epistemology: What is 'Strong Objectivity'?" in Alcoff and Potter's *Feminist Epistemologies,* 58 and 66.
23. For such a relational ethic of care, see for example Carol Gilligan, *In a Different Voice,* and Nel Noddings, *Caring: A Feminine Approach to Ethics and Moral Education.*
24. See Jane Flax, "Political Philosophy and the Patriarchal Consciousness," in *Discovering Reality,* 269–71.
25. Vrinda Dalmiya and Linda Alcoff, "Are Old Wives Tales Justified?" in Alcoff and Potter's *Feminist Epistemologies,* 220.
26. Elsewhere I have proposed retrieval of the word *conation* as the way to name the "intended learning outcome" of religious education. This ancient term, now rarely used, originally included a cognitive, an affective, and a behavioral dimension. It captured the person's whole "will" to life. See *Sharing Faith,* especially chapters 1 and 3.
27. Maritain, Education at the Crossroads, 48.
28. I urge that we abandon this language pattern and use such words as *disciplines, sciences, topics, themes,* etc. instead of *subject* for what is being studied.
29. This is the insight of Jean Piaget, renowned Swiss-born developmental psychologist (1896–1980). See *To Understand Is to Invent.*
30. See, Bishop Edward K. Braxton's fine book *The Wisdom Community.*
31. Maritain, *The Education of Man,* 54.
32. See Michel Foucault, especially *Power/Knowledge.*
33. See Jurgen Habermas, especially *Knowledge and Human Interest.*
34. See John Dewey, "My Pedagogic Creed" in Dworkin's *Dewey on Education.*
35. *The Catechism of the Council of Trent for Parish Priests,* McHugh and Callan translation, 15.
36. Maritain, "The Education of Man," 138.
37. See Thomas Aquinas, *Summa Contra Gentiles,* I, 59.
38. I am being influenced by the significant work of Thomas Lickona on "education for character."
39. Lickona, Educating for Character, 43 and 67.
40. Ibid., 44 and 68.
41. Ibid., 46 and 45.

42. Borg, Meeting Jesus Again for the First Time, 46.
43. See Karen Armstrong, *A History of God.*
44. Confucius, *The Analects,* book 1V, v 1 and 6.
45. Maritain, *Education of Man,* 124.
46. See James Rest, *Moral Development: Advances in Research and Theory.* For this resource and outline, I am indebted to the doctoral dissertation of Harold Daly Horell, *A Pastoral Model of Christian Moral Formation,* 1997.

◁◆▷

CHAPTER SEVEN

A Spirituality for Everyone: "Our Hearts are Restless . . ."

"What is Your Deepest Desire?"

Professor X's body language was an alert from the beginning. He was not going to like what I had to say about "education for ministry"—the topic for this three-day conference with seminary professors from many parts of the Orient. I inquired and found out that he was Professor of Bible at one of the finest seminaries in Asia. His master's and doctoral degrees were from prestigious American universities. Colleagues described him as a brilliant but aloof young scholar, a forceful lecturer who seldom entertained student discussion or questions and who demanded high academic standards. He was their rising star.

I wondered why he so immediately disliked what I had to say. (He explained later that my reputation had preceded me.) It could be that his graduate studies had won out over his culture of origin and had socialized him to favor a narrowly rationalist way of knowing, even in ministry preparation. I was proposing a more holistic approach. It could also be that what I was saying was simply not too brilliant and I wasn't sounding like the expert I should be—this far from home.

He sat through my first three sessions with folded arms and a scowl. I managed to create some lively conversation around the proposals I was making—an unusual pedagogy in this culture— but Professor X refused to participate. At first, I suspected that he was "unreceptive" and then that my assessment was optimistic.

As he left the third session (I had six more to go), he paused just long enough to tell me, with poorly disguised disdain, that he disagreed with my understanding of spirituality, that I was exaggerating its importance in ministerial education and undermining academic rigor which happened to be his priority.

I responded that I shared his commitment. "But why choose between them—why not have both? The scholarly and the spiritual were once partners in all education."

Seeming exasperated, Professor X shrugged and passed on by. He attended no further sessions and I felt relieved. I did find out that he continued to quiz other participants about what we were up to.

The night before I was to leave, Professor X phoned my room and asked rather forcefully to meet with me. Among other things, from what he had heard, I had totally misrepresented the biblical understanding of justice. He referred three times to Scripture studies as his "field"—reminding me of my own amateur status on his turf. I said I was exhausted, needing to pack, and badly in need of sleep—with a fourteen-hour flight ahead of me. He persisted.

I explained that the only time available was that right then (9:30 at night and the end of a long day) or the next day, early, for a brief time since I had a late-morning flight and wanted to buy some gifts. He offered to come for breakfast. I suggested 8 A.M. but he requested 7:30 since his objections to my proposals were many. I finally agreed—with the enthusiasm one has for a root canal.

I awoke and hated the thought of breakfast. My intellectual insecurity was running riot now. What if I had misused the biblical texts? I regretted that we would be eating together. In both our cultures of origin, breaking bread with another still means something that wouldn't be true on that occasion. Ah, well—no choice but to face him!

He arrived ten minutes late and never apologized. Even before we got seated, he was talking down to me. "I must begin by explaining the biblical notion of justice to you," he announced. I thanked him and said—putting a defense in place—"Perhaps I am too dependent on Brueggemann" (one of the leading Scripture scholars on this theme).

He seemed taken aback and asked, "How much of Brueggemann have you read?"

"All of his writings," I said, lying a little—he writes voluminously—"and I've had many conversations with Walter— we're old friends." (Of course I was name-dropping!)

It worked—I knew round one was mine when he changed topics. "Well, my principal objection is to your understanding of spirituality and your proposal to make it a foundation of ministerial education."

I said it should be a foundation of all education and surely of education for ministry. Undeterred, he launched into an oration in favor of academic scholarship and I pretended to listen— preparing my rebuttal. Then, I began to tire of our game.

On the spur of the moment, I decided to gamble. I excused my interrupting him and queried, "Professor X, may I ask you a rather personal question?"

He seemed startled but responded, catching his breath, "Please, feel welcome."

Looking him in the eye I asked slowly and with an air of gravity, "What are some of your own deepest desires in life?" and paused. He was visibly perplexed, and I became worried. Had I crossed inappropriate boundaries? Switched too abruptly from the academic to the spiritual?

Slowly he said, "I'm not sure . . . what you mean."

"Well," I said, "clearly you are a person of strong passions. What fires them? What are the longings of your heart—for yourself, for your family, for your students? And where do you find God in the midst of it all?" as I gave a generic wave of the hand. During the silence that followed, I became aware of my own breathing but managed to wait. Then I noticed him welling up with tears, and my own sentiments were changing too. I began to feel simpatico with him now—I could see the reflections of myself in him and remembered that I knew his pain well. Whatever else, our game was over.

Eventually he found his voice, and he talked—his childhood, relationships with parents and siblings, conversion to Christianity, marriage and children, entering a career in ministry, commitment to scholarship, experiences of graduate school, work now at the seminary, trying to balance family and career. He told all as if trying to discern how God was working in his life, in the

*twists and turns of his faith journey. He said he loved being able
to talk like this and kept asking me to stay longer. I listened as
long as possible, with occasional questions, and shared a few
echoing stories of my own. We spoke and shared like brothers.
Few spiritual conversations have touched me so deeply.*

*I barely made my flight—without the souvenirs. I doubted we
would ever meet again, but was sure I had left behind—at the far
side of the world—a soul friend. I knew we had changed each
other a little. And on the long flight home, I could not help but
wonder if Professor X might teach any differently.*

"What Does This Have to Do with Education?"

This chapter on spirituality is the first of three on what I called in
chapter 1 the "cardinal" characteristics of Catholicism—the following
two take up justice and catholicity. While these define its identity as
do the first five, they function less as distinct emphases and more as
general commitments that permeate the tradition. The Latin *cardinalis*
(from *cardo* meaning "hinge") was used to indicate a unifying
principle or permeating spirit. Similarly, these three—justice,
spirituality, and catholicity—help compose the esprit de corps that
makes Catholic Christianity distinctive, and each is significant to a
philosophy and spirituality for teachers and parents.

At a teachers' conference and expecting some edifying responses, I
began my session by inviting participants to notice their instinctive
reactions to the stated theme of the occasion: "Education and
Spirituality." One immediately volunteered, in a tone more
exasperated than curious, "What has this got to do with us?"

Startled, I said, "Interesting question," but wondered, "Where do I
go from here?" Later, I recognized that it was an interesting question
and a reasonable one to pose, given some standard stereotypes about
spirituality—and indeed about education. Having had more time to
think about it, I take on that teacher's question again here. As the
reader might suspect, I am convinced that spirituality has everything
to do with education—it should be the leaven that vitalizes the whole
enterprise. While spirituality is a generic theme of *Educating for Life*,
in this chapter it is our specific focus.

In the public arena, spirituality has at least become a fad of late
and, hopefully, something much more. Whether "new age" or "old,"

there are spirituality books on the best-seller lists, high-powered executives doing "retreats," ordinary people going for spiritual direction, and enough young people buying Gregorian chant to send recordings to the top of the charts. Spirituality has become a billion-dollar industry, with gurus galore pointing paths to salvation—often quite lucratively for themselves.

Beyond being a fad, I am convinced that this spiritual awakening is significant and reflects people's abiding desire for something more than possessions or personal success. It hints at renewed consciousness of the hunger of the human heart that only Transcendence can satisfy.

Our age has surely tried the fleshpots! Now more people are recognizing what Augustine also learned the hard way—"Our hearts are restless, 'till they rest in Thee." However people name their Higher Power, and even among those who do not believe in a personal God, an unprecedented number are tending to affairs of the soul.

Our spiritual propensity arises from the deepest core of human being. It permeates who we are. It is a longing that allures us, through the depths of ourself, to experience gracious Mystery and ultimate Meaning as the backdrop of our lives and to enter into conscious relationship with the Ground of our Being—with God.

In traditional Christianity, the source of this divine appetite in humankind is called "the soul"—an old word that, ironically, has fallen into disuse in its spiritual sense. Oh, *soul* still refers to something core or true or something that touches the heart, as in "the soul of an organization" or "the soul of generosity" or "soul music." Popular spiritual author Thomas Moore, in the bestseller *Care of the Soul,* writes,

> Soul has to do with genuineness and depth . . . it is tied to life in all its particulars—good food, satisfying conversation, genuine friends, and experiences that stay in the memory and touch the heart.[1]

But notice, no mention of the Transcendent. I use *soul* in its transcendent connotation as what is most divine about us and as what prompts us to turn toward God.

As Moore observes, the phrase "care of the soul" comes from the old description in church law of the work of the priest—*cura animarum*—care of souls. I propose here that it also describes the vocation of educator, that an illuminating perspective on teacher and parent is as priestly minister—and I would add prophetic as well.

The very nature of humanizing education makes it possible for every educator to engage and nurture people as spiritual beings, although most often doing so quite subtly. Of course, spiritual nurture is readily recognized as a responsibility of parents in the home. Likewise, this is expected of religious educators in parish programs, in every parochial and religiously affiliated school. But I propose that teachers in any educational context can help "take care of souls," especially by their relationships with learners and by how they teach—even where religious language or instruction is excluded. All educators are wise to place a spiritual vision at the foundation of their teaching.

In Christian faith, the most precise use of *soul* names the person's *animating and defining principle*. Because humankind draws its life from God's own life, the soul is the very life-breath of God in us. Human vitality emanates from God's own vitality, and this soul is the ultimate clue to our identity as human beings—reflections of God.

As elaborated at length in chapter 2, the classic creation story relates that God fashioned the "person of the earth" and breathed God's own "breath of life" into it, and it became "a living being." (See Genesis 2:7.) The human soul is this breath of divine life by which we are alive. As Jacques Maritain wrote, citing Aquinas, the soul is "our society with God." Further, it "ordains us for God," giving us a homing instinct for the Source from whence we came.[2]

The ancient Greek philosophers spoke of body *and* soul, but separated them as dual entities. Plato even posed the soul as a spiritual captive in a corporeal prison. There is a strain of this dualism in Christian tradition, too, especially from heresies that disparaged the body as evil.

The dominant Christian tradition, however, is that body and soul are not dual entities but are two aspects of God's one gift of life, that they unite as one to constitute "the person." Better to say that we *are* a unity of body and soul than that we *have* a body and soul that unite. Although temporarily separated by death, at the Parousia—the end-time, as the Christian Creed confesses—the body will rise renewed to reunite with the soul, a whole person for eternity.

In this chapter then, *soul* refers to the animating and defining human principle that is the very life of God in humankind. The soul is not a "thing" that we possess or the ghost in the machine of the body. It is instead the spirit and substance of ourselves as persons—"the deep heart's core" (Yeats)—by which we are at once most human and most divine. The soul is the source of all that is distinctly human about us—our ability to experience, to think, to create, to know, but especially to relate and to love, like our God. Our capacity to live as spiritual beings is the soul's preeminent expression, with the soul drawing us inward and outward through our own depths into relationship with others and with Other. The spirit in spirituality is the human spirit for relationship with others and with God.

In Christian tradition, the *spirit* in *spirituality* is also God's Spirit. The Holy Spirit moves within human spirits to entice us into relationship with God and to allow this primary relationship to permeate all relationships—with self, others, and world. Christian spirituality, then, is a partnership between God's Spirit and human spirits—working in kinship. Spiritual growth is a lifelong journey, sustained by God's Spirit through our own, into living as a people of God.

In proposing that all educators can engage learners as spiritual beings—making a spiritual vision their foundation—I draw attention more to the process of education than to its content. This point is significant for educational contexts in which explicit religious education is expected and perhaps more especially where it is not permitted.

First, in parochial schools and parish religious education programs my experience is that concern for religion curriculum is invariably keen around "content" but seldom around "process"—as if instruction in the right information alone will suffice for spiritual formation. This is shortsighted. The teaching process is at least as important as the curriculum content to the spiritual outcome.

Put simply, there are ways of teaching that nurture people's spirituality and ways that sap their souls—a pressing point for teachers in parochial schools and parish programs. Even more so, parents should realize that their participation in the spiritual nurture of children depends far more on the values that permeate their "way of being together" as a family and the ethos of the home than on explicit instruction in religion—although parents participate in religious instruction as well. The pedagogy of every faith context should engage people's souls and foster their growth as spiritual beings.

What then of educational settings that exclude instruction in religion from the curriculum? Can public school teachers still employ a pedagogy that appeals to and educates the spirit of students? I am convinced that they can and should consider doing so, and I will make specific suggestions throughout this chapter.

For now I think of a friend who teaches English literature in a large public high school. His respectful and caring way of relating with students; the depth questions he poses as they encounter the texts of good literature; the personal issues that he invites them to consider for themselves and to make good choices about; the social issues that he raises into their consciousness; the ultimate issues of life that he brings to their attention—in short, his engagement of their "souls" in the educational process—make him an eminent instance of an educator of the spirit, although he never explicitly teaches religion, much less his own Jewish faith. From conversations with Frank, I know that he intentionally teaches as he does precisely because of his own spirituality.

Surely, the great majority of teachers should not relinquish what is most human and divine about people to designated religious educators. The most dehumanizing aspects of Western education stem from its neglect of learners' spirits, with dire psychological and social consequences. Moore writes,

> The great malady of the twentieth century, implicated in all of our troubles and affecting us individually and socially, is 'loss of soul.' When soul is neglected, it doesn't just go away; it appears symptomatically in obsession, addiction, violence, and loss of meaning.[3]

And writing about education at the height of World War II, Maritain warned urgently,

> The preface to Fascism and Nazism is a thorough disregard of the spiritual dignity of [humanity], and the assumption that merely material or biological standards rule human life and morality.[4]

It would seem that no educator can neglect to care for souls.

Certainly, the spiritual depth structure of Christianity recommends education with a vision that fosters the spirit of learners. Pause here to sort out some of your own perspectives on the relevance of care to souls to education.

For Reflection
- Imagine a teacher or parent asking you, "What has spirituality got to do with education?" How would you respond?

- Review the sources of your own response— autobiographical, social, and otherwise. Do you feel any need for a shift in perspective?

- Will engaging people as spiritual beings threaten the academic rigor of education? Why or why not?

Christian Spirituality: A "Catholic" Proposal

Think of the rich diversity among the spiritual traditions of humankind. Every culture finds its own distinct way of expressing and nurturing the spirit of its people. Every religion—whether indigenous or transcultural—fosters its own spirituality, a reminder to Christians that, indeed, God's Spirit blows where she wills. (See John 3:8.)

No one description of spirituality could be sufficiently comprehensive to embrace all possibilities. Christian spirituality, however, has a universal quality that appeals beyond its community confines, particularly to people who believe in a personal God. While welcoming enrichment from other traditions, a Christian spirituality can be a "case study" to highlight the correlation of spirituality and education and to serve as a lens through which educators from many traditions may look afresh at their educating.

A young professional woman with a strong feminist consciousness told me, "The only reason I remain a Catholic is for its spirituality." I probed a bit. She often experiences the institutional structures of her church as patriarchal, exclusionary, and alienating—yet, "I keep coming back and hang in with the tradition because of its power to nourish

my soul." Surely, one of the richest aspects of Catholic Christianity—
capable of transcending its institutional limitations—is its spirituality.

Such spiritual treasury is not easy to describe, much less to define,
with its wealth of emphases, styles, and approaches. It may be
recognized most readily in notable instances—its official and
unofficial saints. But there is no more diverse crew. Every character
type of humankind—with all the foibles and virtues, sins and graces
of the human condition—is represented.

For every Francis of Assisi who relinquished the things of the
world and eschewed the halls of power, there is an Ignatius of Loyola
who saw everything with potential for the glory of God and set out to
educate the future leaders of society.

For every Teresa of Avila or Julian of Norwich who gave
themselves to the contemplative life, there is the Catherine of Sienna
and Joan of Arc who got embroiled in the ecclesial and social politics
of their day.

For every Mother Teresa who consoled the poor and dying, there
is a Dorothy Day who committed to reform the social structures that
are the root cause of poverty.

Saints have come from every race and ethnic background; were
rich and poor; educated and illiterate; famous and obscure; vowed
religious, married, divorced, and single. They lived out their lives in
an endless variety of vocations.

I suggest a collection of characteristics that, woven together, may
amount to a Christian spirituality. There is a Catholic tinge to their
theological underpinnings at times, but they are essentially
Christian—shared by many Protestant brothers and sisters in the Body
of Christ.

The opening characteristics, which are not explicitly Christian,
find echo in many other religious traditions as well. My listing is
cumulative and the characteristics often overlap, the first and last
making the same point in different ways. As I describe them, I begin
to hint at how teachers and parents can allow spirituality to permeate
how they educate.

Spirituality As God's Desire

Human spirituality originates from God's side of the relationship. Out
of unconditional love, God takes the initiative and reaches out to

every person, inviting us into right and loving relationship with Godself and with each other. This initiative reflects God's unrelenting desire to draw all people to Godself that they may experience and respond to God's love as "fully alive" human beings.

This divine outreach is not out of God's need, as if an insatiable divine ego craves the flattery of human attention—ludicrous. Instead, God draws us to Godself out of love—for our own good. God knows that we live most humanly—most completely according to our nature—and most freely through being in loving relationship with God, by putting God at the center of our lives.

Faithful to its principle of sacramentality, a Christian perspective emphasizes that God's desire and outreach to humankind is mediated through the ordinary and extraordinary of life, through common and sacred symbols, in every arena and level of existence, on the Mondays and the Sabbaths of our lives. When educators encourage learners to really notice what is "going on" around them, to gaze contemplatively at creation and culture, to look discerningly at their lives in the world, to appreciate the gift of the ordinary and everyday, they engage and nurture them spiritually.

Spirituality as Human Desire

Through the divine life within humankind, God has implanted a desire for God, a human affinity to turn toward God, a hunger that cannot otherwise be satisfied. Our desire for God—the reflection of God's desire for us—is the pervasive human desire in that all our longings are ultimately for God. Although we may allay these longings in many ways—both wise and foolish—only God can finally and fully satisfy them.

Our great spiritual reservoir then is the human heart, with all its desires and longings. This advises educators to turn learners to their interiority, to their own souls. When teachers and parents encourage learners to take seriously and probe their human desires for signals of truth, goodness, and beauty, they foster their spirituality,

Spirituality As Divine/Human Partnership

Essentially, *spirituality is people's relationship with God*, or with however they name the Ultimate Value at the center of their lives. For believers in a personal divinity, this relationship entails placing God first in one's life—with allegiance to no other "gods" (the First Commandment encapsulates the other nine)—and entering into the equivalent of a one-on-one friendship with God as one's mooring that anchors everything else.

This divine/human association is best described as a partnership. Not that we are equal partners—humans always depend on God's help—but rather that God chooses to wait upon human participation in the friendship and upon our cooperation in unfolding God's will for the world. God invites us into right and loving relationship and helps us to respond. Yet the response is by our own free choice and agency.

Educators nurture spiritual growth as they raise consciousness about the contemporary versions of the perennial idolatries, as they help learners resist the allure of false gods and discern where their "real treasure lies." They foster spirituality, too, as they help people to contribute their own talents, gifts, and best efforts to the shared life of humanity and to do so with a sense of partnership—certainly with others and perhaps with an Ultimate Ground of Being.

Spirituality As a God-Conscious Way of Life in Relationship

Note first that spirituality is one's way of life—an aspect in need of emphasis. Spirituality is often made to sound esoteric and removed from life—confined to the interior self rather than lived out in the everyday. Perhaps this is the emphasis in some traditions, but from a Christian point of view, our spirituality is realized in how we live our day-to-day lives.

Then it can be described as a God-conscious way of life, which means consciously allowing one's partnership with God to permeate every aspect of existence, being alert to God's presence in the everyday, knowing that we live in a "divine milieu"—the beautiful phrase of the great French Jesuit, Teilhard de Chardin (1881–1955).

God-consciousness encourages us to live with more mystery than mastery, to embrace paradox and our own finitude, to realize that we are not "god" but that we can depend on Someone Other than ourselves. And yet it also encourages us to cherish our own selves as of infinite worth and dignity—not earned but a gift. Our very being alive gives glory to God.

The essence of spirituality is our relationships—not only with God, but with self, others, and the world. Or perhaps more accurately, our spirituality as relationship with God is realized in and should leaven all our relationships. From this perspective, holiness is measured by the loving and life-giving quality of our relationships.

For educators, whatever they do to heighten learners' awareness of an Ultimacy to their lives, to encourage them to see the more in the midst of the world, to educate them to live relationally *for life for all* engages and fosters their spirituality

Spirituality As Necessary for Human Wholeness

Spirituality is not necessary like food or drink, but in the sense that without tending to our souls we live less humanly. Humans are spiritual beings. To neglect our spirituality is to be less than who we are. There is even a danger in not caring for our souls. If the innate desire for God is unmet, the temptation is to allay it in other ways— fame or fortune, power or prestige, work, drugs, or alcohol. None will satisfy, and when we make such substitutes a "god," they destroy us. As the French mathematician Blaise Pascal (1623–62) wisely wrote, "There is a God-shaped hollow in the human heart that nothing else can fill."

On the other hand, a vibrant spirituality lends a foundation for integrating all the bits and pieces of our lives, helping us to live a whole and balanced life. A spiritual center nurtures a satisfying sense of purpose, a coherent way of making meaning, a persuasive warrant for responsibility and ethic. We become more human through experiences and expressions of awe and reverence, of supplication and thanksgiving, of wonder and worship—when we reach out of ourselves toward the Transcendent.

Educators in parochial schools, parish programs, and Christian homes can overtly foster learners' spirituality as integral to a holistic education, giving them access to the spiritual resources of their faith community. On the other hand, teachers in nonreligious contexts should remember that "the spiritual" is not synonymous with "religion" and that there are many ways to attend to people's spiritual needs—without overt "God talk."

I have an agnostic friend who says of listening to good music, "That's *my* going to church." He reminds me that the aesthetic and spiritual are first cousins! When educators help learners to enjoy and appreciate the arts, the beauty of nature, and the creativity of human culture, they care for souls in life-giving ways. When educators encourage people to find meaning and purpose beyond the self, to maintain a balanced lifestyle, and to live with integrity, they care for souls.

Spirituality As Human Universal

Every person is equally desired by God—no one more so than anyone else. And made in God's image, everyone is capable of growing in God's likeness. Rather than a rarefied business for monks, nuns, and religious gurus, spirituality is a universal possibility and invitation to all humankind.

Regardless of particular religious tradition or none, God desires and enables all to live in right and loving relationship with God—and so with self, others, and creation. Spirituality is ontological—it belongs to humankind's very "being" (Greek *ontos*). It is more accurate to call ourselves spiritual beings who have a human life than human beings who have a spiritual life.

This universal aspect invites educators to view all people as essentially spiritual, and this can transform one's pedagogy. The great Moravian educational reformer John Amos Comenius constructed his humanizing approach to education around the conviction that every person is made in God's image and likeness. He said that to so convince teachers would revolutionize education. The more teachers and parents can approach learners as essentially spiritual—engaging their depths, with reverence for their divine nature and convinced of their divine destiny—the more likely they are to foster their spirituality.

Spirituality As Call to Holiness—with Justice and Compassion

In the Hebrew Scriptures, the spiritual vocation is holiness of life: "Be holy, for I, the Lord your God am holy" (Leviticus 19: 2). This is ever the horizon of the spiritual journey. Human beings tend to their spirituality to become holy—like God.

At heart, biblical holiness is living in right relationship with God, self, others, and the world. Bible scholars point to Micah 6:8 as a great summary of how one becomes holy. God addresses all humankind and says, "This is what Yahweh asks of you: only this, to act justly, to love tenderly, and to walk humbly with your God."

Note well that *holiness of life* and *living justly* are equivalent demands of the covenant with God. Both amount to *right relationship*—justice and spirituality are not realized apart from each other. For Hebrew faith, holiness and justice are two sides of the same coin—the mandate of the covenant.

What is this "rightness" that should mark all relationships—vertical and horizontal—with God and each other? Clearly, it means living the law of the covenant, well summarized in the Decalogue. A point made in chapter 2 bears repeating. Both classic texts of the Ten Commandments—Exodus 20 and Deuteronomy 5—begin with a statement that is key to interpreting their purpose: "I am the Lord your God, who brought you out of . . . slavery."

Thus, to remain free and live with true freedom: take only God as your God, reverence the sacred and keep a Sabbath, honor parents, respect life, live with faithfulness, be honest and just in all dealings, tell and live the truth, respect others' personal commitments and their property. But surely holiness of life invites beyond this minimum of the Ten Commandments.

Yes indeed! In Hebrew faith, people are to become holy not only because God is holy, but in the same way that God is holy. How God relates with humankind is the model for how our relationships should be with God, self, each other, and the world. And God's holiness/justice is not the scales-balancing of blind "Lady Justice"—giving everyone exactly their deserts. Rather, God's relationships are marked by generosity and—even more—by largess and munificence. This great generosity of God is reflected especially in God's compassion for humankind.

Scripture scholars now highlight that the Hebrew word for compassion—so often attributed to God—has the same root as the word for womb (*rachum*, compassion; *racham*, womb). So, God relates to us with the love and tenderness that a mother has for the children of her womb. God's people should be holy with the same kind of compassion.

As developed in chapter 8, and again taking God's example as *the* human ideal, those most deserving of compassion are people most in need of it—the poor and disadvantaged. To care for the needy is a privileged way to tend to one's spirituality—to grow in holiness of life.

When educators teach learners to live justly, when they encourage compassion for those most in need, when they raise social consciousness and promote commitment to the common good, they engage and nurture their spirituality.

Christian Spirituality As "The Way" of Jesus Christ

It seems strange to place this characteristic in the middle of the list, as if only one among many, when it is the touchstone of Christian spirituality. But all of the previous characteristics are entailed in living as a disciple of Jesus. Although they could be drawn from other religious traditions, they are central to the Christian Gospel. Since the following five are specifically Christian, my list could be described as a pyramid—with following "the way" of Jesus at the top.

"The way" was the generic phrase that the first Christians used to represent how Jesus lived and what he lived for, why he died and was raised to new life. Jesus is ever the prototype of holiness for Christians. Baptism calls us to be disciples—apprentices—of his "way."

As indicated many times previously in this text, the defining symbol of Jesus' way of holiness is the reign of God—doing God's will of peace and justice, love and compassion, freedom and fullness of life, on earth as it is done in heaven. The great law of Jesus' way of holiness is a radical version of the law of love—radical in that love of God, self, and neighbor measure each other, with no limit as to who is neighbor. The pervading spirit of Jesus' way of holiness is epitomized in the Beatitudes and the subsequent Sermon on the Mount. (See Matthew 5:1–7:29.)

In the Beatitudes, Jesus proposed holiness and happiness— wholeness—as trusting in God, opposing evil, living with compassion, doing justice, making peace, and being faithful to God at all costs. Then, in the Sermon that follows, Jesus called disciples to be light to the world and salt to the earth by obeying and teaching God's commandments; by being reconciled as needed; by avoiding sin (including within one's heart); by being trustworthy and faithful; by turning the other cheek; by going the extra mile; by loving even one's enemies; by giving alms to the needy; by praying regularly and fasting; by putting God first—especially ahead of money; by depending on providence; by not judging unkindly; and by doing unto others what you would have them do to you: the golden rule.

For Christian faith, Jesus is not only the exemplar of holiness but also its enabler. Jesus is the Christ, God's Anointed One, who saves from slavery to sin and sets people free to live a holy life. Within his person and through his life, death, and resurrection, Jesus Christ has permanently bonded God and humankind in right relationship. In Christian faith, Jesus is the catalyst in history of God's grace, now empowering humankind to live in right and loving relationship with God, self, each other, and the world. Jesus Christ is the sacrament of Christian holiness, the One who both shows "the way" and lends the grace to follow.

Every educator in a parochial school, parish program, or Christian family has the opportunity and the responsibility to educate in "the way" of Jesus Christ, to encourage gospel values. But beyond Christian educational contexts, whenever educators help learners to live their lives according to their sense of highest calling; when they educate people in how and what to love—*for life for all*; when they encourage passionate pursuit of real human happiness according to transcendent values instead of money, power, or pleasure, they engage and nurture their spirituality.

Spirituality as Faith Community in the World

As one might expect, emphasis on the communal aspect of Christian faith (chapter 4) lends similar emphasis to its spirituality. Like many other traditions, Christian spirituality is centered in the person's relationship with God. However, this divine/human relationship is never realized in isolation or fueled by individual effort alone, but through the relationships and sacramentality of a Christian community.

For all of the Church's sins and shortcomings, God works through it to sustain the spiritual journey of Christians, providing them a "home within God's family" where they can support each other in their relationship with God. Christian care of souls—including one's own—is always a communal effort. Spiritual growth is nurtured most readily in and through the faith community—of saints and sinners—that stretches into eternity.

Christian community exists not for its own sake but to be a sacrament of God's reign in the world. So Christian spirituality calls the whole Christian community to realize the values of God's reign in every arena of life and on every level of existence. Although spirituality is often posed as an individualized affair ("between me and

God") or as pursued out of self-interest (some version of "to save my soul"), Catholic Christian spirituality is realized through the Church in the midst of the world.

Again, educators in Catholic or Christian schools, in parish programs, or Christian families have a responsibility to nurture Christian learners in ecclesial identity—to be members of the Church with a sense of responsibility for its mission in the world. There can also be opportunities for educators in the public context to encourage learners to belong to their particular faith communities and to do so with a heightened sense of solidarity with all humankind. when they take such opportunities, they nurture their spirituality.

I know a high-school social studies teacher who often begins Monday classes by inviting students to share some of what they heard in their houses of worship over the weekend. He invites them to reflect on the experience from a social perspective—what the sermon or symbols might mean for society, for the world. He engages this exercise in order to raise consciousness about the social responsibilities of religious faith; it is always one of the liveliest conversations of the week.

Spirituality as Whole and Wholesome

Like Christian faith (chapter 5), Christian spirituality is a holistic affair, engaging the person's head, heart, and hands—a "whole" way of life. Concomitantly, Christian spirituality at its best is profoundly wholesome. Contrary to the stereotype of holiness as becoming a "church mouse" and getting no enjoyment out of life, Christian spirituality calls to a vibrant and vital lifestyle—to embrace, enjoy, and celebrate life and to be life-giving for others. Becoming holy means becoming fully alive—"to the glory of God." As Jesus said, "I came that you might have life, and have it to the full" (John 10:10). Renowned Catholic theologian Josef Goldbrunner wrote a small book years ago entitled *Holiness Is Wholeness*. The title says it all.

Christian parents and teachers have a responsibility to present Christian faith as a "whole and wholesome" affair, to nurture learners in a very positive and live-giving spirituality. Then, as educators teach in ways that develop learners' gifts and human potential, inspiring them to be fully alive human beings with a sense of joy in life, they engage and nurture their spirituality.

Spirituality As a Life-Long Journey

In the kind of "no-holds-barred" conversation one can have with a total stranger on an airplane, someone volunteered to me, "I was saved by Jesus Christ in Kansas City, June 9, 1978."

I was intrigued by the claim, with the precise date and place, but also found it very strange. I was raised in the tradition of the old code of church law which legislated that a person must be at least three days dead before being considered for canonization. Personal claims to the spiritual heights were always taken as a sign of the opposite— and the sin of pride to boot. Every day brings its new challenge to live one's Christian faith, with no resting on laurels already won.

The spiritual journey is lifelong. It is marked, of course, by high points and turning points, but its conversions are ongoing and ever in need of renewal. God's saving grace is a gift each day that invites our lived response. Given the human condition, there are days and ways in which we do not respond faithfully. We sin, yet God never gives up on us. And sin, thank God, need not waylay us from the spiritual journey. To the contrary, mainstream Christian spirituality emphasizes the need to recognize one's sinfulness and shortcomings and to be ever ready to repent and change one's life. The greatest saints were noted for awareness of their sinfulness, in that they recognized how far they had yet to travel to be "holy as Yahweh God is holy." In this lifelong journey—home to God—no one is "finished" on this side of eternity.

Again, it is self-evident that Christian parents and teachers can offer curricula that encourage learners along their spiritual journeys, ever leaving the impression that it is a life-long affair. However, when any educator teaches people for life as an open horizon—with unfolding possibility to grow as a whole and integral person, to live each day as a gift, to be open to surprises and to new opportunities for fullness of life, and especially to have hope for themselves, others, and the world, he or she engages and nurtures their spirituality.

Spirituality as Sustained by Prayer, Communal and Personal

A common convention is that our spirituality is synonymous with our prayers. This is not so—*spirituality is consciously living our lives in relationship with God.* On the other hand, all religious traditions insist that prayer—of some kind—is essential to taking care of the soul, to sustaining and fostering spirituality. Prayer is necessary to maintain a

God-consciousness about life. As human love needs presence and communication, so, too, does our relationship with God. conscious presence and exchange are the essence of prayer. All Christian denominations accent both communal and personal prayer as integral to the spiritual life.

The prime instance of Christian communal prayer is participation in the liturgy of the Church, its high point being Sabbath worship of word and sacrament. For Catholic Christians, the Mass is a climactic event that symbolically gathers up the divine/human encounters of the everyday and creates a heightened experience of "our lives to God, and God's life to us, for the life of the world."[5] Beyond Sabbath worship, the Christian community celebrates other sacraments and has other "public works" (the Greek *liturgeo*) like the liturgy of the hours—pausing at various times to praise God and sanctify the day.

Personal prayer can take myriad forms. Even within Christianity, this "turning of the mind and heart to God" (the old catechism definition of prayer) has many traditions and styles. Traditionally, the defining sentiments of Christian prayer are *praise*, *gratitude*, *repentance*, and *petition*. Contemporary spirituality suggests adding *decision*.

Two time-honored prayer genres are meditation and contemplation. Meditation is a more proactive kind of conversation between a person and God, in which she or he "talks" to God—often focused on a text of Scripture or an experience or issue of life—and discerns the movements of one's heart for God's "response." Contemplation is more a peaceful presence with God—without any conversation—enjoying a quiet being together, much as lovers might be silent and yet enjoy each other's company.

Educators in a religious context can teach and encourage learners in a life of prayer. Christian families can pray together—the best way to form the young and sustain each other as "pray-ers"—and surely it is appropriate for teachers and students in parochial schools or parish programs to pray together.

I begin my parish program gatherings with a prayer and—although a bit of an anomaly now in a university setting—likewise my graduate courses in religious education and pastoral theology at Boston College. Every catechetical context can introduce learners to traditions of personal and communal prayer, and can do sacramental catechesis so that, as Vatican II urged, "all the faithful be led to full, conscious and active participation in . . . the liturgy."[6]

What of prayer in the public-school context—a hot political issue? Wherever one comes down on the controversy, I believe the debate has been framed with too minimalist an understanding of prayer—only as something that is "said" at a particular moment and with explicitly religious language. As many of my previous suggestions indicate, a teacher can take a "prayerful" approach to teaching and allow the underlying sentiments of prayer to permeate his or her pedagogy—without any "God language."

So any teacher who encourages people to be self-reflective in their hearts, to listen to their own depths, to have a sense of awe and reverence about the world around them, to live with gratitude, to avoid becoming one's own "god," to have a feeling of interdependence and belonging to a whole universe with coresponsibility for its well-being engages and nurtures people as "pray-ers."

Spirituality as the Work of God's Holy Spirit

Our spirituality is perennially nourished by the presence to us of God's Holy Spirit. The Holy Spirit inspires people's spirits, encouraging them to respond to God's invitation to relationship. In the farewell discourse of the Fourth Gospel, Jesus promised, "I will ask the Father and he will give you another Paraclete to be with you always, the Spirit of truth" (John 14:17).

In Christian faith, the Holy Spirit came in a special way on the first Pentecost Sunday (fifty days after Jesus' resurrection) and has remained ever since, sustaining, inspiring, and guiding humankind in its journey "home" to God. In the spiritual life, our own efforts at progress are made possible and far outweighed by the gifts of the Holy Spirit.

Based on Isaiah 11:1–3, Christians have listed the special gifts of the Holy Spirit as: wisdom and understanding, good judgment and courage, knowledge, wonder, and reverence for God. Notice that all of them, in one way or another, are educational gifts! And in the lives of those who respond to Her promptings,[7] the Holy Spirit brings forth these fruits: "love, joy, peace, patience, kindness, generosity, faithfulness, gentleness, and self-control" (Galatians 5:22–23).

Catholic Christianity emphasizes the value of "spiritual mentoring" (more traditionally called "spiritual direction") in caring for the soul and, especially, for discerning the movement of God's Holy Spirit in one's life. The old Gaelic name for the spiritual mentor is *anam cara*—literally, "friend of the soul"—someone who knows well and cares for the very depths of the person.

Spiritual mentoring is usually focused into a regular time of conversation (about an hour once a month) in which the "soul friend": (a) welcomes the person to share about life from their depths of soul, (b) prompts reflection on their lived relationship with God, and (c) encourages recognition and response to God's abiding love— to deepen their relationship. The dynamic of such spiritual mentoring presumes that God's Spirit is moving in people's lives, and that getting them to name and reflect on what is "going on" there heightens their awareness of God's presence and aids their discernment of how to respond in daily life.

Drawing all of these characteristics together, *Christian spirituality is consciously living one's life in relationship with God, empowered by the Holy Spirit and following "the way" of Jesus, the Christ. Allured by God's desire within human hearts, the Christian spiritual journey is into right relationship with God, self, others, and creation, permeated by justice and compassion. It is sustained by prayer—personal and communal—and lived through a Christian community for the coming of God's reign in the world.*

Some of the Historical Story and Signs of New Hope
The substantial characteristics of Catholic Christianity reviewed in previous chapters—and the emphasis on justice and catholicity to come (chapters 8 and 9)—are the foundations of a rich spirituality as proposed.

- A positive understanding of the person—as essentially good and oriented toward God—encourages a life-affirming kind of spirituality.

- Emphasis on the partnership of God's grace and human agency accents that we can choose to participate, again by God's grace, in "the work of our salvation" (Philippians 2:12).

- The principle of sacramentality encourages the spiritual conviction that God comes looking for us through life in the world, and by God's grace we can respond through our own humanity, everyday experiences, and the created order.

- Emphasizing the communal aspect of Christian faith lends a relational accent to its spirituality, not only with God but with a faith community, with others and the world, thus discouraging a privatized piety—ever a temptation.

- Appreciation for tradition gives access to the spiritual treasury that each generation can inherit from those gone before, for the "new age" is not the first whom God has called to holiness of life.

- Wisdom is a great spiritual value and its grounding in critical rationality may prevent spirituality from veering into the bizarre—a distinct possibility.

- Emphasis on justice encourages a spirituality marked by outreach to the neighbor in love, compassion for those in need, and social responsibility for the common good.

- Emphasis on catholicity encourages openness to learn from the great variety of spiritualities that God's Spirit enkindles in the hearts of humankind.

As with each of these substantial characteristics, however, the Catholic Christian community has often failed to live up to the best of its own spiritual tradition. Though Catholicism carries a rich spiritual legacy, it has a particularly debilitating flaw that urgently needs address—and there are hopeful signs that the Spirit is doing something in our time. I am thinking of its exclusivity that expressed itself in two ways: (a) the parochial attitude that only Catholic Christians are called to holiness and that the only path is a Catholic one and (b) by giving such emphasis to the vowed religious life as *the* path to holiness that "ordinary" baptized Christians felt like second-class citizens of God's reign.

Although I hope that the Catholic Christian community will always cherish the vowed living of the evangelical virtues—poverty, chastity and obedience—as a special charism of God's reign, such appreciation should not demean the married nor single life. God calls everyone to holiness of life by whatever "way" is their vocation. The good news is that the Second Vatican Council attempted to redress both instances of exclusivity and was a major catalyst toward an inclusive spirituality.

First, the ecumenical spirit of the Second Vatican Council encouraged an unequivocal appreciation for the spiritual journey of every human being, of God's particular love and saving grace for each person, and of the many rich traditions among humankind for responding to God's invitation to "right relationship." Catholics at last realized, without ambivalence, that everyone can make their way "home" to God, Christian or not, both inside and outside of the Church.

The universality of God's love and saving grace has long been a dogma of Christian faith and yet always seemed threatened by the sectarian axiom "outside of the church there is no salvation." This was first officially promulgated by Pope Boniface VIII in 1302. It was aimed, however, not at people of other religious traditions at all but at forcing a recalcitrant French king, Philip IV, to submit to papal authority. (If he refused, he would be drummed out of the Church as an apostate and "lost.") Subsequently, its interpretation in preaching and catechisms tended to broaden beyond apostates and be directed negatively against people who had never been Christian, casting doubt on the universality of God's saving grace. Officially, however, Catholicism condemned its literal interpretation—you must be Christian to be saved—as heresy[8] and taught that non-Christians of good will are saved by living their own faith. (I return to this issue in chapter 9 on catholicity.)

The tendency to idolize the Church, however, encouraged Catholics to be overly dependent on the ecclesial institution for their spiritual welfare and to assume that those outside of it are always at least "ten points down" with God. In contrast, although Vatican II reaffirmed a rich theology of the Church, it refocused it as the community of Jesus' disciples at the service of God's reign and underscored the universality of God's love and work of salvation—for everyone. Besides encouraging people to become more mature in their relationship with the institutional church, the Council encouraged them to learn from other traditions and communities of faith for their spiritual journey. The Council's *Declaration on Non-Christian Religions*[9] "gives primary consideration . . . to what human beings have in common." All persons "comprise a single community and have a single origin . . . and final goal: God . . . whose providence, manifestations of goodness, and saving designs extend to all" (#1).

Regarding the great religions of the world, the Council states, "The Catholic Church rejects nothing which is true and holy in these religions" but rather looks upon them "with sincere respect." The Council then calls for "dialogue and collaboration with followers of other religions" (#2)—a recognition that Christians have much to learn from ecumenical exchange. This ecumenicity in theology prompted a similar openness in spirituality, raising Catholic consciousness that all human beings are "spiritual," are called to holiness of life, and may respond in multiple ways. All Christians have much to learn from the diversity of the spiritual path.

A second and perhaps the primary source of spiritual renewal among Catholic Christians is their relearning that the call to holiness is not reserved to an elite few but is the vocation of every Christian. Again, Vatican II was a powerful catalyst by returning to a more "radical" theology of baptism. The early Christians took baptism most seriously, understanding it as a call to transformation and holiness of life, and to full participation in the mission and ministry of the Church in the world.

This radical understanding of baptism was threatened after the Emperor Constantine issued his famous *Edict of Milan* (circa 313), granting tolerance to all religions. Thereafter, Christianity emerged as the official religion of the Roman Empire and baptism became a cultural expectation rather than a call to transformation of life and participation in the Church's mission of God's reign in the world.

Adding to the diminishment of baptism, gradually all Christian ministry was placed exclusively in the hands of clergy as a social class. Now Catholicism lost its sense of the "priesthood of the laity," reducing further the import of one's baptismal vocation. Thankfully, the Protestant Reformers retrieved and saved the "priesthood of all believers" as a central doctrine for the whole Church.

One reason the monastic movement emerged in Christianity was to maintain a radical theology of baptism and its call to holiness. Much the same can be said of the vowed life taken on by the religious orders of men and women who modified the monastic charism—away from cloister—to carry on ministries in the world.

Although monasticism and the vowed religious life will always remain cherished charisms within Catholicism and over time have lent it its most precious spiritual treasury, an unfortunate side effect was to encourage Catholics to think that holiness of life is pursued only by "the religious." There were, of course, some countersigns, but in large part, spirituality was seen as the preserve of an elite few. "The religious" were the one's entrusted with "care of souls"—their own and others—and "the laity" were simply cared for. It was so significant then that Vatican II encouraged the Church to return to an inclusive spirituality—one that invites every baptized person to be an active agent of their own spiritual journey.

Even the title of chapter 5 of the Council's *Constitution on the Church* was significant: "The Call of the Whole Church to Holiness."[10] It taught that by baptism, "All the faithful of Christ of whatever rank or status are called to the fullness of the Christian life and to the perfection of charity." Then, emphasizing a worldly kind of spirituality, the Council added, "By this holiness a more human way of life is promoted even in this earthly society" (#40). It restated that "all of Christ's faithful, whatever be the conditions, duties, and circumstances of their lives . . ." are to "grow in holiness day by day" (#41).

The *Catechism* echoed these sentiments of the Council, describing baptism as "the gateway to life in the Spirit" (#1213) and "giving them [the baptized] the power to live and act under the promptings of the Holy Spirit" (#1266). Such attitudes are helping to fuel a spiritual awakening throughout Catholic Christianity, and prompting a more inclusive spirituality.

Originally the spiritual and scholarly were partners in Church-sponsored education. In fact, for the first thousand years or so, spirituality permeated all Church-sponsored education—because it was located primarily in the monasteries. This ceased with the shift to the university and "academia," beginning in the twelfth century.

However, as its spiritual tradition becomes revitalized and accessible to everyone, Catholicism is also rediscovering some strengths from its subtradition of monastic education that deserves to be brought to the fore again. Reclaiming its spiritual heritage renders fresh access to an original philosophy of education. And as I suggested in the previous chapter, why not carry forward the best of both monastery and university—contemplation and critical rationality? Though a theme throughout *Educating for Life*, here we give specific focus to what such a remarriage of spirituality and education might mean.

For Teachers and Parents

"What has spirituality got to do with education?" Readers may still think of them as "strange bedfellows" and hear proposals for their partnership as pious platitude. Even the hints already offered for engaging learners as spiritual beings could seem laughable amidst the present style of Western education, which is so dominated by technical rationality—what works and what is marketable. That many successful graduates of contemporary education can live empty lives—spiritually bankrupt—is never raised as an issue for reform. This depth structure of Catholicism, however, recommends that a life-giving spirituality should permeate all education—its process and content, purpose and environment—and should define the vocation of every teacher and parent.

For Reflection

- What might it mean for teachers and parents to approach learners as spiritual beings? For the educator's soul? Style? For the teaching/learning environment?

- Imagine some adjustments that a holistic spirituality might suggest for your own teaching.

- Is it too late—or even advisable—for Western education to retrieve its spiritual heritage, to reunite the assets of monastery and university? Take your own position, giving your reasons for or against.

For the Educator's Soul

It may sound simplistic, but the primary implication for the educator's soul may well be *take care to nourish your own spirituality*, as well as taking every opportunity—ones that occur and ones you create—to nourish the spirituality of learners.

Nourish Your Own Spirituality

Teachers and parents simply must care for their own souls. To educate in a humanizing way, it seems imperative that educators pay attention to their interiority and have sources to nourish their own depths, patterns to experience awe and express reverence, practices to cultivate a sense of ultimate value in who they are and what they do in learner's lives. In brief, it will be difficult for teachers and parents to care for learners' souls if they do not take care of their own!

All the great religions of humankind have "practices" that they recommend for nurturing the spiritual life. Indeed, one's spiritual life and growth in holiness originates from God's desire to draw us to Godself in love. And yet, the general sense among all religious traditions is that, from humankind's side of the covenant—as our response to God's grace—there are particular practices, usually to be repeated in a disciplined way, that are effective in caring for the soul. Within Christianity and because of its emphasis on both God's gifts and human efforts working in covenant partnership, Catholicism puts particular emphasis on spiritual practices.

There are myriad spiritual practices within Christian tradition. The few I now suggest are suited to anyone interested in care of their soul, although I have chosen ones that might be particularly helpful to educators and that could be practiced by any teacher or parent—regardless of religious tradition.

•*Attend to the Sacramentality of Life.* Take time to notice and relish the more that is always there: in the great experiences of the world—the splendor of nature, beauty of the arts, and the achievements of culture; in love and friendship; in compassion and generosity; in peace and justice; and in the little things of life as well—a walk on a spring morning, a good cup of coffee, the hug of a child, a stimulating conversation, and a thousand other "signals of transcendence" that come our way daily.

Because spiritual well-being depends so much on one's intentionality and consciousness, take the time to pause; to notice; to attend to the desires of your heart, the relationships with self, others, and God, the life you are living and the world around you. Thomas Moore writes,

> Care of the soul . . . is not primarily a method of problem solving . . . but to give *ordinary life the depth and value that come with soulfulness* . . . [11] (emphasis added)

• *Take Time Each Day for Personal Prayer.* Prayer is any turning of the mind, heart, or body toward one's relationship with

God. It can be done in as many ways as there are people—when, where, or however one can deliberately turn to God for personal encounter. Beyond "saying" prayers in the formal sense, turning to one's own interiority for personal conversation or contemplation with God is effective in spiritual growth. It would seem most appropriate for educators to raise up their learners to God in prayer.

• *Join with a Faith Community for Worship.* Many religious traditions emphasize that God comes to humankind and we go to God primarily as a people—through community. In Christian faith, the climactic expression as a people of God is in the "public work" of worshiping together. To join with a community of faith in this peak divine-human encounter can be a potent source of spiritual nurture.

• *Find a Soul-Friend.* This is someone with whom one can "bare the soul." Earlier I expressed my preference for the ancient Gaelic term "soul friend" instead of "spiritual director" since their function is not so much to direct as to draw out one's own discernment, to invite someone to recognize and probe God's movements in their lives and how to respond. A "soulfriend" should be a person of some wisdom and spiritual integrity themselves, but above all be a good questioner and listener.

• *Do Works of Justice and Compassion.* All the great religions teach that seeing to the welfare of others, and especially of neighbors most in need, is a privileged way of nurturing one's soul. It must be that love in action—personal and social—actualizes the divine in ourselves and so brings us closer to God. While the values of justice and compassion should prevail throughout our lives, it is a spiritual discipline to perform particular acts of this quality. And although they may look outside of their work as educators, teachers and parents will find ample opportunities within it as well to practice justice and compassion.

• *Try to Maintain a Balanced Life.* This has become a most difficult spiritual discipline in our frenetic society—often with undue expectations of its educators. It includes taking quality time for oneself—for health care and exercise; for personal maintenance; for cultural enrichment; for hobbies, recreation, and fun; and for family and friends. Spiritual balance means having discipline in one's food and drink, responsibility in lifestyle, and saying "no" instead of taking on too much. It means redefining "success" away from fame or fortune, power or prestige, and focusing instead on becoming an integrated and happy person, developing all one's gifts, contributing to the common good.

For educators in particular, balance means taking seriously their responsibility to learners but yet not exaggerating their function in other people's lives. Educators carry profound responsibility for the individual good of learners and for the common good as well. And yet, it is possible to exaggerate this responsibility—even out of good will and generosity—to where teachers or parents take on too much accountability for the "outcome" of their efforts or have an inflated standard of "success."

Educators can take over functions that learners should be doing—thinking for themselves, learning how to learn, making up their own minds, reaching personal decisions. Such imbalance ill serves learners and can be destructive to educators. There is a fine line between empowering learners as their own people and overpowering them—making them too dependent or indebted to teacher or parent. Walking this tightrope is an aspect of the educator's spiritual discipline of a balanced life.

• *Take a Sabbath.* This discipline supports a balanced life, too, but deserves its own listing, especially for educators. Taking Sabbath rest is a rich spiritual practice in most religious traditions. Biblically, it counts as the third commandment in the Decalogue: "Remember to keep holy the sabbath day . . . for Yahweh your God. You shall do no work that day . . ." (Exodus 20:8–10).

A traditional Christian interpretation is that Sabbath abstinence refers to "servile work"—taken to mean "manual labor." The catch, however, is that education was not considered "manual labor" and so could be done on the Sabbath. But then, so many teachers I know use their Sabbath to "catch up" on their academic work—not getting the rest they need personally and professionally.

I remember how "Big Din" Burke, my high-school French teacher, would wax eloquent, in French, on a Monday morning about his Sunday game of golf. I was fascinated with how he appreciated the aesthetic and the ethic of the game. His overt intent was to teach us conversational French, but he also taught, and I suspect he intended as much, the importance of taking a Sabbath.

• *Find a Community of Personal Support.* The Christian emphasis is that the journey into holiness is communal. It requires companionship. Perhaps the first place to look for supportive fellow travelers is within one's faith community. In larger congregations and parishes, more and more people are finding face-to-face communities of spiritual support in what are being called "base communities."

Teachers are likely to find their "base community" within their school or program. Parents, however, may be most in need to intentionally seek out such support—and parents of younger children especially. In highly mobile societies that also favor retirement homes for the elderly, many young parents are without ready access to the wisdom of their own parents and grandparents and are often located far from siblings and old school friends. All the more reason that they actively seek out a community of support. My point here is that finding and investing in a supportive community is a spiritual discipline.

• *At Day's End, Do an Examen of Consciousness.* Historically, the "examination of conscience" was a review of one's life for its sinfulness, but it's contemporary and more fruitful emphasis is on becoming aware of God's presence and the movements of God's Spirit in one's daily life. It amounts to looking intently at the events of one's daily life and reviewing them with God as conversation partner—trying to see the events as God saw them. It can unfold as follows:

—Become quiet and comfortable, placing oneself consciously in God's presence;

—Thank God for the gift of the day and ask to discern how God's Spirit was moving therein.

—Review the events with God as conversation partner.

—End with whatever prayer arises from the heart.

For the Educator's Style

Let educators be intentional about engaging and fostering the spirituality of learners and integrating it into their teaching style. Beyond the hints already offered, I make two general suggestions about style. Then I will interpret the six-part schema proposed in chapter 6 for getting people to think but this time with focus on engaging learners' souls.

Honoring people as spiritual beings. This means a teaching style *more of drawing out than pouring in, more of making students agents than recipients of knowledge, of getting them to see for themselves more than telling them what to see.* This is another way of saying that a spiritual outlook on teaching asks educators to trust people's innate capacity for learning and to remember that their spirit is enlivened by the Spirit. This "Teacher within" can be trusted to bring forth much that teachers typically presume they must provide.

In his short text *De Magistro*—"The Teacher"—St. Augustine based his pedagogy on "the truth that presides within" every human being. Augustine wrote to his son Adeodatus, who inquired about how to teach, that the teachers primary role is "to question you in a way adapted to your capacity for hearing the Teacher within you." Then, when we do discern something as true or false, it is because of the "everlasting Wisdom" within each of us and which "every rational soul does, in fact, consult." Even when teachers directly instruct students, "They who are called pupils consider within themselves whether what has been said is true. This they do by gazing attentively at their interior truth . . ." In a memorable flourish on behalf of engaging the interiority of learners, Augustine asked rhetorically, "For who would be so absurdly foolish as to send [their] child to school to learn what the teacher thinks."[12]

Incorporate silence into your style. Old stereotypes encourage teachers to presume that learning takes place while they are talking, that "teaching is telling." And, not to blame teachers, modern society is also uncomfortable with silence. We prefer any kind of noise. But people's souls crave silence and quiet, time to reflect, to listen to their own hearts, to hear the sounds of nature—to allow opportunity for the "Teacher within." Spiritually sensitive teaching encourages silence, whether providing formal periods of quiet or simply giving learners time to think instead of "jumping in" too soon.

Doreen is a religious educator in a tough, technical school with adolescents who are generally antagonistic toward formal religion. Over the years, however, she has taught them how to meditate and to do so together as a class. Students come to love it, and often when they feel pressure or know they are acting up, they will ask for a time of meditation.

She gently invites them to assume a comfortable body posture, to close their eyes, to notice their breathing, to relax their whole bodies, to begin to imagine a peaceful scene, to let themselves be drawn in by it (maybe to imagine meeting with a friend like Jesus), to notice and express the longings of their hearts. After about twenty minutes, she brings them back out of the meditation and invites their sharing— always rich and inspiring.

A Spiritual Schema for Teaching

Beyond the two general suggestions above, see if the following schema may encourage a style of teaching that cares for the soul.

- *Engage and Invite Learners to Express Their Interiority.*
  Prompt people to turn to their own interiority, to dip into the depths of themselves, to employ their own spiritual vitality. When teaching gets them to listen to their own hearts, to pay attention to their deepest desires, to notice the movements and sentiments of their spirit (when teaching engages souls), it is most likely to be humanizing and *for life for all*. As appropriate, it further enhances the pedagogy as learners can bring their soul sentiments to expression.

  Employing people's soulfulness and inviting expression can be done without invading their privacy and without

351

explicitly religious language if that is inappropriate. Questions like the following turn people to their own interiority and invite personal expression.

What does your heart tell you about . . . ?

What is your own deepest conviction about . . . ?

What do you like best or least about . . . ?

What are your best hopes or worst fears about . . . ?

Young children will often express their interiority in what they draw or paint or make. Invite them to explain what they are expressing artistically. Artistic expression can be a powerful way for any age group to express their souls. In general, anything that brings self-knowledge fosters spirituality. Karl Rahner, one of the greatest theologians of the twentieth century, was fond of saying that self-knowledge is tantamount to "revelation."

Let me make a special pitch here for storytelling as a powerful way to both engage and invite people's souls to expression. The stories of others can turn us to our own, and sharing our own stories can turn us to our souls. Moore writes,

> Storytelling is an excellent way of caring for the soul. It helps us see the themes that circle in our lives, the deep themes that tell the myths we live.[13]

> What teacher or parent is there that does not have opportunity every day to tell a good story and to invite learners to do likewise!

- *Encourage People to Reverence the Ordinary, to Notice the Mystery.* Invite people to attend to, relish, care for, even to contemplate the ordinary and everyday things of life. The mystery of Being is reflected in all things and experiences. Teachers and parents can encourage learners to approach life and the world with a sense of awe and reverence—to appreciate their gifts, to expect mystery.

    So much of contemporary culture and, thus, of education, is ruled by pragmatism—what works; by empiricism—what can be seen and counted; by materialism—what pays off in what we euphemistically call "goods" but mean possessions. Educators committed to educate learners as spiritual persons will be countercultural to such epistemologies. While maintaining a balance between realism and naiveté, teachers can structure curricula—by questions, assignments, resources, experiences, and so on—that encourage learners to seek out the mystery in the ordinary, to be open to life's unfathomable meaning and surprises, to appreciate the gift of the world.

- *Encourage Learners to Probe and Weigh Their Personal Sentiments.* Sensitive to readiness and context, teachers and parents can invite learners to explore their own depths. This is not to challenge the sentiments of their hearts, but to enhance and deepen them, to sort out what is misleading from what gives life. It is well to scrutinize personal feelings and sentiments for what prompts them and whether they are truly one's own, to weigh them for what is true and good, and for their likely consequences if acted upon. The give-and-take of good conversation is most effective to stimulate such personal evaluation. It is also likely to trigger imagination of new possibilities and to broaden the horizons of one's soul.

- *Consider Care of Souls in Choosing* What *to Teach.* Chapter 5 proposed that a defining function of teaching is to give people ready access to the legacy of the humanities, sciences, and arts. All teachers make choices about what to teach from this "funded capital of civilization." Teachers—and parents too—can draw out of this storeroom what inspires hearts, fascinates minds, stimulates imaginations, raises spirits, encourages hope, and accesses wisdom. Conversely, they can draw out only what "pays off" or "works" or will be "useful." If left standing alone, such resources quickly deaden the soul.

- *Encourage Spiritual Discernment and Decision Making.* These two dynamics are so similar that they can be grouped together here. Central in spiritual mentoring, they are prompted by such questions as the following:

Where is God inviting you at this time?

What are you coming to see as God's desire for you?

What would be a faithful and life-giving response?

Such overtly spiritual questions would certainly be appropriate in a parish catechetical program, but clearly would not be in most educational settings. And yet, could such spiritually based discernment and decision making find appropriate equivalents in an educational context?

I believe so! I am thinking of questions and reflective activities that encourage people to bring together their lives and the legacy of learning and to listen to their own interiority as they discern what is true, good, and beautiful. And why not turn people to their own souls as they make choices and commitments, to listen to their depths to choose what is responsible to self and others? Employing people's souls to participate in shaping their own destiny as human beings is surely to honor and encourage them as spiritual beings.

For the Educational Environment
Spiritual formation can certainly be done through the ethos of a family, and is integral to the raison d'être of every parish religious education program and religious school. Surely the spiritual should be the defining purpose of all religiously sponsored education. Religious schools must provide a general education, but that which defines their special identity and thus reason to exist as "separate" schools is their commitment to overtly nurture the spirituality of their students and to do so throughout the curriculum. Religiously sponsored schools loose their warrant unless they are places of spiritual nurture.

I once asked a couple—of moderate income—why they made such sacrifices to send all five children to Catholic schools, with high tuition costs. Both said in order to give their children a good education and foster their Catholic identity as well. I asked, "What if they don't remain Catholic as adults—will the schools have failed in their religious purpose?"

One immediately volunteered, "Oh, no, not as long as they have given them spiritual formation—to live their relationship with God."

After further conversation, both agreed that "for spirituality" was their primary reason for sending their children to Catholic schools.

Surely "for spirituality" is a central purpose of all religiously sponsored education.

In religious schools and parish programs, the entire curriculum—including the environment—can be made to serve spiritual formation. But taking the "hardest case" scenario: Is it possible for teachers in public schools to create an environment that educates students as spiritual beings—as well as teaching the four R's or whatever their explicit curriculum may be?

At first blush, the tempting response is a resounding "no." But consider that if teachers permeate the school and classroom environment with three more R's—Respect, Responsibility, and Reverence[14]—the ethos may be far more likely to care for souls, without ever using religious language. I reflected on the first two in the previous chapter as moral guidelines. I return to them here for their spiritual potential, and this time add reverence for a trio.

Respect means having esteem and due regard for oneself and for others, for one's own and others' rights, and not violating the created order. Stated this way, respect could sound a bit minimalist—as Thomas Lickona writes of it—"what keeps us from hurting what we ought to value."[15] But it is a necessary foundation for living humanly. To educate people in respect will foster their spirituality as well as their morality.

When a school or classroom environment is suffused with respect for students and staff and teaches respect for all humankind and God's creation, it is conducive to spiritual development. It is so precisely because it nurtures an essential aspect of "right relationship" with self, others, and the world. If it engages persons' souls to inculcate respect for all expressions of life and creation, it disposes them for right relationship with the Ground of Being as well.

Responsibility, as Lickona describes, is more "active" than respect.

> It includes taking care of self and others, fulfilling our obligations, contributing to our communities, alleviating suffering, and building a better world.[16]

There is a deep altruism, then, to responsibility—taking initiative to care for others, society, and creation, as well as for oneself. When an educational environment encourages participants to be responsible for their own and the common good, it fosters another aspect of "right relationship" that spirituality entails—it pushes beyond the minimal of respect to reach out with love that does justice.

Even psychologically, to have a healthy psyche (the ancient Greek word for *soul*) people need to be drawn out of themselves into loving relationship with and care for others—into responsibility. Stated negatively, a school environment that does not promote responsibility or that socializes students only to "look out for number one" is likely to deaden the soul and stunt spiritual as well as moral growth.

Reverence pushes beyond respect and responsibility, although it presumes and undergirds both. The etymological root of *reverence* means to recognize the deepest truth (as in *verily*) about something and then to take a second look—*re*—to see the plenitude beyond the obvious and immediate. Reverence always has religious or spiritual overtones. Surely to reverence oneself and others means first to recognize the dignity of human beings and then to "look again" and recognize their Creator. And the same is true of reverencing creation!

All educational environments, in one way or another, are designed to pursue truth. Can they be fashioned to teach reverence—that second look which sees the ultimate truth about people, life, the world? I believe they can, and the key is likely that teachers and parents model it in their relationships with learners, that the school, home, and parish themselves treat every person with reverence. Perhaps you have other suggestions?

For Reflection
- How do you imagine your educational environment can be enhanced as a place which nurtures spirituality?

- Where do you now stand on the issue of the relationship between spirituality and education?

- Is there a decision emerging for you regarding the spiritual aspect of your own teaching?

Notes

1. Moore, *Care of the Soul*, XI.
2. See Maritain, *The Person and the Common Good*, 15–22.
3. Moore, *Care of the Soul*, XI.
4. Maritain, *Education at the Crossroads*, 114.
5. This is my own proposal for the dynamics of liturgy. See *Sharing Faith*, chapter 12.
6. "Constitution on the Liturgy," # 14, Abbott, *Documents*, 144.
7. Note that *ruach* and *pneuma*—the Hebrew and Greek respectively for "spirit"—are both feminine nouns.
8. I am thinking of the famous case of Fr. Leonard Feeney (1897–1978) who was excommunicated and dismissed from the Jesuits in 1953 for a too-strict interpretation of this axiom.
9. See Abbott, *Documents*, 660 ff.
10. Ibid., 65 ff.
11. Moore, *Care of the Soul*, 4.
12. Augustine, *The Teacher*, 177, 179, 180, 177, 185.
13. Moore, *Care of the Soul*, 13.
14. Here I note my indebtedness to the writings of Thomas Lickona on respect and responsibility. (See especially *Educating for Character*.) I add to this reverence.
15. Lickona, *Educating for Character*, 67.
16. Ibid., 68.

❖

CHAPTER EIGHT

A Faith That Does Justice:
"Beyond the Scales"

Dangerous Memory

It was late July in Boston, a hot and humid afternoon, summer school, 1978. I was a very junior professor—note the less desirable teaching time. The course had gone well, I thought, but on this second to last day, eyes were beginning to glaze over with that "gone fishin'" look—including Russ. I determined not to take it personally, but that kind of detachment takes years—if then.

I was explaining the notion of "dangerous memory." They are personal or communal memories with an endless capacity to disturb complacency and birth new life. When we return to them, they challenge our compromises with the status quo, help us to remember what we should not forget, and inspire recommitment to who we ought to be—they revitalize. Like the biblical story of Exodus. When the Hebrew people really remembered—not just a facile recall—how God had brought them out of slavery, it helped them to refocus on their covenant, to become aware of their sins, and to recommit themselves to live in freedom as a people of God. "Dangerous"—especially to complacency and compromise.

Then I invited students to take some quiet time (I would lose Russ, for sure) and recall a "dangerous memory" from their lives. "This is a significant memory from your own or your family's past. It's just dozing there—no pun intended—largely forgotten; yet to recall it now could bring new life—even on such an afternoon. Choose and remember it first—some of its details— and then dwell in the memory again for a short while."

I paused. All seemed too quiet. After a while I said, "Now, as you experience this memory again, is it life-giving for you? Perhaps it challenges a complacency? Invites a commitment?"

Silence—but not an empty kind. I began to realize that they had not left for the beach. In fact, they were deeply engaged. I invited them into groups of three with the caution, "Share only what you are comfortable talking about. Feel free just to listen." The conversation started slowly in hesitant whispers, but reached a crescendo with a riot of laughter and tears. Eventually they were ready to come back together.

I asked for a volunteer to share with the whole group. A long pause—but I felt I should wait! Finally Russ began. His voice quivered with emotion; many times it got caught and the tears rolled, but the group encouraged him on. "My grandmother came to America from near Vilnius in Lithuania around 1917. Her name was Constance. She was about fourteen at the time." He told about why she left, the terror of the journey, Ellis Island and no English, how she had married a Russian émigré, Stanley, a refugee from the Bolsheviks. Eventually they settled in Somersville, Connecticut, both working in the woolen mills. The mill owner owned everything else as well—their housing, the town's general store and bank, the police. They were totally dependent on him; he controlled their lives.

Constance was a handsome young woman. Once when she was alone, one of the mill owner's family cornered her and demanded sexual favors. Terrified, she refused. He beat her—beat her so badly that sixty years later she still shuddered in pain on recounting the blows and had scars that never went away. And there was no point in going to the police. Russ trailed off and fell silent.

About ten years later, Russ finished up a doctorate at Boston College with a dissertation entitled "Dangerous Memory: A Pedagogy for Social Justice." And some twenty years afterward as I requested permission to use this story, he was a little miffed when I asked if he could still recall that sultry, summer afternoon. He retorted, "Whaddya mean—it changed my life." And I went looking again for "dangerous memories" of my own.

"Beyond the Scales"

All of us have "dangerous memories" that can disturb the comfortable and comfort the disturbed in us, can challenge complacency and renew commitments. One such memory that those of religious faith often forget or explain away is the teaching of all the great religions that faith demands justice. The major traditions vary in their particular memories for justice, ways to describe it, and level of emphasis, but all teach that to live in faith demands giving everyone their due.

Moreover, all go beyond this minimum of equity and teach compassion for the poor and needy. And yet throughout history, religion has been used to legitimize the worst of injustices—racism, sexism, economism, or whatever the root, and the most brutal of wars. Clearly, people of all religions regularly forget their "dangerous memory" that faith demands justice and peace. Humanizing education should be an antidote to such forgetfulness!

From the beginning, Christianity has had a strong social justice tradition. Its Jewish roots lent the memory of the great prophets of Israel and their insistence that God is a God of justice, that to be in covenant with God demands living with *shalom*. There was also the example of Jesus, his great compassion for the poor and suffering, and the "dangerous memory" of his death—a political execution for political crimes—and God's reversal of all the powers of evil, including social, with Jesus' resurrection.

There is a strong Christian tradition of affirming the *imago Dei* tenet as the foundation of social morality, convinced that being created in God's image gives everyone the right to be treated with dignity and a mandate to treat others the same. Catholicism has avoided emphasizing an individualized salvation, as if a person can save one's own soul without care for others' welfare. Instead, God's work of salvation is realized within society and through community. God's saving intentions require Christians to be their brothers' and sisters' keepers—obligating significant social responsibilities.

The early Christian Church pushed back against many of the injustices and oppressions of its day, providing direct services to the hungry and sick, to orphans and widows and working for social reforms on behalf of those most in need.

> Church leaders were instrumental in getting laws passed
> that protected the rights of widows and orphans, that
> curtailed slavery, that reduced abortions, and that
> provided for the humane treatment of criminals.[1]

We also find in many early Church documents a strong note of radical pacifism. Christians were forbidden to bear arms, and soldiers who desired baptism were required to resign from the army.[2] Radical pacifism was later overshadowed by Augustine's theory of the "just war" (writing circa 400 C.E.), but Augustine, too, began with the premise that Christian faith forbids war and then proceeded to define conditions for making an exception to this pacifist rule of faith. And his other writings reflect strong commitment to the social responsibilities of Christian discipleship.

Throughout the Middle Ages, the monasteries served as havens of social service, providing hospitals for the sick, shelter for orphans and widows, food for the poor, and ministry to prisoners. They worked for social welfare by providing schools, books, and libraries; by preparing wasteland for cultivation and tutoring farmers; by apprenticing people in the trades and professions. Scholastic scholars, most notably Thomas Aquinas, continued to develop the conceptual aspects of a strong social tradition. Meanwhile, the common people were catechized in the corporal and spiritual works of mercy. These were two lists of seven social actions that today would be called works of justice.

The seven corporal works of mercy are to feed the hungry, give drink to the thirsty, clothe the naked, shelter the homeless, visit the sick, minister to prisoners, and bury the dead. The seven spiritual works of mercy also reflect the values of justice and especially peace: convert the sinner, instruct the ignorant, counsel the doubtful, comfort the sorrowful, bear wrongs patiently, forgive injuries, and pray for the living and the dead. At its best, the Christian community has not understood its mission as narrowly spiritual, or better to say that its sense of spiritual mission has demanded care for social welfare through the works of justice and peace.

Justice is not easily defined, nor the peace to which it leads. We likely know them most keenly in their absence. Aquinas, echoing Aristotle, defined the virtue of justice as "the strong and firm will to give every one their due."[3] But then, what is a person's "due"? Aristotle favored calculating this arithmetically, with each person receiving from society in proportion to what he or she contributes. A slightly more generous version was based on merit, with the blindfolded Lady Justice weighing the scales according to what everyone deserves.

But what about human needs—when someone does not contribute enough or "weigh" enough to meet their own? Do the strong and wealthy have any responsibility in justice to the weak and poor?

I will unfold a Christian understanding of justice in this chapter, but note in anticipation here that it not only includes but goes beyond "everyone their due." This is because Christianity combines justice with the great commandment of love, convinced that God's relationship with humankind should be the model for our relationships with each other. And so Christian justice has a quality of largess, of being generous toward needs rather than scrupulously weighing the scales.

Ironically, though, Christian love or *charity* (the favored term) that should have been the icing on the cake of justice came to overshadow it and to imply an optional kindness—typified in almsgiving—with little sense of social justice as an obligation. Indeed, the requirement of justice continued in Christian faith but as honesty between individuals, without adverting to unjust social structures. As long as Christians did not steal or cheat, as long as they gave a little to "charity," their social responsibilities were considered fulfilled.

Consciousness of social justice as an essential responsibility of Christian faith began to reawaken with the Industrial Revolution. The new economic structures and relations between capital and labor demanded that the Church think more in social terms. Both Protestant and Catholic communities began to recognize that works of mercy and acts of charity must reach beyond the personal and be realized at the structural level as commitment to justice.

The emerging social sciences lent the tools to analyze how social systems work. As the "wider picture" of social reality became clearer, so, too, did awareness that the structures of society favor some and victimize others, that cultures and societies often discriminate against individuals on grounds such as race, ethnicity, class, and gender. Slowly, the Church began to realize that justice is not satisfied by honesty in personal dealings and private charity alone. It demands as well participation in struggles to transform sociocultural arrangements that cause people to be hungry or homeless, oppressed or victimized in the first place.

Beginning in earnest with the great social encyclical of Pope Leo XIII, *Rerum Novarum (Of New Things)* issued in 1891, Catholic

Christianity developed a rich corpus of social teachings—emphasizing and elaborating the social responsibilities of Christian faith. At about the same time a similar sentiment came to the fore within mainline Protestantism heralded by the "Social Gospel" movement.[4] Since then and supported by the work of socially conscious theologians, the papacy, church councils, and synods have continued to develop the responsibilities of Christian faith to the contemporary political, economic, and international orders. This teaching reflects developments in the Church's own social consciousness.

Initial focus on the rights of workers in the late nineteenth century shifted with the two world wars to the international community, then to the threat of nuclear destruction, and now attends to the problems of postindustrial society, responsibility to the environment, and the need for solidarity among all peoples. Although prompted by Christian faith and guided by biblical norms, much of this social teaching is stated in philosophical language and draws upon the natural law understanding of the person and society. Its asset is being able to engage the wider civil society with concepts and language that do not presuppose Christian faith.

In continuity with an ancient tradition, contemporary Church social teaching has established justice as a core commitment—a depth structure—of Christian faith. Two frequently quoted ecclesial statements capture the spirit of this new day for social justice. The first is that "Christian love of neighbor and justice cannot be separated. *For love implies an absolute demand for justice*—namely, a recognition of the dignity and rights of one's neighbor." And these stirring words:

> Action on behalf of justice and participation in the transformation of the world fully appear to us as a *constitutive dimension of the preaching of the Gospel,* or, in other words, of the Church's mission for the redemption of the human race and its liberation from every oppressive situation.[5] (emphases added)

Surely education of any kind should be suffused with commitment to justice, regardless of its source of inspiration—philosophical, religious, or basic human conscience. At a minimum, learners whose primary education leaves them without respect for the laws of the land are likely to end up in jail. Or stated more positively, the very survival of society demands citizens who support and live within a system of justice, and education is crucial in this formation. However, education inspired by something akin to a Christian commitment to justice will reach far beyond this minimum—"beyond the scales." But first, pause to observe your own sentiments on this crucial issue for education of all kinds.

For Reflection

- What is your own most basic understanding of "justice"? How did you come by it?

- Recall a "dangerous memory" that could enhance your commitment to social justice. What does it ask of you personally? As a teacher or parent?

- From your own experience, can you describe some instances of the interrelation between education and justice? Do some social analysis on one of your examples.

A Christian Understanding of Justice: One Proposal

Any Christian understanding of justice should arise from the Bible and then be complemented by philosophical sources. This "revelation and reason" approach is keenly reflected in the social teachings of contemporary Catholicism.

From the Hebrew Scriptures

For Hebrew faith, justice is an absolute mandate because God is just and those in covenant with the God of justice must live justly. To forget such a central injunction or to pretend that justice is not demanded by the covenant amounts to blasphemy, implying that God favors injustice. God is just and expects justice of God's people; the great Hebrew Scripture scholar Walter Brueggemann writes, "In biblical faith, the doing of justice is the primary expectation of God."[6]

God "is a God of justice" (Isaiah 30:18) who "secures justice and the rights of all the oppressed" (Psalm 103:6). God delights in the realization of justice (Jeremiah 9:23), loves it (Psalm 99:4), and hates injustice (Isaiah 61:8).

This God of justice calls the Israelites into covenant to live as God's own people. God makes the promise to them: "I will set my dwelling among you . . . . Ever present in your midst, I will be your God and you will be my people" (Leviticus 26:11–12).

With this, they realized that God's presence and covenant bonded them in intimate relationship with God and more deeply with each other as a people. Such a relationship with such a God demands that all relationships be "right." Keeping the covenant and living justly are the same affair—living in "right relationship" with God, self, others, and creation.[7]

What, then, would make relationships "right" for justice's sake? In the Hebrew Scriptures, the model and measure of rightness (righteousness) in human relationships is God's relationship with humankind. How God relates with humankind is the ideal by which we are to relate to others and creation.

And God relates with humankind, not as a blindfolded judge balancing a scale to measure our legal deserts, but with compassion, mercy, and loving-kindness, with largess and munificence. The God of compassion has "espoused" the people "in right and in justice, in love and in mercy" (Hosea 2:21).

Even toward the sinner—the one who chooses "wrong" relationship—God is not vengeful, but "a merciful and gracious God, slow to anger, rich in kindness and fidelity" (Exodus 34:6).

Faithful human partners with God must strive for such generosity in their everyday relationships with themselves and others. A covenant kind of "right relationship" gives what is due and then "flows over" like a gentle rain. (See Isaiah 45:8.)

Justice with compassion is a special mandate toward those most in need of it—the "poor." In the midst of God's munificent ways of relating with all humankind, God has what the great Jewish scholar Abraham Heschel (1907–72) calls "a burning compassion for the oppressed."[8]

The Bible says that God has special favor for those whose lives are most threatened—"the poor" (Psalm 140:13). Clearly the defining sense of poverty is economic, but the Bible also, and often, adds favor for "the widow, the orphan, and the alien in the land" (Jeremiah

7:6)—broadening beyond economic disadvantage to those suffering oppression from sexism, racism, and more—all the disadvantaged. God hears the cry of the poor and oppressed (Exodus 22:21–22) and comes to their aid (Psalm 113:7). God "lavishly gives to the poor" (Psalm 112:9) because God wills fullness of life for all and so favors most those most in need of favor.

Again, people of the covenant are to imitate God's "option" for the poor and oppressed. As God does, so should God's people do. (See Daniel 4:24.) The justice of the community—i.e., its faithfulness to the covenant—is measured, ultimately, by its treatment of the powerless and poor. The prophets, speaking for Yahweh on behalf of the oppressed, remind the Israelites that to offer true worship to God they must do justice toward all and favor those whom God favors. To offer sacrifices while neglecting the works of justice makes one's attempts at worship "loathsome" to God or, as the old King James edition translated, "an abomination" (Isaiah 1:13).

In the Hebrew Scriptures, the consequence of living in right relationship with God, self, others, and creation is *shalom*. Conversely, shalom is the rule of justice as right relationship. This term, usually translated as "peace," means much more—solidarity among all peoples, harmony within creation, wholeness and complete well-being for everyone, the best of everything that is best for all.

The Hebrew understanding of shalom evolved over the centuries from a sense of personal safety to a social meaning of public harmony marked by the absence of war and by right relationship among humankind and with creation. There is, then, in biblical faith, a symbiosis between justice and shalom. As the prophet Isaiah taught, the way to lasting peace is to work for justice. (See Isaiah 32:17.)

A promise runs throughout the Hebrew Scriptures of a realized Messianic time when "kindness and truth shall meet; justice and peace shall kiss" (Psalm 85:11). Then justice will be "secure" and peace without end. (See Isaiah 9:6.) Meanwhile, the covenant places urgent responsibilities upon adherents now. The classic statement of what Yahweh asks is found in Micah 6:8, a text taken by scholars to summarize the whole prophetic tradition.

In a dramatic passage (Micah 6:1–8), Yahweh puts Israel on trial for "forgetting"—forgetting the dangerous memory of how Yahweh had set them free from slavery in Egypt (6:4); forgetting what a God who liberates from oppression requires of God's people. Israel tries to plea-bargain or, better still, to buy off the Prosecutor by increasing its sacrificial offerings.

But then, in the climactic punch line of Micah 6:8, Yahweh looks out over the head of Israel and addresses all humankind, saying "This is what Yahweh asks of you, oh humankind: only this, to act justly, to love tenderly, and to walk humbly with your God." These three mandates cannot be separated; justice, love, and faith are parts of a piece and of peace—the covenant of "right relationship"—demanding a faith that does justice with love.

From The New Testament

In Jesus' life and preaching, his central passion was for the *reign of God*. Likewise, it was the touchstone of his commitment to justice and peace. There is no doubt that God's reign was understood at the time and by Jesus as demanding justice for all. When Jesus made the reign of God the core passion and purpose of his life, he knew that it symbolized God's shalom intentions for humankind and all creation— love and fullness of life, wholeness and holiness, community and interdependence, values personal and social, spiritual and political, to be "done on earth as in heaven."

In Christian faith, the reign of God was why Jesus lived, died, and was raised up again. Thereafter, the Risen Christ symbolizes God's ultimate guarantee that God's loving will of shalom for all will be finally realized. Within Jesus' overarching commitment to the reign of God, here I highlight his special favor for the poor and oppressed, his gift of peace, and his preaching of the law of "right relationship" as radical love.

According to the Gospel of Luke, before Jesus was born, his mother Mary praised God for doing "great things" in her conceiving, for deposing the mighty from their thrones, raising up the lowly, and feeding the hungry as promised. Mary surely had a radical image of God as demanding social justice. (See Luke 1:46–55—the Magnificat.)

Then a "heavenly host" proclaimed "peace on earth" as the divine favor being realized with Jesus' birth. (See Luke 2:13–14.) As noted many times, toward the end of his life, Jesus presented an account of God's final judgment as rewarding "the just"—because of their care for the poor, the alien, the imprisoned, and all in need—and condemning those who fail to do these works of social justice (Matthew 25:31–46).

"Peace" was the farewell gift of the historical Jesus (John 14:27) and the first gift of the Risen Christ to the disciples (John 20:19).

Between his birth and death, Jesus' whole life was one of right and loving relationship with God, self, others, and creation—with special outreach to the poor, oppressed, and marginalized. His care for the poor was accompanied by "hard sayings" regarding money and possessions (Mark 10:25—"easier for a camel . . . "). Moreover, he resolutely rejected every form of discrimination.

Jesus' ministry was a countersign to the sexism, racism, and all the other forms of oppression in his social context. He presented his life and mission as fulfilling the Jubilee Year promise of Isaiah (61:1–2) of bringing "glad tidings to the poor," "liberty to captives," "sight to the blind," and "release to prisoners" (Luke 4:18–19). In the Beatitudes, he said that the reign of God belongs to the poor. He promised satisfaction to those who work for justice and declared peacemakers to be God's own people (Matthew 5:9). No longer is it "an eye for an eye and a tooth for a tooth," but loving one's enemies. Jesus' disciples should make God's relationship with humankind the model for their own with others (Matthew 5:38–45).

Jesus' first disciples came to recognize that the reign of God in Jesus is a life of justice, peace, and joy (Romans 14:17) and that they must "put on justice" to preach Jesus' "gospel of peace" (Ephesians 6:15). They saw Jesus as the catalyst of peace among humankind and with God (Ephesians 2:14–18)—that God reconciled the world to Godself in Jesus and has given disciples the same "ministry" of changing enmity to friendship (2 Corinthians 5:18). If the New Testament adds anything to the Hebrew understanding of justice as "right relationship," it is emphasis on agapaic love—that the covenant be fulfilled with love without expectation of return.

There is great passion in the biblical call to justice—it can light a fire in the tummy. It lacks, however, the precise and analytical categories needed for discerning, administering, and living the virtue of justice in everyday life. Such precision is more readily suggested by the philosophical tradition of the West.

Yet how important that Jews and Christians experience their faith in God as primary motivation for commitment to justice! For those who look to the Hebrew Scriptures and then for Christians who also look to the New Testament as their sacred texts of faith, it is inspiring to encounter the God of loving justice revealed there and the biblical mandate of justice required of God's people. One can get an understanding of justice from Aristotle, but not a passion to favor the poor or to go the extra mile through compassion. One can find among the philosophers helpful distinctions like commutative, distributive, and legal justice, but no great "dangerous memories" like Exodus, Good Friday, and Easter!

I highlight the biblical mandate because Catholic Christians, more than most, need to reclaim this inspiration for justice. For much of its history, Catholicism has drawn its social tradition primarily from the philosophy of natural law. This reflection of God's law within humankind by nature can provide the basis of a public sense of justice. Stated in philosophical language, with conviction reached through persuasion rather than biblical authority, it becomes accessible in the marketplace of society. But for motivation as well as clarity, Catholic Christians need their social teaching to reflect the inspiration of both sources—biblical and philosophical.

Catholic Social Teaching

There is a two-thousand-year-old tradition of Christian social teaching. However, the advent of capitalism and of the modern nation state prompted a more critically conscious body of teaching on the social responsibilities of Christian faith. As already noted, this new moment began for Catholicism with the encyclical *Rerum Novarum* in 1891 and has continued since then, evolving in depth and breadth.

The early documents were heavily philosophical in language and argument, but as modern biblical scholarship permeated Catholic consciousness, the church's social teaching came to reflect both the natural law tradition of philosophy and the biblical mandates of peace and justice. The following tenets may amount to a summary.[9] As reader, imagine their implications for teaching and education.

Honor the Sacredness, Dignity, and Priority of the Person

We must honor the sacredness, dignity, and priority of the person. All of us have intrinsic dignity and every human life is sacred. In philosophical terms, a person's capacities for knowledge and self-reflection, for love and freedom, attest to a singular status. Theologically, the person has infinite worth and pride of place in God's creation because made in the image and likeness of God.

Although all creation is good and to be cared for, concern for humankind is the preeminent consideration.

Human Dignity Gives Rights and Responsibilities

Human rights are claims to the spiritual and material goods that persons need to realize their dignity. Human responsibilities are duties that we have toward God, self, neighbor, and creation, precisely because of our status and capacities. Emphasis on both rights and responsibilities is important. Without responsibilities, rights become selfish. Without rights, the person gets sacrificed to the collective.

The Person Is Essentially a Social Being

By nature, humankind is both "persons-in-community" and "community-of-persons." The society and state are fundamental extensions of this social nature of the person rather than voluntary associations based on a social contract—a la English philosopher John Locke. The *society* is all the collective relationships—political, economic, cultural, and legal—that structure the shared life of a populace at local and national levels. The *state* is the aspect of a society that exercises political authority.

Justice Demands Care for the Common Good and the Public Order

The "common good" combines respect for every individual with care for the social well-being of the collective. Personal and common good are not competitors but partners, each supporting and tempering the other. More recently, the concept has emerged of the "international common good," again highlighting that the good of individual nations and the good of the entire "global village" are symbiotic and must work in solidarity.

The "public order" is a subfeature of the common good and refers to the state's responsibility to oversee public safety, public morality, and the tenets of legal justice for all. Every group in society is responsible for the common good, but the state is primarily responsible for public order—drawing limits to the power of the state and safeguarding the function of particular groups within it.

Subsidiarity and Societal Agency Serve Justice

Justice is served both by subsidiarity and by societal agency. The principle of subsidiarity encourages addressing social needs at the lowest level effective, instead of expecting everything to be done at the macro level of the state. In other words, let local organizations and groups do the most they can, retaining as much freedom and initiative as possible throughout society.

On the other hand, the principle of societal agency reflects the state's responsibility to step in and provide whatever else is needed for personal and common good. To American readers, subsidiarity may sound a little like a Republican sentiment, whereas societal agency sounds more Democratic. Note that Catholicism affirms both principles!

The tradition of Catholic social teaching has found it helpful to distinguish various aspects of "basic justice" corresponding to different kinds of relationships in society. Three key distinctions are commutative, distributive, and social justice.

- *Commutative Justice:* This kind of justice demands *honesty and fairness in all exchanges between individuals or private groups*. It binds us in our day-to-day dealings with others and applies to businesses, manufacturers, or organizations. It excludes cheating and stealing, lying and dishonesty. When I choose a box of cereal at the grocery store, commutative justice entitles me to an accurate description from the manufacturer of the nutrition facts on the label; the store owner should have the item priced at no more than a reasonable profit—even if there is a food shortage; and I should pay rather than shoplift. Similarly, commutative justice requires employers to pay their employees a just wage with decent working conditions, whereas it requires employees to render honest and diligent work. Failure to fulfill commutative justice demands restitution—insofar as possible—to the party wronged.

- *Distributive Justice:* This kind of justice requires *society to insure that its social goods—culture, economic wealth, and political power—are fairly distributed*. Society must see to it that all its members have the resources to meet their human needs, to enjoy their rights, and to fulfill their responsibilities.

  Distributive justice requires fair distribution of burdens and benefits according to people's bounty and wants. Although likely not a favorite example, income tax arises out of commutative justice—taking in proportion to people's ability to pay, giving through social programs in proportion to people's need to receive.

> •*Social Justice:* This kind of justice pertains to the responsibility of *society to create structures that protect the dignity of all and allow each member to participate according to needs, talents, and choices.* Although the notion has ancient roots, the term "social justice" was introduced in the papal encyclical *Quadragesimo Anno* of 1931, prompted by growing awareness of how social structures influence the quality of human life.

Social justice condemns every kind of discrimination on any basis (sex, race, ethnicity, class, orientation, religion, or condition) and every structural arrangement (legal, economic, or political) that exploits or excludes anyone from full participation in society. Stated positively, social justice requires that the structures of society be arranged to welcome the full participation of all.

Contemporary teaching on social justice pays particular attention to economic structures and is cautious toward the two great competing ideologies, condemning both unbridled capitalism and totalitarian socialism. The *Catechism* states initially: "A theory that makes profit the exclusive norm and ultimate end of economic activity is morally unacceptable." And then, quoting Vatican II, adds:

> A system that "subordinates the basic rights of individuals and of groups to the collective organization of production" is contrary to human dignity.[10]

Every segment of society is responsible for pursuing social justice—individuals, voluntary associations, business and professional groups, religious and cultural organizations, the state, and society as a whole. In a sense, social justice is the overarching category that demands structural arrangements within which commutative and distributive justice are more likely to be fulfilled.

The last four features of contemporary social teaching reflect more the biblical and theological sources of a *faith that does justice for peace.*

The Reign of God Mandates Justice
The reign of God as central passion to the life of Jesus gives disciples the mandate of justice. Many times throughout, I have referred to the

reign of God as the central symbol of the mission and ministry of Jesus. Here I highlight that Jesus understood God's reign as a profoundly social as well as spiritual symbol, as beginning to realize God's intentions of shalom within human history—"on earth as in heaven." This underscores the social responsibilities of Christian faith, requiring commitment to justice and peace as well as to personal holiness of life.

The symbol of God's reign, of course, was never lost from Christian preaching and teaching, but was minimized to refer only to life after death—favoring Matthew's phrase "kingdom of heaven" and understanding this solely as a place of reward for souls later.

In recent years, the conviction has deepened that God's intentions of *fullness of life for all* should begin now—within history—as well as being completely realized in eternity. Vatican II gave this sense of God's intent as warrant for one of its clearest statements on social justice:

> With respect to the fundamental rights of the person, every type of discrimination, whether social or cultural, whether based on sex, race, color, social condition, language, or religion, is to be overcome and eradicated as *contrary to God's intent.*[11] (emphasis added)

People of Faith Must Make an "Option for the Poor"

People of faith should make an "option for the poor." At first considered a radical idea of liberation theologies, "option for the poor" is now liberally laced throughout even conservative church documents. For example, there is no major theme in the *Catechism* that does not catechize favor for the poor. The text makes clear that this is not charity but "a work of justice," demanding preference for people most in need: "Those who are oppressed by poverty are the object of a preferential love on the part of the Church." Like the Bible, the *Catechism* defines poverty first in economic terms, but then broadens it to include "not only material poverty but also . . . the many forms of cultural and religious poverty."[12]

Justice and Peace Are Symbiotic

Mainstream Christianity has deepened the conviction that the Bible condemns war and violence of every kind and that a people of God must be a people of peace. Although there has always been a Catholic

Christian pacifism, it remained a subtradition within the more dominant "just war" position—for which I earlier cited Augustine. It claims that, under certain stringent conditions, war might be justified as the lesser of two evils (waged as a last resort, for a just cause, have reasonable hope of success, and with the good intended proportionate to the evil done).

Catholicism's many "holy" wars throughout history (e.g., the Crusades) indicate that it has often forgotten the biblical presumption that war is evil. Further, the advent of nuclear weapons makes the principle of proportionality much more difficult to fulfill. What could possibly justify the vast destruction of innocent lives that would result from nuclear war?

The American Catholic bishops in their courageous pastoral letter *The Challenge of Peace* declared, "We do not perceive any situation in which the deliberate initiation of nuclear warfare, on however restricted a scale, could be morally justified."[13] They also make clear that peacemaking is the duty of every person of faith and that peacemaking is integral to the work of justice—citing Isaiah 32:17: "Justice will bring about peace."

Recent church documents also condemn "institutional violence"—recognizing that social structures that deny people justice are a form of violence. The American bishops' peace pastoral lists some common institutional violences.

> Violence has many faces: oppression of the poor, deprivation of basic human rights, economic exploitation, sexual exploitation and pornography, neglect or abuse of the aged and the helpless, and innumerable other acts of inhumanity. Abortion in particular blunts a sense of the sacredness of human life.[14]

Christian commitment to peace and justice also demands putting an end to the evil of domestic violence. This horrendous and rising epidemic terrorizes people physically and emotionally in the very sanctuary of their own homes—where they should feel safest. Most often perpetrated by men on women and children, domestic violence is a serious breach of justice and peace. People of faith must eschew it in their own lives and help eradicate such violence from church and society.

Liberation Theologies Heighten the Emancipatory Intent of Christian Faith

There are many expressions of liberation theology, but all share two convictions. First, liberation theologians allow the consciousness that emerges from struggles for justice to influence their interpretation and presentation of Christian faith. This introduces into theology a host of voices heretofore unheard—the poor and oppressed, the marginalized and exploited—and these voices leave no doubt but that Christian faith should be emancipatory.

Second, liberation theologians are convinced that the Word of God in Scripture and Tradition always favors justice. It should empower people to participate in God's work of "liberating salvation."[15] Such a "hermeneutical lens" highlights emancipatory aspects of Christian faith often overlooked heretofore, and unmasks what has been used to oppress and victimize.

Although still suspect in official circles, liberation theologies have deepened the consciousness of the whole Church—Protestant and Catholic—that Christian faith must struggle against all forms of oppression and on behalf of freedom. Liberation theology is as diverse as the struggles from which it emerges. I highlight four main instances.

- *Liberation Theology from the Lives of the Poor:* Emerging from sociopolitical contexts like Latin America where the great majority suffer severe economic poverty, this theology mounts a concerted critique of economic structures that exploit the poor and are driven by unbridled profit. It poses the alternative of just and liberating structures and challenges Christians not to be accomplices in exploitation but to join the political struggle for economic justice for all.

- *Feminist Liberation Theology:* This theology reflects and contributes to the rising feminist consciousness throughout the world. It emerges out of the struggle of women—and some men—to fight against sexism and misogyny and to forge the full freedom of women, including genuine mutuality with men. Feminist theology mounts a devastating criticism of the patriarchy of the Church and challenges the ways Jewish and Christian traditions have been interpreted to legitimate the oppression of women and domination by men. Religious feminism is convinced that faith in God demands commitment to the demise of sexism and draws upon the aspects of Scripture and Tradition— and there are many—that enhance women's struggle for human liberation.

• *Liberation Theology from the Struggle against Racism:* One central example is the theology that emerges out of the African-American community and the struggle against racism in North America. It critiques and heightens awareness of social structures and cultural mores that discriminate against people on the basis of race or ethnicity, and it empowers the struggle for true racial equality and affirmation. These theologians, too, are convinced that Christian faith must be interpreted as opposing racial discrimination and demanding participation by Christians in the struggle to end all instances of racism—in Church and in society.

• *Liberation Theology of Creation:* Emerging out of the struggle to "save the planet," this theology is driven by the urgency to steer human practices away from wasting and destroying our air, land, and water—and the ozone layer over it all— before it is too late. Out of religious faith, these theologians challenge anthropocentrism—an exaggeration of human preeminence that allows people to selfishly indulge their appetites to the destruction of the environment. Eco- theology calls humankind to the biblical mandate of good stewardship of creation. This perspective also encourages a "creation spirituality," with emphasis on experiencing the divine presence in nature and taking responsibility out of faith conviction for Planet Earth.

In Summary and Humility

From these biblical, philosophical, and ecclesial resources, we can draw together a summary of Christian commitment to justice. *By faith in God and following "the way" of Jesus toward God's reign, Christians have the mandate to be partners in God's intentions of shalom by living a faith that does justice for peace. Such justice demands unqualified commitment to the dignity and sacredness of every person; working for the common good; honesty in one's personal dealings with neighbors and groups; actively helping to create social structures that distribute fairly society's resources and promote the rights and responsibilities of all; bringing to every level and arena of life a deep commitment to the full liberation of humankind and the integrity of God's creation, with special favor for those most in need.*

There is ample historical evidence that the Catholic Christian community has failed—often miserably—to live up to its own creed concerning justice as required by faith. One can say defensively that the Church in each era was "the product of its time," but it should have known better too. Indeed it has a record, as noted earlier, of serving the needs and defending the rights of the poor and oppressed—the tradition of social justice goes back to the very beginning of the Church. And yet, its blessing of slavery and practice of slave ships, its violent and sectarian crusades, its inquisitions and witch-hunts—the latter leading to the destruction of millions of innocent women—cannot be set aside but should bring lament and genuine repentance, *metanoia* as a transformation of heart and ways.

How embarrassing it is now to read the *Malleus Maleficarum*. This was the theological and legal document used by the Church for detecting and trying witches. Written by two Dominican theologians circa 1486, it was the only Church document on which both Catholics and Protestants agreed during the Reformation period. It is laden with the most horrible misogynist rhetoric portraying women as inherently evil and naturally prone to witchcraft.

Likewise, how lamentable it is that for centuries the Church quoted the "curse of Canaan" from Genesis 9 to justify slavery and was hesitant to unequivocally condemn the practice until the modern social encyclicals.

Although these failures are outdated now—and are not "the whole story"—yet contemporary Christians forget them to their peril. Remembering them can prevent any glib reliance on the Holy Spirit to prevent the Church from partaking in dreadful injustices. Christians have done them in the past and could do similarly again, if not alert to the possibility and to our own blindnesses.

The Christian Church is under mandate by its faith to oppose all forms of oppression and discrimination. As Vatican II declared,

> Every type of discrimination, whether social or cultural, whether based on sex, race, color, social condition, language, or religion, is to be overcome and eradicated as contrary to God's intent.[16]

With special urgency, the Church is bound to practice justice within its own structures. How else will it be a credible witness on behalf of justice in society? It was out of concern for the Church's credibility— for its sacramentality to the world—that the Second General Synod of Catholic Bishops (1971) declared:

> While the Church is bound to give witness to justice, [it] recognizes that anyone who ventures to speak to people about justice must first be just in their eyes.[17]

Anything that smacks of injustice within the Church's own life is a countersign to the reign of God. It seems imperative that education *for life for all* encourage social consciousness and commitment to justice.

For Teachers and Parents

Every Christian school, parish program, and family, and every Christian educator *for life for all,* should be committed to educate for justice and, I suggest, along the lines proposed. Not an option, justice is a mandate of Christian faith. From the beginning, the Church understood its ministry of education as participating in God's mission of saving the world. The divine edict of justice requires education for personal and social transformation. Beyond the context of explicitly Catholic education, all Christians who teach anywhere—school, home, or program—in whatever capacity, are required by their faith to educate for justice, albeit without imposing their religious language on participants.

But I further propose that *every teacher and every system of education are responsible to educate for justice in society*, to help form the character of persons to live justly. Although educators may draw upon diverse philosophies and theologies for their notions of justice, my hope is that the understanding proposed in this chapter can at least be suggestive and perhaps inspire many from other traditions as well. How ironic if a society does not expect its education to form people in rudimentary justice—being honest and truthful, not stealing or cheating, paying taxes—and yet puts citizens in jail when they break the laws of the land!

Concern for justice runs through every chapter here—much has already been suggested by way of educating in this "cardinal" virtue.

—Justice permeates education when its anthropology values and helps to develop the whole person, treats people with respect and dignity, and teaches them to respect the dignity, rights, and responsibilities of others.

—Justice is taught by sacramentality that enables people to "see" and respond to the poor and oppressed of society and to imagine how to change unjust social structures and oppressive cultural mores.

—Justice is taught as the educational community reflects "right relationship" and educates students in their civic responsibility to the common good.

—Tradition should be taught in ways that highlight justice as an integral aspect of its legacy, providing models and suggesting ways to live justly.

—Justice should permeate education's rationality by encouraging learners to think for themselves, to be "thoughtful" about ethical issues, to reach for wisdom that both knows the truth and does the good.

—Likewise, spirituality is a call to "right relationship"—the biblical sense both of holiness and of justice. To allow spirituality to permeate education may lend people the most powerful inspiration for living justly.

—Catholicity (chapter 9) requires justice as care for all humankind and as respect for diversity.

And yet, to reflect explicitly on what justice itself recommends for teachers and parents seems worth our while.

Taking something like the notion of justice as proposed, what would be some implications for educators in home, school, or parish? First, pause to assemble some of your own thoughts.

For Reflection

- What are your own sentiments about the place of justice in your work as an educator? Describe why and how it belongs. Review some of the personal and social influences on your position.

- Recall a notable instance when you brought concern for justice to your teaching or parenting. What do you learn from that experience as you reflect on it now?

- What do you imagine a commitment to justice asks of an educator's soul? Style? Of the educational environment?

For the Educator's Soul

I have three suggestions to propose: one for the educator's own heart and two that are more pertinent to his or her educating.

Educators Need a Personal Passion for Justice

In their own lives, teachers and parents need to have a personal passion for justice. Without "fire in the belly" for justice, educators are less likely to educate others in this "cardinal" virtue. I remember a civics teacher in high school who knew well and taught clearly the social teachings of Catholicism. But he never showed any real passion for justice. We "caught" his lack of enthusiasm.

At a minimum, teachers of justice need to have a sense of fairness and care for the well-being of individuals and society. But a passion for justice requires a deep empathy for those who suffer injustice, an aptitude to cross over and "walk a mile in the moccasins" of the oppressed and violated. To sustain such empathy is difficult indeed. I suggest a few spiritual resources for educators to "keep on" in a passion for justice.

- *Ask for God's help.* It may sound a bit pious, but a passion for justice is maintained only with the help of "Higher Power"—of whatever name. If we overinvest in our own efforts, the enormity of the task will overwhelm and paralyze. As always in the life of faith, but especially in

something like justice education, we must avoid the favorite
Catholic heresy of "good works" (as if we must do
everything by our own efforts) *and* the favorite Protestant
heresy of "cheap grace" (as if God should do everything for
us). Instead, remembering God's covenant with humankind,
let educators themselves help learners to bring the struggle
for justice to prayer, asking for God's help while making
every good effort. Likewise, let them allow their prayer time
to heighten consciousness of injustice and renew
commitment to justice.

- *Redefine "success" and remember that even small efforts are
worthwhile.* In modern society, "success" with a problem
means a complete solution—to have no more problem.
Anything less is considered a bit of a failure. So when we see
that the "whole problem" cannot be solved soon (e.g., world
hunger), there is a tendency not to even try.

  Justice educators must redefine success, becoming
convinced that the simplest of efforts are worthwhile—that
everyone can do something. And the smallest of victories
should be celebrated. Some plant the seeds, others water,
others may reap the harvest, and it is always God who gives
yet the increase. (See 1 Corinthians 3:6.)

  Introducing young children to the three R's of environmental care—reduce, reuse, and recycle—may seem little in
the face of acid rain, toxic waste, pollution of air and water,
destruction of rain forests, and depletion of the ozone layer,
but such education is worthwhile for now and forms their
future character. Someday those children will be presidents
of companies or political leaders or parents—with an environmental consciousness. What a difference they will make!

- *Remember personal oppression and experiences of suffering.* In
recent years, some liberation theologians have posed the
question of whether or not "the privileged" can ever be
committed to justice—if they can have real empathy for the
poor and oppressed. Although a reasonable question, might
there not be a bit of cynicism behind it? I am convinced that
all people of good will, whatever their economic or social

status, can have a passion for justice, enlivened by remembering their own experiences of suffering and oppression—their own "dangerous memories."

To the needy, the oppressions of the wealthy seem privileged indeed—and verily so—but all human suffering is real and, when remembered intentionally, can be a source of empathy for others who suffer. I have an affluent friend who gives much of her personal time and resources to working with indigent women who are victims of domestic violence. Her passion is fueled by the memory of such violence as a child in her own home, albeit a wealthy one.

• *If possible, do some direct work with the poor or oppressed.* This advice is surely for privileged people like myself, since people who are poor and oppressed do not need to seek out "direct contact." But working in academia and living where I live could readily insulate me from the poverty and racism of my city. I find regular volunteer work in a guest house for the homeless to be helpful in maintaining my consciousness of suffering and my commitment to educate for justice.

Educators who do not feel comfortable with such volunteer work can find other ways to "hear the cry of the poor" (Psalm 69:34). For example, men can listen intentionally and with open hearts to women's experiences of oppression; Caucasians, to people of color about their experiences of racism; straight people, to gay people on their experience of exclusion and vilification. And surely every home can try to model "right relationship" in its own family life.

• *Avoid elitism and debilitating guilt.* Faith that does justice is a lifetime conversion for everyone. No one can claim to have "arrived" on this issue. Who does not have some complicity in sinful social structures and practices? As Jesus said to the accusers of the woman caught committing adultery, "Let the one among you who is without sin be the first to cast a stone" (John 8:7).

Justice education should never foster a "better-than-thou" attitude; none of us can afford to "cast the stone." Nor is putting guilt trips on people an effective way to form character. It even smacks of injustice. Oh, there is a sense of guilt that everyone should have about his or her sins, personal and social, but let it be a healthy kind that prompts repentance and working for transformation. There is a debilitating guilt which paralyzes and encourages fatalism—avoid it.

Having successfully defended a fairly radical dissertation on justice, a doctoral candidate on whose committee I had served invited me to a celebration lunch at a very elegant and expensive restaurant. Concerned that the bill would be too large for her still-student budget, I suggested that we relocate to a more moderate place. She insisted on staying and commented, "Justice doesn't mean that we shouldn't eat here for a special occasion. Justice means that everyone should get to celebrate in places like this," I was persuaded to stay and recognized again the truth of that moving song from the early days of the workers-union movement sung especially by the women strikers, "Give us bread and give us roses." Concern for the hungry should not make those who have enough food feel guilty, but rather should encourage their efforts so that everyone has enough to eat, and then some of the aesthetic pleasures of life as well.

For the work of educating, I suggest two commitments that justice invites from the educator's soul.

Educators Must Be Just with Those They Educate

Teachers and parents should be just in their immediate relationships with those they educate. Surely, the most effective way to teach for justice is to model it, to embody it in every relationship. And all educators have ample opportunity to practice what they preach on this score. There is ever a power dimension to teaching, no matter how democratic and participative a teacher might be. The very dynamic of giving access to sources of knowledge has a power to it, and then add in evaluation that so often accompanies teaching.

Teachers and parents are in a position of power, and learners can be so vulnerable. Therefore, educators must be scrupulous to maintain justice in every aspect of their educational relationships. And beyond being fair, "right relationship" for educators demands generosity as well, a willingness to go the extra mile, never to give up on someone, to forgive and forget. Teacher power is a given, but one can choose how to use it. Justice requires using power to empower learners rather than control them.

Every teacher and parent should see to it that the immediate environment—classroom, meeting place, or home—exemplifies respect for people's dignity, promotes their rights, encourages their responsibilities, offers them a peaceable and safe context in which to learn together. Crucial to this environment is the mode of discipline. It must be marked by commutative justice—fairness—and yet mixed with compassion.

Justice also requires that the teacher give all equal access to the community's traditions of knowledge and wisdom—the humanities, arts, and sciences. And in regard to the equity issue that concerns students most—assignments, examinations, and evaluations—teachers must maintain the strictest justice. What an injustice to victimize a student in her or his grade!

Educators Need to Care for "Poor" Learners

Educators can make an "option for the poor" by having a special care for "poor" learners. A teacher at a teachers' workshop on justice asked in a protesting tone, "But who are my poor?" I immediately answered, "First, your students," and I meant it. Many schools, programs, and families include the economically poor, but all have the physically poor, the emotionally poor, the spiritually poor, the self-esteem poor, the personality poor. (Remember the cruelty to unpopular students.)

An educator's greatest favor should be for those he or she is most capable of favoring—the academically poor—the ones who need extra help with academics or discipline. Help to "poor students"—we even use the term—can be offered in many ways: a little extra time or tutorial, encouragement and help on assignments, rewarding effort and not merely outcome. Even in my university context, not a day goes by but that I have opportunity to favor a student who needs some extra help. When faithful to my commitment to the "poor," I take it.

For the Educator's Style

All education is capable of teaching for or against justice, which is to say that education is always "political"! Both the *what* and *how* of education affect who people become and how they live in society—big-time politics! There is nothing inevitable, however, about education being good politics—*for life for all.* Justice requires intentionality on the part of educators and especially regarding their teaching style.

In choosing what to teach from the humanities, arts, and sciences—either consciously or unconsciously—teachers can choose curricula that perpetuate injustice. They can present tradition in ways that legitimate oppressive arrangements; motivate only for production and profit; or perpetuate sexism, racism, and other injustices.

Or, they can emphasize aspects that humanize and challenge social oppressions, that open up learners' minds, that encourage wisdom for life. Even when teachers aspire to be "objective" as a norm of scholarship, they give their curricula a "spin" that shapes the characters of learners. Let the spin be *for life for all.*

A history teacher I had in my Irish high school was an engaging and scholarly historian, but after his course on European history it would be difficult not to have a negative image of "the English." I know of a math teacher who is notorious for favoring the boys in his class, saying often, in one way or another, that the girls are not as capable of mathematics or will not need to know math. Both are political in their spin, but not a politics *for life for all.*

Words and language patterns carry "political" content, and educators must be especially attentive to that implicit but powerful aspect of their curriculum. They can teach justice or discrimination simply by how they say things. Modern society has become fairly alert not to use racist language, stereotypes, or stories, but is much in need of consciousness-raising regarding sectarianism—especially anti-Semitism, ageism, negativism regarding the specially challenged, and other forms of discrimination. Sexism is an exigent case in point, because it is built into the very "rules" of English grammar. (For example, English has no gender-inclusive singular personal pronoun.)

To use *man* and *mankind, he* and *himself* when one intends to speak generically is to render women invisible and to propose man as the norm of humanity. The same is true of defining women in relation to men, as "man and wife" or "Mr. and Mrs. John Smith." Using generic terms such as policeman, mailman, and *congressman* maintains discrimination in careers. Stereotyping women as emotional, soft, and dependent and men as rational, tough, and self-sufficient is a political curriculum that is humanizing for neither. And the examples could go on! Language is a pressing issue for teachers because we are persons of public speech—words are our "stock-in-trade." The language we use may be *the* most effective politics of what we teach.

In addition to language, justice educators need to be alert to and make choices about all aspects of the implicit curriculum. So often the "real" politics are taught covertly rather than overtly in the explicit curriculum. A friend Susanne brought my attention to a children's math book in which almost all the examples and assignments had something to do with buying and selling, owning and investing—all to the owner's advantage and without any semblance of ethical consideration.

Such an implicit curriculum teaches that making money is the way to make meaning out of life and that mathematics is simply a tool of capitalism. The politics would surely be more humanizing if the examples engaged the children's imaginations across the breadth of life, if the economic examples prompted them to think about and question their socioeconomic reality (see the math example that follows), and if the assignments encouraged creativity, fun, and playfulness.

Likewise, regarding how to teach—this, too, is a political and justice-laden issue on which educators must make choices. Compare a teaching style that encourages people to think and to think critically for themselves in contrast to one that tells them what to think and discourages questioning of their world or society. Or compare a teaching style that invites learners to express themselves, listen to others, and work together to a style that silences them, stymies their opinions, encourages individualism and competition. And the contrasts could go on. One's teaching methods must be reviewed for whether or not they are educating justly.

Educators can make deliberate choices regarding what and how to teach that promote justice in society and character formation of learners in the virtue of justice. As a general principle, I propose that teachers and parents choose to teach for justice by teaching justly—which is to say, let justice suffuse the whole curriculum in both content and process.

Content for Justice

I have already proposed that educators should consciously teach aspects of tradition that encourage justice and call attention to injustice. Such a curriculum guideline would seem more operable in disciplines like history, literature, and social studies. These are perspectives on the human condition and can make explicit proposals about ways to live justly.

Even in the humanities, however, teachers must make deliberate choices to ensure that what they teach educates for justice. Mary, a junior-high history teacher in a white suburban school, chooses to teach a course on "Great Black Leaders in America." In Mary's efforts to get it approved, the principal protested, "But there are no black students in our school." And my friend responded, "All the more reason to have this course in the curriculum."

I am convinced that all teachers, regardless of their discipline or context, can find ways to educate for justice through the content they teach and do so without appearing to "drag it in." A friend, Maryanne, who teaches second grade encouraged students to criticize a reader she was using because its few people of color were represented doing menial work. In other words, she deliberately chose to turn the book's graphics—a significant aspect of its "content"—into a social studies lesson around racial injustice. She could have let this slip by but then that, too, would have been a political choice.

In contrast to the math book just cited, Laura tells of a math teacher—her father—who often poses "problems" suggested by stories in the morning newspaper. They can run like this: "Jack makes $500 a week and works 35 hours. Jane does the same job for the same amount of hours and makes $375. What is the percentage difference in their salary per hour?" Invariably someone will ask, "Is this true?"

"Yes—did you see the story in this morning's newspaper?"

Then comes, "Why is this allowed?" The conversation ensues, and justice has been "infused" into the math curriculum.

Process for Justice

All the proposals in previous chapters about the teaching process—to engage the whole person, encourage active participation and conversation, build community, prompt critical reflection, invite appropriation and decision making, nurture respect and responsibility, and other such suggestions—are suffused with commitment to justice and seem likely to educate justly. Here I highlight only the need for pedagogies of social consciousness. This auspicious-sounding phrase means encouraging people to become aware of what is just and unjust in society and disposing them to act for social transformation.

Many times and from different angles, I have urged critical reflection as integral to a pedagogy *for life for all*. Here I highlight that it as an asset to "consciousness raising" education because it encourages people to think contextually—to really analyze what is "going on" in their world and why; to become aware of how their historical situation shapes themselves, their lives, and their knowing.

In my own teaching, to encourage students to "think contextually"—in and about their social location—I tend to favor four simple-sounding questions. They are usually focused on some specific social issue or event and I pose them in a variety of ways: "What is really going on here—and why?" "Who is benefiting?" "Who is suffering?" And then, perhaps the most socially self-reflective question, "What is influencing my own perspective?"

Undoubtedly, the social analysis intended by such questions is more readily done by adults. Developmental psychologists advise that social reflection requires a mature stage of cognitive development—in Piagetian terms, after the onset of "formal operational thinking," beginning around age fifteen. But surely the seeds of social reflection can be sown much earlier, and the tree is in the seed.

Ilene teaches fourth grade. An annual event at her school is when students spend a day at work with their parents. During subsequent classes she takes time to ask for stories and thoughts about their experiences. She invites the children to review the ways that society decides who gets to do what work; why some people have more fulfilling and remunerative jobs than others; how things like gender, race, education, and social background influence people's work and vocation. She noted, "This reflection on their experience with their parents at work is probably the most effective thing I do all year by way of raising their social consciousness." Her students would learn less from their experience by way of justice if Ilene did not include such critical social reflection as part of the curriculum during class time.

An adult educator I know who works with the catechumens of his parish has a reputation for asking them two sets of questions—regardless of the theme: the first in which he invites their opinions, feelings, or thoughts about the topic or issue at hand; the other in which he invites, "Tell me the story that brought you to think or feel, or act as you do?"

Participants often pull his leg that no matter what they say or express, they have to "tell the story behind it." He is fostering their social consciousness—likely a cousin to Christian conversion? I know a parent whose teenage children report that "Mom always asks us what we think. When we tell her, she asks 'Is that really your own opinion?' and then we have to think all over again." She is fostering their social consciousness. Observe the function of good questioning!

For the Educational Space

The whole environment of a school, program, or family—every aspect of their explicit and implicit curriculum—should educate for justice and form people's character in living justly. Many critics charge that too often education is co-opted as a tool of its political context, as an agency of socialization that prepares persons to "fit in" as obedient automatons of their situation—social or ecclesial—rather than preparing them for social transformation.[18]

I think education should prepare people to participate effectively in society—get a job, make a contribution, have a life. But far beyond this, it should also be prophetic, educating them to become aware of every instance of oppression and injustice, to oppose each instance, and to create structures and cultural mores that promote "right relationship" for all. Every symbol and instance of the shared life of a school, parish, or family should be scrutinized to ensure that it is not domesticating but educating, and educating *for life for all*.

In particular, I draw attention to the growing practice in schools, public and parochial, and in parish programs of making a service component integral to the curriculum. Outreach to the neighbor in need is possible in many families as well. This involves learners performing direct service as an aspect of their education. In American high schools, colleges, and parishes, nothing has done more to educate for justice and to heighten learners' critical consciousness than such programs. I have two brief suggestions for their effectiveness.

First, give learners direct experiences of real service with real people, and the more immediate the better. So going to a soup kitchen and feeding hungry people is more likely to raise social consciousness than working on a fund-raiser for some charity—although the latter is also a service. I know a family who spends a few hours on Sundays after church working together in a shelter for the homeless. It is most likely that their children will grow to adulthood with a strong social consciousness.

Second, to heighten the learning from service work, learners need the opportunity to reflect on it and to share their reflections. John Dewey never tired of saying that people learn little from experience unless they "reconstruct" it. Encourage students to reflect critically on their service activities, making opportunity for such reflection an intentional aspect of the curriculum.

According to age level and context, reflection can include social analysis of why people are in need of such service and imagining more equitable structures that reduce the need. From working with college students over the years, I have found that the learning potential of service work is heightened when we take class time for critical reflection on their experience.

For Reflection

- Has your own understanding of justice and its place in your teaching changed or grown from your encounter with this chapter? How? Why?

- What would you challenge in the chapter? What insights would you add to it?

- Can you imagine ways to enhance your own commitment to educate for justice?

Notes

1. Rohr, *Why Be Catholic,* 25.
2. See, for example, *The Apostolic Tradition of Hippolytus,* chapter 16.
3. Thomas Aquinas, *Summa Theologica,* II-2. 58.1.
4. The great Protestant theologian Walter Rauschenbusch (1861–1918) is considered the primary spokesperson for the Social Gospel movement. See, especially, his *Christianity and the Social Crisis,* which was first published in 1907.
5. Both of these statements are from a document entitled *Justice in the World,* which emerged from the Second General Synod of Catholic Bishops (1971). In Gremillion, ed., *The Gospel of Peace and Justice,* 520 and 514.
6. Brueggemann, "Voices of the Night," in *To Act Justly, Love Tenderly, Walk Humbly,* 5.
7. I take the term "right relationship" as a biblical description of justice from a fine essay by the renowned scripture scholar John R. Donahue entitled "Biblical Perspectives on Justice."
8. Heschel, The Prophets, 201.
9. For the substance of much of this list, and particularly in describing the first six characteristics, I am indebted to J. Bryan Hehir, "Catholic Social Teachings" in *Encyclopedia of Catholicism.* McBrien, Ed.
10. *The Catechism,* # 2423, 2424. The insert quote is from Vatican II's "Church in the Modern World," #62.
11. "Church in the Modern World," #2, Abbott, *Documents,* 227–8.
12. *The Catechism,* # 2447, 2448, 2444.
13. National Conference of Catholic Bishops, *The Challenge of Peace,* 44.
14. Ibid., 71.
15. It is interesting to note that I take this phrase from a papal document "On the Evangelization of Peoples," often referred to by its Latin title, *Evangelii Nuntiandi.*
16. "Constitution on Church in Modern World," #29, Abbott, Documents, 227–28.
17. Justice in the World," in Gremillion, The Gospel of Peace and Justice, 522
18. See for example the writings of education theorists Maxine Greene, Ira Shor, Henry Giroux, or Nel Noddings.

CHAPTER NINE

A "Catholic" Openness:
"Here Comes Everybody"

Many Mansions

Maybe I always look a bit lost at O'Hare Airport, but I seem to attract more evangelists there than anywhere else. And they are more persistent too—perhaps something in the Chicago water? This one was young and attractive with a chic, leather shoulder bag. She walked right up to me and said, "Excuse me, sir—are you saved?"

Startled, I exclaimed, "Whaaaat?" and she repeated the question. I thought about it quickly and said, "Well, some days more than others," and hurried past her.

Intrigued by my response, or so she said later, she fell into step with me, or more of a trot. "Where you travelin' to?" "Boston," I panted, "and my plane should be about to leave!"

"Well," she said, "you may never find Jesus in Boston."

"It could be difficult," I agreed. She kept coming!

I arrived at the gate with evangelist in tow just in time to hear the announcement: "The 4:30 flight to Boston is delayed until 6:15." Ah, captured! I said I had work to do, but she said she had too—to save my soul. I was beginning to admire her faith commitment and to wonder about my own. So, throwing caution to the winds, I asked, "What makes you do this?"

Her response was a cascade of Bible verses, carefully crafted to prove that I must "accept Jesus Christ as my Lord and Savior"—preferably today—or I could be lost to eternal damnation. She met my protests with Bible rebuttals and a commanding air of certainty. I was a bit daunted by her ability to call up just the right quote as needed and give book, chapter, and verse. "But it says in Romans, chapter 8, verse 2 . . ."

My being impressed showed, and she presumed my biblical ignorance. "I can see you don't know the Bible." Before I could agree or protest, she swung the bag from behind her back, dived in and came up with a Bible for me. She began explaining where to begin and how I should proceed, step by step, to find Jesus as the answer to everything—promise to fulfillment.

More to catch her breath, she asked, "Do you have any religion at all?"

"Well," and I paused to choose my words carefully, "I'm trying to become a Catholic Christian!"

This perplexed her, "Whaddya' mean?"

"I was raised a Catholic," I responded, "but I'm realizing how difficult it can be to become a real one—a good one. It's a lifetime journey."

She cautioned me, "But as a Catholic you don't follow the Bible."

I admitted, "Well—too often poorly, but I'm practicing."

I continued, "Becoming a Catholic Christian means growing to love and care for all humankind—cherishing their diversity, relishing life and maturing into its fullness—for oneself and others, embracing the world as gift and responsibility—convinced that you can make a difference for life for all. It means being a good steward of God's creation—enjoying and protecting it, and ever remaining optimistic—especially about people.

"It requires letting go of parochialism to embrace everyone as brother and sister, replacing narrow-mindedness with openness to learn from those who are very different. It means expecting surprises, finding joy in the everyday, living with a spirit of gratitude and celebration. A true Catholic is convinced that God loves every person equally and God's family embraces all humankind."

"But," she protested, "the only way to be saved is to accept Jesus Christ as Lord and Savior."

"Well," I responded, becoming confessional myself now, "I have faith in Jesus and my home within God's family is indeed the Christian one, but is this necessary for everyone? I don't believe a loving God could allow the vast majority of humankind to go astray and lead only a few of us aright? Surely God draws home

to Godself all people who live their faith with integrity—
Buddhists, Hindus, Moslems, and everyone of good will?"

She responded, "No, God doesn't," but added after a pause—
as though out of Bible verses —"That's a mystery." And so it
went, back and forth, each of us now angling for a convert—and
out of some genuine care for the other.

It was time to board. The polemics had subsided, and we were
more like soul-friends. She wished me luck with becoming some
kind of a "real" Christian—I'm sure she meant other than a
Catholic one. I wished her well, too, and said I admired the
courage of her convictions, that I was confident we would both be
"saved," and likewise all these strangers swirling 'round us—
oblivious that we were debating their eternal destiny.

She asked, "May I give you a Bible verse to pray with on the
plane, a parting gift?"

I hesitated—maybe a parting shot—but accepted. I
recognized the text without checking, Acts 4:12, referring to Jesus,
"There is no salvation through anyone else . . ." I was right!

Well, two can play that game! So I asked if I might also give
her a verse. She looked incredulous and protested, "But you said
you didn't know the Bible."

I corrected, "No, you said I didn't know it—I said I sometimes
live it poorly."

"What's my verse?" she asked curiously and with a smile. I
hesitated but offered, "Spend a while with John 14:2," and I
boarded the plane.

Later, I wondered about my swapping Bible verses to win
points in an argument. I hadn't done that before. But I also
wondered how my evangelist friend might have interpreted Jesus
saying, "In my Father's house, there are many mansions." Did it
invite her to affirm the "catholicity"—the inclusivity and
diversity—of God's human family?

"Here Comes Everybody"

Humankind, at its best, reaches for "catholicity." Our deepest desire is
to transcend sectarianism and parochialism and live instead with
authentic love of self and other and in solidarity with all people. It is
certainly not easy to be catholic, and Catholics may do no better than

most. But let us not be self-righteous about anyone falling short of such an ideal.

The truth is that we experience our human condition as transient and threatened—finally by death. The precariousness of existence, what German philosopher Martin Heidegger called the "thrownness" of life, prompts understandable sentiments of self-interest and self-preservation. Then, both nature and nurture bond us with our own kind—family and clan—and we figure that hanging in with them is our best defense against all that threatens. We develop loyalties to "the tribe," to its worldview and way of making meaning out of life. It is difficult not to settle into an "us versus them" stance toward the world.

Developmental psychologists claim empirical evidence that the great majority of people spend their lives at this conventional stage of human consciousness—clinging tenaciously to an identity forged by whatever "our group" says and does and believes. Though far short of the maturity of a universal perspective,[1] such conventionalism is an enticing strategy—and it has warrant beyond survival. Even Christian faith teaches that our first responsibility is to love those most immediate to us—the brothers and sisters whom "we can see" (1 John 4:20). The prophet Isaiah preached that true religion includes "never turning your back on your own" (58:7).

Catholic Christianity, too, affirms and celebrates particularity—so necessary for personal identity. At its best, it is not an amorphous universalism but *a grounding in the particular that opens to the universal*. It should provide deep roots that nurture branches to reach beyond parochialism to inclusivity in care and consciousness. So significant for education, catholicity also entails an openness to truth wherever it can be found (regardless of its sources) and a willingness to learn from people whose perspectives on life and ways of making meaning are different from one's own.

To become catholic is surely among our highest callings as human beings. It is integral to humanity's religious vocation in that transcending narrow self-interest should be an aspect of reaching for the Transcendent. And enabling people to become catholic is surely one purpose of humanistic education. What a worthy ideal for teachers and parents—to foster learners' particular identity in ways that open them to be universal in care and perspective.

Catholic comes from two Greek words, kata and holos. Holos means "whole," as in parts working together and can also mean "everyone." Kata is used in many ways (e.g., every, according to, including, as if), but with holos—forming katholos—seems most accurately translated as "welcoming everyone."

Many dictionaries take catholic simply to mean "universal." They are influenced by how Aristotle used the term to designate something that can be said of every member of a class. (Death and taxes are catholic—universals.) This is a limited use, however, that emphasizes what is uniform, whereas the word can also reflect breadth and diversity. For example, a "catholic music lover" is someone who likes all kinds of music. It can also mean "worldwide," but this is best understood as keeping membership open to everyone, regardless of background, more than a hegemonic insistence that everyone belong. So it seems that the richest meaning of catholic is the one closest to its etymology—"welcoming everyone."

St. Ignatius of Antioch (circa 35–107), a great bishop and martyr of the early Church, was the first to use "catholic" of the Christian community. At the beginning of the second century, Ignatius was arrested in Antioch for being a Christian and brought to Rome to be fed to the lions in the Colosseum. As he traveled (circa 106), he wrote a kind of "thank-you" letter back to Christian communities who had offered him hospitality along his journey to martyrdom.

In his letter to the Smyrnaeans we find this statement: "Where Jesus is, there is the Catholic Church."[2] The surrounding text indicates his meaning that when the spirit of Jesus prevails in a community, it is complete—the "whole" Church is there. We can presume that Ignatius had experienced Jesus' catholicity in the hospitality offered by the Smyrnaeans.

Inclusion and outreach—catholicity—were certainly the spirit of the historical Jesus. He sought out and preached to all classes of society, of every ethnic background. Elizabeth Schussler Fiorenza, a great New Testament scholar of our time, proposes that one of the most extraordinary features of Jesus' public ministry was that he brought together an inclusive community of disciples.[3] Just his table fellowship was an unmistakable sign—in the social context—of his hospitality and inclusion; a damning accusation against him was that he "ate with tax collectors and sinners" (Mark 2:16).

At the end, the Risen Christ commissioned the young community to make outreach to "all peoples" (Matthew 28:19), welcoming everyone of every station to discipleship. On the first Pentecost, when the Holy Spirit came upon Jesus' disciples and initiated the Christian Church, the crowds present in Jerusalem experienced an amazing phenomenon. Although from many ethnic backgrounds and languages, each person heard the disciples preach in the listener's native tongue. (See Acts 2:1–13.) It seems significant that the first miracle of the new Christian community was to make everyone feel welcome and included.

After Ignatius, the designation "catholic" for the Church caught on. It must have struck a chord. Christians used *catholic* of the Church in general and in a local place, highlighting that both the Church universal and particular should be complete and welcoming to all. St. Cyril of Jerusalem (d. 386) explained that the Church is catholic because it is confined to no one place or nation, welcomes people of every class ("rulers and subjects, learned and ignorant"), forgives every kind of sin, and promotes every kind of virtue.[4] The great creeds of Christian faith included it as a "mark" of the Church, as in the Apostles' Creed, "I believe . . . in the holy catholic Church," and the Nicene Creed, "We believe in one, holy, catholic, and apostolic Church."

St. Augustine used catholicity as an argument against the Donatists, a group of overly ardent Christians in North Africa who were claiming that theirs was the only true Church and that only saints could belong. He argued that the true Church must be catholic in the sense of welcoming saints and sinners alike and that the Donatists themselves could not be the Church of Jesus because they were limited to one geographical area. Augustine also used catholicity to encourage Christians to be open to the truth, wherever it can be found.[5] A contemporary of Augustine, St. Vincent of Lérins (d. 450), said that a belief is orthodox Christian faith if it is "catholic," and he meant something that has been "believed everywhere, always, and by all."[6]

After the Reformation, few Protestants used *catholic* to describe the Church—apart from its recitation in the creeds. It was as if the term was too associated with a hegemony they had just rejected. By contrast, Western and Eastern Catholics began to use it as a polemical argument for their orthodoxy, claiming that Christian denominations that do not possess this "mark of the true Church" are heretical.

Vatican II moved beyond such polemics and proposed catholicity more as a challenge for the entire Church than as an accomplishment of any denomination, a vision of what the entire Christian community ought to be rather than a "one up" point to win arguments. This is also the perspective of the *Catechism*. Instead of claiming it as a permanent achievement, the Church is ever challenged and "called to realize" its catholicity.[7]

I will draw heavily from the documents of Vatican II because they gave such fresh impetus to the Church becoming catholic—in the richest sense of the term. The Council also taught that the Church's catholicity is not simply for its own sake, but should be a service to all humankind—as a sign of the interdependence and bondedness of all peoples.

The *Constitution on the Church* states that though the Church "may . . . look like a small flock," nevertheless it is "a lasting and sure seed of unity, hope, and salvation for the whole human race." Its deepest bonds are profoundly human ones of "life, charity, and truth," and it ought to function in the world as a "source of unity and peace" among all peoples. In this challenge to be catholic, the Church must "never cease to renew itself."[8]

For Reflection

- What are some of your own immediate associations when you hear the term "catholic"? Review where they come from!

- Note some ways in which your faith community is catholic. Ways in which it is not—yet. Reflect on why.

- What in your social context promotes catholicity? What prevents it?

Characteristics of Catholicity: One Proposal

Drawing upon Catholic Christian tradition, I make a proposal of what it means to become catholic. Although having more than its share of sectarianism and parochialism, Catholic tradition is most faithful to itself when it favors catholicity. For each characteristic, I begin with its theological underpinnings and then highlight its human conviction that can be shared by anyone—confessional Christian or not—about what it means for life. The latter is my primary interest, not to make theological points but human proposals—to support educating *for life for all*. Catholicity is a profoundly human sentiment that can be embraced by people of all faiths, albeit for different theological or philosophical reasons.

Universality of God's Love: *Care for Everyone*

The Bible reflects the human experience of being deeply loved by God. As if a bit of hyperbole could help to drive home this conviction to their own people, the sacred authors—especially of the earlier books—can make God sound fiercely partisan to the Hebrews, only occasionally making explicit that God similarly favors everyone else. Some Christians have laid claim to these texts and taken them literally, aggrandizing God's favor to themselves alone and foolishly thinking that they are the only people whom God loves. In contrast, the dominant biblical and ecclesial traditions favor the universality of God's love. That God loves all people is a core conviction—a dogma—of Christian faith.

The initial biblical portrayals of humankind as made in God's image and likeness (see Genesis 1:1–31, esp., v. 26–27) and as alive by God's own life breathed into the "earth person" (see Genesis 2:7) continues throughout the Hebrew Scriptures. Isaiah acknowledges to God that "we are all the work of your hands" (64:8). The psalmist praises God who has "knit me in my mother's womb . . . wonderfully made" (139:113–14). Toward the end of the New Testament, we find St. John's culminating three-word description of God that had been unfolding throughout salvation history—"God is love" (1 John 4:16).

Uniting these convictions from the beginning, throughout, and at the end of the Bible, we realize that God's life within humankind represents God's love for all humanity. Made in God's own likeness, every human being lives by the love of God. Our very life blood is God's love coursing through our veins. To claim that some people are not loved by God is blasphemy!

The overarching biblical witness, then, is that God takes all humankind into loving partnership even while choosing a particular people to symbolize this universal covenant. Note that the very first biblical covenant is made with all humanity. God points to the rainbow in the sky and says to Noah, "This is the sign of the covenant I have established between myself and all mortal creatures that are on earth" (Genesis 9:17). And God does not break covenants.

For Christian faith, the theme of the universality of God's love gets writ large in Jesus. That Jesus as a human being was bonded with all humanity and was also the incarnation—the living embodiment—of God's presence makes him a profound symbol of God's love for all humankind. When he began his public ministry, John the Baptist introduced him as "the one who takes away the sins of the world" (John 1:29).

Jesus presented himself as "the light of the world" (John 8:12). He preached that all people "from the east and the west and from the north and the south" are welcome in the reign of God (Luke 13:29). And he compared God's reign to a mustard tree that grows from the smallest of seeds (about the size of a grain of pepper) to be big enough to hold all the birds of the air. (See Mark 4:30–32.) Jesus left his disciples a Great Commandment of Love to live by, requiring love of God, self, and neighbor—including enemies.

God's universal love lends the mandate to people of God to live likewise—to love without limits or borders. There should never be "us and them" but only "we"—bonded as one human family. Catholicity means caring deeply about the well-being of all people, the most immediate and furthest away. The only ones more deserving of care are those most in need of it—the "poor" of any kind or circumstance. Catholicity has an open horizon and genuine altruism in its care. It requires concern for the human family as a seamless garment.

Universality of God's Saving Will: *Work for the Welfare of All*
A companion conviction to the universality of God's love is that God wills the salvation—the present and ultimate well-being—of all people. This is to say that God's Holy Spirit is moving among and working for the welfare of all humankind—here and hereafter. Vatican II refocused God's saving will for all. It reminded Christians of "the affection with which God seeks out all people" and "the universal design of God for the salvation of the human race."[9] It opened its *Declaration on Non-Christian Religions* with the foundational principle

that "[God's] providence . . . manifestation of goodness, and . . . saving designs extend to all [people]."[10]

Christians have struggled to affirm both *the universality of God's saving will* and their *faith in Jesus as the one Savior of humankind:* "There is one mediator between God and the human race, Christ Jesus" (1 Timothy 2:5–6). Or the "gift" my friend at the Chicago airport gave me, "There is no salvation through anyone else than Jesus Christ" (Acts 4:12).

The fruitful balance of holding to both convictions was threatened by the 1302 dictum of Boniface VIII "Outside of the Church there is no salvation." As I noted in chapter 7, however, this was originally a declaration aimed at apostate Christians—not people outside of Christendom—and specifically at forcing a recalcitrant French king, Philip IV, to obey the pope. Rather than claiming that everyone outside of Christianity is "lost," Catholicism has condemned as heresy the notion that every person must be visibly incorporated into the Church in order to be saved—precisely because it denies God's will to save all.

The most persistent theological proposal for affirming both the primacy of Christ and the universality of salvation has been "baptism of desire." This is the concept that all people who resolve to do God's will— as best they know it—have a virtual desire for baptism and are saved by their implicit faith in Jesus. Essentially, Vatican II took this position:

> Those also can attain to everlasting salvation who through no fault of their own do not know the gospel of Christ or His Church, yet sincerely seek God and, moved by grace, strive by their deeds to do His will as it is known to them through the dictates of conscience.[11]

Although other religious traditions might hear this as hegemonic on the part of Christians, it at least allows the latter to get around a theological conundrum. Perhaps Jesus himself said it more felicitously, as in the quote I offered to my friend at O'Hare, "In my Father's house, there are many mansions" (John 14:2).

A related theological problem for Christians has been to affirm God's saving will and yet to explain how some people may, in their freedom, refuse God's desire to save them. This is a theological quagmire and too tangential to review here (one's position regarding the relationship of nature and grace—see chapter 2—may decide where one comes down). Because theology is "faith seeking understanding," the relationship between God's saving grace and human free will is an important theological issue; constructing some understanding of such matters of "faith" rightly occupies theologians.

For our interest here, however, it is important to note that Catholic Christianity has consistently rejected all versions of predestination—the notion that some are lost because God predestines them to be lost. Summarizing Catholic tradition, the *Catechism* states rather bluntly, "God predestines no one to go to hell" (#1037) and explains that predestination would violate human freedom and deny God's will to save all. In summary, God offers spiritual salvation to everyone—Christian or not—who does not refuse it.

God's saving intent for humankind and the ability that everyone has to respond has great spiritual relevance, and the corresponding philosophical truths are profound as well. By birth, everyone has a mandate to work for the common good, and we need never accept any social situation as hopeless.

On the personal level, no one should despair because of life's difficulties—we always retain our agency and can do something to improve our lot, if only to say "no" to debilitating circumstances. It always remains true that human efforts can improve the quality of life for all—we can make a positive difference. The human spirit (through which God's Spirit moves in the world) enables people to be "makers of history" rather than simply its creatures, to "make things happen" instead of fatalistically accepting whatever comes our way.

A catholic person works for the human rights of all without exception and never loses hope for the welfare of any individual or social situation. Socialization is never so strong as to predestine someone for ruin. How prevalent is the attitude that a debilitating social background destines some people to fail in life, as if their social context seals their fate. Such fatalism is not a catholic attitude. there is always hope. With help, things can be turned around for the better. Rejecting all versions of fatalism—theological or sociological—is most significant for educators.

The welfare of humankind is ever a mosaic. While any piece remains missing, the mosaic is incomplete. Though no one can take on every cause, catholics have a sense of responsibility for the whole picture. No struggle for justice and freedom can be beyond their concern.

Universality of God's Self-Disclosure:
Be Open to All Knowledge and Wisdom

Regarding divine revelation, there is a core Christian sentiment that what began in the Hebrew Scriptures was brought to "perfection" in Jesus. Vatican II declared:

> Jesus perfected revelation by fulfilling it through His whole work of making Himself present and manifesting Himself; through His words and deeds, His signs and wonders, but especially through His death and glorious resurrection from the dead and final sending of the Spirit of truth. . . . The Christian dispensation, therefore, as the new and definitive covenant, will never pass away, and we now await no further new public revelation.[12]

With this sentiment, the Council was summarizing what had been a Christian conviction throughout history—that divine revelation is complete in Jesus.

And yet, the Council assiduously avoided the noncatholic attitude that Christians know it all already or that God has revealed Godself only to Christians or that they have nothing to learn from other religions. First, contra a static and closed-minded posture, the Council taught that the Church's appropriation of its "deposit of revelation" continues to unfold and develop throughout history.

> The tradition which comes from the apostles develops in the Church with the help of the Holy Spirit . . . For there is *growth in the understanding* of the realities and the words which have been handed down. (emphasis added)

Then the Vatican II declared:

> As the centuries succeed one another, the Church constantly *moves forward toward the fullness of divine truth* until the words of God reach their complete fulfillment in her.[13] (emphasis added)

For Christians, there always remains a lot to learn! This can be noted as a rather amazing admission for the Catholic community since it had often pretended to already possess the "fullness of truth"—ironically, a non*catholic* sentiment.

The Council then went on to encourage genuine openness on the part of Christians to learn the divine wisdom of other religious traditions. With this catholic sentiment, the Catholic church finally recognized, however belatedly, that Christianity is not the sole proprietor of divine revelation. In this, it was only echoing the ancient biblical sentiment that God's wisdom "deploys herself from one end of the earth to the other" (Wisdom 8:1). With an ecumenical spirit, the Council stated that "the Catholic Church rejects nothing that is true and holy" in other religious traditions because they "often reflect a ray of that Truth which enlightens all people."[14] Vatican II urged Christians to engage in "truly human conversation" with all peoples of good will and "to learn by sincere and patient dialogue what treasures a bountiful God has distributed among the nations of the earth."[15]

Such openness toward other religious traditions does not diminish the normativeness of Jesus Christ for Christian faith. As the Council stated, the Church "proclaims and must ever proclaim Christ as 'the way, the truth, and the life.'"[16] And yet, affirming Jesus as the perfection of God's self-disclosure in human history does not preclude appreciation for God's revelation in other traditions. In fact, their very faith in Jesus should lead Christians into

> dialogue and cooperation with the followers of other religions, and in witness of Christian faith and life, acknowledge, preserve, and promote the spiritual and moral goods found among these [peoples], as well as the values in their society and culture.[17]

Theological recognition of God's self-disclosure in other religions calls philosophically for an openness to truth wherever it can be found. Being catholic means a willingness to learn from perspectives on life very different from one's own—a sentiment articulated forcefully by St. Augustine sixteen hundred years ago. Catholicity means that no one group has a corner on the truth. We are all learners and we learn best from each other.

A catholic outlook is open to surprises, to be confronted, to be enriched, to be changed by the entire breadth of human knowledge and wisdom. A catholic perspective is the antithesis to closed-mindedness. It seeks out and welcomes the truth regardless of its human sources—because all truth has one divine Source.

An Entire People of God: *Be in Solidarity with All Humankind*
As elaborated in chapter 4, Catholicism emphasizes the communal aspect of human existence and adds that being Christian—as well as living humanly—is impossible apart from community. This ecclesial nature of Christian faith was a central teaching of Vatican II. Dipping back into the earliest tradition, the Council's two principal images for the Church were "new people of God" and "Body of Christ"—both radically communal.

The communal nature of the Church mandates that it strive for vibrant unity within itself. Vatican II recognized that "the divisions among Christians prevent the Church from exercising the fullness of catholicity proper to her." This prompted the Council to make ecumenism—"a desire for the restoration of unity among all the followers of Christ"—one of its "chief concerns."[18]

It emphasized, however, that unity as the Body of Christ does not mean uniformity. In fact, the very catholicity of the Church requires diversity. This important nuance has been reiterated by many official Church documents since the closing of Vatican II—1965. For instance, "The unity of the Church is realized in the midst of rich diversity. This diversity in the Church is a dimension of its catholicity."[19]

The Church's commitment to solidarity within itself should be an effective sign of unity for all humankind. The *Constitution on the Church* taught that all people are to live with the mutuality of a people of God. "The Church is a kind of sacrament of intimate union with God, and of the unity of all [human]kind, that is, she is a sign and instrument of such union and unity."[20] Later it added that "all are called to be part of this catholic unity of the People of God, a unity which is harbinger of the universal peace it promotes."[21]

Philosophically, catholic commitment to community and unity encourages cooperation and mutuality among all peoples. A catholic outlook insists that we are all one human family, bonded together by flesh and blood as sons and daughters of God. Our partnership should be universal—with every person of good will, to work together *for life for all*. Real catholic solidarity means willingness to make alliances with any party who shares similar commitments to the common good, not for strategic advantage but to advance the well-being of humankind and of God's creation. One can think of the United Nations as a hopeful symbol of such catholicity.

A catholic solidarity resists every instance of division and discrim-ination, of dualism and hierarchical ordering, but at this time in human consciousness, it is particularly important to work for mutuality and partnership between women and men. Sexism is the most pervasive instance of discrimination in the human family—the antithesis of catholicity. Only the naive could underrate the enormity of the task of forging true equality between men and women—in every culture. Yet, catholic sentiment demands commitment to and struggle on behalf of this ideal.

Local Church as Entire: *Cherish Roots*

From the beginning, Christianity has attributed catholicity to the local church. Everything that it means to be Church is represented and complete in each local instance. Echoing this long tradition, Vatican II stated that

> the Church of Christ is truly present in all legitimate local congregations . . . . In these communities, though frequently small and poor, or living far from any other . . . the one, holy, *catholic,* and apostolic Church gathers together.[22] (emphasis added)

This appreciation of the local and particular is also reflected in Catholic commitment to inculturation—reviewed in chapter 5. By indigenizing Christian faith into every context, incorporating "the customs and traditions, wisdom, learning, arts and sciences"[23] of all peoples, Catholicism affirms every cultural situation as partner in God's work of salvation. This affirmation and absorbing of what is particular—the local scene—has lent Catholicism its charism to bond diverse peoples and yet encourage in each a strong sense of cultural identity, to be not only Catholic Christian but "Irish—or Italian, or American, etc.—Catholic."

The theological affirmation of what is local and particular translates philosophically into an appreciation for one's own culture and context. The catholic sentiment is to cherish one's roots, to draw upon and be proud of them—without becoming sectarian. Although none of our cultural origins is perfect, a catholic attitude is to appreciate them as one's "home" within the human family, as necessary to avoid getting lost on the journey of life. Catholicity as claiming one's roots is in marked contrast to the anomie encouraged by modern culture—and surely serves *for life for all.*

It was often noted of the late Tip O'Neill, former Speaker of the U.S. House of Representatives, that he never lost touch with his roots in Cambridge, Massachusetts. Although he was a universal person in so many ways and walked the halls of power with ease and distinction, he delighted in coming home to his neighborhood in North Cambridge, going for breakfast at the local diner, greeting old friends along the street. He coined the phrase "All politics are local." Tip was a "Catholic" in every sense of the term.

Universal Church as Catholic: *Grow Branches*
The flip side to Catholicism's affirmation of particular roots is its commitment to universality, to growing branches of outreach to all humankind. At the core of its catholicity, Catholic Christianity understands itself as universal in scope, with no limits of time, place, or people; as ever reaching into an open horizon of human history. According to Vatican II, "The Church transcends all limits of time and of race, [it] is destined to extend to all regions of the earth and so to enter into the history of [human]kind."[24] There is no person or people not invited to embrace its faith, no location beyond its mission, no vista beyond its horizon.

Similarly, every expression of human culture and creativity can enrich and be wedded with a life of Christian faith. As the Council stated well, Catholic faith should "uncover, cherish and ennoble all that is true, good, and beautiful in the human community."[25]

Likewise, everything fitting and moral to the human vocation—trade or profession, skill or art, sport or recreation, lifestyle or occupation—can be integrated with Catholic Christian identity. I think of an active Catholic I know who works as a pit boss at the local casino. Joe, raised a Southern Baptist, often jokes, "Thank God I became a Catholic—or I might be unemployed."

Although for many denominations casino pit boss would be an impossible profession to incorporate into Christian faith, the Catholic perspective is that, though hazardous and surely a challenge, it is possible for Joe to integrate his faith with his work, helping him to maintain his integrity and honesty, influencing how he treats people, prompting him to look out for the addicted and irresponsible, and so on. Although "fools rush in where angels fear to tread," yet if Joe's faith is up to the challenge, there is much good that he can achieve in his position.

Such latitude of Catholicism also has a catholic echo for the human condition. Since my next point emphasizes inclusivity toward all peoples, here I highlight openness of attitude—to life and to the world. A catholic person or community transcends boundaries, is never "hog-tied" by any time or place, keeps an open horizon. Catholicity promotes internationalism—mutual support, exchange and enrichment among all peoples and nations. It encourages delight in and celebration of the diversity of the human family. Although fostering a particular identity, it does so with global consciousness and universal concern.

A catholic person is open to grow, to change and develop, is ever curious about life's new possibilities. He or she has an attitude that anticipates surprises rather than fearing them, retains a childlike sense of wonder at the astounding diversity of human existence. Being catholic means having no limits to learning, never allowing oneself to stagnate on the journey of life. I have a friend Frank who took flying lessons in his early eighties and, having mastered that skill, went on to mountain climbing. I will not be surprised if he announces that he is getting married again. A staunch Unitarian since childhood, Frank has a catholic spirit about life.

People with a catholic attitude, too, appreciate the discoveries of science, enjoy the creativity of the arts, relish the wisdom of the humanities. Without falling into the modernist naiveté that the new is always better, catholics support the human push out into the horizons of consciousness and achievement. They welcome every discovery and invention, evaluating them by their potential to enhance human life and God's creation.

I read recently an author from an Anabaptist tradition lamenting the World Wide Web as a new technological evil that can lead people astray from their faith. Although I appreciate the integrity of his tradition and recognize some wisdom in his caution, my instinctive catholic response was in direct contrast. Like all technologies, the Internet can surely be abused, but essentially it is a gift from God through human ingenuity. This amazing new technology can and should be engaged to enhance human welfare—even to communicate Christian faith—lending new branches of outreach among all humankind.

An Inclusive Community: *Avoid "Totalizing Isms"*

I referred already to the fourth-century fight among Christians in North Africa about whether or not the Church could retain members who had publicly sinned. As a rigorist group, the Donatists insisted that only "saints" could belong. The special butt of their ire were some fair-weather Christians, people who denied their faith during persecution but in better times sought readmission to the Christian community. The Donatists insisted that they be barred. In mounting the counterattack on behalf of mainstream Christendom, Augustine argued that although the Church is *Corpus Christi* (the Body of Christ), it is also *corpus mixtum* (a mixed body) and should welcome saints and sinners alike—even apostates.[26]

Augustine may have favored such catholicity because he had tried both sin and sanctity with equal ardor himself. But he also remembered the early Church sentiment that favored the word *catholic* of the Christian community. As noted, the word *katholos*, which the early Christians found so fitting to describe their community, is best translated as "welcoming everyone." James Joyce may have expressed this sentiment most colorfully, some fifteen hundred years after Augustine, when he wrote in *Finnegans Wake* (1935), "Catholic means here comes everybody."

A catholic inclusivity of all peoples prompts similar open-mindedness regarding opinions. Although often stereotyped as a narrow and closed-minded monolith (and not without warrant), at its best, Catholic Christianity embraces great diversity and breadth of perspectives. Within the Catholic church one can find reactive restorationists who long for the days of an imperial papacy and liberationist radicals committed to left-wing revolutions in both church and society.

In many of the great theological disputes throughout history, its catholicity has prevented Catholicism from taking either/or positions, often holding divergent views in fruitful tension. A leading Catholic theologian, Richard McBrien, summarizes some prime examples of this "both/and" outlook:

> Catholicism is a comprehensive, all-embracing, catholic tradition, characterized by a both/and rather than an either/or approach. It is not nature or grace, but graced nature; not reason or faith, but reason illumined by faith;

not law or Gospel, but law inspired by the Gospel; not Scripture or tradition, but normative tradition within Scripture; not faith or works, but faith issuing in works and works as expressions of faith; not authority or freedom, but authority in the service of freedom.[27]

To welcome everyone regardless of their status and to exclude no one on any social basis is ever a pressing mandate for institutional Catholicism. The pages of history leave no doubt that the Catholic Church can readily commit all the forms of exclusion which have marked its social context—whether based on race, ethnicity, class, economics, gender, age, or sexual orientation. But surely the most pressing issue for prophetic attention within the structures of Catholicism today is the eradication of sexism and patriarchy. To be credibly catholic, the Catholic church must practice and be seen to practice (i.e., be a sacrament of) the full inclusion of women in every aspect of its mission and ministry. To continue otherwise seems eminently "non*catholic.*"

Many of the human values that mirror the theological inclusivity of Catholicism have been anticipated already. Here I highlight that catholicity should oppose all "totalizing isms" in society, in particular, puritanism, sectarianism, and fundamentalism. *Puritanism* is a self-righteous attitude that insists on total adherence to a rigorist position; it is essentially antihuman. Regarding *sectarianism,* let me reiterate a point made in chapter 1. With this term I in no way disparage the rich sectarian tradition that runs throughout the history of Christianity. Significantly, many of the sectarian groups have been most free of sectarianism. By the latter term, I mean a hardened attitude that absolutizes the true and the good in one's own group and disparages anyone who does not belong to it. It can be more destructive than puritanism in that sectarianism encourages active bigotry, often to the point of violence, toward anyone who is "different from us."

And because it spills over so readily into politics, I include *fundamentalism* here—a regrettable but growing phenomenon among the three great monotheist traditions: Christianity, Islam, and Judaism. Like its religious expression, social fundamentalism is a rabid intolerance for all modernist tendencies. It presumes that the true and the good are found in a literal interpretation of some original texts or by a return to a previous era—imagined as "golden." Catholicity is antithetical to all such "totalizing isms."

A Hospitable Community to All:
Take Initiative to Care without Borders

From its etymological root, "hospitality" means to welcome guests, with liberality toward strangers (*hospes*)—guests from outside one's community. The Hebrew Scriptures put a mandate on people of God to offer hospitality to "the alien." In Job's great speech of apologia, he claims, "I opened my door to wayfarers" (Job 31:32).

In the first Christian communities, hospitality was considered an important practice of discipleship. The epistles often urge Christians to "exercise hospitality" (Romans 12:13), and one of the conditions for becoming a bishop was to be hospitable (Titus 1:8). Such texts were written when hospitality to strangers was often a life-or-death issue—long before motels—yet it remained a sentiment within the heart of Christianity, a mark of its catholicity throughout the ages.

Beyond offering succor to "strangers," catholicity requires taking initiative to reach out with care to other peoples and especially to those most in need. This proactive outreach is epitomized in the example of the historical Jesus. Scholars point out that it was the practice of teachers in his day to have students come to them, but Jesus went out into the highways and byways, seeking those most in need of his presence—as he said himself, going out "to the lost sheep of the house of Israel" (Matthew 10:6).

In many of his miracles, Jesus is approached with a request, but as often again he takes the initiative to reach out. See, for example, his outreach to the woman bent over in Luke 13:10–17. In one of his most beloved parables—the Good Samaritan—the latter, who could have passed by like the priest and Levite, *went out of his way* to help the person in need. As a member of a despised ethnic group reaching out to one of his very despisers and taking initiative to do so, this Samaritan lives on forever as the epitome of catholicity as well as of love of neighbor—so symbiotic to each other.

The human value reflected in catholic hospitality and outreach has been well noted already. Here I highlight that all people live more humanly the more hospitable they are to those who are "different" from them and the more they reach out to strangers in need. Catholicity urges outreach beyond ourselves and our community, to stretch far beyond our own people, to actively look for opportunities to help others—without exception. It invites beyond rights and responsibilities to compassion and generosity, to go that extra mile, to love even enemies.

"Catholicity": A Summary

Being catholic entails an abiding love for all people with commitment to their welfare, rights, and justice. It welcomes human diversity, is open to learn from other traditions, and lives in solidarity with all humankind as brother and sister. A catholic cherishes her or his particular culture and roots of identity while reaching for an open horizon and a global consciousness. A catholic community is radically inclusive of diverse peoples and perspectives; is free of discrimination and sectarian sentiment; and welcomes "the stranger" with outreach, especially to those most in need.

Although it claims to reflect catholicity as a distinguishing mark, Catholicism's institutional expression often falls far short of sacramental witness to its realization—and likewise myself as a member. Perhaps it is clearer now why I told my friend at O'Hare Airport that "I'm trying to become a *catholic* Christian." The same can be said of my church—it is trying to become catholic, with signs and countersigns of progress. Likewise, Catholic schools must confront their lack of catholicity, and for this can be inspired by the example of hospitality to all typically found in the public schools of the Western democracies.[28]

For example, one often finds Catholic schools that exclude students who have learning challenges, whereas the local public schools usually welcome them and have concerted support programs—an instance of catholicity. Although it may be an ideal—achieved to perfection by no church or community, school or program, parish or family—yet the human heart—and most certainly the heart of an educator—should not settle for less than catholicity.

For Teachers and Parents

Being a cardinal characteristic of Catholicism, catholicity has already permeated the pedagogy proposed throughout the book.

The value of catholicity is reflected
— in a positive anthropology that affirms the essential goodness of all people and engages the whole person in the teaching/learning process;

413

— in a sacramental outlook that values every aspect of life in the world and looks to the "more" within the ordinary;

— in commitment to an inclusive community and to a communal way of learning; in a pedagogy that honors tradition—with breadth without limit and depth back over time;

— by a way of knowing that encourages people to think for themselves, to seek wisdom wherever it can be found, and to join the universal human quest for truth, goodness, and beauty.

And a catholic education engages the human spirit—the soul, the ultimate source of human solidarity—and educates for justice for all.

So, catholicity readily correlates with the other seven depth structures of Catholicism. And yet, catholicity can lend its own specific emphasis to humanizing education and to the vocation of teachers and parents. Pause first to note some of your own intuitions and insights about its implications for educators.

For Reflection

• In what ways do you recognize yourself as a catholic educator? Why?

• Imagine your school or program or family has decided to make a commitment to a thoroughly catholic education—a truly humanizing one that educates *for life for all*. Can you suggest a symbol or slogan to help sustain such commitment?

• What do you think catholicity asks of teachers' or parents' hearts? Of their style? Of the educational space?

For the Educator's Soul

I have two proposals for teachers' and parents' souls as persons, and two more pertinent to their vocation as educators. You will add from your own life and wisdom. I close this section with a special note on what catholicity might imply specifically for Christian religious educators—the people in the faith community entrusted with teaching Christian faith.

Develop Global Consciousness

Catholicity invites teachers and parents to a global consciousness. This means to look through the village to the world, to live and care for "the particular" in ways that open out to "the universal." The lifelong conversion of a catholic educator includes the following: to recognize oneself as a citizen of the global village; to feel bonded with all people and to care for their welfare as neighbors; to appreciate diversity and be open to learn from other cultures and wisdoms; to cherish one's roots and yet to transcend parochialism; to exclude no one and offer hospitality to all. Not that we should have achieved as much before beginning—waiting that long, one might never get started. But teachers and parents will do well to make such catholicity their heart's desire and strive toward it—the best way to foster it in learners.

Early during my first experience of schoolteaching—and feeling very lost—I was blessed to attend a workshop led by an old Christian Brother who had spent a lifetime in the classroom. Regretfully, I have forgotten his name, but I remember him as a creative artist in his approach to teaching. His key theme was to actively engage students, and he encouraged us student-teachers to allow our imaginations to run riot in creating interesting ways to teach whatever we were teaching.

The details of the workshop have long faded except for a piece of wisdom he repeated so often that it etched in my memory and remained: "To be a good teacher, you have to know what's goin' on in the students' own world—and in the big world outside of them as well." The first part I had heard before, but the second was new to me. I took him to heart and began raising issues "from the big world" with my students—national and international conflicts and crises, politics and human-interest stories from the news of the day. That old Brother had sown the seed of a global consciousness in me, and perhaps I did likewise in some of them.

A similar example is from another religious brother—Brother John, a Franciscan this time—who takes a large globe into his junior-high religion class on the first day of school each year and places it in the center. He explains that the globe will be a primary symbol of their time together and that he will put it in place for every class.

None of the young people expects a globe as a central symbol in religion class, so he has already engaged their interest and aroused their curiosity. As the year unfolds, he often draws to their attention world news items of social injustice, upheaval, or natural disaster—helping them to find the location on the globe. And no matter what theme of faith they study, Brother John brings them back to the question, "What does this mean for the world?" Every year his young people choose to devise programs of outreach to suffering and oppressed peoples in faraway places. Most likely, they have also grown in a global consciousness—a catholic consciousness—and from a faith perspective.

Educator as "Leading Learner"

Teachers and parents themselves are invited to be lifelong learners. A professor friend is fond of saying, "When you stop learning, stop teaching." If we close down our own learning, we become staid and routine, and our teaching becomes boring—even to ourselves. To teach something with infectious excitement, with *hilaritas*—hilarity—as Augustine recommended, it certainly helps if we expect to learn something ourselves.

Catholicity recommends breaking down the hierarchy between teachers and students, between educators and learners, and realizing that we are all learners together. Elsewhere I have written of the teacher as "leading learner."[29] The Latin *ducare* means to lead; my point is that the educator leads best as the number one learner. We educate most effectively when we allow ourselves to be addressed by our own statements and questions, by the statements and questions of our co-learners, and by the affairs of life and texts of tradition that constitute the curriculum.

Encourage Curiosity

Specifically for teaching, catholicity recommends that educators enliven in learners a spirit of curiosity—an unrelenting interest in the limitless horizons of life. All of us, at one time or another, have likely suffered through teaching that was "deadly," that could kill the spark of human interest. In my opinion, the most "deadly" teaching is what tells too much too finally, as if teaching is telling. The teacher knows it all, tells it all, and leaves the impression of no more to learn. As the great British philosopher Alfred North Whitehead commented of this kind of teaching, learners are taught to simply "pack away knowledge like items in a trunk." Case closed, but curiosity killed!

On the other hand, hopefully all of us have experienced educators—teachers and parents—who enlivened our interests and fanned our curiosity. What a great gift when we foster learners' innate desire to know! Real catholic educators stimulate an insatiable curiosity, a determination to go on mining the inexhaustible mysteries of life.

No age before us has had comparable resources for rendering ready access to the legacy of the sciences, arts, and humanities. Just compare a monk or nun in a medieval monastery taking half a lifetime to copy a text that today could be run off on a copying machine in a few minutes. With such technology readily available, we would expect that the educator's overt role in giving learners access to traditions of knowledge, art, and wisdom has receded—what with fine curricular texts, vast library resources, audio and video communications media, instant technology for storing and retrieving information, the Internet, and more. This adjustment in consciousness is still unfolding for many educators. For example, why should I expect my university students to transcribe a lecture I might deliver when I can readily make copies of my notes, distribute them, and have a conversation instead?

But, I am convinced that the teacher will always have an irreplaceable function in arousing and maintaining, guiding and resourcing curiosity. This point is well-demonstrated by the experience of home-school parents. They find that if good resources are available, the amount of didaction is greatly reduced and their primary function is to encourage learners' curiosity and guide their interests.

Provide Tools to Continue Learning

Catholicity encourages educators to provide learners with the tools needed to continue learning all of their lives. *Adult education should begin in kindergarten* in that children learn how to learn and become aware that there need never be an end to their learning. My friend Philip King, who has spent a lifetime teaching people the Bible, advises, "Teach everything so that the teacher coming after you can build upon it and add to it, rather than having to deny or undo what you taught."

He cites the example of the Bible story of creation. Even if teaching it to the youngest children, Philip counsels, do not teach it as literally true—somebody later, and surely the science teacher, will deny its data. Instead, present it as a great story with truths that they can continue to "learn" all of their lives, not of science but of faith— God as loving Creator, the goodness of ourselves, our responsibilities for each other and for creation. Then later, those children will encounter the discoveries of science or critical biblical scholarship as enhancing rather than threatening their journey in faith.

The key to forming the *habitus of lifelong learning* (an old scholastic term that includes both disposition and ability to do something) may be to encourage learners to make their own the basic principles and logic of whatever they are learning. One of the many valuable insights of Jerome Bruner, noted Harvard professor of psychology who did pioneering work in cognition, was that all the disciplines of learning have their own essential structure—ways of thinking, methods of investigation, and criteria. Essentially, every discipline reflects its own particular way of knowing.

Further, Bruner was convinced that each method of knowing can be taught to even the youngest children—at their own level of understanding—as if within the most complex ideas there is a radically simple one. Bruner's oft-quoted dictum, which has become a rubric of contemporary education, is that "any subject can be taught effectively in some intellectually honest form to any child at any stage of development."[30] The basic structure of any discipline is what people need to learn in order to keep on learning.

When children learn to diagram a complex compound sentence, they are learning the structure and syntax of a language. With this as their own, they can go on learning to speak and write well. When people come to see for themselves the logic behind a mathematical equation, they begin to think mathematically and will continue doing so in other contexts. Or when students learn basic theological principles, methods, and criteria, they begin to think theologically for themselves and are more likely to have the *habitus* of theology throughout their lives.

And now a reflection on what catholicity asks of Christian religious educators. This is an aside, but surely worthwhile. If any Christian community is to move toward catholicity, much depends on its religious educators and how the community shares its faith.

I am convinced that the catholic challenge for religious education is to help nurture people in particular Christian identity but to do so in ways that assiduously deter sectarianism and open them to appreciate and learn from the universality of religious faith—to be so grounded in the particular as to be open to the universal. This calls religious educators to do the following:

- Inform and form people in a thorough knowledge and deep love for their own *Christian tradition,* and yet never as a hardened ideology or "final" version of divine truth or as if Christianity is the only way to know and love God.

- Inform and form people in the identity of their *Christian community,* giving them a sense of home and belonging within God's family, but ever reminding them of God's "many mansions" and never teaching that "our group" are the only "people of God."

- Teach explicitly and throughout the curriculum *the universality of God's love,* encouraging deep respect and genuine care for all others—with no limit, as Jesus taught, to who is neighbor.

- Teach explicitly and throughout the curriculum the *universality of God's saving will,* encouraging commitment to God's reign of peace and justice, love and freedom, wholeness and fullness of life for all people—here and hereafter.

- Teach explicitly and throughout the curriculum *the universality of God's self-disclosure,* fostering respect for other religious traditions, readying people for dialogue with diverse perspectives.

For the Educator's Style
Again, much has been said already suggesting what catholicity might mean for teaching style. By way of emphasis, one point each about

content and process seems worth reiterating. As usual, the particular situation, school, parish program, family, theme, and participants must be taken into account.

Content for Catholicity

Catholicity recommends teaching curriculum that has as much depth and breadth as possible—within the limits of the curriculum and context. No one can teach everything about anything or be encyclopedic in knowledge, art, and wisdom. Yet every educator within her or his discipline and situation can have an expansive rather than a constricted scope of curriculum, inviting learners to push out to the cutting edge of what they already "know." Parents constantly have opportunities to help children expand their horizons, to convince them that there is always more to discover and learn. How refreshing it is, too, for a teacher or parent to say to learners, "I don't know." It dispels the stereotype of "know-it-all" and affirms that everyone has an open horizon. It also encourages openness in children if parents limit their own opinions to as few absolutes as possible.

Catholicity recommends that education welcome diversity of views and perspectives among participants—lending breadth to the curriculum. When educators show respect and hospitality for the diverse opinions of learners, it gives the latter confidence in their own contribution and encourages respect for the contribution of others—even those with whom they disagree.

Process for Catholicity

The teaching process reflects catholicity when it employs a variety of teaching methods and appeals to various learning styles. An educator can have a consistent and integral approach to teaching while employing many different methods. For instance, one can be committed to active participation by learners, or to giving direct access to traditions of wisdom or to encouraging personal appropriation and yet realize these commitments by many different methods.

Think for a moment of the myriad ways that a teacher can foster good conversation. Conversation is the style. the ways of effecting it— round robin, fishbowl, one-on-one, interview, role-play, cross-talk, and more—are methods. While maintaining integrity of approach, an educator can use a variety of methods, honoring the many learning styles among participants.

For the Educational Space

Like the other depth structures of Catholicism, the whole educational environment of the school, parish program, or family can be made to reflect catholic sentiments and commitments. Conversely, an ethos that encourages self-interest and parochialism, that limits learners' hearts to their own kind, closes their minds to lifelong learning, and that practices discrimination or indifference to the welfare of others is surely not a catholic environment.

When I was a very young boy, no more than six or seven, my family heard about a devastating famine that had broken out in some part of Africa—I forget the details now. My father—an inveterate reader of the daily newspaper—brought it to our attention and asked us to decide what we wanted to do for "those poor people dying of hunger on the other side of the world."

I remember him getting out an atlas and helping my brother Jimmy and myself to find Africa and the location of the famine, and yes, it seemed a great distance from our Irish village. But he kept repeating that "we are all children of God, and no one should be dyin' of hunger." I know we did something by way of contributing our pennies to the cause, but more significant was the catholic attitude my father was encouraging in us. He made us aware that a vast world extended beyond our small village and that we should care for all its people.

To create an environment that nurtures people's identity within a particular community and simultaneously encourages global consciousness and care requires particular attention to symbols. The hundred and one symbols that make up the life of the school, program, or family must be reviewed for their catholicity. An environment's symbols include everything that expresses and creates the life-world of a community.

Some symbols are so subtle or become so taken-for-granted to be no longer noticed by those closest to them, but they have an effect—subconsciously—nonetheless. An aspect of the educator's service to his or her community is to encourage it to review its symbols from the perspective of what they "teach" and whether or not they foster a humanizing worldview, value system, and identity.

Clearly, the leadership within a school, parish, or family is most responsible for such stewardship of community symbols. However, all participants can contribute to the catholicity of an environment. I think immediately of the often repeated instance of young people shaving their heads when a classmate is undergoing chemotherapy so that she or he does not feel left out. What a great symbol of catholicity!

As for every depth structure, space requires intentionality on the teacher's or parent's part, some imagination and attention to detail—even to things that may seem insignificant. With a bit of thought and effort, every environment can be made to reflect catholicity. Stop and look at your own school, parish, or family and imagine how you can enhance it as an environment that *nurtures its participants in solidarity and justice for all; respects and welcomes diversity; encourages openness and lifelong learning; and practices inclusion, welcome, and outreach to people in need.* I can immediately think of a half-dozen things for attention in my own context. Perhaps you can too!

For Reflection

- What do you agree or disagree with in these reflections on catholicity for education and the vocation of educator? Reflect on what brings you to take the positions that you do.

- What insights or proposals would you add to those here about catholicity and its challenge for teachers and parents?

- What decisions are emerging for your own teaching and environment in response to the challenge of catholicity?

Notes

1. For a classic expression of such a "stage" theory of human development, see James Fowler, *Stages of Faith.*
2. Ignatius of Antioch, "Letter to the Smyrnaeans," 8:2. in *Apostolic Fathers*, II/2. 311.
3. See Elisabeth Schussler Fiorenza, *In Memory of Her.*
4. St. Cyril of Jerusalem, *Catechetical Lectures*, 18: 23.
5. See chapter 1, endnote 31.
6. St. Vincent of Lérins, *Commonitories*, II, 3.
7. *The Catechism*, # 812.
8. "Constitution on the Church" #9, Abbott, *Documents*, 26.
9. "Decree the Missions," #10 and 3, Abbott, *Documents*, 598 and 586.
10. "Declaration on Non-Christian Religions" #1, Abbott, *Documents*, 661.
11. "Constitution on the Church" #16, Abbott, *Documents*, 35.
12. "Constitution on Revelation," #4, Abbott, *Documents*, 113.
13. "Constitution on Divine Revelation," #8, Abbott, *Documents*, 116.
14. "Declaration on Non-Christian Religions," #2, Abbott, *Documents*, 662.
15. "Decree on the Missions," #11, Abbott, Documents, 598.
16. "Declaration on Non-Christian Religions," #2, Abbott, *Documents*, 662.
17. Ibid., 663.
18. "Decree on Ecumenism," 4 and 1, Abbott, *Documents*, 342.
19. "Directory for the Application of Principles and Norms on Ecumenism," in Neuner and Dupuis, *The Christian Faith*, 364.
20. "Constitution on the Church," #1, Abbott, *Documents*, 15.
21. Ibid., #13, Abbott, *Documents*, 32.
22. "Constitution on the Church," #26, Abbott, *Documents*, 50.
23. "Decree on the Missions," #22, Abbott, *Documents*, 612.
24. "Constitution on the Church," #10, Abbott, *Documents*, 26.
25. "Church in the Modern World," #76, Abbott, *Documents*, 289.
26. St. Augustine's writings against the Donatists were many, but perhaps his most precise statement can be found in a treatise "On the Unity of the Church."
27. McBrien, *Catholicism*, 1190.
28. For this insight, I am indebted to a comment of Catherine Cronin Carotta, Boston College Summer School, 1997.
29. See Groome, *Christian Religious Education*, chapter 12.
30. Bruner, *The Process of Education*, 33.

❖

CHAPTER TEN

The Proposals in Review: "Keeping On" as Educators *for Life*

"If You Love Them"

Gussie Mootz was one of the loveliest and most delightful human beings I've ever met! Her name "Gussie" seemed onomatopoeic to her personality; she had an infectious wellspring of life. More than twenty-five years later, I still carry an indelible memory of her beautiful rounded face, the glint in her eyes, the impish smile, and oh, her hair—Gussie ever remained a dashing redhead.

Her faith and love for God were writ large in her compassion for people. It was clear that her largess of heart emanated from a spirituality well-honed by the struggles of life—she had experienced her share—and by disciplined care of the soul over many years. There are those rare individuals of such spiritual maturity that they enable others to experience a felt sense of God's presence. Gussie was such an icon of God's love, and a lot of fun besides.

When I met Gussie, she had long since retired from schoolteaching—but her reputation lived on. She was a legend in the folklore of Dodge City, Kansas, having spent her whole career in its public school system. By all accounts, she was an extraordinary teacher, famed for her ability to challenge students to reach for their own excellence. The story was that she was particularly effective with slow learners and "discipline problems."

Generations later, people still boasted about having Gussie as their teacher, and she had an uncanny ability to remember them too. I heard a child tell of Gussie paying her the compliment, "Oh, you're just as bright as your grandma was when she was in first grade."

For as long as anyone could remember, Gussie was a volunteer catechist in the parish program at Sacred Heart Cathedral and had helped with catechist formation. I came there fresh out of seminary—with all the insecurity this entails, but as typical, most intent on a camouflage. A year later, when becoming director of the parish religious education program, I allayed my anxiety with the thought of having Gussie to help.

I approached my first teachers' meeting—being in charge—with trepidation. I felt I had to win their confidence and was required to demonstrate my expertise as a religious educator—and I had so much of it back then! My anxiety was that subconsciously at least I knew how little I knew.

I met with Gussie beforehand to "review the agenda"—mainly to avoid making a fool of myself. She listened awhile, and then startled me by asking, "Why are you so nervous?"

In a moment of abandon—or maybe I sensed her genuine care—I decided to be honest: my lack of background, my fear of failure, not knowing what I was doing—really. Trying to end on a hopeful note, I said, "But I think I'll do okay if I can get the students to like me."

Gussie smiled and said, "That would be nice. But perhaps you might think of it the other way around—that you'll do fine if you learn to love them."

What a great idea! I resolved, there and then, to try to do as much for that year—renewable. Some twenty-five years later, Gussie remains a model of how to do it well.

"Reach for the Stars"

My reader surely agrees that I have proposed a challenging—even idealistic—spiritual vision for the educator and for the school, parish program, and family as well. I think of it as eutopian. I have spelled this word throughout with the *eu* because the roots of the more common *utopia* literally mean "no place"—an ideal beyond reach, whereas *eu-topos* means a "true place"—an ideal worth striving for. Being an educator is surely a eutopian vocation. Although the ideal is never fully realized by anyone—or by any school, program, or family—yet such a spiritual vision can inspire everyone to reach for their best selves as educators, to become "stars of heaven" (Daniel 12:3).

Becoming a *for-life-for-all* educator is surely a lifelong conversion—I know! I use conversion intentionally because of its spiritual connotation. Maturing as a teacher or parent is a spiritual journey. Of course, life is as much for everyone—a perennial process of conversion, but perhaps more than in most vocations, educators are called to holiness and wholeness of life precisely through their vocational work. Their praxis of educating is both source and expression of teachers' and parents' own spirituality.

In *Educating for Life* I have proposed a spiritual vision for educators, drawing inspiration from the depth structures of Catholic Christianity. This may appeal most readily to Catholic educators–teachers and parents who are Catholic Christians by faith confession and who educate in schools (parochial or public), parishes or families. I am convinced, however, that such a spiritual vision can have universal appeal. It reflects spiritual commitments that find echo across a broad spectrum of religious traditions and could be embraced by or at least might inspire the work of any educator, regardless of religious identity. And though they might never call theirs a catholic pedagogy—even with a small c—they will experience it as a humanizing one—a way of educating *for life for all.*

Embracing the spiritual vision of *Educating for Life* would mean allowing the philosophical convictions suggested by such depth structures to become operative convictions that seep into one's soul and then permeate how, what, why, and where one teaches—the whole curriculum.

So, a positive anthropology; a sacramental consciousness; commitment to relationship and community; appreciation for tradition; cultivating reason for wisdom of life; and the cardinal commitments of fostering holistic spirituality, formation in social justice, and inculcating a catholic worldview—all need to become embedded in an educator's persona and permeate how one fulfills her or his vocation. As teachers or parents make these commitments operative in the practice of education, they become their spiritual vision, nurturing their own holiness and wholeness of life. Conversely, as the educator's spirituality matures, these commitments are more consistently realized in her or his teaching.

For Reflection

   •Remember a few of your own "saints" in teaching—your Gussies. What strikes you as most important to take from their modeling of this noble vocation?

   •What are some of your eutopian hopes for your own educating? What aids their realization? What hinders?

   •Name some of the commitments that mark your vocation as educator. How did you come by them?

A summary of what each of the eight depth structures of Catholic Christianity suggests for the educator's soul, style, and space will give a cumulative sense of the spiritual vision proposal to teachers and parents throughout *Educating for Life*. I will hit only the high points in review!

For the Educator's Soul

A *humanitas anthropology* recommends for the educator as person an abiding spirit of affirmation, appreciation, and celebration of life and of human beings. Such positive perspective on the human condition recommends a perduring commitment to the whole person, to the learner as agent-subject, and to education that fosters human rights and responsibilities.

A *sacramental cosmology* recommends that a teacher or parent personally cultivate a sacramental consciousness—a sense of the "more in the midst"—and a spirit of contemplation toward life. For their teaching, it suggests encouraging learners to look for meaning and for "the more" in life, to use their imaginations and aesthetic gifts, and to develop an ecological consciousness, becoming good stewards of creation.

A *"community-of-persons" sociology* urges educators to be committed public servants who educate in ways that promote the "common good." Teachers and parents can educate for communities of common care by fostering cooperation and partnership among learners.

Appreciation of *history's legacy of tradition* calls for core curriculum in general education that is humanizing; available to all;

and lays the intellectual, moral, and aesthetic foundations needed for every vocation. For Christian religious education, appreciation of tradition recommends access to the whole Story and Vision of Christian faith and then to other traditions as well.

Appreciation of history and tradition also invites teachers and parents themselves to grow as educated and cultured participants in life. Their teaching should help to conserve the most humanizing traditions and to draw new life from them—a dual responsibility.

A *wisdom epistemology* invites educators to a deep passion for truth—to pursue it, to live it, to teach it. Their teaching should reflect commitment to "the whole truth": cognitive, relational, and moral.

Taking *spirituality* seriously invites teachers and parents to care for their own souls and to see their vocation as a spiritual one—enabling learners to live into the mystery and depths of life, to become "fully alive" to the glory of God.

To *educate for justice* invites teachers and parents to a personal passion for justice. Their teaching and environment should be marked by right relationships. They must teach for justice at every level of human existence and can make a personal "option for the poor" themselves by special care for learners who need extra help and encouragement.

Catholicity invites educators to a global consciousness and ever to be "leading-learners." Such teachers and parents foster learners' openness of mind and heart, stimulate curiosity, and help prepare them for lifelong learning.

For the Educator's Style

Rather than a summary list from previous chapters of what the eight depth structures of Catholic Christianity might imply for the educator's style, here it may be more helpful to weave together a humanizing pedagogy that could be used—with adaptation—to mediate a great variety of educational events. First, I offer two general proposals apropos a style of teaching *for life for all*—one about the ethos of a teaching event; the other, regarding the essential dynamic of a humanizing pedagogy.

The Ethos and Essential Dynamic of a Humanizing Pedagogy

By way of overall ethos, a humanizing approach to teaching suggests a community of co-learners in conversation. Stylistically, this means encouraging everyone present to actively participate, creating conversation and fostering partnership, stimulating and welcoming the contributions of all.

The essential dynamic of a humanizing pedagogy is to mediate between people's lives in the world and the legacy of tradition—in the humanities, sciences, and arts; and for religious education, in the Story and Vision of its community of faith over time. For convenience, let us call this pedagogy mediating between Life and Tradition. The educator renders the service of helping people to bring themselves and their Life to Tradition—seeking what they need to live humanly, and to bring Tradition to Life—appropriating what is life-giving for self and others.

So, for a humanizing pedagogy I suggest an overall dynamic of from Life to Tradition to Life, to Tradition to Life to Tradition, and so on—in an endless and creative exchange between learners' own lives in the world and the legacy of those before and around them. In religious education, the dynamic is bringing Life to Faith and Faith to Life—again, in an ongoing cycle.

Many authors and experiences have influenced my recommending a Life/Tradition/Life process of teaching. Paulo Freire's pedagogy, with his emphasis on beginning with and ever returning to peoples' own praxis in the world, has been particularly influential. But Gussie ranks near the top of my communion of teachers who encouraged this simple and innocent-looking—yet so challenging and potentially transforming—pedagogy.

Commitments of a "For Life for All" Style of Teaching

Taking it that an educator commits to creating communities of participation and conversation and to using a generic process that intermingles Life and Tradition, what might be the design that they bring to structuring an educational event—a class, session, or presentation, an intentional exchange, encounter, or conversation? My response is to propose seven commitments that might mark a *for-life-for-all* style of teaching. There are likely others too, and subcommitments within each, but these seven combined would likely amount to a humanizing pedagogy: *engaging, attending, expressing, reflecting, accessing, appropriating,* and *deciding.*

While I set them out separately, no single one can be realized without some of the others. For example, to personally engage is to get learners to begin attending to life and reflecting upon it. to give access to tradition is to encourage reflection and to enjoin learner's engagement and attention. appropriation requires giving access to tradition and encouraging reflection, and so on, with each of these commitments depending on and overlapping with each other. And yet, for clarity and by way of emphasis, these commitments can be distinguished if only to heighten the consciousness of educators to include and combine them within their teaching style.

Although they do have a logical pattern as I lay them out—e.g., engagement should mark the beginning and decision is more likely toward the end—in a real-life teaching situation, these seven commitments would never be realized in any fixed sequence or be confined to one moment—engagement must continue throughout and decision can emerge any time.

These are pedagogical commitments to be honored regularly throughout an educational event or across a number of meetings and not a lockstep process to be followed in sequence. Setting the seven out as a schema can heighten the intentionality of the educator and, while avoiding a rigid pattern, may suggest the dynamics of a humanizing pedagogy.

Engaging

The key commitment here for the educator is to draw learners into active participation from the beginning and to maintain their "interest" throughout. Little of life-significance can be learned when people are not personally engaged in the educational process. On the other hand, when the pedagogy reaches into the core of learners, when it gets them really interested and involved, significant learning is almost inevitable and the outcome more likely to be of wisdom. And the more the whole person is engaged—head, heart, and hands— the more likely that a humanizing education is being achieved. The pinnacle of personal involvement is to enlist people's souls—the very core of their "being."

It seems obvious, but nonetheless worth stating, that personal engagement requires turning learners to something of genuine interest to them. Think about it—have you ever learned anything of substance or significance for your life when you were not really interested? At best rarely, and somewhat miraculously!

The most likely way to stimulate interest is to turn people to their own resources and to their situations in the world—to their Life. Of course, much depends on the topic and context, the occasion and participants, but we are engaged most readily by what is of real interest to us—to our existence.

Honoring people's interests, however, poses a "two-edged" task for the teacher or parent. I am convinced that educators must not only engage learner's felt interests but must stimulate and educate their interests as well. I cite again the example of my friend who teaches music in junior high school. She begins in September with the music in which students express immediate interest—"alternative" music— but by Christmas has them listening to Mozart.

When I enter the university classroom to teach undergraduate theology, students may have little interest in the topic of the day, but with some effort to dip into their lives I can usually get them interested. As I am sure is required of every educator, I try to honor what learners are interested in, but I also try to get them interested in what I should teach. The clue to honoring both "sides" of people's interest is to employ their own lives. This takes imagination and preparation, with the educator pausing often to wonder "How can I engage learners' lives so that I teach what they are interested in and they become interested in what I teach?"

The great Maori educator Sylvia Ashton Warner built her approach to teaching literacy around everyday words from children's immediate world. She would begin by having young children choose and "bring" to school each day at least one word that they would like to be able to spell and write. She accepted their important words as the literacy curriculum—regardless of propriety. She found that children were eager to learn their life-interest words, and she made the underlying insight the foundation of her very effective pedagogy.[1] In a different culture, the original insight of Paulo Freire's pedagogy— centered on life praxis—was similar to that of Ashton Warner.

Active involvement in an educational event does not mean everyone being hyperactive or talking incessantly. All persons have their own style of learning and participating. The quieter ones—the introverts on the Myers-Briggs personality indicator—can be just as actively engaged in learning as the expressive extroverts. It is simply that the participation of introverts is more internal and more selective in expression.

Attending

An old stereotype put upon teachers is that they are forever struggling to get students to "pay attention"—usually to what the teacher is telling them. I propose that encouraging learners' attention should be an educator's commitment, not as something that they "pay"—as if it costs a lot—but rather attending to everything that comes into their experience, initiative, and consciousness.

The educator is like a troubadour who awakens people to "take a look" and "make a difference," to observe, absorb, and actively engage in their world. I use *world* here as in chapter 3 to mean, first, people's own immediate existence (the personal life inside and outside of them that they experience and contribute to) and then their social, political, and cultural world, which includes the traditions of humanities, sciences, and arts that are the "funded capital of civilization" over time. And I use *attending* with both its passive and active connotations—both to absorb one's world (as in "being attentive") and to help care for and create it (as in "tending" to).

So, far beyond concern for what the pedagogue is saying, a *for life for all* educator is committed to learners "attending" as looking at, listening to, and drinking in their world and as engaging in, contributing to, and being responsible for their life-world.

To attend begins with the five senses of touching, tasting, smelling, hearing, and seeing. Getting learners to pay attention to the data of their senses—both what comes their way and what they initiate or look for—honors the first moment of human attending. Beyond this, the educator must encourage learners to attend to the whole "world of meaning" that they are creating and that comes to meet them from their encounter with and active participation in life and, broadening out, from the cultures created by humankind over time—the worlds of meaning reflected in the traditions of wisdom, knowledge, and aesthetic that is their human heritage. Getting people to attend to their whole life-world—receiving and creating it—is a core commitment of the for life for all educator, essential to a humanizing pedagogy.

It is possible to attend to the world in a purely instrumental way—to figure it out, conquer and control it, to use it for one's own benefit. It is also possible to approach the world defensively and with suspicion. Neither is the attending of an education *for life for all*.

More humanizing by far is to attend to the world as a gracious mystery, with curiosity, with appreciation, and even with relish; to enter into a relationship of receiving and contributing, as gift and responsibility, respecting the world for what it is and oneself as an agent within it—an enriching exchange. I know a woodwork instructor in a technical high school who teaches students to always pause over a piece of wood—to notice its grain and texture and the beauty of it— before proceeding to work on it. He gets them to "pay attention"!

Attending to the world can merge into a sacramental outlook on the part of learners, when the educator encourages them to see the "more" in the midst of the ordinary, the giftedness of the everyday. Stretching deep into a sacramental perspective, educators can encourage learners to attend to the world in a contemplative way—to encounter it with the gaze of wonder and awe, to enter into a conscious sense of presence to the mystery of it all.

Lest this sound far-fetched, note that a core conviction of the great Italian educator Maria Montessori was that even the young child is, at heart, a contemplative. Her whole "Montessori method" is based on creating a personal and sensory encounter between the child and their world, allowing the child to absorb it through the kind of contemplation associated with play.

Anyone who has ever observed a small child methodically repeat an exercise, over and over—like pouring water from a glass to a bowl and back again, mesmerized by the activity and as if lost in time—will not doubt Montessori's sense of the child as contemplative. So, beginning from the most fundamental activity of the senses—"taking a look" at the data—and stretching to the heights of contemplation, the educator is to encourage learners to attend to their world. The "exchange" that emerges is the lifeblood of humanizing education.

Expressing

The stereotype is to think of teaching as telling and learning as listening, forgetting that self-expression is essential to learning for oneself. Only by "putting it out there" do we recognize it ourselves and come to know more deeply. From its Latin root, *to express* literally means going out of oneself to be present with others. In expressing, we express our very selves, and so we contribute to our own becoming—fully alive.

What learners express can be their thoughts, feelings, and doings from their world within and without; their "naming" of what is "going on" in the world around them or what happens as they encounter the traditions of wisdom, knowledge, and art in their world of meaning. *How* learners express themselves can be by any mode of human communication. The readiest and most obvious mode is speaking, but imaginative educators will encourage all modes of expression: writing, composing, drawing, painting, creating, miming, gesturing, physical signs, and more.

To emphasize expressing is not to neglect receiving, but to recast the latter into an exchange mode instead of a one-way delivery and reception. Certainly, in a conversational process, expressing presumes people are willing to receive, but conversely, it counts on a readiness to receive on the part of those willing to express. Think about it— expressing oneself in conversation can never be a "one-way street"— or it is not a conversation.

We can receive by many modes too. Listening is the most obvious, and then reading, deciphering, calculating, reviewing, sharing together, entering into an experience, physical touch, and so on. We receive much from our life-world mentally and physically, but likely we acquire what is most humanizing through the heart. Heartfelt receiving requires empathy and compassion toward life, having a "listening heart"—the gift that Solomon asked of God, making him famous for his wisdom ever after (see 1 Kings 3:9).

When at all possible, I invite participants to express themselves early in an educational event and then often throughout. Sometimes the first commitment of engagement may need to be more teacher-directed to get things going. But as soon as learners are engaged and attending to the curriculum theme, the educator might consider encouraging them to express themselves. In my university context, even professors who invite student comments typically assume that this should come after their lecture—a lot of receiving and often quite passive. But with a bit of imagination, whatever the theme or context, teachers can encourage learners to express themselves from the beginning and throughout.

Even when I find myself in a convention context, with organizers and participants expecting a lecture-type presentation, I often pause after bringing attention to my theme—hopefully, in an engaging way—and invite participants to take some notes of what they already know or believe or feel or do regarding the topic. Then I pause from time to time and invite participants to share with a neighbor what they are thinking or feeling or intuiting in response to my proposals (note appropriation dipping into access and being realized as expression—all mixed up together).

Reflecting

To know as a person, learners must reflect on what they are learning. Knowledge passively received without becoming one's own through reflection is less humanizing. Regarding every aspect of their lives in the world and every aspect of the humanities, sciences, and arts that they encounter, learners need to think for themselves. And as raised up from a number of angles throughout *Educating for Life*, as learners think for themselves, educators should prompt them to use their whole mind—reason, memory, and imagination.

Reflection includes listening to the ruminations of the body—to the skills, intuitions, and common sense that are stored there. The body has its own wisdom, felt intuitions, and corporeal-carried memories from all that it has lived through. Note that the word *biography*, from the Greek *bios graphia*, literally refers to what is "written on bodies," as if the body forgets nothing. To prompt learners to draw upon and reflect on their own biographies—to "tell their own story"—is to include their bodies in the process of reflection. Reflection also means becoming aware of feelings and emotions and probing them for both wisdom and deception.

As noted many times in other chapters, reflection becomes "critical" in the discerning and creative sense as people consciously take account of their historical context—when their reflection includes probing their everyday lives and what is going on in their world. Personal critical reflection uncovers my own wisdom and interests, my biographical knowledge and influences, and imagines new possibilities for me.

Social critical reflection analyzes one's public world, sees its linkages and systems, gets a sense of the "whole picture," and does so with both appreciation and question, judgment and imagination of communal possibilities. Together, personal and social reflection can be described metaphorically as becoming aware of one's "story" and "vision."

Although clearly age-related and with people's capacity for it developing in stages, the seeds of reflection can be sown early by encouraging children to think for themselves, albeit in a concrete manner. I overheard a wonderful parent, Mary, having a conversation with her three-year-old son, Conner, who persisted in requesting a rice crispy treat just before his lunch. She took him aside from the company for a one-on-one conversation. I was within listening distance. More by reflective questions (like "Why do we not want you to have a treat just before lunch?" and "Why should we wait until after lunch?") than by directives, Mary helped Conner to see why his request could not be met until later. To my amazement, and although still a bit reluctant, he agreed to wait until "yater" (not yet pronouncing *L*s). I wager that he is already on his way to being able to think for himself, and to think critically.

Reflection, like all of these teaching commitments, should permeate the entire educational event. There is a kind of logical sequence to first attending to something from life or tradition and then reflecting on it, but reflection is already present in the very act of attending and is needed throughout all seven commitments of a humanizing pedagogy. This is simply to say that educators should encourage learners to think all the time.

Accessing the Wisdom, Knowledge, and Aesthetic of the Ages

Every generation of humankind is entitled to have access to the legacy of wisdom, knowledge, and aesthetic assembled in the humanities, sciences, and arts. In religious education, people's entitlement is first to the Story and Vision of their own faith community and then, as fitting, to that of other faith communities.

This legacy of history should be represented as an inexhaustible source of new life. Teachers and parents have a pivotal function in seeing to it that learners get to draw deeply and in life-giving ways from their "family" inheritance. No one school, parish program, or family can possibly teach the complete legacy of humankind, and no one person can appropriate more than a fraction of it. But everyone deserves to have access to sufficient educational resources for a breadth and depth of tradition—general and religious—enough, at least, to sustain a decent quality of life.

I use the term *access* because it has the connotation of encounter between learners and tradition, with learners as active agents who rediscover the tradition for themselves more than having it "poured in" or "delivered." Educators also need to be clear and intentional about why they are giving learners access to tradition and allow their purpose to shape how they do it.

I suggest that teachers and parents not settle for people "knowing about" their heritage but that, echoing a recurring refrain since the beginning of the book, they intend that this heritage touch people's lives, form their "being," be an influence *for life for all*. Educators can give access to tradition in ways that encourage learners to make it their own—choosing what it means for their lives and for the world.

Appropriating

As learners engage, attend, express, reflect, and have access to tradition, the abiding intent of the educator must be to bring them to their own knowledge and wisdom, to have them appropriate from Life and Tradition what they see, understand, judge, and decide—*for life for all*. Appropriation means learners coming to knowledge and wisdom as embraced rather than submitted to, as experienced with conviction instead of accepted on outside authority. That teaching encourage such personal appropriation seems key to its affecting people's "being" in life-giving ways.

The teacher or parent promotes appropriation more by questioning than telling, more by inviting than exacting, more by guiding than directing. Appropriation often entails waiting—the discipline I find most difficult as a teacher—for learners to come to see for themselves, to make something their own. But there is no shortcut to wisdom or formative knowledge. I have a teacher friend who often says, "People are never ready to know more than their own lessons." This often requires great patience on the part of an educator, but as any artist will attest, no great work of art can be hurried.

In the overall pedagogy I am proposing, appropriation is most likely to take place as people move from Tradition back to Life again. It is the beginning of the third moment in the "from Life to Tradition to Life" dynamic. However—worth repeating—appropriation should not be limited to any particular moment, but should be the conscious intent of the educator throughout—present from the beginning.

Deciding

A pedagogy that humanizes must invite people to choices and commitments. If educators do not invite learners to decision, they settle for them "knowing about" things in their heads. They stop short of uniting "knowing" with "being," of wedding knowledge with responsibility—of wisdom. Given the endless variety of educational events, the choices and decisions that emerge can be myriad, with varied or combined emphases—cognitive, affective, or behavioral. However, the pedagogy should dispose people to choose as fitting to the particular event.

Prompting learners to decision should be an invitation—not an expectation—respecting participants' freedom of choice. To do otherwise would be unjust. And although there is a logic to decision making toward the end of an event, I reiterate that the *for life for all* educator has this purpose from the beginning and allows it to shape the pedagogical process throughout.

Caring for the Teaching Space

Throughout the book, space has pertained more to the overall environment of the school, parish program, or family than to the vocation of individual educators. Self-evidently, however, teachers can care for the quality of their own immediate space (typically a classroom or meeting place) and can contribute to the overall educational environment (typically a school or parish), helping to create an ethos more likely to form the character of participants for life for all. Helping to create a life-giving space is certainly the opportunity of parents. Although they must contend with other major influences upon the ethos of the home (e.g., American children watch, on average, thirty hours of television each week), yet parents can take initiative to create a home environment that educates for life for all.

In summary from the previous chapters, teachers and parents can enhance their educational space in humanizing ways by doing the following:

— Helping to build community—human and, as fitting, religious;

— Welcoming diversity, practicing inclusivity, offering hospitality to all;

— Giving people encouragement, challenge, and a sense of their own dignity;

— Nurturing character in the values of respect, responsibility, and reverence;

— Teaching in ways that are just and that help to form learners in living justly;

— Giving opportunity for service and direct care for others;

— Encouraging openness, thoughtfulness, and moral reflection;

— Attending to the aesthetic of the space, and nurturing imagination;

— Fostering moral and spiritual formation, especially by example.

For Reflection

• What helps you to "keep on" as a teacher or parent?

• From your experience as an educator, if you had one piece of advice to give to a beginning teacher or parent, what would it be?

"Keeping on" As Educators For Life For All

In chapter 7, I suggested some spiritual practices that can help educators care for their own souls. What I offer here in closing is not so much "practices" as spiritual attitudes that can sustain teachers and parents to "keep on" in their work of educating for life, not only to survive but to thrive—albeit experiencing times when surviving seems the order of the day. You will add other suggestions for helping to "stay the course" of humanizing education from your own tradition and experience.

Think of Educator As a Vocation

Catholic Christians have a strong tradition of using the term vocation, but, regretfully, in typical parlance it got reduced to mean becoming a priest or vowed religious. Now, with the reclaiming of an "inclusive spirituality" and of a more traditional understanding of baptism (chapter 7), Catholicism reflects growing awareness that everyone has a vocation. From the Latin *vocatus* meaning "called," every person has a vocation to make the most of their lives for the reign of God—fulfilling God's life-giving desire for all humankind and the integrity of creation.

For a few, their vocation may entail living the evangelical virtues of poverty, chastity, and obedience—the vowed life will hopefully always remain a cherished charism in Catholic Christian understanding of vocation. Far beyond this, however, God calls everyone to live the great theological virtues of faith hope and love in some life-world particular to each person.

We find our vocation when we discern our own deepest desires, gifts, and aptitudes, and correlate these with what is worthwhile and needful in the world. The "desire" for what to do with one's life and the "needs" one encounters for response will be particular to each person, and God's invitation to all is to let desire and need meet and mesh. Thomas Landy elaborates insightfully and precisely with educators in mind:

> Vocation is that sense that nourishes us in our best moments. We sense that we are for some reason meant to do what we are doing, that our work is of inherent value to others and to us, not merely a way of passing the days or collecting a check. The origin of that sense of purpose lies outside of ourselves—it is not merely an invention of our own selves—yet is intimately connected to who we are as individuals, to our own particular gifts, talents, and sources of contentment. . . . For religious people, the notion of vocation is inherently tied up with our relationship with God.[2]

Surely being an educator—teacher or parent—is an eminent instance of Landy's description of vocation. What work could be of more "inherent value to others," and, may I propose, more "tied up with our relationship with God."

The vocation of educator is its own particular way of living the great virtues of *faith, hope,* and *love.* It requires faith in "the Teacher within" who inspires learners to respond—by God's grace; faith in oneself as equal to the challenge—by God's grace; and a profound faith in learners as inherently good and having great possibilities for living humanly—by God's grace.

Being educator is a vocation to hope and never to lose hope that in the end "all will be well." This is the lovely phrase of the amazing fourteenth-century mystic Julian of Norwich (circa 1342–1420).[3] Julian, often using feminine imagery for God, imagined all people and creation to be "enfolded" as in God's womb. Her extraordinary sense of God's mothering love gave her the unshakable conviction that "all will be well." St. Paul counseled that hope is truly a virtue only when challenged—when one cannot "see" what is hoped for. (See Romans 8:24–25.) By the very nature of their work, the vocation of educators is "long-term." They simply must take the "long view" in order to stay the course.

And perhaps most of all, educator is a vocation to love—often stretched and tested to the limits. Is it simplistic to say, as Gussie Mootz said to me, "You'll do fine if you love them"? I do not think so. I have relearned so often the wisdom of her words!

Do Not Overinvest in "Success"

I put success in quotes to signal, as commented in chapter 8, that educators need to redefine it away from its connotation in popular consciousness. The exaggerated notion of "success" in Western society is to solve a problem or meet a challenge completely. In Western education, the stereotype of success means every learner turning out "well"—measured socially by the power, fame, or fortune they achieve.

Educators, of course, should hope to be successful with all learners, but must define this as whether or not their efforts are humanizing in learners' lives, whether people make a "life" for themselves and contribute *for life for all*. And even with the best of efforts, mysteriously, no teacher or parent can "win 'em all." Perhaps educators have something to learn from the humility of the child throwing sand dollars back into the ocean one at a time. to educate even one life for the better is always a great achievement—especially "to that one"! And it lasts for eternity.

Reflect Often on Your Own Praxis

Heralded by John Dewey, a truism of educational theory is that we learn little from experience unless we reflect on it. Surely it behooves educators to take time regularly to reflect on their praxis of educating and how it is faring. Over the years, I have found this discipline most helpful in "keeping on" and in nurturing my lifelong conversion as an educator.

Coming away from a class or workshop, sermon or retreat, I find myself asking questions such as "What did I try and what happened?" (naming present praxis) and then reflective questions such as "What went well and why?" "What did not go so well—even poorly—and why?" "Were my own contributions and interventions fitting?" "Did I relate appropriately to other participants?" "What can/will I do differently next time?" The potential of such reflection is enhanced if shared with another person or support community. My spouse, Colleen Griffith, and I regularly share review of our teaching and learn much from reflecting on each other's praxis.

Remember Your Partnership with God

To be teacher or parent is to be a special instrument of God's grace in learners' lives. Ultimately, to educate is God's own work. Education is an eminent way that God realizes the divine desire for people to come to fullness of life. So, God's Holy Spirit—not the human agent—is always the primary educator. Often place yourself and your educating in the hands of "The Educator."

Remembering our partnership with God should lighten educators' sense of burden for the outcome of our efforts—much to our relief. Oh, because grace works through nature, teaching is no laissez-faire business. Educators are always responsible to make our own best efforts. But the "learning outcome" does not depend on our efforts alone, nor even on those of learners. There is an "actual" grace—an everyday divine gift—that works through educational events. "The Educator" is ever present to our efforts.

In chapter 1 we noted the promise of the Book of Daniel to educators that "those who teach others unto justice shall shine like the stars of heaven forever" (12:3). To conclude this spiritual vision for teachers and parents, I mix in the farming imagery of St. Paul. It seems apt for educators whose work is never more than one moment in a person's education. Our efforts may be like one seed in a planting, or a time of nurturing what others have planted.

In our wisdom, we know that we cannot "force results"—they are always by gift—nor can we enjoy a final harvest this side of eternity. And yet we can take heart from our partnerships—with God, with other educators, and with learners. Sustained by our spiritual vision, we can keep on, knowing that sometimes we sow, other times we water, and God "gives the growth." (See 1 Corinthians 3:6–7.)

For Reflection

- What other suggestions would you add to help sustain educators in educating for life?

- What is the next step in your own spiritual journey as a teacher or parent?

- With whom would you like to share the spiritual vision that has emerged from your conversation with *Educating for Life*? How will you share it? When?

Notes

1. See Sylvia Ashton Warner, *The Teacher*.
2. Thomas M. Landy, "Collegium and the Intellectual's Vocation to Serve," 21.
3. Julian uses this phrase often throughout her work *Showings*.

INDEX

Pacem in Terris, 114

pacificism

    radical, 28, 56, 61, 86, 88–89, 91, 185, 187, 256, 305, 334, 343, 362, 368, 374, 384

Pakistan, 9–12, 21, 40, 48

    educational system, 10, 50

    government, 10, 41, 45, 48, 52, 73, 193, 213, 255, 307

papacy, 17, 240–242, 364, 410

papal, 47, 236, 240, 342, 373, 392

    authority, 39, 41, 56, 111, 181, 188, 217, 232, 239–244, 273, 299, 342, 370–371, 411, 438

    charter, 47

    magisterium, 240–242, 264

parochialism, 41, 44–45, 394–396, 399, 415, 421

parochial schools, 252, 325, 331, 338, 427

Parousia, 324

Pascal, Blaise, 331

patriarchy, 43, 188, 376, 411

"peaceable kingdom," 305

Pedagogic Creed, 39, 64, 213–214, 297, 317

pedagogy, 12, 25–26, 38, 45, 62, 103–105, 107, 142, 162, 164, 232, 235–236, 311, 313, 319, 326, 332, 339, 350–351, 360, 389, 413–414, 427, 429–433, 437–439

pedagogies, 103, 105–106, 167, 388

    humanizing, 10, 13–18, 20–21, 26–27, 29, 36–37, 44–46, 48, 53, 61, 73–74, 92, 105, 136, 154, 156, 205, 219, 221, 229, 232, 234–236, 244–249, 255–256, 261–262, 274, 277, 281, 284–285, 288, 290, 292, 298, 300, 303, 308, 324, 332, 345, 351, 361, 386–387, 414, 421, 427–431, 433–437, 439–440, 442

    monastic, 47–48, 234–235, 281–282, 295, 316, 343–344

of social consciousness, 194, 363, 388

Pelagius, 88–89

Pentecost, 339, 398

    Sunday, 117, 177, 237, 252, 339, 349

people of God, the, 54, 79, 176–177, 179, 184, 189, 213, 224, 347, 365, 401, 406, 419

Perkins School for the Blind, 97

Petrine, 240

    doctrine, 42, 47, 62, 76, 224, 343

    office, 240, 301, 313

philosophers, 20, 37, 70, 104, 118–119, 122, 132, 134, 137, 149, 151–152, 160, 175, 180, 193, 235, 270–271, 275–277, 304, 324, 370

    ancient, 26, 39, 45, 73, 77, 111–112, 122, 132, 134, 137–138, 149, 152, 160–161, 180, 183, 190, 192–193, 233, 242, 248, 250, 261, 272, 275, 277–279, 304, 317, 324, 347, 356, 364, 373, 405

    Enlightenment, 48, 80, 105, 176, 193, 217, 243, 273–278, 280, 284, 286, 300–301, 303–304

    modern, 25, 28, 45, 59, 70, 80, 112, 115, 119, 123, 144, 152, 158, 176, 187, 196, 216–217, 223, 236, 250–251, 257, 264, 276, 296, 351, 370, 378, 382, 386, 392, 407, 423

    pre-Socratic, 270

    scholastic, 59, 126, 151, 235, 241, 282, 362, 418

philosophy, 10–13, 16, 18–21, 23, 26, 29–30, 41, 44–46, 59, 61–62, 64, 70–71, 73, 85, 96, 118, 137, 148, 150, 160–161, 175–176, 190, 192, 217–219, 221–222, 226, 235, 241, 251, 264, 282, 301–302, 316–317, 322, 344, 370

    for teachers and parents, 11, 18, 36, 45–46, 62, 93, 103, 120, 131,

BIBLIOGRAPHY

Abbott, Walter. *The Documents of Vatican II*. Translated by Joseph Gallagher. New York: America, 1966.

Adams, Dennis M. *Cooperative Learning: Critical Thinking and Collaboration across The Curriculum*. By Dennis Adams, Mary Hamm, with the collaboration of Martha Drobnak and Althier Lazar. Springfield, Ill: C.C. Thomas, 1996.

Alcoff, Linda and Elizabeth Potter, eds. *Feminist Epistemologies*. New York: Routledge, 1993.

Apostolic Fathers. Edited by Jack N. Sparks. Nashville: T. Nelson, 1978.

Aquinas, Thomas. *Summa Contra Gentiles*. Notre Dame, IN: University of Notre Dame Press, 1955–57.

―――. *Summa Theologica*. 5 vols. Translated by the Fathers of the English Dominican Province. Westminster, MD: Christian Classics, 1981.

―――. "The Teacher." In *Basic Writings in Christian Education*. Edited by Kendig Brubaker Cully. Philadelphia: Westminster Press, 1960.

Aristotle. *Nicomachean Ethics*. Cambridge, MA: Loeb Classical Library, 1982.

Armstrong, Karen. *A History Of God: The 4000-Year Quest of Judaism, Christianity, And Islam*. New York: A.A. Knopf, 1993.

Ashton-Warner, Sylvia. *Teacher*. New York: Simon and Schuster: 1963.

Athanasius. *On the Incarnation*. Translated by a Religious of CSNV, Crestwood, New York: SVS Press, 1982.

Au, Wilkie. *By Way of the Heart: Toward a Holistic Christian Spirituality*. New York: Paulist Press, 1989.

Augustine. "The First Catechetical Instruction." Translated by Joseph P. Christopher. In *Ancient Christian Writers*, vol. 2. Westminster, MD: Newman Press, 1962.

―――. "The Teacher." In *Ancient Christian Writers*. no. 9. Translated by Joseph M. Collernan. New York: Newman Press, 1949.

―――. *Teaching Christianity*. Hyde Park: New City Press, 1996.

―――. *The Confessions of Saint Augustine*. Translated by John K. Ryan. Garden City, NY: Doubleday, Image Books, 1960.

―――. *The Enchiridion on Faith, Hope, and Love*. Gateway edition. Translated by Henry Paolucci. Chicago: Regnery, 1961.

―――. *City of God*. Edited by Vernon J. Bourke. Translated by Gerald G. Walsh et al. Garden City NY: Doubleday, Image Books, 1958.

Bailyn, Bernard. *Education in the Forming of American Society*. New York: Vintage Books, 1960.

Benedict, Saint. *The Rule Of St. Benedict in Latin and English*. Edited by Timothy Fry. Collegeville, Minn.: Liturgical Press, 1981.

Borg, Marcus J. *Meeting Jesus Again for the First Time*. San Francisco: HarperSanFrancisco, 1994.

Boys, Mary C. *Educating in Faith: Maps and Visions*. San Francisco: Harper and Row, 1989.

Braxton, Edward K. *The Wisdom Community*. New York: Paulist Press, 1980.

Bridges, David and Terence McLaughlin, eds. *Education and the Market Place*. London/Washington: Falmer Press, 1994.

Brown, Raymond. *The Churches the Apostles Left Behind*. New York: Paulist Press, 1984.

Brueggemann, Walter. "The Legitimacy of a Sectarian Hermeneutic: 2 Kings 18–19." In *Education for Citizenship and Discipleship*. Edited by Mary C. Boys. New York: Pilgrim Press, 1989.

————. *To Act Justly, Love Tenderly, Walk Humbly*. By Walter Brueggemann, Sharon Parks, and Thomas H. Groome. New York: Paulist Press, 1986.

Bruffee, Kenneth A. *Collaborative Learning: Higher Education, Independence, and the Authority of Knowledge*. Baltimore: John's Hopkins University Press, 1993.

Bruner, Jerome. *The Process of Education*. Cambridge: Harvard University Press, 1977.

Bryk, Anthony S., Valerie E. Lee and Peter B. Holland. *Catholic Schools and the Common Good*. Cambridge, Mass: Harvard University Press, 1993.

Buber, Martin. *I and Thou*. Translated by Walter Kaufman. New York: Charles Scribner's Sons, 1970.

Canfield, Jack and Victor Hansen, *Chicken Soup for the Soul: 101 Stories to Open the Heart and Rekindle the Spirit*. Carmel, NY: Guideposts, 1993.

Church Teaches: Documents of the Church in English

Compiled by John F. Clarkson, et. al. Rockford, IL: Tan Books, 1973.

Clement, of Alexandria, Saint. *Stromateis*. Books 1–3. Translated by John Ferguson. Washington, DC: Catholic University of America Press, 1991.

Code Of Canon Law: A Text and Commentary. Edited by James A. Coriden, Thomas J. Green and Donald E. Heintschel. New York: Paulist Press, 1985.

Coleman, James S., Thomas Hoffer, and Sally Kilgore. *High School Achievement: Public, Catholic, and Private Schools Compared*. New York: Basic Books, 1982.

Coleman, James S. and Thomas Hoffer. *Public and Private High Schools: The Impact of Communities*. New York: Basic Books, 1987.

Confucius. *The Analects*. Translated with an introduction by D. C. Lau. London: Penguin Books, 1979.

Congar, Yves M. "The Magisterium and Theologians—A Short History." *Theology Digest* 25:1 (Spring 1971): 15–20.

Convey, John J. *Catholic Schools Make a Difference: Twenty-five Years of Research*. Washington, DC: National Catholic Education Association, 1992.

Cully, Kendig B., ed. *Basic Writings in Christian Education*. Philadelphia: Westminster Press, 1960.

Cyril, Saint. *The Works of Saint Cyril of Jerusalem*. Translated by Leo P. McCauley and Anthony A. Stephenson. Washington, DC: Catholic University of America Press, 1970.

Dewey, John. "My Pedagogic Creed." In *Dewey on Education*. Compiled by Martin S. Dworkin. *Classics in Education*, no. 3. New York: Teachers College, Columbia University, 1971.

————. *Experience and Education*. New York: Collier Books, 1974.

Donahue, John R. "Biblical Perspectives on Justice." In*The Faith That Does Justice*. Edited by John C. Haughey. New York: Paulist Press, 1977.

Dulles, Avery. *Models of Revelation*. Garden City, NY: Doubleday, 1983.

Dupre, Louis. "Catholic Education and the Predicament of Modern Culture." *The Living Light* 23:4 (June 1987): 295–305.

Durkheim, Emile. *Moral Education; A Study in the Theory and Application of the Sociology of Education*. Translated by Everett K. Wilson and edited by Herman Schnurer. New York: Free Press, 1973.

Dwyer, Barry. *Catholic Schools: Creating a New Culture*. Newtown, NSW: E. J. Dwyer, 1993.

Flax, Jane. "Political Philosophy and the Patriarchal Consciousness: A Psychoanalytic Perspective on Epistemology and Metaphysics." In *Discovering Reality*. Edited by Sandra Harding and Merrill B. Hintikka. Boston: D. Reidel, 1983.

Flynn, Marcellin. *The Effectiveness of Catholic Schools*. Homebush, N.S.W., Australia: St. Paul Publications, 1985.

Foucault, Michel. *Power/Knowledge: Selected Interviews and Other Writings 1972–1977*. Translated and edited by Colin Gordon. New York: Pantheon Books, 1980.

Fowler, James. *Stages of Faith: The Psychology of Human Development and the Quest for Meaning*. San Francisco: Harper & Row, 1981.

Frankl, Viktor. *Man's Search for Meaning: An Introduction to Logotherapy*. Boston: Beacon Press, 1992.

Gadamer, Hans G. *Truth and Method*. New York: Crossroads, 1989.

Gilkey, Langdon B. *Catholicism Confronts Modernity*. New York: Seabury Press, 1975.

Gilligan, Carol. *In a Different Voice: Psychological Theory and Women's Development*. Cambridge, MA: Harvard University Press, 1982.

Giroux, Henry. *Theory and Resistance in Education: A Pedagogy for the Opposition*. South Hadley, MA: Bergin & Garvey, 1983.

Goldbrunner, Josef. *Holiness is Wholeness*. Notre Dame, IN: University of Notre Dame Press, 1964.

Goleman, Daniel. *Emotional Intelligence*. New York: Bantam Books, 1995.

Greeley, Andrew and Peter Rossi. *The Education of Catholic Americans*. Garden City: Doubleday, 1986.

Greeley, Andrew. "My Research on Catholic Schools." *Chicago Studies* 28 (1989): 245–63.

Gremillion, Joseph, ed. *The Gospel of Peace and Justice*. Maryknoll, NY: Orbis Books, 1976.

Groome, Thomas H. "Looking Back on Twenty-five Years: A Personal Reflection." *The Living Light* 32:2 (Winter 1995).

————. *Christian Religious Education: Sharing Our Story and Vision*. San Francisco: Harper and Row, 1980.

————. *Language for a "Catholic" Church*. Revised Edition, Kansas City: Sheed & Ward, 1995.

————. *Sharing Faith: A Comprehensive Approach to Religious Education and Pastoral Ministry*. San Francisco: Harper San Francisco, 1991.

Habermas, Jurgen. *Knowledge and Human Interest*. Translated by Jeremy J. Shapiro. Boston: Beacon Press, 1971.

————. *The Theory of Communicative Action*. Boston: Beacon Press, 1984.

Hamm, Mary. *The Collaborative Dimensions of Learning*. Norwood, NJ: Ablex, 1992.

Harakas, Stanley. *Toward Transfigured Life: The Theoria of Eastern Orthodox Ethics*. Minneapolis: Light & Life Publishing Co., 1983.

Harding, Sandra and Hintikka, Merrill. *Discovering Reality: Feminist Perspectives on Epistemology, Metaphysics, Methodology, and Philosophy of Science*. Boston: D. Reidel, 1983.

Harding, Sandra G. *The Science Question in Feminism*. Ithica: Cornell University Press, 1986.

Hehir, J. Bryan. "Catholic Social Teachings." In *Encyclopedia of Catholicism*. Edited by Richard P. McBrien. San Francisco: HarperSanFrancisco, 1995.

Heidegger, Martin. *Basic Writings*. Translated by John Macquarrie and Edward Robinson. New York: Harper & Row, 1962.

Heschel, Abraham Joshua. *The Prophets*. New York: Harper & Row, 1962.

Hippolytus. *The Apostolic Tradition of Hippolytus*. Translated by Burton S. Easton. Cambridge: Cambridge University Press, 1934.

Hopkins, Gerard Manley. *Poems and Prose*. London: David Campbell, 1995.

Horell, Harold Daly. *A Pastoral Model of Christian Moral Formation*. Doctoral dissertation, Boston College, 1997.

Irenaeus, Saint, *Five Books of Saint Irenaeus, Bishop of Lyons, Against Heresies*. Translated by the Rev. John Keble. Oxford: J. Parker, 1872.

John Paul II, Pope. *On The Coming Of The Third Millennium* : Washington, DC: Catholic Conference, 1994.

————. *On Social Concern*. Boston: St. Paul Books, 1987.

Johnson, Elizabeth. *She Who Is: The Mystery of God in Feminist Theological Discourse*. New York: Crossroads, 1993.

Julian of Norwich. *Showings*. Translated and edited by Edmund Colledge, O.S.A. and James Walsh S.J. Paulist Press: New York, 1978.

Kavanagh, Patrick. *Collected Poems*. Martin, Brian & O'Keeffe: London, 1972.

Kearney, Richard. *The Wake of Imagination: Toward a Postmodern Culture*. Minneapolis, MN: University of Minnesota Press, 1988.

Kushner, Harold S. *When Bad Things Happen to Good People*. New York: Schocken Books, 1981.

Landy, Thomas M. "Collegium and the Intellectual's Vocation to Serve." *Conversations* 10 (Fall 1996): 15–24.

LeClercq, Jean. *The Love of Learning and the Desire for God: A Study of Monastic Culture*. New York: Fordham University Press, 1982.

Levinas, Emmanuel. *The Levinas Reader*. Edited by Sean Hand. New York: B. Blackwell, 1989.

Lickona, Thomas. *Educating for Character: How Our Schools Can Teach Respect and Responsibility*. New York: Bantam, 1991.

Locke, John. *Two Treatises of Government*. Edited with an introduction and notes by Peter Laslett. New York: Cambridge University Press, 1988.

Lonergan, Bernard. *A Second Collection: Papers*. London: Darton, Longman, and Todd, 1974.

————. *Method in Theology*. New York: Seabury Press, 1972.

Luther, Martin. "To the Councilmen of All Cities in Germany That They Establish and Maintain Christian Schools," In *Basic Writings in Christian Education*. Edited by Kendig Brubaker Cully. Philadelphia: Westminster Press, 1960.

Maritain, Jacques. *Education at the Crossroads*. New Haven: Yale University Press, 1960.

———. *The Education of Man; Educational Philosophy*. Garden City: Doubleday, 1962.

———. *The Person and the Common Good*. New York: Scribner, 1947.

McBrien, Richard P. *Catholicism*. Revised Edition. San Francisco: Harper San Francisco, 1994.

———. *Caesar's Coin: Religion and Politics in America*. New York: Macmillan, 1987.

McLaughlin, Terence, Joseph O'Keefe S.J., and Bernadette O'Keeffe. *The Contemporary Catholic School*. London: Falmer Press, 1996.

Montessori, Maria. *The Montessori Method*. New York: Schocken Books, 1964.

Moore, Thomas. *Care of the Soul: A Guide for Cultivating Depth and Sacredness in Everyday Life*. New York: HarperCollins, 1992.

Murphy, Christopher. *An Interpretation Approach to Religious Education*. Doctoral dissertation. Boston College, 1997.

National Conference of Catholic Bishops. *The Challenge of Peace: God's Promise and Our Response*. Boston: Daughters of Saint Paul, 1983.

Neuner, Josef. *The Christian Faith in the Doctrinal Documents of the Catholic Church*. Dublin and Cork: Mercier Press, 1973.

Newman, John Henry. *The Idea of a University*. New York: Longmans, Green, and Co., 1947.

Noddings, Nel. *Caring, a Feminine Approach to Ethics and Moral Education*. Berkeley: University of California Press, 1986.

O'Brien, David J. and Thomas A. Shannon ed. *Catholic Social Thought: The Documentary Heritage*. Maryknoll, NY: Orbis Books, 1992.

Parks, Sharon. *The Critical Years: The Young Adult Search for a Faith to Live By*. San Francisco: Harper & Row, 1986.

Piaget, Jean. *To Understand is to Invent*. New York: Penguin Books, 1973.

Plato. *The Republic*. In *Great Dialogues of Plato*. Translated by W. H. D. Rouse. New York: New American Library, 1956.

Powell, Marjorie. *Teacher Attitudes : An Annotated Bibliography and Guide to Research*. New York: Garland, 1986.

Rahner, Karl. *Belief Today*. New York: Sheed & Ward, 1967.

Ramsey, Ian T. *Models and Mystery*. New York: Oxford University Press, 1964.

Rauschenbusch, Walter. *Christianity and the Social Crisis*. Louisville, KY: Westminster/John Knox Press, 1991.

Rest, James. *Moral Development: Advances in Research and Theory*. New York: Praeger, 1986.

Rohr, Richard. *Why Be Catholic? Understanding our Experience and Tradition*. Cincinnati, OH: St. Anthony Messenger Press, 1989.

Roman Catechism. Translated and annotated by Robert J. Bradley and Eugene Kevane. Boston: St. Paul Edition, 1985.

Schillebeeckx, Edward. *Christ, the Sacrament of the Encounter with God*. Kansas City: Sheed, Andrews & McMeel, 1963.

Schiro, Michael, *Curriculum for Better Schools: The Great Ideological Debate.* Englewood Cliffs, NJ: Educational Technology Publications, 1978.

Schreiter, Robert J. "Faith and Cultures: Challenges to a World Church." *Theological Studies* 50:4 (December 1989): 744–60.

Schussler Fiorenza, Elisabeth. *In Memory of Her: A Feminist Theological Reconstruction of Christian Origins.* New York: Crossroads, 1983.

Senge, Peter M. *The Fifth Discipline: The Art and Practice of the Learning Organization.* New York: Doubleday, 1990.

Shea, John. *The Legend of the Bells: Stories of the Human Spirit.* Chicago: Acta Publications, 1996.

Shor, Ira. *Empowering Education: Critical Teaching for Social Change.* Chicago: University of Chicago Press, 1992.

Tertullian. "The Prescription of Heretics." In *Documents of the Christian Church.* 2nd ed. Edited by Henry Bettenson. New York: Oxford University Press, 1963.

Tracy, David. *On Naming the Present: Reflections on God, Hermeneutics, and Church.* Maryknoll, NY: Orbis Books, 1994.

————. *Plurality and Ambiguity: Hermeneutics, Religion, Hope.* San Francisco: Harper & Row, 1987.

————. *The Analogical Imagination: Christian Theology and the Culture of Pluralism.* New York: Crossroads, 1989.

Trible, Phyllis. *God and the Rhetoric of Sexuality.* Philadelphia: Fortress Press, 1978.

Troeltsch, Ernst. *The Social Teachings of the Christian Churches.* 2 vols. Translated by Olive Wyon. London: George Allen, 1931.

Vatican Congregation for Catholic Education. *The Religious Dimension of Education in a Catholic School.* Washington, DC: USCC, 1998.

Vincent of Lérins. *Commonitories; in Fathers of the Church.* Translated by Rudolph E. Morris. New York: CIMA, 1949.

Viviano, Benedict T. *The Kingdom of God in History.* Wilmington, DE: Michael Glazier, 1988.

Ward, Mary. *Till God Will: Mary Ward Through Her Writings.* Edited by M. Emmanuel Orchard. London: Darton, Longman and Todd, 1985.

Whitehead, Alfred North. *Process and Reality: An Essay in Cosmology.* New York: The MacMillan Company, 1929.

————. *The Aims of Education and Other Essays.* New York: The Free Press, 1929.

Yeats, William B. *The Collected Poems Of W. B. Yeats.* London: Macmillan, 1963.